Lewd Looks

AMERICAN SEXPLOITATION CINEMA IN THE 1960s

Elena Gorfinkel

University of Minnesota Press
Minneapolis
London

Introduction
"Coy Leericism"

New York City, mid-1960s, black-and-white 35mm film stock and a familiar sexploitation scenario: young Candy leaves her small town. We see her departing on the train. She is fleeing the fate of her mother, a prostitute who has committed suicide. She opines in voice-over about a new life in New York City, which holds the promise of another identity and respite from the shame bestowed by maternal disgrace. Candy (Barbara Morris), with dark hair and cropped bangs, evokes a low-budget Anna Karina circa Jean-Luc Godard's early 1960s films. She moves in with an old girlfriend, her enchantment by the city's roiling creative energies and architectural marvels rendered through street scenes, vertiginous views of skyscrapers, female flânerie. Introduced to the world of the single urban working girl by the women whom she befriends, Candy resorts to nude modeling and escorting. After two failed romances, with a philandering nude photographer and a sculptor more piqued by his art than by Candy, she returns to her party girl life while secretly edging toward despair.

This film's penultimate "orgy" scene is one of prototypical bohemian carousal: a drunken swinging pot party in the girls' middle-class apartment, replete with mid-century details and decorative flourishes. The camera sits at hip or "couch" level, surveying the pairings and unpairings of potential sexual partners. Men and women abandon decorum to grind on each other and make out. They laugh ostentatiously, gesturing come-ons in thick, slowed motions, at the pace of striptease. The women dance to records and circulate from man to man, bouncing on their laps. Whiskey glasses are filled and cocktails disbursed, big crystal ashtrays overflow, and we hear the sounds of a saucy percussive jazz sound track. Candy switches from one man to another, tentatively settles down with a young man on the carpet. An older man in sunglasses and white tennis shorts arrives,

FIGURE 1. Candy resorts to nude modeling in *One Naked Night*.

laughing and leering, his eyes concealed. As the women's outer garments inch off, couples pair to make out and grope in available corners in kitchen and hallway. A 16mm film projector is set up on the coffee table, and the group eagerly gathers around to watch. The lights go off and a "stag film" unspools—in it a woman plays strip chess with an older man. There is a cutaway to the man in sunglasses, watching and laughing. The stag film's action, we are to impute, encourages if not enjoins the group's sex action. In the dark, underneath the illumination of the projector's beam, which filters and draws shafts of light through the smoky air, Candy's friend Laura makes out with a man on the floor. We see her skirt getting pulled up over her legs. The diegetic film runs out, creating a blur on the wall as light is thrown through the projector's gate, an illuminated rectangle. Another girl, the exhibitionist Peg, with a blonde bouffant hairdo, leaps up in front of the projector's beam and into the light, entering the doubled "frame." She slowly dances and strips off her blouse and then her bra, casting high-contrast shadows onto the blank white rectangle behind her.

The film's knowingness—an elemental scene of film spectatorship, the recognition of the female erotic body as the undergirding substrate of cine-

INTRODUCTION 3

FIGURE 2. *One Naked Night*'s scene of looking, the female body doubled as spectacle and screen.

matic spectacle—seems to collapse onto that which it describes. The live, dancing, stripping girl reflexively *replaces* the film, her body supplanting the diegetic movie, providing her own screen for projection. As her bra comes off, we see the shadowed shapes of other figures, a man at the edge of the screen, pulling her back down below the frame. The lights come back on. A montage of sexual grappling ensues. We see male hands grasping at bra hooks in close-up, waist-up kissing and much heavy breathing, bare feet rubbing each other on caftans, a woman's hand ecstatically grabbing a crocheted blanket in close-up. Metonymic extremities signal a distinctly sexual pleasure that must remain off-screen. This cumulatively paced crescendo indicates sexual action, but it is organized by ellipsis, evasion, and the sense of the film's presentation of an illicit view. One scene of looking—at the film within a film and at a writhing, dancing female body, bidden to move and to undress for the camera and the on-screen spectators turned participants, reflexively points outward to another implied scene, of the film spectator's look at this lascivious fiction of excess, sensation, sexual circulation, and consumption.

This self-conscious scenario of looking and sensational corporeality is at once both chaste, as nudity remains minimal but strategic, and unsavory, in the film's exposition of single girls caught in a seamy trade of sexual commerce. The scene appears in the sexploitation film *One Naked Night* (filmed in 1963 but released in 1965) directed by Albert Viola, and it is emblematic of the gambit of the sexploitation cinema of the 1960s, which overflows with scenarios such as this one: a young, sexually curious but naive young woman in the big city becomes embroiled in sex work of one kind or another and an industry of erotic spectacle and is finally corrupted, used up, discarded. The film is also fairly illustrative of 1960s sexploitation films' preoccupation with the conjunction of sexual labor, spectatorship and performance, and the contradictory nature of a mode of address that sits between the illicit and the permissible. The film is conversant with popular sexual discourses of its time and uses these as novel currency, evoking the trilling intonations of lurid pulp paperbacks, pinup photography, and sexual science manuals in a post–Kinsey Report, post-*Playboy* era, yet one still cognizant of the *limits* of cinematic conventions proscribing screen sex.

Making sense of this film, and many like it produced in this decade, necessitates recognizing their location at the precipice between different regimes of sexual representation and in the context of the history of the obscene image. Sexploitation film has been bracketed as a precursor or bridge to a more authentic or explicit mode of sexual expression, in the hard-core hypervisibility of pornographic features that emerged in the early 1970s. As a chapter in the history of film pornography, sexploitation's uniqueness as a finite phenomenon can contribute to a broader understanding of the place of sexual representations in American film history and culture. If, as Linda Williams has suggested in her work on pornographic film and sexual representation, the transition from the *obscene* to the *on/scene* is the story of cinema as a sexual medium, what can sexploitation films such as *One Naked Night* and its dialectic of seen and unseen (and obscene and on/scene) tell us about the transformations of cinema, the film spectator, and forms of sexual expressivity in the 1960s?[1] What do we make of the sexploitation text that traffics in the constant deferral of the explicit sexual act into off-screen space? How does the simulation of the signs of sex operate within the sexploitation film, and what kinds of desires, knowledges, and affects does it produce? In short, how to historicize and theorize the *implicit,* rather than explicit, image? This book examines the historically overlooked sexploitation film to tackle these questions and to unravel the material and discursive relations between bodies, looking, and spectatorship that these films impudently present. Sexploitation films made the sensational body and female sexuality public and visible in distinct and unprecedented ways, tensing it in a constant vacillation between concealment and revelation.

Sexploitation Film, between Cinematic and Social History

Although sexploitation cinema is central to this history of an ever-greater visibility of sexuality "on scene" in the 1960s, it has been scantly treated in film history and film studies. The *American Film Institute Catalog of Motion Pictures Produced in the United States 1961–1970* reveals pages upon pages, hundreds of film titles that fall into the category of the sex film or sex exploitation film. These hundreds of films constituted a cottage industry and locus of independent film production at the forefront of a newly sexualized media and popular culture in American public life. Despite the renaissance of low-budget sex films that proliferated in that decade, sexploitation films' value as a historically, culturally, and aesthetically significant branch of independent film has been largely overlooked. This explosion of sex cinema has also not been accounted for in histories of American or 1960s cinema—most overviews and textbooks bear minimal mention of this bountiful "adults-only" cinema that flourished on the margins of an ailing Hollywood system. For example, Paul Monaco's important macro-account of the cinematic decade in the History of the American Cinema series contains not a single mention of sexploitation in its 359 pages.[2]

Sexploitation films' importance to film history and to the transformation of 1960s cinema is deep and manifold. The emergence of sexploitation films as a viable niche in the 1960s augments and complicates a picture of the rise of independent production in the postwar period. The American film industry faced considerable challenges in the postwar era, struggling with the impact of the major studios' divestiture of their holdings in exhibition in the wake of the Paramount decree of 1948 and the broadened expressivity bestowed to cinema by the *Miracle* Supreme Court decision of 1952.[3] A product shortage throughout the 1950s, as Hollywood produced fewer and fewer pictures, led to the expansion of the art house market and the widening exposure among American audiences to foreign films.[4] It also led to the rise of and greater space available for independent producers, who dove into low-budget genre territory, from monster horror and science fiction potboilers to teenpics.[5] Exhibitors, especially neighborhood theaters, confronting the paucity of product, became receptive to independent, foreign, and exploitation fare, creating a window for the emergence of sexploitation. The influx of racy art films from nations such as France, Italy, and Sweden, as well as changing legal definitions of obscenity, led to a rising tide of films with more robust sexual or mature content across modes of production, among which sexploitation films became some of the most brash and direct.[6] The precipitous decline in American moviegoing was linked to the stratification of a newly unpredictable film public whose greater access to television and a widening array of leisure activities, from sports to pop music, siphoned their undivided attention from the silver screen. Filmmakers were thus both unmoored and liberated from a one-size-fits-all demographic and imagining of audience taste. In these years, the youth, family, and adult markets emerged as distinct fields, and film product diversified away and apart from the major studios, in the increase in independent productions. Before the arrival of feature-length hard-core porn, the lowly sexploitation film defined and constituted an "adults-only" cinema and its terms of sexual expression, liberalizing the American screen.[7]

Sexploitation film thus made visible the "maturation" of cinematic subject matter, in the decade when the movies seemed to suddenly "grow up." Low-budget operators, based primarily in New York and Los Angeles, sexploitation filmmakers and producers seized on an opening in legal doctrine regarding obscenity. As Hollywood's Production Code floundered and a ratings system eventually took shape, the gap created by the Hollywood studios' product shortage in these years allowed the sexploitation producers to make risqué and salacious films that could fill ailing neighborhood theaters. As a mode of production, sexploitation extended the tradition of classical exploitation cinema and its network of producers and distributors from an earlier era but also operated as a distinct field of practice from other independents that were gaining visibility in these years, such as larger-budgeted exploitation operators like Roger Corman and American International Pictures, and from the more personal, artisanal, and noncommercial approach of avant-garde and underground cinemas strongly associated with sexual expressivity and experimentation in this decade.[8] Sexploitation films presented something distinct from these neighboring modes, an erotic expression emboldened by the market but hampered by budgetary limitations and whose aesthetic aspirations were often circumscribed by generic and economic necessities.

Eric Schaefer provides a historical framework for understanding the antecedent mode to sexploitation, in what he identifies as the "classical" exploitation film tradition, which operated in varied forms from 1919 to 1959. Exploitation film, as he illuminates, was a mode of production that worked on the margins of Hollywood, capitalizing on the subjects of sex, drugs, disease, and vice, which the Hollywood industry—beholden to the Production Code—could not broach.[9] Schaefer illustrates how exploitation films charted the transition from a production- to a consumption-based sexual economy in their subject matter and mode of address, exposing "cultural ills," taking a moralist stance on them, and simultaneously encouraging their audiences to consume and implicitly enjoy. This paradigm of a cinema that attempts to veil its economic intentions through the alibi of moral circumspection and morbid narrative resolutions, while simultaneously offering "cheap thrills," is one that persists, with some alteration, into the period of the sexploitation picture, as this book will show. Classical exploitation films often made use of a pedagogical "square up," a framing device through narration or intertitles that offered an absolution for the spectator's morals for watching salacious, sensational images of sexual disease, vice, nudism, or the dangers of marijuana.[10] While this device disappears in sexploitation, its residue remains, couched instead in a language that incorporated changing obscenity standards and the contours of 1960s legal limitations in the form of "socially redeeming value." Schaefer's periodization and exhaustive account of the parameters of classical exploitation facilitate this book's examination of the period that follows and the emergence of sexploitation cinema.

What came to be called *sexploitation* by the late 1950s—an abbreviation of "sex-exploitation"—developed on the heels of a 1957 New York State Board of Appeals decision marking the presentation of nudity in film as not, in and of itself, obscene.[11] The following decade, roughly 1960 to 1970, witnessed the production of hundreds of sexploitation films.[12] Their plot pretexts functioned to present the maximum nudity and sexual content, at times mixed with violence, allowable by law, often promising a bit more than the law sanctioned. Narrativizing sex through transparent plots, pretexts, and generic gimmicks, sexploitation films codified a softcore aesthetic ethos and elaborated excessive scenarios of social change represented through changes in sexual practices. The films and their fulsome promotional address—in trailers, advertisements, and the films' titles themselves—lured audiences with promises of sexual spectacle, using the bait of scenes of female nudity, primarily exposed breasts and buttocks, and of risqué topics borrowed from tabloid headlines, sex manuals, and current events. The melodramatic scripts of "sex and its discontents" that engine the generic attractions of sexploitation run the gamut, with returns to common motifs, among them the flight of the unsatisfied wife into the arms of sinister men or the fate of the insatiable nymphomaniac (*Agony of Love*, William Rotsler, 1966; *Love Me . . . Please!*, Victor Petrashevic, 1969), the fall of innocents into a den of depravity involving promiscuity, prostitution, bohemianism, and the occult (*Orgy at Lil's Place*, Jerald Intrator, 1963; *Olga's House of Shame*, Joseph P. Mawra, 1964; *The Sex*

Perils of Paulette, Doris Wishman, 1965), the submission of men to sadistic women (*Faster Pussycat! Kill! Kill!,* Russ Meyer, 1965; *Venus in Furs,* Joseph Marzano, 1967; *She Mob,* Harry Wuest, 1968), narratives of rape, revenge, and torture (*Mondo Keyhole,* Jack Hill, 1966; *The Touch of Her Flesh,* Michael Findlay, 1967), the currency of the newly emancipated working girl refigured as a sex worker (*Rent-a-Girl,* William Rose, 1968; *The Hookers,* Jalo Miklos Horthy, 1967; *The Sexperts,* Jerald Intrator, 1966), the sexual psychopathology of peeping toms (*Strange Compulsion,* Irvin Berwick, 1964; *Electronic Lover,* Jesse Berger, 1966), the underground exchange in "white slaves," and sexual bondage through blackmail (*Olga's Girls,* Joseph P. Mawra, 1964; *How Many Times,* Don Walters, 1969). Perversion; sexual deviance; nonnormative sexual practices such as sadomasochism, swinging, and wife swapping; emergent identities such as lesbianism, bisexuality, and cross-dressing (and, to a far lesser extent, male homosexuality); and the sex industry itself provided hardy material for sexploitation's wide generic variations—from melodramas to pseudo-documentaries and sex exposés to noir-ish, violent action films. But central to all is the anxious status of autonomous female labor and desire, unhinged from the reproductive certitude of family and marriage, most often set loose in the permissive urban space of the city—as is Candy in the streets of New York in the opening of *One Naked Night*—but also left to wallow in hothouse scenarios of "suburban sin."

These kinds of sexual and gendered representations are inseparable from the social contexts within which these films were made and the larger cultural and political forces that constituted public life in the 1960s, including its many "revolutions." This period witnessed a heightened visibility and proliferating discourses surrounding sexual practices and identities, the civil rights movement's battle for racial justice and equality, the women's movement's rising consciousness, and the emergence of gay liberation politics, as well as a youthful insurgency—as young people disinvested from the ideologies and values of their parents and, "turned on, tuned in, and dropped out," joined student activist organizations, and protested the Vietnam War.[13] Youth also gravitated toward forging countercultures, through creative practices such as art, performance, rock music, and psychedelia. Though often pathologized as deviant in this era of radicalization, young people were the defining and sought-after demographic of the 1960s, and their tastes and habits created the architecture of American popular culture's preoccupations and anxieties.[14] These developments were refracted and filtered in sexploitation cinema's ideological attitudes toward youth cultural practices, new sexual identities, social and racial mobility, and the economic and erotic lot of single women. Sexploitation cinema in many ways capitalized on a cultural fascination with the lives

INTRODUCTION

FIGURE 3. Blazing promotional come-ons for *The Skin Game* and other sexploitation titles featuring nudity and vice address passersby at the State Theater, Washington Street, Boston, 1965. Mayor John F. Collins Records, Collection 0244.001, City of Boston Archives, Boston. Reproduced under a Creative Commons 2.0 License.

and practices of the young as well as the generic stakes of sexual difference, particularly the fate of sexually active, primarily white women.[15]

The sexual revolution in particular has been ascribed in no small measure to the transformation of the media and popular representations in the 1960s. Hilary Radner suggests that it was not politics per se but popular culture that was most instrumental in positing the personal as the political and constituting the consuming self as a new sphere of value and pleasure, pleasures most overtly oriented in sexual form. Eric Schaefer also asserts that the "mass media served as the most important and visible battleground on which the sexual revolution took place."[16] Sexploitation films, one of the key sites of sexual representation, participated in and prognosticated the arrival of this "revolution," even while the films, politically and ideologically, often remained suspicious of sexual liberation's value or social effects. Counter to the liberatory discourses often associated with the cultural products of the sexual revolution, this book examines the unique status of sexploitation film in its pessimistic, frequently shame-drenched imaging and imagining of the changing conception of social relations, sexual identities, and gender roles in the 1960s. *One Naked Night,* for example, ends with Candy, after waking up on the floor after the sex party, in a state of humiliated self-abnegation, perceiving herself as no different than her prostitute mother. Her solution is to jump to her death off the balcony of her shared apartment, her stilled body, in the final shot, captured in an overhead high angle—resembling a modernist, Michelangelo Antonioni composition. Such morbid, punitive endings were common in the mid-1960s, as they could appease censorial restrictions and stave off charges of obscenity, moralist punctuation that provided narrative buffer for the mode's indulgence in sexual excess. However, by the late 1960s, the gambit of guilt and shame began to abate as more competitors entered the sex film market in the wake of legal, cultural, industrial, and political transformations that expanded the sphere of the permissible, although an air of suspicion and self-consciousness remained.

This book also locates sexploitation films within the film culture of the 1960s, accounting for how these films circulated; gained notoriety; and were perceived, made sense of, and talked about in the decade's public culture. Sexploitation's very publicness, in presenting audiences with sexual content and female nudity previously prohibited or unseen, challenged notions of film spectatorship and definitions of obscenity. Fluctuations in censorship practices and state and federal obscenity law placed sexploitation films within a highly visible and public sphere of contest and debate over what constituted aesthetic and social value in a period of an expanding consumer culture and leisure economy. Functioning at the margins and in the gaps between other modes of production, sexploitation's importance and influence are paradoxically bound up in its marginality, its cultural status, and the currency and pervasiveness of its sexualized representations as the 1960s wore on. Reliant on the residual prohibitions on sexual content, sexploitation films codified what would later become identified as a soft-core aesthetic, contra the hard-core of pornography. Yet the greater sexualization of Hollywood and other wide-release films and the emergence of feature-length hard-core would economically eclipse the novelty of sexploitation by the early 1970s. Therefore this book surveys the period and films produced roughly from 1959 to 1972, the latter a crucial year in the commercial success of publicly exhibited feature-length pornography.

The renegade economic logic of the sexploitation film—one that Hollywood attempted in the late 1960s to appropriate for its own failing market—was founded on a principle of lowest investment yielding the highest return in profit.[17] Bottom feeders within the sea of a market economy, sexploitation producers drew on the traditions of recycling, reediting, and repackaging, trick tactics and expedient forms culled from previous eras of the exploitation trade.[18] The huckster mentality and the entrepreneurial attitude of carnival sideshow and vaudeville circuit are a strong residue in sexploitation's marketing strategies and mode of address to its audience, even as newer and younger filmmakers and producers entered the field over the course of the decade—and many notable New Hollywood talents, such as directors Francis Ford Coppola and Brian De Palma as well as cinematographer László Kovács, notably worked early on making lowly "nudies."[19]

Andrew Sarris, in a not-too-belated postmortem written in 1971 on the valence of the sexploitation film as a lost form, would call this quality of sexploitation's address a "coy leericism."[20] *Lewd Looks* traces the peculiarity and historicity of sexploitation's mode of address to its audience, this very "coy leericism." The courting and production of an illicit mode of looking through promises of erotic spectacle articulates a moment marked as much by shame and prohibition as it was by license and liberation. It is a mode also underwritten by the self-conscious novelty of the sexual commodity. Sexploitation film continually managed its audience's "foreknowledge of spectacle," as Paul Watson terms it, through the promotional promise of unseen and sexualized sights.[21] Sexploitation producers would consistently negotiate the expectations and disappointments of the ticket-buying public through aesthetic strategies of syntactical tease and erotic deferral. These strategies of tease, which Tom Waugh identifies as the regnant rhetoric of 1960s sexual culture, were constitutive to the films' style, ethos, mode of address, and construction of a skin flick spectator.[22] The historical spectator was tasked to navigate and negotiate this dialectic of plenitude and absence, circumvention and titillation.

Sexploitation films, I argue throughout this book, foreground the conditions of looking at erotic spectacle, making the subject and object of sexual looking the crux of their drives, self-consciously underscoring their own status as cultural artifacts caught in a period transitioning from restriction to license. If we understand spectatorship as a form of erotic consumption, these films make this consumption possible, visible, and sensational, in their appeal to the viewer's visceral faculties through the construction of erotic spectacle housed in salacious narratives of vice and excess, through the spectacle of the female body gripped by sexual desire, and through the incorporation of the spectator as figure into the films' narratives. In the process, sexploitation films widened the terms of legitimate male consumer desire, paving the way for an exponentially proliferating marketplace of sexual media, a marketplace and consumer identity that would face much pushback and critique in the 1970s porn age.

My analysis emphasizes the ways scenes of looking at erotic labor abound in sexploitation cinema and contends that the film spectator is central to sexploitation's generic, industrial, and social identity. Following on the work of Karl Schoonover, whose analysis of the international reception of neorealist cinema reveals the construction of a spectator—the bystander, outsider, witness—whose humanism can be authenticated by geographically distant images of "imperiled corporeality," this book attends to the construction of a libidinous mode of address in a more explicitly prurient mode of production that bears no pretense of elevation.[23] The book investigates the figure of the film viewer within sexploitation films' narratives, in the mode's address to its audience, and in assorted historical reception spheres of sexploitation cinema. In legal situations, in social science, in municipal debates, in the popular press, and in trade journals, the "adult film audience" is inaugurated by the publicity attached to and the economic success accorded the sexploitation film. It is not that this figure of the "adult consumer" emerges historically only at the moment of the sexploitation film but that the peculiarly public characteristic of sexploitation focused popular interest on the activity and effects of film viewing in its relation to sexualized film content, which had often been reserved for exclusive, private, and primarily male consumption.

Sexploitation thematized this consumption and made the issue of visual access to the sexual its primary subject—in its narratives, in its mode of address to its audience, and in its promotional identity as purveyor of barely legal spectacle, designated "for adults only." Although the historical audience of sexploitation seems perhaps the most ephemeral element of this mode of production, I argue that this spectator is defined by the mode of address, marketing strategies, and narrative ploys of the films as well as being a product of cultural discourses regarding the emerging sexual marketplace within popular media. Across the book, I map the appearance and management of the figure of the sexploitation spectator in the contexts of film censorship and other forms of regulation, in the films themselves and their thematization of erotic consumption and the vagaries of new modes of erotic looking, and through the critical reception of sexploitation as a filmgoing experience and cultural phenomenon throughout the 1960s.

Historically, the 1960s marked a period in American film history when film audiences were becoming economically unpredictable due to the postwar slump of divestiture after the Paramount decree and the competition of television, an era when target markets, segmentation, and classification gained prominence.[24] Thus the figure of the adult film spectator operates as an extreme pole in the designation of the taste for a certain kind of film entertainment, set in stark contrast to the sixteen- to twenty-four-year-old demographic Hollywood had identified as the bulk of U.S. moviegoers in the 1960s. Alongside imported art cinema, sexploitation was central in the 1960s in transforming and heightening the visibility of the category of "adults-only" entertainment. As Mark Betz and Schoonover each detail, the proximities of exploitation cinemas to art cinemas at the level of promotion and exhibition in the 1950s onward highlight their "shared discourses" and modes of audience address.[25] "Adults only" as a designation for audiences prior to the development of the ratings system in sexploitation cinema and art cinema provides one instance of the confusions generated by sexual content in marking other kinds of classed taste boundaries.[26]

By the time the President's Commission on Obscenity and Pornography had taken account of the threat of numerous forms of erotica in varied media to public health and the national character in 1970, the soft-core stylizations and crude renderings of sexual melodrama in sexploitation had begun to blend with hard-core pornography, which would soon overtake it.[27] Numerous sexploitation makers, such as Radley Metzger (as Henry Paris) and Joe Sarno, continued on into hard-core productions; many others did not. Whereas the filmmakers who made sexploitation and who began to make commercial pornography represented different generational groups, the audience transitioned more smoothly from the soft-core to the hard-core venue in the late 1960s and early 1970s. As with pornography, sexploitation was made with a male audience in mind, although unlike the historically privatized screening contexts for stag films and amateur porn, it opened up the possibility, in its publicness, for female audiences to attend.[28]

As a product of these social, cultural, and industrial circumstances, at the level of textuality, sexploitation often tends to narrativize this historical spectator as a thematic figure, positioned as either the peeping tom or leering voyeur who is impotent to act—like Russ Meyer's bumbling protagonist in *The Immoral Mr. Teas* (1959)—or the sexual psychotic whose actions confuse sexual drives and violent ones, as seen in the murderous psychotic lead in Michael and Roberta Findlay's "Flesh" trilogy, *The Touch of Her Flesh*, *The Curse of Her Flesh*, and *The Kiss of Her Flesh* (1967–68), and, later, even as permissiveness takes hold, of the "curious female" whose erotic inquisitiveness leads her toward embroilment in risky sexual scenes (*Love Me . . . Please!*; *Vibrations*, Joe Sarno, 1969). Such are the grave dangers in the satisfaction of desire and the lifting of restraint within the ideological worldview promulgated by sexploitation films. Narratively, the sexploitation film constantly contravenes the distinction between "seeing sex" and "doing sex," articulating the fundamental quandary that motivates the troubling nature of the sexual image and its incitement to mimesis. Looking at the sexual image in this particular historical moment thus has contradictory and incendiary implications, which sexploitation films self-reflexively map. In this sense, sexploitation is always circumstantially dialoguing with itself about itself.

As this book elaborates, sex in sexploitation cannot end happily or in a gesture toward the plenitude of pleasures: owing to the extenuating threat of censorship and the necessities of legal protection, a loosely rendered moralism is deployed to do the work that the sexually explicit cannot. In this sense, sexploitation largely presents a diegetic and discursive space distinct from the utopian and naturalist tendencies ascribed to pornography, the space, in Steven Marcus's coinage, of "pornotopia."[29] Instead of a sexual economy dependent on an endless exchange and multiplication of sex acts that we see in hard-core pornography, sexploitation films provide a more stringent economy, which enumerates teleological outcomes and is dependent on logics of scarcity and what I term *guilty expenditure*. By the late 1960s, however, pressed by changes in permissiveness and competition with Hollywood and other independents, sexploitation films slowly begin to alter their approach with respect to the abundance of the sexual marketplace and acquiesce to the terms of the market in the broadening explicitness of its sexual situations and an at times "lighter" approach to sexual experimentation.

Sexploitation films and their fundamentally contradictory nature and budgetary constraints produce fissures between what is said and what is shown, between sound and image, between the promise of the trailer and the film itself, between narrative events and their outcome. They thus raise questions about the historicity of spectatorial expectations regarding sexual content in a moment hovering between prohibition and license and speak to the specific cultural climate of the 1960s, a moment marked by the tension between the overt and the covert in sexual representations. Thus this book argues that sexploitation as a mode provides a fascinating semiotics of the currency of the public revelation of sexual, frank, and salacious imagery heretofore more distinctly cordoned off within private domains of consumption.

In addition to adding to the larger film historical record in its account of sexploitation cinema's rise and decline over the course of the 1960s and its contribution to the culture of the era, this book intervenes in research that theorizes and historicizes sex in cinema within the areas of the history of independent production as well as in adult film studies and porn studies. The work of two film scholars in particular has laid the pathways for this project. Linda Williams's foundational *Hard Core: Power, Pleasure, and the "Frenzy of the Visible,"* on pornography, and Schaefer's essential study of the classical period of the exploitation film, *Bold! Daring! Shocking! True! A History of the Exploitation Film, 1919–1959*, serve as chronological bookends for the sexploitation "period" and provide conceptual frameworks for this book. Although more recent studies that consider some aspects of exploitation cinema, porn, cult, and adult film have emerged, Schaefer and Williams's works still considerably define this field of research.[30]

Williams's 1989 book addresses the "problem" of pornography through a Foucauldian analysis of the genre's process of truth production and the paradox of the visibility of sexual pleasure. Williams attends to the generic features of the hard-core form, particularly in the films from the "golden era" of hard-core in the 1970s. Working through Freudian and Marxian models of sexual economy, Williams reveals embedded structures and systems of meaning within explicit moving images. Her insights raise the question as to whether one can posit a comparable ontology of the soft-core image. If hard-core's generic modus operandi invests in the presumption of the "truth of sex" in its visible evidence, then sexploitation's syntactical organization, as I here argue, offers an entirely different experience of the mediation of the sex act. In the constant teasing of the spectator with images of unmaterialized promise, of the approximation, rather than the definitive transcription, of the sex act, sexploitation films generate their own energies and receptive affects, apart from the documentary associations of the hard-core image. Sexploitation films are also clearly allied with what Williams has termed the classed and corporeal subject matter of the "body genre,"[31] a form of "sleazy," low, sordid American culture. This very crass, sleazy sensibility challenges conventions of cinematic taste and aesthetic value. Jeffrey Sconce, in his articulation of the value of sleaze as a hermeneutic for comprehending exploitation films' ethos of subterfuge, writes,

> Sleaze . . . by necessity evokes a whole range of textual issues, from the industrial mechanics of low-budget exploitation to the ever shifting terrains of reception and taste. . . . Sleaze is a feeling one has about a film that requires judging, if only in one's imagination, that there is something "improper" or "untoward" about a given text. Often sleaziness implies a circuit of inappropriate exchange involving suspect authorial intentions and/or displaced perversities in the audience.[32]

In this sense, the nature of the implicit, of sexploitation's reliance on duplicity, on subterfuge and switch and bait, opens up certain complexities and contingencies of interpretation. That complex process of reading mixed signals and the curiosity of an historical encounter with the contradictory, sometimes anarchic sexploitation text orient the approach of *Lewd Looks* to its objects. Sexploitation films provided a public space—the adults-only theater—where the proximities of desires and distaste, spectacle and its disavowal, subterfuge and sensation, could intersect for its curious spectator. As such, different moments of reception and confrontation with the eccentric sexploitation text, in different scenes of looking, become the object of my analysis in the following chapters. Across varied methodological and historiographic scales, I track the figure of this spectator, as product of censorial regulation, of moralist anxiety, as a textual construct and thematized figure, as subject of critical and sociological speculation, as well as a motoring fantasy of retrospective reception.

Finally, I engage with the notion of sexploitation films of the 1960s as a corpus of texts and contexts constituted through a discourse of obsolescence. Sexploitation cinema's boundedness by its own historical conditions of possibility, as an extinct, finite mode of production, and the fragility of its tightrope walk on the border of the permissible and the obscene in the 1960s, produced an experience of sexual spectacle contingent on its own acknowledged evanescence. This sense of ephemerality emerged not only from the self-consciousness of the films regarding their conditions of exhibition and potential regulation but also from the fleeting nature and the sense of illicitness in the erotic images themselves. The historical place of sexploitation films within this decade of tumult and transition, and in the contexts of a fracturing and diversifying film industry, gives the films the quality of what fans and critics frequently remark on as their status as peculiar "time capsules": they are documents of changing attitudes regarding gender and sexuality and manifestations of ideological resistance to these nascent transformations. The notion of obsolescence is useful here not as a rhetoric of devaluation of these complex films and their contexts but as a way to understand the shifting valences and contingent meanings of sexual images in the public sphere of 1960s American culture, in terms of their historicity and their purchase on the recognition of cultural change.

Retro Archive, Cult Afterlives

While this book considers the historical conditions of sexploitation's public life in the 1960s, it is necessary to contextualize the reemergence of sexploitation films into wider circulation in more recent years with respect to the question of the sexploitation archive. The lack of a legacy or a sense of historicity in advance for sexploitation films has been simultaneously cultural and institutional, a product of the marginal and culturally disreputable nature of adult cinema in the long view as well as a consequence of the inadvertent actions and decisions of the producers and distributors themselves. The independent nature of the sexploitation enterprise in the 1960s and 1970s did not predispose filmmakers and producers toward a cultural, preservationist mind-set. Sex films such as *Body of a Female* (John Amero and Michael Findlay, 1964), *All Women Are Bad* (Larry Crane, 1969), *Moonlighting Wives* (Joe Sarno, 1966), and *The Sexploiters* (Al C. Ruban, 1965) were seen to some degree as disposable commodities, made to fill a market need in a moment when nudity and sexual situations were in short supply. Some filmmakers worked for hire, or on a film-by-film basis with producers' funding, so did not necessarily own the rights to their own helmed efforts. Some less canny producers themselves saw little future value in their films, which became suddenly obsolete in the wake of hard-core pornography in the 1970s and by the heightened frankness of big-budget and studio pictures by the late 1960s and early 1970s. Ascertaining existing business and production records is also a difficult and tricky endeavor—as these records exist among surviving filmmakers and those foresighted enough to have saved this documentation, although many did not. As with pornographic cinema more broadly, both the explicitly sexual and outré nature of the film material, its maligned status, and the noncanonical nature of the films have resulted in wariness and caution on the part of archivists and preservationists.[33] Very few of these films are housed in film archives, nor do they have a coherent or summary archive attached to them that might catalog representative or atypical works. Some films and promotional materials exist within larger archives, some oriented, like the Kinsey Institute Library, around inquiry into sexuality research. The salacious and sexual nature of much adult cinema has no doubt given archivists and preservationists pause, even as our knowledge of the volume of films to be preserved, the number of presumed "lost films," or ones that still need to be rediscovered has grown. Some films were sold or lost without an archival imprimatur or institutional stewardship—and the smaller number of circulating prints has also limited their capacity for archival rediscovery, although "lost" films have continued to emerge in specialty video niches, but also through scholarly rediscovery, as is the case with a newly recovered 35mm print of *The Orgy at Lil's Place* found recently at the Kinsey Institute.[34] Other bodies of texts, such as most of the sexploitation films Andy Milligan made with producer William Mishkin, are definitively lost: Mishkin's son Lewis destroyed the prints after his father's death. Data and research gathered and disseminated about sexploitation cinema have circulated piecemeal through the efforts of a small number of vigilant film scholars, amateur historians, for-profit video distributors, private collectors, and sex film devotees. This has slowly begun to change recently, as the establishment in 2014 of an Adult Film History special interest group in the Society for Cinema and Media Studies and a growing group of younger scholars undertaking aspects of this research attest. In the age of crowdfunding and retro-nostalgia, newly organized archives are also emerging—for example, the American Genre Film Archive devoted to low-budget exploitation films and based in Austin, Texas.

Most significantly, public knowledge regarding sexploitation followed the reopening market for these films in their recirculation on cult and underground video circuits in the 1980s and now, more recently, in wider digital formats. Sexploitation films gained a robust second life on home video beginning in the mid- to late 1980s and into the early 1990s, as cult audiences, niche fans, and nostalgic enthusiasts for American trash or low culture found in the films an alternative appeal counter to the slick surfaces of studio productions. These audiences and collectors espoused a particular zeal for sexploitation films' quasi-documentary qualities as "time capsules" of the 1960s, their anachronistic and politically passé sleaziness, their transgressive demeanor of rebellious independence, their financial limitations and their aesthetics of impoverishment. In magazines such as *FilmFax, Psychotronic Video,* and *Shock Cinema,* and in the *Re/Search* compendium *Incredibly Strange Films* as well as various B-movie and "bad movie" guides, sexploitation films were among the low-cultural cinematic texts that were extolled and excavated, seen as a refreshing counter to the "corporate" pablum of late 1980s and 1990s multiplex cinema. *Incredibly Strange Films,* perhaps one of the first such publications, released in 1985, was in many ways a paean to the anachronism of sexploitation cinema—with interviews and profiles of sexploitation directors such as Doris Wishman, Joe Sarno, Herschell Gordon Lewis, and Russ Meyer.[35] For audiences of paracinema, as Jeffrey Sconce has termed it, sexploitation represented a field of practice more obscure and more appealing in its unkempt independence and illegitimacy than the discourses around the emergent talents of the New Hollywood directors or art house auteurs.[36] The era of home video opened up access to unknown and unexplored corners of autonomous and then seemingly anonymous productions, yet ones that revealed the work of intrepid operators and creative talents invested in making films in whatever venue might allow it, and despite certain limitations of means. With the widening video circulation provided by early exploitation film distributors and collectors, most notable among them Something Weird Video, but also Sinister Cinema, Video Vault, and independent collectors and video traders, this amateur, fan-oriented sphere became the logical location for the earliest amateur historical and vernacular discourses on sexploitation's mode of production, often gathered under the broader rubric of cult or psychotronic cinema.[37] The psychotronic milieu, a tributary of postmidnight movie culture, operated at the interstices of the rise of *Mystery Science Theater 3000* and exhibited both retrospective nostalgia for the vintage of 1960s turbulence and idealism and a relish for atypical cinematic conventions; this milieu gave ground to the establishment of a sexploitation cinephilia.

The research for this book began in this largely predigital, persistently analog moment, with fanzines and mail order small print catalogs, in local video stores (such as Reel Life and Kim's Video and the well-stocked rental behemoth Tower Video in New York City) and purloined bootlegs, as well as in distinct local places like the Anthology Film Archives in New York City and urban underground film and queer film festivals. Pursuing sources and industry data on microfilm and fiche and in small corners of larger libraries and archives, the discovery of small details often took circuitous routes. That moment of this project's inception seems a far cry from the plethora of detail, however inaccurate or tendentious at times, that circulates today online on IMDb, various cult and exploitation websites, collector and fan review sites, and specialty blogs and compendia on varied aspects and ephemera connected to sexploitation cinema, and as a subset of grind house, cult, adult, or generally weird cinema histories. Much has changed in terms of the access provided to and vernacular knowledges circulating around the films and milieus that produced these peculiar, maddening, and oddly seductive films. At the same time, beyond filmmakers such as Radley Metzger and Russ Meyer, as Eric Schaefer has noted, who represented the summit of the industry and its apex of cinematic craft, and were made legible through the terms of auteurism (as I discuss in chapter 4), many more sexploitation films have remained obscure despite these niche audiences and publics. Their obscurity is reproduced as a residual and countercultural value in their second life—a reproduction of the underground status of these filmic objects, a doggedly recursive replaying of their place in time and their status as "trash."[38] Yet they also serve as grist for the mill of urban and cosmopolitan specialty tastes in a debauched scene of the historical past—made evident as much in the anecdotal and ethnographically oriented books such as Josh Alan Friedman's *Tales of Times Square* and Michelle Clifford and John Landis's *Sleazoid Express* and in the grind house fever that followed the release of Tarantino and Rodriguez's retro-fitted double feature.

Such "grind house nostalgia," as David Church and others have called it, has also witnessed a certain revivalism in sexploitation's public programming, as in the "Deuce" series at the independent microcinema Nitehawk Cinemas in Williamsburg, Brooklyn. Sexploitation- and adult film–specific blogs and online magazines, such as *The Rialto Report,* also indicate new and younger audiences, if not a third "millennial" wave of enthusiasm.[39] The 2009 sexploitation retrospective at the British Film Institute curated by Julian Marsh, which screened representative works by Meyer, Sarno, and Metzger, and the series "This Is Softcore" at Lincoln Center in New York City, which profiled Radley Metzger's films in 2014, signal a widening repertory audience. In addition to a series of documentary films produced around and about the subject of sexploitation, exploitation, and grind house cinema, including films such as *Schlock! The Secret History of American Movies* (Ray Greene, 2001), among others, and the recent *That's Sexploitation!* (Frank Henenlotter, 2013, produced by Something Weird Video) and *The Sarnos: A Life in Dirty Movies* (Wiktor Ericsson, 2013), also demonstrate a popular interest in sexploitation's history.[40] In such a ripe moment, one would hope that the sexploitation film, some fifty years later, is soon to arrive.

My interest in sexploitation films emerged out of the convergence of a subcultural and academic space of analysis and out of these questions of past moments of reception—in the cross-pollination of a feminist film theory classroom and the local underground film festival. Championed by feminist avant-garde filmmakers Peggy Ahwesh and M. M. Serra, the rediscovered sexploitation director Doris Wishman, one of the very few women working as director and producer in this primarily male-dominated industry, was soon to visit my graduate feminist film theory classroom (this was 1998). In anticipation, I went to see her film *Double Agent 73* (1974) at the New York Underground Film Festival, where Wishman was featured as a special guest. Her singular position as sole woman in a male-dominated mode of production was fascinating and stupefying, an intrigue compounded by the uniquely vertiginous style of her work and the peculiarity of the film itself. *Double Agent 73*'s conceit involved the implantation of a spy camera in the protagonist's (exotic dancer Chesty Morgan) very large breasts, making them a somatic weapon wielded by the actor contra spectator, and made the film an unwitting exercise in screen theory.[41] What may have begun as a theoretically driven interest in this mode of production and the formal architecture of its erotic spectacle became a broader concern with the complex social and political context out of which Wishman's films, and many others' films, were molded. Numerous questions emerged, among them, what was the milieu and the conditions that gave rise to such a film and its highly baroque premises and gimmicks, all bound up in the spectacle of the naked female body? What kind of audience attended and engaged with these simultaneously excessive and rhetorically complex films? The fusion and intermingling of a subcultural, cinephile milieu and a scholarly, academic one ultimately provoked this exploration into the history of the sexploitation film and its relationship to its spectator.

In the beginning of this project, I was bootlegging VHS tapes from my Kim's Video rentals—who employed a full wall in the back corner, just outside of the hard-core porn backroom, devoted to Something Weird tapes. In the late 1990s, sexploitation's diffusion occurred through videotape, and this was certainly the key intervention of Something Weird Video in the field, the Seattle-based video distributor, run by the late Mike Vraney, that from the early 1990s onward bought many sexploitation film prints outright and in bulk from whomever they could and built perhaps the largest commercial collection of sexploitation, exploitation, scare films, and other filmic arcana.[42] Their evolving catalog contains an impressive assortment of sexploitation but also drug films, hygiene films, imported spy films, trailers, 16mm and 8mm adult loops, and early porn. A fruitful collaboration with the producer David Friedman and the acquisition of numerous works by Joe Sarno, Harry Novak, Doris Wishman, Barry Mahon, and many others secured their place as the scrappy Criterion Collection of sexploitation film, with less emphasis on pristine restoration and more on voracity. Catering to a retro-nostalgia fueled in the VHS era for the shocks and titillations of yesterday, the stock in trade of Something Weird relied on the premise of the time capsule and of giving voice to the horizon of the past spectator's desire, however bewildered, aroused, or embarrassed.

At the time of writing, sexploitation films by varied filmmakers and from diverse distributors are available for instant viewing through many digital, online streaming, and on-demand services, such as Fandor, Netflix, Amazon Prime, and Hulu, as well as whole films that appear and disappear on YouTube and other online video sites. The changes to the video market and the reign of streaming delivery have no doubt had an impact on the ways that sexploitation gained value via video circulation, and its larger effects remain to be seen in relation to the acquisition of physical media. The establishment of grind house–oriented or exploitation-centered streaming channels, such as Exploitation.tv and The Grindhouse Channel, is an attempt by independent distributors to adjust to the changing climate of home entertainment. Nevertheless, this sea change in digital access to the films, like the proliferation of access to production information regarding films via online fora, is remarkable and has no doubt made sexploitation a more popular and widely viewed form in the popular cultural public sphere and particularly among niche, specialty audiences, even if it does little for actual preservation or the sexploitation archive. Yet what persists, at some level, is the sense of sexploitation cinema's remaining and relative obscurity as an aesthetic form, even as canons and countercanons of significant filmmakers (Sarno, Wishman, Metzger, Meyer, the Findlays, Lewis, Milligan), actors (Audrey Campbell, Pat Barrington, Marsha Jordan), and producers (Novak, Friedman, Weiss) have found a new audience in the digital context of collector, niche, and narrow-casted tastes. Specialty distributors and conservationists, such as Something Weird, Alternative Cinema's Retro Seduction line, Cult Epics, Vinegar Syndrome, and Distribpix, are all recirculating the legacy of 1960s and 1970s sex cinema in more visible ways, available for purchase on Amazon, at Best Buy, and at other mainstream retailers. What made sexploitation films forgotten was in part the perception of their negligible status as culturally valuable texts or objects and their sense of obsolescence and anachronistic function once hard-core arrived. The work of intrepid collectors and enthusiasts, as well as that of for-profit video businesses with a vested interest, such as Something Weird, has immeasurably reconstituted the history at the level of access and what can be watched and rewatched.

But it is still the labor of film history to recover the wider aesthetic, cultural, and industrial significance of these works—their importance in a wider field of film practice and in their innovation in the battles against censorship and the policing of obscenity law. This book focuses on the formation of sexploitation cinema as a complex aesthetic and cultural phenomenon, which had a force and drive of its own. This approach has its limitations in terms of its granularity, but it is committed to giving a wider sense of sexploitation's public existence as an object of scrutiny, a field of practice, discourse, and concern in wider debates about sexuality, obscenity, spectatorship, and film culture of the period. It accounts for the tenor of sexploitation's circulation in the public life of media forms and traces the discourses that accrued around it, particularly concerning the fractious status of adult filmgoing itself.

Lewd Looks joins a range of scholarship that explores from varied perspectives the film culture and sexual politics of the 1960s, its status as representation, culture, and cult.[43] It aims to elaborate on a period that is underrepresented in the histories of American cinema, perhaps due to its "transitional" and thus liminal status between "classical Hollywood" and New Hollywood and on the margins of other independent production scenes.[44] As an entry in the contextualization of the history of adult film, soft- and hard-core, it addresses the relationship between economic, industrial, legal, representational, and discursive shifts that allowed the emergence of a previously shadowy category of film and spectator. This book assesses the importance of sexual content to the American film scene of the 1960s and establishes how this content was regulated, classified, and managed by regulatory and public agencies in the name of a collective national propriety. Additionally, as a contribution to theories of the obscene image, it conjoins the cultural and symbolic work that these images perform with an understanding of their circulation within a public sphere of cinematic consumption.

Sexploitation film thus remains a low-cultural, "bad" object without a housing archive or a unitary method that might arrogate its meaning. As an ephemeral, and, until recently, disposable cultural form, sexploitation as an object of knowledge requires its "collectors" to be comprehensive and expansive. Affectionately allied with the "trashy," the research paradigm that sexploitation demands necessitates multiple methodologies. This project employs reception studies as a mode of film history that intersects with both cultural studies and historiography; theories of the image and of gender and sexuality; and the historicization of the discourse of the film audience. In a sense, this book is as much answerable to a cultural history and the history of sexual representation and politics as it is to film studies. Barbara Klinger, in retooling and reorienting reception studies to the aims of cinema studies, connects the goals of reception with the goals of film history more generally.[45] Klinger argues for the necessity of a "total history" that attempts to bring together as many aspects of a film's social existence as possible, acknowledging the impossibly idealist nature of the task, one that must nevertheless be pursued to achieve a "materialist approach to textuality." Piecing together the history of sexploitation film and its reception requires the mobilization of varying and diverse sources and texts. One challenge that emerges is how to integrate and synthesize primary materials from disparate areas of research into a cohesive historical narrative. For the purposes of this book's analytic, the film spectator is deployed as a historical figure who operates as a point of synthesis, a figure who emblematizes the crisis of the film industry as a whole as well as being a figure for the projection of the specific anxieties of the sexploitation film and of the problem of "consuming sex."

By reconstructing some of the conditions and contexts of sexploitation films' public life, one can, in Klinger's words, pursue the sense of sexploitation's "semiotic environment" in which relations between different audiences and viewers of sexploitation encountered the films and their traces.[46] The engagement here with discourses of reception studies attempts to bridge the gap between understanding empirical spectators and imagined ones through the dense discursive materiality of sexploitation's public life. By thinking the textual spectator produced in and by the films, the "peek snatcher" or the "girl with hungry eyes" alongside the historical spectator whose traces appear in archival accounts, I would like not to foreclose on the relation between the materiality of actual social practices and the animating stakes of the discursive and of cultural fantasy.

Chapters

The chapters herein move through a set of contexts through which sexploitation's public status was mediated and talked about. Chapter 1 discusses the importance of regulatory and censorship contexts to the constitution of sexploitation film as a mode of production and set of aesthetic strategies. The chapter analyzes the history of sexploitation producers' wrangling with censor boards, various obscenity suits and legal interventions, and other forms of regulation and self-regulation. While the history of censorship is only one framework through which to understand sexploitation's mode of production, this chapter argues that a horizon of prohibition on sexual content was constitutive to sexploitation's identity. The chapter thus surveys the appearance of sexploitation in these highly public and contentious disputes about sex, cinema, and aesthetic value and investigates how sexploitation producers both capitalized on and negotiated accusations of obscenity amid a transforming national standard of screen permissiveness. Detailing the history of legal decisions that wore away at the acceptability of nudity and sexual situations; specific contestations of sexploitation producers, such as Radley Metzger and Ted Paramore, with state censor boards; and the late-1960s climate of local and community uprisings against adult films, this chapter analyzes the terms through which an idea of proper and improper viewers was produced within censorship discourse around the threat of sexploitation as a new type of filmgoing activity. Therefore censorship, regulation, and the history of obscenity law are deployed as one sphere of reception of sexploitation films, yielding a set of expectations regarding spectatorial response and aesthetic value.

Chapters 2 and 3 examine the aesthetic and thematic manifestations of sexploitation films over the decade, tracing the development of the films' style and modes of address. They survey the range of films created in the 1960s and their unique textuality, attending to the shifting terms of representation of nudity and the sexualized female body in its varied subgenres and cycles. Elaborating some generic and ideological characteristics of sexploitation films of the 1960s, these two chapters contend that sexploitation films, in their constitutive interest in presenting forbidden spectacle, often thematized their own conditions of reception and more broadly made the "problem" of consuming sex—in scenarios of looking, peeping, erotic consumption, and scenes of sexual exchange—their anchoring tension or paradox. Chapter 2 tracks the shift from the early-1960s "nudie cuties," such as *The Immoral Mr. Teas, The Adventures of Lucky Pierre* (Herschell Gordon Lewis, 1961), and *Bunny Yeager's Nude Camera* (Barry Mahon, 1963), among others, with their formulaic and comic presentations of female nudity, to the darker, more violent variegations in mid- to late-1960s films often called "roughies," such as *Lorna* (Russ Meyer, 1964), *The Defilers* (Lee Frost, 1965), *Sin in the Suburbs* (Joe Sarno, 1964), and *Bad Girls Go to Hell* (Doris Wishman, 1965). Chapter 3 examines the rising interest in female sexual desire and agency, and alternative sexual practices in the continuation of the roughie form and in films that begin to deal with female desire and agency, and forms of sexual "deviance," such as lesbianism and sadomasochism, in quasi-documentary and sex exposé variants and that take up the countercultural zeitgeist of more liberatory attitudes, such as swinger films. Chapter 3 considers films such as *White Slaves of Chinatown* (Joseph P. Mawra, 1964), *Free Love Confidential* (Gordon Heller, 1967), *Office Love-In, White Collar Style* (Stephen Apostolof, 1968), and *Monique, My Love* (Peter Woodcock, 1969). Both chapters analyze films that articulate a certain concern with the transforming sexual marketplace and the reconceptualization of gender and sexual roles within the cultural context of the 1960s. Embedded within the narrative and syntax of sexploitation films, despite their overwhelming and chaotic variety, is a reflexive interest in the consumption of sex and its conditions of visibility within an economy that vacillates between notions of scarcity and abundance. Over the course of the decade, sexploitation's preoccupation with corporeal spectacle, sexual consumerism, and female sexual autonomy is paramount and gets mapped across a broad expansion of interest, from male peepers and perverts, in chapter 2, to the emergence of female observers and female sexual agents in the 1960s, discussed in chapter 3. The conclusion of chapter 3 points to ways sexploitation films narrate their place in a wider sex film market, as in the meta-backstage drama *Starlet!* (Richard Kanter, 1969).

Chapter 4 elaborates on the critical and cultural reception of sexploitation film as a phenomenon over the course of the 1960s, assessing how sexploitation films, their audiences, and their exhibition contexts entered the public imaginary and became indicative of the larger social problem of sexual media as well as the more specialized problem of filmic taste. Drawing from varied archival sources, it examines different discourses of filmgoing that obtained within this marginal mode of production. Rather than presuming the shorthand of the audience as dupe, which sexploitation filmmakers themselves often perpetuated in their promotional appeals to the "slack jawed trade,"[47] it points to places where sexploitation film, as a type of filmgoing experience, began to be negotiated through a language of aesthetic distinction and connoisseurship. In these discourses of reception, the figure of the adult film audience becomes an animating object of projection, speculation, and anxiety but also is newly constituted as a taste public and a consumer. It treats the way the reception of Russ Meyer and Radley Metzger films positioned them as "auteurs" of the mode as well as offering unique accounts of countercultural forays into the sex film scene in the mid- to late 1960s. The last section of the chapter examines how the federal inquest into obscenity set its sights on the empirical audience as an object of knowledge. While acknowledging the ultimately fragmentary nature of these transcriptions of sexploitation's reception, this chapter illuminates the conditions—and the anxieties—of moviegoing within the newly constituted adult film marketplace as well as sexploitation's determinative role in defining it.

Thus this book investigates a set of interlocking contexts for the emergence and decline of the sexploitation film, using the optic of reception and the figure of the spectator. In approximating some of the conditions of sexploitation films' reception across the decade of the 1960s, it reconstructs some of the ways that these contradictory films, which trafficked in libidinal excess and forms of diegetic restriction, were received, perceived, and regulated by their various publics and how they spoke to the era's anxieties about gender, sexuality, and the obscene image. Finally, *Lewd Looks* problematizes some commonplaces around our notions of the 1960s as an untrammeled, liberatory sphere by pursuing the semiotics and affective resonance of sexploitation's bounded images, its illicit views, and the horizons of the historical spectator. Sexploitation, as *Lewd Looks* suggests, was always an anachronistic, belated form, about to expire and about to begin, caught between different regimes of representation and between a wary circumspection about social and sexual change and a capitalization of its profit-making potentials. Moralizing and hedonistic, hearkening to a time before such roiling transformation, yet also prefiguring a possibly more sexually egalitarian, if unreachable, future in the fantasized eruption of corporeal pleasures, sexploitation's contradictory identity articulates the capacity of new cinematic forms both to trace sedimentation and to promise the novel shocks of contingency. At the heart of these films lie the fleshiness and obdurate materiality of bodies both recalcitrant to and in excess of the hold of the gawker's gaze.

CHAPTER ONE

Producing Permissiveness
Censorship, Obscenity Law, and the Trials of Spectatorship

Sexploitation films of the 1960s, much like their classical exploitation forebears, were marked by, and their industrial identity constituted through, the horizon of prohibition and regulatory limitations on screen content operative at the time. A catalog of both an emergent category of filmic content (erotic display) and an archive of the paradoxically as yet unseen (hard-core sex and penetrative intercourse), sexploitation films narrate a unique history of iterative expression around sexuality. Through the suggestiveness of off-screen space, strategic nudity, and simulated sex, sexploitation films and their history retrospectively recount an archive of an absence, the absence of the kind of sexual representation that contemporary audiences have come to associate with the "adult cinema." Defined in part by state and local censorship practices, informal and self-regulation, and other limitations on screen content, sexploitation films provide documentation of the transformation of cinematic conventions of sexual representation. These films instrumentally impacted and contributed to what has been called the decade's "liberalization of the screen."

Solid historical, sociological, and observational accounts of film censorship and regulation in this period, and in American film history more broadly, have substantially explored the specific debates and changing tides of obscenity law.[1] This chapter explores the role and position of sexploitation within this larger history to examine the multiple avenues through which sexploitation forged its fragile identity as the purveyor of "barely legal," forbidden sexual spectacles as well as the means through which legislative, community, and government bodies and the film industry attempted to regulate and control these representations. Central to these historical and discursive conflicts over what made an image, a book, or a film obscene was an emergent curiosity and anxiety about the spectator of "adult" media, the erotica consumer, whose etiology and psychological makeup would become one of the primary subjects of the late-1960s federal investigation into the traffic in erotic materials, culminating in the final reports of the Presidential Commission on Obscenity and Pornography in 1970. The place of sexploitation film in establishing a market for sexually explicit materials, by the late 1960s and early 1970s, would ironically lead the way toward its declining profitability as a stand-alone purveyor of sexual spectacle, as more explicit and hard-core works came into public exhibition. Yet the impact of these films and the developing public and legal interest in the characteristics of their audience signaled a historic transformation in both the role sexuality played in American cinema and the definition and classification of sex films as well as their viewers. This chapter considers how sexploitation film took part in larger conflicts regarding obscenity and censorship and how the genre benefited from and defined itself in relation to regulatory controversy and restriction. Censorial discourses around sexploitation films constructed an emerging vision—partly imagined, partly sociological—of the adult film audience. That prohibitions can be seen as productive rather than overwhelmingly repressive is a familiar historical insight, one derived from Michel Foucault's epistemology of sexual knowledge forms. Though this point has become customary in analyses of cultural and political regulation of cinema and media, it remains useful in providing a framework through which to deal with the historical period and the mode of production in question, a mode that trafficked in the illicit and forbidden.[2]

"Why Was This Censored?"

No film more directly encapsulates the constitution of sexploitation as a product of film censorship and obscenity legislation, and emerges as a contradictory discourse *about* that network of regulation, than does Barry Mahon's film *Censored* (1965).[3] The film was a timely statement on the politics and mercurial nature of film censorship, released as it was in the year that the New York State Censor Board was virtually disbanded and in which "prior restraint" was deemed unconstitutional.[4] The film was also appropriately the subject of an obscenity case in Maryland in 1966. Mahon, one of the most prolific directors of sexploitation films in New York, a World War II fighter pilot, entered the film business as pilot, then manager, and later producer of Errol Flynn's films in the 1950s. After Flynn's death, he went on to produce a wide range of low-budget nudie films, sex exposés, and grimy urban melodramas, stories of crime, erotic vice, and sexual ruin often filmed in the environs where he worked—

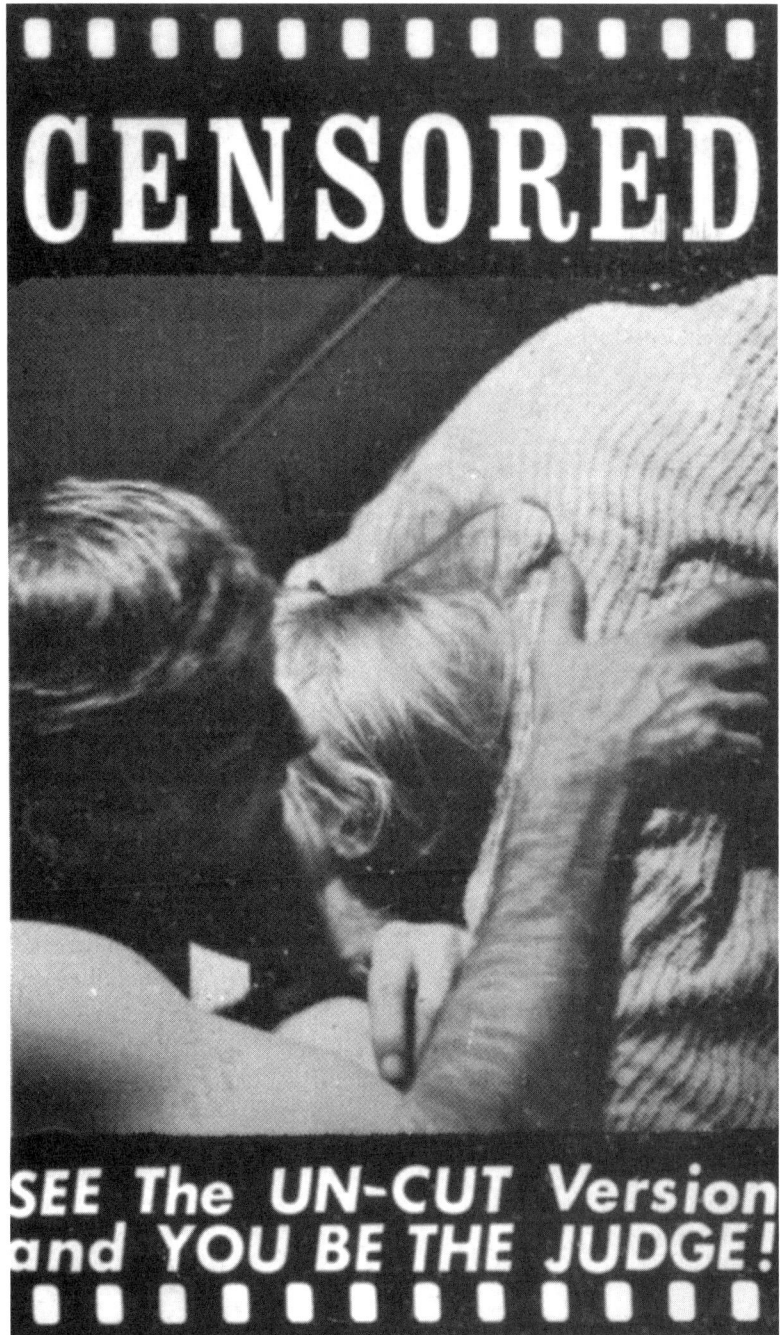

FIGURE 4. Barry Mahon's *Censored*, press book advertising mat. Courtesy of Something Weird Video.

midtown Manhattan as well as Times Square and Greenwich Village. In the mid-1960s, Mahon managed a staff of apprentices and personnel of around fifteen and directed ten to twelve films per year, working out of his office in the Film Center at 45th Street and 9th Avenue.[5] Mahon abandoned his sex film business in New York to make children's films in Florida in 1968.[6]

Emblematic of Mahon's shrewd shoestring approach, *Censored* was a fake documentary, a meta-text of sorts, employing a simple yet rich gimmick. The film's premise and its execution crystallize the industrial circumstance of sexploitation films and define the ways these films positioned themselves discursively within film culture and commerce. Presented as a documentary of curated film excerpts, *Censored* alleges to offer its audience a selection of scenes that have been cut out from existing films due to the intervention of censorial authorities. The film and its purportedly archival contents were actually entirely fabricated by Mahon, or as he claimed in his later Maryland obscenity case, "re-enacted," within the "compilation film" format.[7] The film offered up not so much a fictionalization of sexploitation film's conditions of production and exhibition as an exposition of the circumstances of the films' vulnerabilities as public, regulated texts. Professing to show segments removed from previously banned films, it becomes testimony to the artfulness of the exploitation gimmick, a treatise on the peculiar relationship of sexploitation cinema to the social limitations that it would otherwise claim to defy. A Frankenstein monster of sorts, a sewn-together body of imagined celluloid fragments, the film revivifies a collection of possible and approximated offenses to the delicate public and regulatory psyche. *Censored* is unique in that it so blatantly and directly foregrounds censorship as a compelling narrative unto itself, baldly acknowledging that the taint of censorial controversy was a marketing boon for film exhibitors' profits.

The film begins, self-reflexively, with a title image of a film canister with *Censored* tagged onto it. The shot shifts to the front of the desk of a middle-aged white man, who begins speaking directly to the camera and discussing the U.S. Constitution in relation to film censorship. Taking on a middlebrow tone, the narrator, actor Sid Berry, leads the audience through the situation of film regulation circa 1965. Berry appeals to his viewers through an idiom of cultural citizenship and democratic judgment. Berry claims to offer the audience the ability to judge for themselves rather than have the films judged for them by other parties, such as censor boards, police officers, and others, pinpointing one of the resonant cultural aporias about the adjudication of obscenity itself, that is, its subjective, evaluative nature. Through this manner of seemingly impartial direct address, the film provides its imagined spectator a degree of distance from the material being shown. Berry asks,

> Still where does the fine line between constitutional freedoms and pornography lie? Now I'm not a judge, nor a moralist. I've only compiled an interesting and certainly controversial collection of scenes which at one time or another had been cut out by the producer because their film had been censored by a local political body or police organization. Now keep in mind times are changing, what is out today will be commonplace tomorrow. The people's concept of morality is not a stable thing. . . . As you watch the scenes you are about to see, and the others which I will show you, I will ask for your decision—should they have been censored? Now before I start, if any of you feel that the scenes you are about to see are more shocking than expected, or you find will perhaps leave you morally disturbed, please feel free to leave the theater. We must also insist that the audience be adults only.

The refrain of "why was this censored?" which is also used liberally in the film's theatrical trailer, creates a mode of address that is markedly detached, aligned with the posture of free inquiry. By deflecting to the film audience, and giving them the role of adjudicators of offensive material, the film gestures toward the inquisitive and morally righteous stance of the vice squad, the bluenose, the community decency committee, and the courts, while simultaneously endorsing the rights of free expression in the arts. Yet the material evidence of the film indulges the audience in its presumed desire to see the taboo, perverse, and socially marginalized images that have been promised. By replicating the position of judgment, usually associated with the mind-set of the censor, *Censored* masquerades as both a public service announcement and an exposé on contemporary events. Appealing to its audience as an ideal viewer or "average citizen" under the guise of public pedagogy, the film mobilizes the discourses of obscenity law as articulated by the 1957 Roth test, "whether to the average person, applying contemporary community standards, the dominant theme of the material, taken as a whole, appeals to the prurient interest."[8] That the viewer of sexploitation films could be branded an "average citizen" is, in the provisions of the discourse of the time, a contradiction in terms, an oxymoron at best. Thus the film draws attention to the patently obvious disavowal of the very average—often white, middle-class, male—audiences who were attending sexploitation and nudie films at this time.[9]

The film's address buffers the viewer from his own ostensibly prurient impulses and installs a viewing position in which judgment is the operative lingua franca. This operation both alienates the audience from

FIGURE 5. Sid Berry, authoritative narrator and guide in *Censored*, press book still. Courtesy of Something Weird Video.

its bodily desires and lewd thoughts, through the intellectualization and contextualization of the footage, and presents these (fake) excised scenes as fragmentary and deracinated from their filmic "origins" and narrative contexts. As unsupported fragments and images decontextualized from their narrative framing, they take on the quality of spectacular moments with *more* of a hypothetical capacity to incite lust and arousal. In fact, Mahon's mobilization of the footage seems to go directly against the portion of the Roth doctrine that necessitates that the film be "taken as a whole" in ascertaining its obscene content. By presenting these images *out* of context—granted that they never *had* an original context to begin with—*Censored* challenges the legal justifications of proper filmic interpretation in relation to screen sex.

Such contradictoriness was a central characteristic of sexploitation films' ideological stance, yet it also attests to how the genre created a space for itself through a number of textual and extratextual alibis. For Mahon's film, the documentary mode, pedagogical format, and contemporary censorship context itself all legitimate the scenes viewed in different ways. More than questioning whether the scenes incite lustful thoughts—the index of an obscene text's intentionality—the film questions the audience about whether its content would or does incite the censor's scissor. This is a circuitous route back to the problem of the obscene film as an enticing, arousing, pandering object, mediated through the inquest into the mind, and implicit lusts, of the censor. The censor and the prurient viewer become a unified entity through this device of address and framing. From this intellectualized remove, the erotic text is both delivered to the viewer and quarantined from legal or moralist scrutiny. However, this device did not prevent the film from being taken up as obscene in the state courts, as we will see later.

The "banned" footage that constitutes the film vacillates between the banal and the ludicrous and is often marked by a haphazard syntactical construction. Certain scenes are repeated and reused throughout the film, giving the film a recursive, didactic function. Additionally, continuity between scenes is functionally negligible, justified by the compilation format. One excerpt portrays a nudist camp, in which the traffic of bodies through diegetic space supports the prohibitive conventions of the time around erotic representation—women enter and exit a room where they are undressing, although only backsides and breasts are glimpsed. To avoid showing pubic hair, Mahon only films these scenes from behind or from the side. In one scene, two nude women attempt to jump a fence; the shot remains stationary and positioned behind them. The narrator asks, "Is nudity per se wrong? Can it be when taken on a completely artistic basis? Why? Is their art any less of an ideal? . . . The following scenes were found objectionable. What do *you* think?" The film offers up incrementally more extreme scenarios that mime the then developing styles and generic strategies of the sexploitation film: an unclothed artist's model is being painted, a photographer instructs his nude model, a woman is raped in a hallway, nude young women are tied up in a "white slavery" scenario in what looks like the lower level of a houseboat, and another woman is assaulted by an intruder in her kitchen. This progression of sequences self-reflexively duplicates the development of the sexploitation film and its subcycles in the early to mid-1960s, along the line of an increasingly challenging, risqué content, and aligns, respectively, with the changes from the nudist camp film and nudie cutie to the artist's model film to the more violently oriented "roughie." Through such a consecutive, meta-chronological arrangement, the film inadvertently narrates the story of sexploitation as an industry and a mode of production, with particular aesthetic benchmarks and defining characteristics, as well as showing directly the visible impact of changing obscenity laws on films' sexual content.

When the excerpts transition to scenes of nudity combined with violence, the narrator asks the audience whether the scenes were cut due to overwhelming brutality or due to the presence of exposed flesh. A psychopath has kidnapped two girls whom we see from overhead, through the frame of a lower level of what appears to be a houseboat, as he ties them up. Two particularly preposterous and obviously staged excerpts push at the boundaries of the film's already ragged claims to veracity; one features a "madman" inexplicably sawing off the leg of a young girl as she screams and throwing the dismembered leg—visibly fake and plastic—into a furnace, while the other presents a scene of a female Nazi officer, with a swastika banner hanging behind her, proceeding to brand and maim a young, naked woman who is roped up before her. The shot is taken from behind the victim and framed in a doorway, showing the girl's bare backside, while the actual contact of the torture implement (a hot poker?) with her flesh remains unseen, as smoke rises up after contact, again reinforcing the limitations of what can and cannot be shown. Again, Sid Berry states, "The basic censors are the people themselves . . . where is the point where the bulk of the audience will walk out? Or worse yet, not enter the theater?" This constant gesture toward the index of audience response conflates the act of the censors and the proscribed actions of the film viewer, while also deferring to the argument that the audience is the most appropriate censor in merely not choosing to see a particular film or image.

The film returns to scenes of a more sexual nature, of implied bedroom sex, and quotidian views of nude female bodies laying aloft on various beds, their bodies fragmented, heads often cut off by the frame, as we hear their banal conversation. The camera takes a more devoted and tactile attention to naked legs and breasts held in unmotivated, and seemingly fragmentary, medium close-ups, as Berry continually interjects "why was this censored?" *Censored* becomes a self-reflexive text paradoxically at the same time that it performs a feat of decided earnestness. Enacting the cat-and-mouse relationship between filmmakers and the censors through its generic convention (educational film, reportage, pseudo-documentary), the film also retells this story as a newsworthy slice of current events through its narration—no different, it would like us to think, from an exposé article in *Time* magazine.

The film concludes with Berry summarizing the scenes we have seen and reflecting on their status within the spectrum of the potentially obscene, ending with the following credo, which serves again to indicate the libertarian ethos of the film:

> Now you have it—as many of the facts as I can offer in an hour's time. Does censorship exist in your community? Is such a body legal? Have you been imposed upon by some minority group? . . . Just remember, you have a right to say, to see, to hear, and to read what you wish.

FIGURE 6. The staged scene of kidnapping, one of many hypothetically excised excerpts in *Censored,* press book film still. Courtesy of Something Weird Video.

Censored articulates the conflicts and layers of subterfuge at work between sexploitation filmmakers and the censors of the time. It also illuminates the ways the spectator of sexploitation is imbricated in this dynamic, constructed as both an "average citizen" and an impartial observer by the film but also, on another level, disavowed. Through its mode of address, Mahon's film allows its audience to occupy contradictory spectatorial positions—the regulation-seeking censor, the seeker of education or sociological enlightenment, the "merely curious" naïf, and the wayward "average person"—while most directly denying the figure of the sensation-seeking erotica spectator. The film denatures the position of the film viewer, turning the sexploitation audience into a judicious average public, appointed as citizenry, emboldened to speak as consumers within a democratic market for their choice of cinematic expression. *Censored* historicizes and dramatizes its own conditions of reception—a reception sphere that included, as I will argue in this chapter, not only the expected nudie film ticket–buying audience but also censor boards, community and religious groups, the police, the film industry, and the lay public, all of them implied in the address of the film.

Fittingly, the exhibition of *Censored* faced controversy in the state of

Maryland in 1966, when the film was charged as obscene by the state licensing board. The crux of the dispute was whether an unorthodox gesture by the trial judge, in assigning a jury the role of expert witnesses and evidence bearers, was legal or in fact unconstitutional. When the decision of the state censor board was taken to the circuit court, the judge allowed the twenty-five-person jury to serve as "expert witnesses" to watch the film and ascertain whether it was indeed obscene—perversely and inadvertently replicating the injunction of Berry, the film's narrator, to his audience to judge on their own. Despite the exhibitor's protest regarding this assignation of expertise, the court ruled that the film was obscene. After two appeals, the obscenity decision was reversed.[10]

It is not only ironic that the film, which hinges in its content on an authoritative pedagogical address, through the means of a "pseudo-expert" narrator, should get caught up in a court case that hinges precisely on the validity and definition of expert evidence in ascertaining obscenity. Furthermore, the filmmaker's use of "reenactments" rather than actual film footage was not considered an obstacle to its "redeeming social importance." The court further declared that the film's anticensorship stance was not without social value, determined with reference to previous obscenity rulings in cases such as *Jacobellis v. Ohio* (1964), involving Louis Malle's film *The Lovers* (1959), and *Memoirs v. Massachusetts* (1966), concerning John Cleland's novel *Fanny Hill: Memoirs of a Woman of Pleasure*. The court, in its final decision, ended up providing its own interpretation of the text, stating that although the film possessed "a most generous display of female epidermis, both fore and aft, the whole thing is about as titillating and exciting as a ton of coal."[11] The court's adjudication of the prurient appeal of *Censored* amounted to a defense of the film, not on the grounds of its artfulness or lack of it, but through the available terms of constitutional protection for motion pictures.

If, on the textual level, *Censored* represents the raison d'être and contradictory identity of the sexploitation film, one part bluenose and one part lecher, how did sexploitation, as a mode of production, develop this particular relationship to the censors? How were the films managed by these regulatory bodies, as well as through modes of industrial policing and informal self-regulation, as *potentially* obscene? What were the effects, impacts, and products of these conflicts? In the following, I argue that sexploitation films developed around them a particular discourse, aesthetics, and mode of address that would evade the censors but also appeal to the viewer based on the supposition of *virtually* illegal or *almost* forbidden sexual content. Furthermore, I examine the vernacular and official discourses that circulated around sexploitation, branding it an "offensive" and renegade branch of the film industry, particularly in its proximity to other modes of production, such as the Hollywood studio film and other independent and foreign features. Out of these discourses of the obscene and the immoral would emerge a composite vision and collective imagining of the adult film audience, a figure broadly defined by, and caught between, a responsible, respectable maturity, on one hand, and the infectious potentiality of sexual license, particularly its pernicious impact on corruptible youth, on the other.

The Law of Filmic Obscenity and Its Evolution

While *Censored* offers a core sample of the legal and industrial circumstances faced by sexploitation films in the 1960s, a more detailed account of the landscape of obscenity law and censorship practices needs to be elaborated to understand the emergence of sexploitation as a new player within this filmic and cultural context. Although the 1960s has customarily been seen as a time of a loosening of restraint and a "freeing" of the screen, this much-heralded process did not happen without contention and dispute. Many heated conflicts transpired between community groups, municipal and religious organizations, state and city politicians, and local law enforcement agencies, all wishing to apply pressure on film producers and exhibitors to stem the tide of adult content in film, in response to changing federal statutes regarding the definition of obscenity. The tensions could be seen through a differentiation between the discourses around film obscenity on the national level, in the legal pronouncements of federal courts, and in the reactions of local communities and municipal agencies to the broadening of cinematic expression. Public intellectuals, acting in defense of sexual freedom in the arts, often took voluble positions against censorship—for example, as Paul Goodman's 1960 Reichian call for the elimination of repression in "Pornography, Art, and Censorship" and in Susan Sontag's defense of the literary pornography of the Marquis de Sade and Georges Bataille in "The Pornographic Imagination."[12] Despite the triumphalism of a narrative that would champion the broadening of expression in the arts, each victory for First Amendment rights and constitutional protection was customarily challenged and contested on the state and local levels. The terms of definition of obscenity, as a textual category and mode of classification of literary and visual works, had begun to change significantly in the 1950s. The Paramount decree of the late 1940s forced the divestiture of the major studios' exhibition holdings and facilitated an expansion of independent theaters showing non-Hollywood product.[13] On the heels of divestiture and the subsequent consent decrees, the influential 1952 *Miracle* film decision had altered the conception of film as a constitutionally protected realm of speech. In this case, the U.S. exhibition of Roberto Rossellini's forty-minute film *The Miracle* (*Il Miracolo*, 1948) was charged with blasphemous obscenity. When appealed to the U.S. Supreme Court, the justices finally acknowledged that movies as a cultural form should be granted constitutional protection as free speech, alongside the press and other "organs of public opinion,"[14] and thus overruled a thirty-seven-year precedent established by the 1915 *Mutual Film* decision.[15] This latter decision, in the early period of the American film industry's development, denied a "public status" to film, claiming that film was a business, predominantly entertainment, and therefore not protected as speech. Numerous historians have addressed the implications of the *Mutual* decision in terms of its underlying ideology of controlling an unruly, and oftentimes lower-class, immigrant audience, an anxiety managed through the branding of the film medium as inherently more prone to inciting passion and as having a capacity for social influence and "evil" because of its mass cultural nature.[16]

By the 1950s, the status of film as "a medium for the communication of ideas" facilitated an emerging view of film as artistic expression. The art house theater and the foreign film import complicated the film industry's understanding of the definitions of filmgoing, the constitution and desires of the film audience, and discourses of "film as art."[17] By the late 1950s, the notion of obscenity as a category of unprotected expression had been further narrowed to cover only sexual subjects and representations, as court decisions around literary and filmic works identified the key node of offensive material to be of a predominantly sexual nature. The landmark *Roth* decision attempted to proscribe, under certain terms, what obscenity was—or at least how obscenity could be located and managed within a literary or filmic text. In 1957, *Roth v. United States*—which involved obscenity charges against bookseller Samuel Roth for sending erotic literature in the mail—ushered in what Edward de Grazia and Roger Newman have referred to as a period of "constitutionalization" of the movies and of literature. In this ruling, Justice William Brennan, writing for the majority, defined what could be considered obscenity and fine-tuned what could not, thus establishing what would come to be known as the Roth test: "whether to the average person, applying contemporary community standards, the dominant theme of the material as a whole appeals to prurient interest."[18] Brennan further suggested that any discussion of sex was not in and of itself grounds for an accusation of obscenity, contrary to the blanket prohibitions proffered by pro-censorship groups, such as the

Legion of Decency, and by the terms of the MPAA Production Code well into the mid-1950s. Brennan wrote in the majority decision,

> Sex and obscenity are not synonymous. Obscene material is material which deals with sex in a manner appealing to prurient interest. The portrayal of sex, e.g., in art, literature and scientific works, is not itself sufficient reason to deny material the constitutional protection of freedom of speech and press. Sex, a great and mysterious motive force in human life, has indisputably been a subject of absorbing interest to mankind through the ages; it is one of the vital problems of human interest and public concern.[19]

Another narrowing of the definition of obscenity was meted out by *Kingsley International Pictures v. Board of Regents,* in which the Court ruled that censorship on the basis of "ideological" grounds of defining obscenity was unconstitutional. Despite the New York State Board of Regents's claim that the French film *Lady Chatterley's Lover* (Marc Allégret, 1955; based on the D. H. Lawrence novel) was obscene in its depiction of adultery as an immoral act, the U.S. Supreme Court decided that the film could not be suppressed due to its "advocacy of an idea." The film could only be contained if it "actually incited to illegal action or was presented in an obscene manner."[20] According to legal scholars de Grazia and Newman, the notion of "ideological obscenity . . . was dead."[21]

With this broadened purview on the rights of creative expression, the task of adjudicating what was obscene and inappropriate for public consumption, as determined by the Court guidelines—albeit vague ones—was in the film industry thus gradually decentralized from the self-regulating activities of the Production Code, creating confusion and radically different conclusions of what was deemed obscene by individual state censor boards and in localized communities. In a central dispute of the mid-1950s, a Production Code seal was denied to United Artists for Otto Preminger's films *The Moon Is Blue* (1953) and *The Man with the Golden Arm* (1956). Owing to Preminger's protests and his refusal to make substantial cuts, the studio released them without PCA approval, despite the censure of the Motion Picture Association of America (MPAA), whose member studios were required never to release a film without a seal. When *The Moon Is Blue,* banned in Kansas for its supposedly sexual content and use of "objectionable" language, was finally brought to the U.S. Supreme Court, the Court's ruling in favor of the film again reinforced the terms of the *Miracle* decision.[22] This case, as well as the now more widespread distribution of independent and foreign films without a Code seal, rendered the Production Code of the Hollywood studios "antiquated" and ineffective, continually struggling to "keep up" with the independents operating and thriving on its borders. Hollywood cinema in this period had also grown increasingly "mature," as tony adult dramas with a greater quotient of frankness in part in a way to distinguish its product from television. Perhaps motivated in part by these tensions around the efficacy of the Code, Geoffrey Shurlock, then head of the PCA, introduced in the late 1950s a revised Code with a slightly more flexible version of the "Don'ts and Be Carefuls." By 1961, the Code had been amended to allow representations of homosexuality and other "sex perversions," if handled in a "restrained, discreet" manner.[23]

As the high courts would release per curiam decisions in these years, the onerous task of adjudicating obscenity was distributed across numerous locations, at state and city censor boards, but also was taken up as a self-designated responsibility of police, local officials, religious organizations, and community and parent groups. In some cases, even theater owners, particularly in smaller, suburban towns, would voluntarily classify the films they were showing to appease vociferous local audiences wanting to know what films were and were not appropriate for children. Ad hoc groups, both for- and non-profit, would form in these early years of the 1960s to make sense of the welter of film product and would distribute published monthly or weekly guides for parents, such as *The Green Sheet* or the film review section of *Parents Magazine,* categorizing films into whether they were suitable or inappropriate for children and voluntarily presaging the installation of the long-awaited ratings system by the MPAA in 1968.[24] The battle over the public exhibition and circulation of licentious or erotically suggestive films foregrounded this emerging conflict between a national and local conception of the obscene. Because of the organization of film distribution according to regions, and the differing rules of various city and state censor boards, the outcomes of specific obscenity cases around the same films were often radically different from one another, further complicating the goals of the federal courts to establish a uniform national standard.

At the same time that Hollywood attempted to hold the line and renegotiate the terms of its Production Code in respect to offensive content, its directors and producers were looking toward diversifying to compete in this new climate with more mature fare. The new "frankness" of films such as *Tea and Sympathy* (Vincente Minnelli, 1956), *The Strange One* (Jack Garfein, 1957), *Cat on a Hot Tin Roof* (Richard Brooks, 1957), *Peyton Place* (Mark Robson, 1957), *The Best of Everything* (Jean Negulesco, 1959), and *Lolita* (Stanley Kubrick, 1962) doled out a heavy dose of sexual innuendo, if not yet in deed or explicitness, most certainly in suggestive themes and narrative content. By proclaiming that "the movie making fraternity should abandon its comfortable assumption that the mental age of its audience is twelve,"[25] as Columbia executive William Fadiman did in 1959 in the *Saturday Review,* the task at hand was both seeking out an adult audience and producing one.

Yet the bolder challenges to the status of censorship practice across multiple states and to the constant redefinitions of obscenity came from independents and foreign film producers and exhibitors. Sexploitation films, with their risqué subject matter and female nudity, became a major target for state and local censorship, although their makers did not always have the economic means or the inclination to pursue higher court appeals and challenges. Some of these cases would form a range of U.S. Supreme Court doctrine on the propriety of sexually explicit images in the public realm. The public stature and mass appeal of cinema became a key justification of the contest over the permissiveness of recent films, which presented nudity and previously classified scenes of "immorality." In these instances, the key figure of debate was the potential film viewer, especially a potentially underage one, who could be corrupted or debased by contact with images of sexual license.[26] The content of these contested texts was always subtended by both a juridical and vernacular rhetoric about their "effects," a discourse in which the implied spectator was irrevocably and undeniably caught.

Nudist Camps, Nudity, and the Emergence of the Nudie Cutie

One of the main legal events credited with precipitating the rise of the sexploitation film was a crucial ruling in a case revolving around the fictionalized nudist camp film *The Garden of Eden* (Max Nosseck, 1954).[27] The film was a relatively innocuous tale of a widowed woman who leaves the home of her overbearing father-in-law and goes for a ride in her car with her daughter. Her car breaks down, and she is helped by a group of people who live in a nearby nudist camp. At first balking at the nude bodies, the young widow eventually grows comfortable in this new environment, and when her father-in-law arrives, the family is rehabilitated and reunited within this alternative, palliative social world. Presenting the context of the nudist camp as a space for retreat and rejuvenation, and showing nude bodies without any purported prurience, the court decreed that the film, by the letter of recent law such as Roth, was not obscene.

Upon its submission to the New York State Board of Regents, some censor board members claimed that the film was "indecent," although all agreed that it was not obscene, and asked the distributor to cut out scenes of group nudity depicted in the film. The censor board, in justifying its complaint, cited a state penal code that forbade any person from willfully exposing "his private parts in the presence of two or more persons of the opposite sex whose private parts are similarly exposed."[28] The distributor refused to make the cuts and filed a complaint at the New York State Supreme Court, which denied this argument of the state censor board and drew a distinction between indecency and obscenity, stating that "'indecent,' standing alone and read literally, is far too broad and vague a term to be made a valid censorship standard."[29] This in turn reinstated that obscenity was the only reason for which prior restraint of motion pictures could be justified and that only under these conditions could a picture be denied a license. Filmic representations of nudity were rendered no longer obscene, despite the New York State Supreme Court's minority opinion protesting that "the picture contains protracted scenes of women in unwholesome, sexually alluring postures which are completely unnecessary to—and in fact a radical departure from the activities of the nudist camp depicted."[30] In response to the claims of the censor board regarding the state penal code around nude exposure in a group, the court majority declared,

> To say that representation of criminal activity is criminal is to abolish the drama and the novel in one stroke. . . . The showing of crimes in book, play or cinema is evil . . . only when it is done in a dirty way or when it glorifies the criminal act. So to characterize *The Garden of Eden* is impossible.[31]

This insistence on the permeability of, or even conflation between, real life and representation was customarily exacerbated in such cases, particularly when the material on display was potentially sexual or involved the nude female body. The court in this case disqualified the slippery logic of the censor board, which could confuse real acts with fictional representations of them. But the ruling also unintentionally created an opening for the emergence of movies that would present nudity for a decided profit. The concern over the impact of erotically charged images on the film audience and in the space of "real life," as well as the supposition that erotic representation was tantamount to the public act—of sex or nude exposure—itself, would persist throughout the decade in subsequent cases and disputes over the propriety of such images in the public realm. As one critic suggests about trends in the discourse of anti-obscenity, the advocates of such laws would like to claim that "obscenity is idealess. . . . Its appeal is physical, not mental. In this view, obscenity is not worthy of protection within the freedom of speech because it is not truly an *expression* of sexuality, but rather is itself a sexual *act,* or at least, an aide [*sic*] to sexual activity."[32] The conflation of sexual ideas, now protected, with the cinema's seemingly transparent representation of sexual acts would plague the enforcement of obscenity law across the nation in the following years.[33]

Now that context and intent would define which images of the naked body were properly obscene, the emergence of the sexploitation film as a genre and a mode of production would tread boldly on this new ground. The development of the "nudie cutie" film, which would borrow from the conventions of the nudist camp film and the burlesque film of the 1950s, was marked by an acknowledgment of its own censorial limitations (discussed in the following chapter). Russ Meyer's *The Immoral Mr. Teas* (1959) was commonly seen as the first film in the "nudie cutie" cycle and the progenitor of the sexploitation genre. Meyer had been an army photographer in the Second World War. He returned home and started shooting "cheesecake" pin-up photography throughout the 1950s, most notably for *Playboy. Teas,* shot in five days for twenty-four thousand dollars on 16mm film blown up to 35mm, and starring an old friend of Meyer's, the bumbling Bill Teas, was made with the help of old-time burlesque proprietor Peter DeCenzie. In the course of two years screening the film, it brought in more than one and a half million dollars and subsequently spawned a wave of more than 150 copycat films in the following few years, Meyer's films among them, including five more nudie cuties with his company Pad-Ram.

The impact of *The Garden of Eden* case was strongly felt well into the early to mid-1960s. Yet the precise parameters between what uses of nudity were and were not obscene, as defined by the case, were troubled. The film *Have Figure, Will Travel* (Leo Orenstein, 1963) was confronted with such an adjudication of its content when presented to the Maryland State Censor Board for licensing in 1964. A travelogue featuring three women who go on a tour of a variety of nudist camps by boat, the film presented scenes of the three in states of undress while at sea, and it was these images, rather than the scenes of the women cavorting nude in the camps, that warranted the Maryland board's disapproval. The board's logic was that nudity in the camps was normative, whereas on the boat, "normal people would not so comport themselves and there was no reason for its portrayal except to arouse sexual desire in the viewers."[34] When taken to the Maryland Court of Appeals, the high court disagreed and reversed the board's ruling. The elasticity of nudity's proper diegetic context as seen in this case shows the extent to which censors were beginning *a low-budget american "art" film heralds a new wave of cinematic sex*

IT USED TO BE that European film makers had pretty much of a monopoly on cinematic nudity and sex. Their products — good, bad or indifferent — have long held the world-wide reputation for revealing far more of the female form than anything produced here. No more.

There is today a group of independent, low-budget producers, ambitious Americans all, who have made broad encroachments in the areas of nudity (sex, we assume, will come along later) on the screen. No Oscar hunters, the members of this West Coast wave are cranking out commercially conceived "art" films concerned mainly with cute chicks dressed in nearly nothing. What's more, these films are being distributed nationally, to the delight of backers and moviegoers alike, and doing big box office at the art houses where they play.

Vital to the warm climate in which this exotic cinematic bloom flourishes is the new liberal attitude of the federal courts toward film censorship. In a series of recent decisions, the courts have ruled: (1) that local censorship of movies, as long practiced in many parts of the U.S., is unconstitutional because

THE IMMORAL MR. TEAS

The Immoral Mr. Teas, as the film's narrator explains, is all about "the simple, uncluttered fellow who merely lives from day to day." In his humdrum routine, delivering dental supplies, he's tempted by the sexy creatures he meets along his route. Then, under anesthetic in a dentist's chair, a fresh fillip is added to his life: the voluptuous dental assistant suddenly appears before him in the nude.

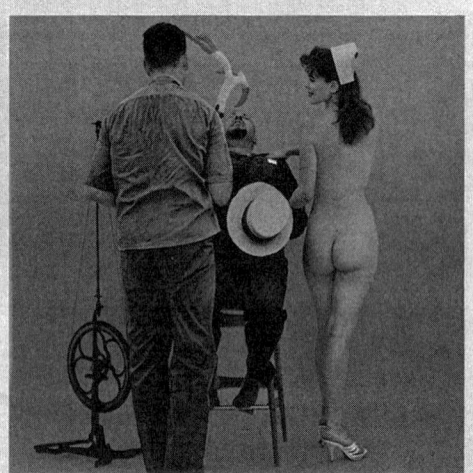

FIGURE 7. Russ Meyer's *The Immoral Mr. Teas*, profiled in *Playboy* in 1960, mocks the piety of the nudist film and introduces the "nudie cutie."

to parse and fine-tune the definitions of obscenity and its impact on an unwitting viewer. The censor's interpretation hinged on a comparison between what people would do in the "real world" versus in the fictional world of the film, as proscribed by the necessary documentary definition of narrative contexts in *Garden of Eden;* yet by 1964, the influx of films with sufficiently fictionalized and nondocumentary nudity spoke clearly to changing standards and practices of using the sensationalized material of the nude body.

The nudie film producers relied on cinema's new protection as art to ply its wares as a business venture, releasing and distributing their films, without a Code seal, to ailing and empty theaters, often couching their narratives in some pretext of art or other documentary or social value. The lack of industry approval also stoked the coals of disapprobation. As one harsh critic in the *Christian Science Monitor* noted in response to the substantial growth of nudie theaters in the Boston area, "cinema critics show by their general shunning of 'nudie' films, that these low budget, low quality productions are not considered art at all, but a crass commercial bid for a particularly dirty dollar."[35] Throughout the decade, the sexploitation film, in whatever incarnation, was met with such distinctions—painted as the black sheep of the film trade, the "spoiler" ruining it for all "serious" film artists. The freedoms and rights accorded to filmic expression by the *Miracle* case allowed the nudie film to trade on that liberty with an eye on quick profits—ironically reinforcing the prior view of the *Mutual* decision that movies were commercially driven and made for entertainment only.

The production of nudies, by Meyer's Pad-Ram, by producers like David Friedman and filmmakers like Barry Mahon and Doris Wishman, who had worked with Walter Bibo and who made eight nudist camp films by 1965, was met with consternation and regulation as they began to be made with great speed in the early 1960s. What began on the West Coast, in Los Angeles, very soon arrived on the East, in New York; these became the central axes of sexploitation production in the decade. Some filmed in Florida using scenic locales and nudist camps to shoot these full-color, comic bawdy films. While nudist camp films followed the formula of self-discovery seen in *Garden of Eden,* nudies were often episodic tableaus, frequently involving the sudden visibility of nudity by incompetent and leering older men performing their ineptitude in a burley, "baggy pants" style as women with breasts and buttocks unveiled appeared in magical and improbable situations of bawdy voyeurism, but always observed from a distance.

It was clear that the Hollywood industry was beginning to warily take notice of these independents. In a discussion of a fledgling "anti-smut" drive in Los Angeles County, a *New York Times* article reported that the head of the committee was Y. Frank Freeman, the chair of the American Motion Picture Producer's Association and vice president at Paramount Studios. Freeman himself would distance himself and his professional colleagues—employed by the majors—from what he would call these "fly-by-night" producers, a refrain that would become common in assessing the relative anonymity and low-budget operations of the nudie and sexploitation field. The article made a point of naming *The Immoral Mr. Teas*, as Freeman and other studio employees commented:

> "Most of us," Mr. Freeman said on behalf of producers, "do not even know the people who are making these movies." . . . John L. Dales, national executive secretary of the Screen Actor's Guild . . . said the cheap movies were being made in "hills, canyons, and barns, not by the motion picture industry but by a few in the market for a fast dollar." Some of these quickie productions utilize models and non-professionals, lured by promises of easy entrée into Hollywood fame. Very few thus far have employed actors of any standing.[36]

Characterizing the nudie producers as an anonymous, unruly group, genuine exploiters ready to capitalize on the optimism of hopeful starlets, Dales and Freeman take on a sizable task in attempting to control a nascent field among which they knew no one. Expressing astonishment at the success of the nudie films, the article highlights the extent to which sexploitation films in this early period posed a threat and provocation to the mainstream film industry, shrewdly articulated by the industry insiders as an affront on *moral* rather than economic grounds. At the same time, the nudie films provided much-needed support to failing theaters across the country. By positioning themselves as "aboveboard" productions of legitimate taste and standing, industry spokespersons like Dales and Freeman could also conflate the economic marginality and aesthetic limitations of sexploitation product as part of a political rhetoric of professionalized labor. The mainstream industry's moral disidentification with the nudie producers and the defensive posture taken linked legitimate art with professionalism and, implicitly, union labor.

Although Hollywood was treading somewhat conservatively in respect to sexual content at this time, despite the release of "mature" dramas such as *Butterfield 8* (Daniel Mann, 1960), *Walk on the Wild Side* (Edward Dmytryk, 1962), and *Splendor in the Grass* (Elia Kazan, 1961), they were nonetheless benefiting from the license taken by the sex film makers in how the films were broadening the boundaries of the nude body's representability. In this particular anti-smut drive, the group was formed and established a fact-finding committee in response to pressure from Los Angeles County for a self-policing motion picture industry and, more tellingly, from the financial pressure of a threatened withdrawal of municipal moneys, in the sum of four million dollars, for the foundation of a Film and Television Museum. The success of this initiative would prove limited, however, as by 1963, the studios would take the public tack of distancing themselves from the nudies through silence, claiming that they had no jurisdiction over their "fringe competitors."[37] The presence of sexploitation on the industry's edges put the burden of evidence and action on the more publicly visible Hollywood outfits, as they were taken to task and held accountable by the community for the infractions of these smaller producers. As this example of industrial self-censorship bears out, the emergence of sexploitation films was seen as a problem borne by the entire film industry.

State Censor Boards

Such attempts at municipal and industry self-regulation of moving images were a developing trend to be seen in the light of the evolution and applications of the *Roth* decision and the developing antiquation of state and city censor boards during legal challenges to prior restraint. Prior restraint was the requirement that obliged independent movie producers and distributors outside of the province of the MPAA to submit a film to a licensing agency for evaluation prior to exhibition. Before the practice of prior restraint was rendered inoperable in 1965, leading to the eventual collapse of most existing censor boards on the grounds of a failure to enact new procedural guidelines to adhere to the new laws of submission and film review, the period between 1960 and 1965 would see an effort on the part of state agencies to continue to police a wildly changing and transforming body of film product. Here we move to an examination of state censoring practice and the texture of confrontation and clashes between sexploitation films and the boards that would attempt to rein in, however incompletely, their indulgence in "sexual license."

The landscape and administrative purview of the state censor board had considerably diminished in this period. By the early 1960s, only four state censoring agencies remained—New York, Maryland, Kansas, and Virginia—with city boards in Detroit, Fort Worth, Chicago, and Providence. Most of the court cases regarding film censorship and obscenity would come from two primary states—New York and Maryland. Maryland's state censor board was a unique case, helmed by three members and renowned for its stringency. The acknowledgment of the board as a body of priggish tastes entrusted with the responsibility of regulating film content was already being disputed on the public stage in 1962. An editorial in the *Washington Post* in 1962 criticized the Maryland board, seeing the agency as an inappropriate arbiter of cultural tastes and values:

> The people of Maryland, who are considered, apparently not yet mature enough to choose their own entertainment, have been protected during the past year by a Motion Picture Censor Board which decides what is safe and suitable for them to see on the silver screen . . . The cost of this operation, for the most part, recouped in license fees, is not to be reckoned with in dollars. It must be reckoned in terms of those who live in the Free State. Many of them can drive across the frontier into the District of Columbia, of course, if they want to see such films as *The Immoral Mr. Teas* or *La Dolce Vita,* which incurred the censors' displeasure. But so far as the films they are allowed to see are concerned, they never know how much may have been cut out to satisfy the censor's prudery. . . . But it may not be feasible at all to see, and to form one's own judgment about, films which someone else has banned from the theaters or from which scenes have been deleted in accordance with someone else's taste. Do Marylander's [sic] really want to pay a board to make choices of this sort for them?[38]

The principal workings of the board, in this opinion, were at odds with the audience's right to self-determination through consumption, in the operative logic of choice within the capitalist marketplace. This "sounding off" was a criticism of the processes of the board, if not more a signal of the antiquation of the censor board as a cultural institution itself, which could not reconcile itself with the changing times and the altering film market. New York was similarly a tough state for film licensing. New York State was a very important launching location not only for the big studios and the independents but also for the influx of foreign film imports, as these films would often go through U.S. Customs inspection there. Additionally, the licensing challenges a film might face there would set the terms for the potential of its distribution and exhibition across the country, regardless of its national or industrial provenance. Exhibitors in other states and regions would look to the New York State Censor Board's decisions as a bellwether, a measure of whether a film was worth picking up in their local theaters. Additionally, other state and city licensing agencies would often compare the film evaluations of the New York State Censor Board to their own impending decisions on offensive film content.

Looking at the workings of the New York State Censor Board in the period between 1960 and 1965, and its decisions on a select number of sexploitation films, we can begin to understand not only under what conditions the films were licensed but also the specific pressures that would come to bear on their producers and distributors. In one way, the operation of the New York State Censor Board was an enterprise of diminishing impact, in that sexploitation filmmakers would sometimes choose not to distribute their films in the state or would use other means (such as making "hot" and "cool" prints) of evading the restrictive, and exceedingly obsolete, criteria to receive a license. Although New York was a boomtown in terms of box office revenue for the industry, sexploitation filmmakers could redirect their energies to other municipalities with less stringent film licensing requirements, as opposed to other sectors of the film industry that were much more reliant on the state's location and influence. On the other hand, sexploitation distributors seeking a license at any cost for the lucrative exhibition sites offered by New York would more often acquiesce to the eliminations requested by the board without much contest. Partly owing to the limited economic means available to sexploitation producers and exhibitors as compared with the major studios and even the foreign film exchanges, and the fundamental ways that sexploitation films required some modicum of restriction to exist, conflicts over the summation of the board or suits against the agency charging improper determination were not always guaranteed with each submission. But they did occur on occasion, and their number increased substantially in the last few years of the board's existence.[39]

On the basis of a survey of a number of films submitted for review by the board, some general patterns and procedures can be ascertained.[40] An outline of the process of submission required by the New York Board of Regents in this period would customarily proceed as follows: the distributor or producer would submit a film script and a print to the agency with an attendant application fee, and the board's committee members would read the script and watch the reels among a group of appointed censors (five sat on the New York state board) and make a preliminary determination as to eliminations—indicating whether the film needed specific cuts of material deemed licentious, whether it was "rejected in toto," or if it was fully approved without cuts. If there were any questions as to how severely to evaluate the film, board members would convene with or refer the film for viewing to the agency's director, Louis Pesce. The summary of the evaluation process, including a list of necessary eliminations and reel numbers, would be sent to the exhibitor, and she would have the opportunity to make the required changes and resubmit the film. The board would rewatch the film and again assess it. If the changes were satisfactory, a seal of approval and license for exhibition would be granted, along with a form letter providing a proviso that all advertising and marketing should also refrain from licentious or otherwise obscene material, as per Section 130 of the State Education Law regarding excessive pandering in advertising.[41] If a film needed to be changed, filmmakers would be obliged to notify the board and get a duplicate license. In the case that the eliminations or edits were not satisfactory to the board, the process of resubmission and review could go on for months and, in some cases, years. In these instances, it was common for the exhibitor to attempt to make fewer cuts than ruled necessary by the board. If a film producer or exhibitor was unhappy with the summation of the censor board, he could appeal to the Board of Regents for a hearing and review of the case, a process that could take up to six months.

The New York State Censor Board was generally quite strict in the rules that governed the evaluations of sexploitation films. Scenes of female nudity, primarily exposure of naked breasts and buttocks, even when scant, as well as the suggestion of sexuality or the expression of sexual desires, orientations, and acts, when combined with nudity, were frequently verboten. "Lewd" acts such as "obscene pelvic thrusting" in the portrayal of erotic dancing, burlesque, or stripping were also an oft-requested cut. Despite rapid changes in film content, nudity and sexual acts remained for the censors excessive and out of place. A representative retinue of eliminations might read as follows—here from a request letter for cuts from "Reel 3D" of Doris Wishman's *The Sex Perils of Paulette* (1965):

> Eliminate all views of Tracy, seated at table, reacting erotically to fondling of her leg and thigh by Sam.
>
> In scene of Sam undressing and embracing Tracy, eliminate all views of him fondling her body, view of her lying on him with her buttocks visible through transparent panties, and views of her with breast partially exposed.
>
> In sequence in which Tracy, intoxicated, undresses and lies on bed, eliminate all views of her with breasts exposed, and all views in which her buttocks are visible through transparent panties.
>
> REASON: Obscene pursuant to Section 122 of the State Education Law.[42]

Although these scenes were removed from the film, creating a considerable ellipsis in plot development, some of them remained in the film's trailer (Figure 8). The quality of the eliminations demanded by the New York board for sexploitation films adhered to the excision of physical exposure and sexualized plot points and connotations.

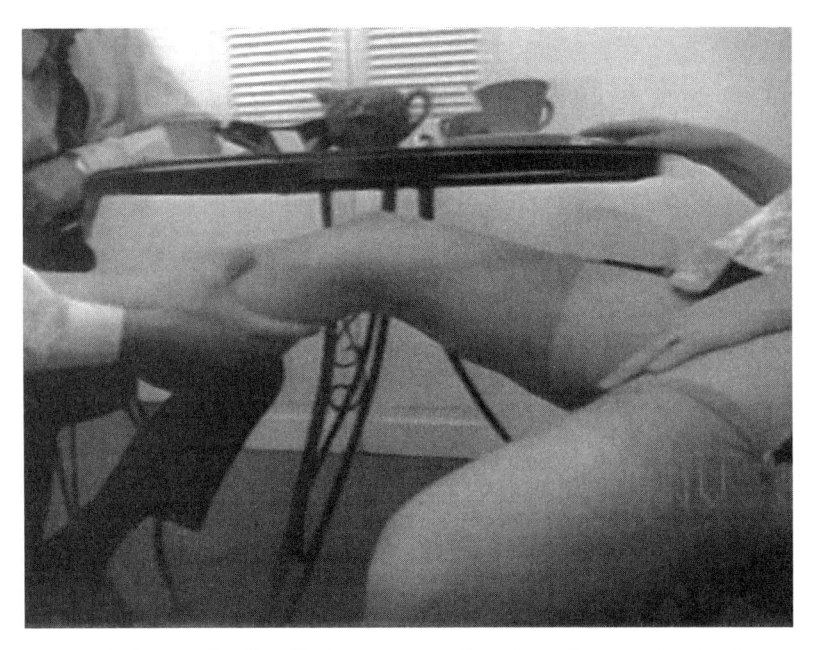

FIGURE 8. A scene the New York state censor found unpalatable, showing Sam fondling Tracy's leg in Doris Wishman's *The Sex Perils of Paulette*, preserved in the film's trailer.

Russ Meyer faced difficulty getting a license for *Mr. Teas* in the state and eventually approached distributor William Mishkin to submit the film in his stead. The board produced a four-page letter enumerating that all nudity or partial nudity be removed. Mishkin agreed to these changes, which shrunk the film to a mere forty-seven minutes.[43] There is evidence that some of the remaining state boards were even more stringent than the New York agency—for example, those in Maryland and Virginia, the latter of which also cut open-mouth kissing and non-sex-related offenses.[44] Subtending the sense of the fragmentary nature of the censor's task, Louis Pesce, the New York State censor board director, had indicated that even though "the Supreme Court has ruled that the books must be 'taken as a whole' in being judged for obscenity . . . Pesce holds he must judge a film scene by scene."[45] The obvious conflict between the notion of the "work taken as a whole," in its textual integrity, and the potentially eruptive quality of an individual shot or scene seem, from the censor's point of view, irreconcilable. In the reduction of a film to its offending parts, the logic of censorial eliminations functionally contributed to the fragmentary nature of the sexploitation text, as discussed earlier in relation to Mahon's

Censored. If the job of the censor was to privilege the fragment, the evolving obscenity doctrine handed down by the Supreme Court certainly complicated the more pragmatic and reductive role of the censor in a focus on the work considered in its "entirety."

Partly due to the marginal status of sexploitation in relationship to Hollywood and more legitimate art imports—Pesce had publicly called sexploitation producers "fly by night operators"—the nudity and sexuality in sexploitation films submitted to the board were consistently positioned as excessive, narratively unnecessary, and a cynical form of exploitation. The only appropriate context for nudity was in the nudist camp, even as late as 1965, and the only appropriate place for sexual acts or intimations was off-screen. Sex as a subject of representation was yet to be legitimated, and the "low" status of sexploitation in this period, culturally and industrially, gave the films an aura of seediness and illegitimacy. At the same time, this system of limitation became a constitutive aspect of sexploitation films' generic identity: precisely *because* of these restrictions, nudity was suggested but scantly offered, sexuality couched in alternating tones of guilty titillation and moralizing disapproval. Associatively, the role of the censor operates as the structurally inverse pole of the adult film audience. Both audiences are in fact looking for scenes of sexual excess— the censor and adult film spectator become a unified entity at the point of apprehension of an obscene or, alternately, arousing image. The censor's sensitivities toward potential violations of taste and moral values forced a symbolic occupation in the shoes of the "average person," an average person who might very well be sitting in the grind house theater.

Sexploitation versus New York State: Challenging the Board of Regents

One trend seen between 1960 and 1965 was that sexploitation producers became increasingly bold in their contestations of the board over editorial decisions by the mid-1960s, and board officials increasingly rescinded certain demands. Louis Pesce, director of the New York agency, commented in a number of different contexts that as the period wore on, he felt the efficacy of the board's job being eroded by ever-changing obscenity laws. An early example of sexploitation producer resistance to the decisions of the New York agency was in the case of *The Twilight Girls* (1957, imported in 1961), a French film directed by Andre Hunebelle that was dubbed and reedited and to which Audubon Films added additional footage for the film's American release. Audubon was the production and distribution house run by filmmaker Radley Metzger and his business partner Ava Leighton. Metzger had entered the film business as an editor, among other jobs cutting scenes for *Bitter Rice,* before joining the motion picture unit in the Air Force during the Korean War. Upon his return, he worked for the New York branch of RKO and as a trailer editor and dubber for Janus Films before starting Audubon with Leighton. One of the most significant, and recognizable, producers working in the broad field of 1960s sexploitation, Metzger was also one of its savviest. Both as a distributor and eventually in making his own films, Metzger's Audubon developed a curatorial and aesthetic imprint in the films he produced and managed Stateside that linked sexuality with a Continental flair and a bourgeois, literary sophistication. Films under the Audubon aegis also had a patina of respectability as well as higher budgets as compared with Metzger's New York nudie contemporaries.[46]

The Twilight Girls (originally titled *Les Collegiennes*) was a sentimental coming-of-age tale set in a girls' boarding school. A young woman, played by ingenue Agnès Laurent, is sent to school after the death of her father and embarks on a clandestine affair with a composer, to the chagrin of her teachers. Magnifying the association of European art cinema with eroticism, Metzger amplified some of the subplots by adding newly shot scenes of nudity (including with future 1970s porn star Georgina Spelvin) and emphasizing a lesbian subtext, a common practice among exploitation distributors seeking to repackage imports with a more salacious sell.

The Twilight Girls was submitted to the New York State Censor Board in October 1961; the agency responded with eliminations they deemed imperative, which included removal of scenes of nudity (bare breasts, buttocks, and a side view of pubic hair in a shower scene) as well as the scene explicitly showing a lesbian encounter between schoolgirls in the dormitory.[47] Although representations of homosexuality were now permissible under the Production Code, the board found the presentation prurient. Metzger appealed; in an affidavit responding to the rejection of a license for the film, Metzger brought on a sustained critique of the operations of the censor board on grounds of anticonstitutionality and in defense of free speech. He stated that it was not for the censor board to act as film director:

> The Director and the Regents of the University of the State of New York of the State Educational Department are without constitutional authority to pick and choose certain portions of a literary work and to substitute their views of a work of art for those of the director, writer and producer. To permit any group of people, official or unofficial, to edit films, books or other media of communication, in effect permits that group to substitute their particular sense of values and ideas to the public in place of the artistic and literary individuals getting their message out to the public.[48]

FIGURE 9. *The Twilight Girls,* a French schoolgirl film imported for the burgeoning sexploitation market by Audubon, featured additional "lesbian" scenes to spice up the film's U.S. release.

Metzger's strident rebuttal of the practices of prior restraint asserted the autonomy of the filmmaker and artist from state or governmental control. Censorship in this sense contaminated the authenticity of the work of art. Prior restraint for Metzger was not only an affront to the First and Fourteenth Amendments but also an operation that silenced or contorted the purity of the art form and the artist's intentions. The irony, of course, was that Hunebelle was himself unseated in the directorial role by Metzger's repackaging of the film for Stateside release. Metzger was making a name for himself in the 1960s through a form of "creative distribution" of repackaged and reedited risqué foreign films. Metzger's politicized outrage at the practice of prior restraint relied on a discourse of film as art and of the imperative creative autonomy of the film artist.[49] His comments slyly disparage the censors' poor taste and capacity for discernment. The power of the cut was not lost on Metzger, the career editor. Despite Metzger's dramatic protests on behalf of the role of the artist, it would be naive to assert that constitutional protections and a lofty defense of free speech on principle were the primary motivators for film producers to pursue legal action against overreaching film boards. Rather, as Richard Randall suggests, the incentives for film producers were predominantly economic ones.[50] Censorship, and the defiance of its authoritative heft and force, could also be used to a sexploitation producer's advantage—as part of the obvious marketing appeal and risqué draw to the film.[51]

The Board of Regents rejected Metzger's claim, and *The Twilight Girls* case made it up to the New York Court of Appeals, which reversed the regents' decision.[52] Audubon's and Metzger's victory over the censors was a double-edged one, as the release of *The Twilight Girls* in New York State was delayed for three years, by the time the court had heard the case and delivered its decision in 1964. The dispute over *The Twilight Girls* points to some of the tensions at play, the prohibitive factors of pursuing action against the censor board, as well as the financial costs. Legal fees; time lost for box office revenue; staff time and salaries; and, perhaps most tricky of all due to the very topical nature of the sexploitation film, the danger of irrelevance and "outdating" of the film's subject by the time of its delayed release were all factors that conditioned challenging or appealing a board decision.[53] As a result, few sexploitation producers would follow the route of legal action, which was considered costly and at times futile, with no definitive guarantee of a positive outcome or timely resolution.

Another example of distributor resistance to the procedures of the New York board was the dispute between the estimable foreign film importer (and Metzger's former employer) Janus Films, which had taken on distribution of the nudie film *Not Tonight Henry* (Merle Connell, 1960), and the censors, who had demanded a substantial number of eliminations for the film.[54] The conflict illuminates the entrenchment of the ideological and procedural position of the censor board, while highlighting the ways certain distributors, as early as 1961–62, were relying on the defense of constitutional protection and free speech for their right to exhibit their films without cuts. The fact that Janus Films, an established art house distribution company, was retained certainly benefited the film and perhaps allowed the resources for the pursuit of an appeal to begin with. Many distributors running on tighter budgets might not have been able to manage the legal expenses and make such an investment in fighting the board or might have negotiated eliminations through other means.

Not Tonight Henry was released as part of the wave of nudie cutie films then expanding in the film market and had received some attention for casting Las Vegas nightclub performer Hank Henry in the title role, physiognomically and stylistically a predecessor to the woebegotten "average schmuck" antics of Rodney Dangerfield. Henry is a henpecked husband whose wife denies him erotic affections, leaving him to his own fantasies at the local bar. These fantasy scenes provided the bulk of the material in the film, each with a comic punch line, as Henry partakes in imaginary dalliances with famous female historical figures such as Cleopatra, Pocahontas, Lucretia Borgia, and prehistoric women. Each period segment ends with some kind of comic comeuppance or thwarting desires. When he returns home, his wife, reading her own book on historical romance, is suddenly more amenable to his erotic advances—and wearing lingerie, she drags him into the bedroom. Constructed in a distinctively burlesque address, with a voice-over narrating the travails of Henry as the archetypal everyman, the film aimed to couch marital woes and mundane male fantasy within the rubric of the comic form.

A few months prior to the submission of the film for review by the New York board, in spring 1961, the film had faced legal controversy in Modesto, California. The producer and distributor were put on trial for obscenity after the film was seized, an act which itself was legally questionable, by the county police. The trial concluded in a hung jury and the prosecutor dismissing the case; he stated that no twelve jurors could ever decide uniformly that the film was obscene.[55] This case clearly bolstered the justifications of the New York censoring agency in calling for a denial of a license.

Not Tonight Henry was submitted to the censor board in August 1961, and after a preliminary determination of edits made by the board, a resubmission of the film in April 1962 resulted in the denial of a license by the board because of insufficient cuts. Janus Films appealed and requested a reexamination and hearing, retaining the prominent obscenity lawyer Stanley Fleishman. The censor board's application of obscenity law did not diverge from its usual targeting of the exposure of nude female bodies. In the review report he drafted, board committee member Julian Miranda argued after screening the film that

> this film purports to present a humorous portrayal of a henpecked man's romantic fantasies. In so doing, it utilizes bawdy *double entendre*, nudity, and semi-nudity in a manner which frequently results in an obscene effect. . . . This film links nudity with coarse humor in such a manner as to make the exposure of women's bodies more than incidental. In each one of these sequences, the interest of the protagonist in the nude women is sexual. The comments of the narrator, while not in and of themselves obscene, are also sexual, and the fact that they are jocular does not mitigate the feeling that we are at a dirty peep show, leering along with the narrator. The eliminations were restricted to the most overt exploitation of nudity.[56]

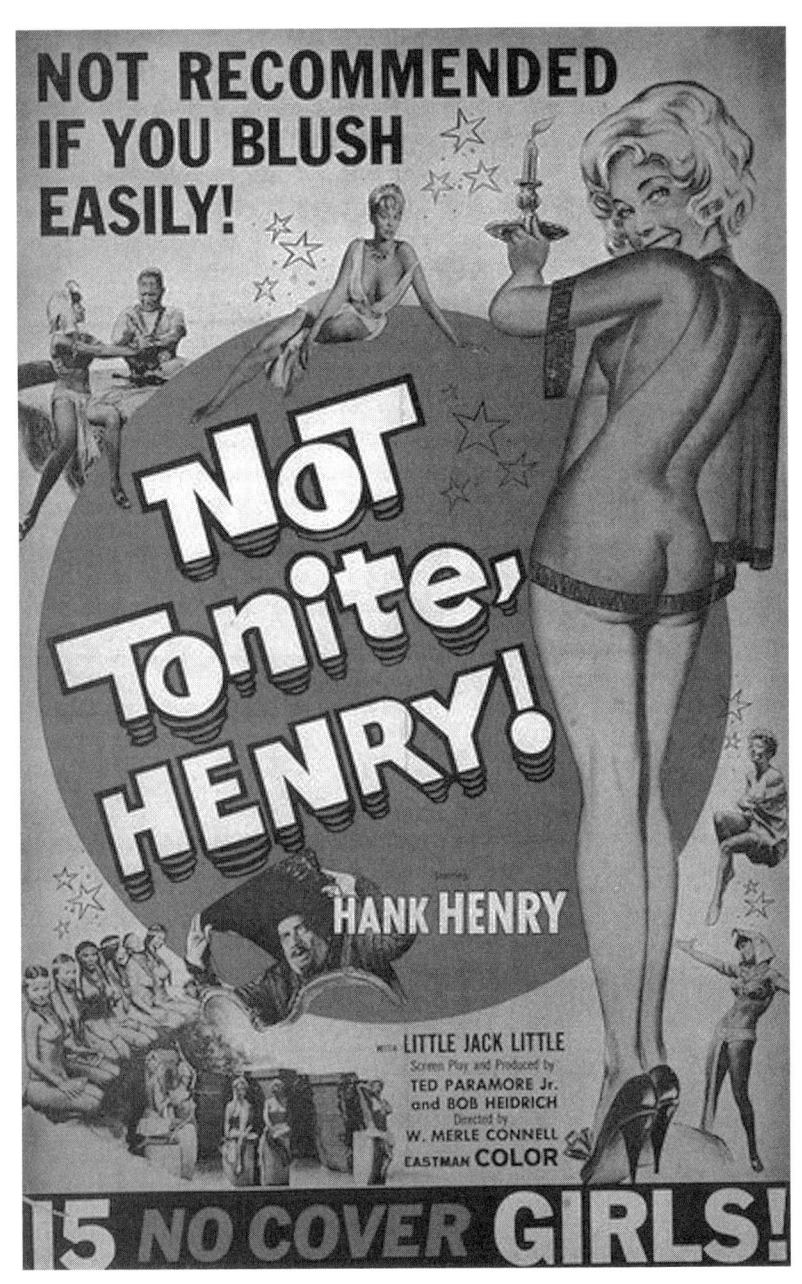

FIGURE 10. *Not Tonight Henry*'s historical fantasy is overwhelmed by the bawdy promise of "15 no cover girls."

Miranda articulates the customarily orthodox position of the board on sexual content and nude exposure, finding problematic the juxtaposition of lewd humor with the leering guaranteed by the inclusion of nudity. That looking at nude bodies could not be elevated into something else but rather reduced the act of viewing to a comparable experience of peep show voyeurism seems to have particularly perturbed Miranda. The wording of this analogy, partaking in a collective phrasing, departs from the more detached tone of the rest of the assessment as it registers distaste for being put in the same category of reception as a libidinal spectatorial public. If the nudity of the film were only incidental, Miranda's interpretation of the film suggests, then the film would be elevated into a legitimate narrative form. Thus the generic alibi proved insufficient for the censors. The censor board's criteria had not moved far beyond the allowances made for nudity by the *Garden of Eden* case five years earlier, in which it was ruled that nudity should not be the object of a gawking viewer but, in its documentary function and narrative veracity, should only act as a function of authentication of the plot or setting. In this way, the New York State Censor Board by necessity, and as can be seen in many other instances, engaged in an institutionalized form of cinematic reception as well as articulating prescribed criteria of taste. These review reports bore resemblance to miniature film reviews, embodying a convergence of film censor as film critic, the two relating to their respective publics through variant foci, preoccupations, sensibilities, and institutional responsibilities, yet, at the crux of it, partaking in forms of filmic evaluation and interpretation.

Louis Pesce also submitted a statement justifying the agency's action. Marginalizing the sexploitation market, Pesce noted that "the subject motion picture is one of a group of films produced recently in Los Angeles, which have run into trouble in several jurisdictions throughout the country, and have been the subject of much adverse comment in motion picture trade journals." Pesce also mentioned the contemporaneous trial around the film in Modesto, California, in February 1962, which resulted in a hung jury, as a means of implicating the film in its broader offense to spectatorial communities outside of New York.[57] For Pesce, the implication was that the film had a characteristic obscenity that could be legible universally, across different national municipalities.

Janus attempted to defend the textual integrity and the "wholeness" of the film. In a lengthy legal memo in support of a reexamination and hearing, lawyer Stanley Fleishman made a sustained case for the unconstitutionality of the New York State obscenity statute as well as suggesting that the practice of prior restraint is also an infringement on the rights of filmmakers. He argued that the film's presentation of nudity was no different from the pinups in *Playboy* magazine and that, based on the standards set by U.S. Supreme Court cases regarding this magazine and others like it, New York's application of the federal obscenity doctrine was incorrect and faulty. Fleishman referenced other legal decisions around First Amendment issues that necessitated the need for a jury, rather than a state agency, to decide what is obscene, in accordance with the notion of a fair hearing necessitated by federal law.[58] This position was also similar to his argument in the Modesto case against *Not Tonight Henry,* in which he contended that the "average person" and the courts may actually be at odds with one another in their attitudes toward obscenity; Fleishman was reported to have "told [the] jury that what the law thinks is obscene can be very different from the average person's opinion."[59] This served as an interesting twist on the "average person" criterion of the operative obscenity laws by casting doubt on the conservative nature of the citizen in local communities as well as the conflation of the censor and his indexical relation to the everyday film audience.

An affidavit of producer Ted Paramore, on the other hand, engaged in a legitimation of the film on the grounds of both its entertainment status and the employment of professionalized labor, arguing that the film was not out of bounds in relation to contemporary standards and trends in film production. Paramore enumerated a number of the legitimating characteristics of the film, including Hank Henry's minor star status and its use of IATSE, the major union representing motion picture workers, and enacted a defense of it on the level of genre. The same comic touch that made the film that much more offensive to reviewer Julian Miranda was for Paramore an asset, a generic identification that in turn distanced it from an appeal to prurient interest—not a function of leering intent but a "spoofing of all the professorial studies of the 'war between the sexes.'"[60]

Listing a series of contemporary films, such as *Jules and Jim* (François Truffaut, 1962), *Viridiana* (Luis Bunuel, 1961), *The Third Sex, Saturday Night and Sunday Morning* (Karel Reisz, 1960), *Room at the Top* (Jack Clayton, 1959), *La Dolce Vita* (Federico Fellini, 1960), *Odd Obsession* (Kon Ichikawa, 1959), and *The Lovers,* Paramore proclaimed that *Not Tonight Henry* was not alone in indexing contemporary standards and tolerance around sexual themes and images. In this move, Paramore affiliated his work with trends in domestic products and with foreign imports "sexed up" for American audiences (such as Audubon's *The Third Sex*). By insisting against the marginalization of his film for its deployment of nudity, Paramore claimed that tolerance of erotic content had become an incontrovertible feature of a swiftly changing American cultural life. Citing a case against a sex magazine in New York State, Paramore stated that the court "nevertheless recognized that tastes differ and that the Constitution is broad enough to protect and does protect freedom of taste and pursuit of happiness, at least where communications are concerned."[61] By focusing on "freedom of taste" rather than freedom of expression or of the film artist, as we saw in Metzger's statement in *The Twilight Girls* appeal, Paramore implicitly referenced the rights of the adult film audience above his own expressive, creative rights. The discourse of taste and the presumption of happiness—affiliated with visual pleasure—are privileged as a site of defense. The claim also mirrored the rhetorical tenor of Barry Mahon's *Censored* in its own coda, in which the audience becomes the final arbiter of acceptability in the directive by the narrator to "see and read and do what you wish" with respect to its choices of sexual entertainments. Paramore's focus on the mercurial logics of taste renders problematic the censor's attribution of value to sexploitation film, as well as the specific film in question, due to the agency's inability to adjudicate questions of aesthetic and consumer preference. This defense of the rights of the film viewer seems on one level a pious and self-congratulatory gesture, but it also underscores one of the final positions that Paramore takes—that is, the status of his film as a form of entertainment rather than a work of high art. Unwittingly invoking the transformations in constitutional protections for films and the historical demarcations of film as entertainment and business, versus film as a definitive art, Paramore entreaties the New York State Censor Board not to disparage the film for its "light entertainment" value, a value that should not be denigrated:

> I do not claim that *Not Tonight Henry* is a great film. I do say it is an entertaining film suitable for viewing by the average person. It is an escape film and we all know that with the hydrogen bomb, the atom bomb and the pressures of civilization, there is much to escape from. If it be argued that the film is only light entertainment, all I can say is that it pretends to no greater heights, and entertainment serves its purpose too. I am proud of the film *Not Tonight Henry* because it has been able to entertain and amuse a vast audience.[62]

Professing a humbleness and appeal to tolerance and the right of the filmmaker to entertain a world-weary audience above all, Paramore's concluding comments in the affidavit struck a chord of naive faith. His claim that the film aspired to nothing greater than entertainment is belied by his affiliation of the film, at least in content, with foreign art films, as discussed earlier. Additionally, his return to the discourse of entertainment as the primary goal of the cinema seems to return the classification and status of movies, as mass medium, to their limited definition by the *Mutual* decision and thus proves to be a risky rhetorical move. That is, by reducing moviegoing to a simple drive for escape from the pressures of modern life, and thus by positioning *Not Tonight Henry* as a product that can ameliorate cultural anxieties by providing cathartic release, the association of the nudie with licentious and "cheap amusement" persists as a stigma. Gesturing toward 1960s Cold War politics, Paramore attempted a bid for social relevance paradoxically through the abilities of the cinema to act as a location of political denial. Such a line of argument predated the defenses of hard-core pornography in terms of "safety-valve" theory, that is, that pornography fulfills a social need by providing spectators a sexual outlet through fantasy and a redirecting of their malevolent or perverse impulses. The unspoken and sublimated address to the way female nudity itself offers a particular spectatorial "release" or indulgence in fantasy indicates the tricky nature of Paramore's point. If we recall the concern of reviewer Miranda over the *kind* of looking that is presumed the film encourages to take place, specifically "leering," then the abstracted potential response of the audience, transformed into a notion of generalized amusement rather than arousal, was a discursive evasion of the specific terms and spectatorial experience of erotic display of nude female bodies. Particularly in the differing discourses of filmmaker and censor (and censor as film critic), it is evident that the terms of dispute were less about the film's content than they were about the potential impact on and responses of an unknown audience—an audience empirically present, in Paramore's testimony of the film's screening venues (the film had already played in 120 cities across the United States), and, in another sense, an audience that was absent and abstract, in the anxieties and fears represented by the censors' view.

Despite these legal proceedings and an extensive appeal on the part of the filmmakers and distributors, in the end, Janus Films acquiesced to the board's demands. It withdrew its appeal shortly after the hearings in June 1962, and after a series of cuts and rescreenings by the board, the film was licensed in September 1962, with the filmmakers having cut a new print with a series of optical superimpositions and effects to block, or at least to make diaphanous, glimpses of breast and buttock nudity. Until 1965, sexploitation producers had to negotiate an as yet rigid system of regulation in New York, while at the same time attempting to recoup their money in other states, which might have different licensing agencies who might arbitrate salacious content differently. *Henry,* made on forty thousand dollars, managed to recoup tenfold on its initial investment on the West Coast, this dispute in New York State notwithstanding.[63]

Substantial evidence attests to the attempts of sexploitation directors to evade or circumvent censorial control after the fact of receiving a license through a practice of using "hot" and "cool" versions of the same print, a well-documented tactic in this emerging industry. Requests for rescreening or review would invariably be confronted with a generally unmoved response from the board. In some cases, however, a process of review and resubmission could go on for many months without much compliance on the part of the sexploitation distributor. For example, Barry Mahon's film *Nudes Inc.* (1964) went through a series of screenings and suggestions for edits, yet Mahon's attempts, perhaps disingenuous, to edit the film were met with repeated calls for revision. The board's review notes for *Nudes Inc.* stated, "Present version unsatisfactory. Conference to discuss possible eliminations of exploitation of modeling views and episodes involving 'phony photographers.' Mr. Mahon, producer to attempt some editorial changes and resubmit."[64] In a subsequent screening after purported changes, the reviewer commented, "Eliminations and added material not satisfactory. Mr. Sugarman advised that problem remains basically the same."[65] As the proceedings wended their way into the following year, another set of edits yielded positive results, contingent on the board viewing a final cut, but it appears that Mahon never resubmitted the film for final licensing as decisions such as *Jacobellis v. Ohio* narrowed even further the jurisdiction of obscenity to the "hard-core," which Justice Potter Stewart famously announced would be evident on its presence, in his claim "I know it when I see it." Indeed, *Nudes Inc.* had numerous playdates in the state of Texas in 1964, where the film's narrative of the life of a nude model in New York City generated a multiweek run.

Other situations involving the resistance of distributors and exhibitors to the control of the board over content emerged in face-offs over film advertising, specifically the editing of trailers. The jurisdiction of the board, as mentioned earlier in respect to the state law on "pandering," extended to the production of film trailers, in that "obscene" material edited from a submitted film was prohibited from being used in the trailer or other forms of advertising, and generally, the distributor or producer was required to submit any trailers to the board for appraisal. Occasionally, distributors would attempt to sneak trailers past the discernment of the board. The trailer for the film *White Slaves of Chinatown* (Joseph P. Mawra, 1964) was discovered by board director Pesce to contain three scenes that were deleted from the film itself, which was passed with revisions in early July 1964. Pesce itemized these scenes in a review report of the trailer, "1. View of Frenchy lying on dungeon floor with her breasts exposed. 2. View of Jackie strung up by her hands, with her breast exposed. 3. View of Olga undressing, exposing her breasts and buttocks."[66] The producer George Weiss assented to the projectionist's cutting of the trailer.

It is also essential to note that by 1964, whereas nudity continued to be a thorny topic, the introduction of sadomasochistic subjects into the content of sexploitation films, which had generically shifted to a subcycle of "roughies," dealing with vice, crime, and physical and sexual violence, were left unassailed by the agency, despite Pesce's claims elsewhere that the law was not strict enough in respect to film violence, which he saw as an equally, if not more, pressing matter in films being made at the time.[67] In a related incident, a citizen's complaint to her state senator regarding the Herschell Gordon Lewis film *Blood Feast* (1963) led to a response from Forty-Third District chairman Henry Wise, who lamented the fact that obscenity law as it stood could not sufficiently remedy an extremely gory and violent film such as this one.[68] *Blood Feast* had notably modified the nudie formula, which was facing box office decline in the mid-1960s. The film has been credited in part with creating the "splatter" horror genre, according to the most common narrative attributed to the film, as it redirected sexuality into a focus on extreme violence, filmed in blaring color, with artificial blood and sense-defying graphic detail.

Citizen complaints were a common form of censorial pressure felt not only by politicians, film theater owners and managers, and the police but also by the censor board itself. A layperson's complaint might lead the board to double back and reinspect a film's trailer or the film print itself. For example, on February 10, 1965, a Mr. Buonanno called the censor board office reporting that the New Apollo Theater on Clinton Street in New York City was showing obscene material. The film in question was *Hollywood Nudes Report* (licensed in 1964 with revisions, produced by Mahon's Cinema Syndicate), and apparently the complainant was viewing the "coming attractions" with his eight-year-old daughter and saw a trailer for the film that featured nudity and exposed female breasts and buttocks. A board official went to the theater and inspected the film to find that the film was being shown in the proper licensed version, without any of the excised material reinserted into the print. However, the evidence sought, the trailer in question, was no longer available, as the film had already started its run at the theater.[69]

The preceding incident explains in part some of the economic pressures attendant on sexploitation filmmakers as well as the ways these producers would work with the structure of limitations established by censorial policy to reap a profit from a film regardless. Sexploitation filmmakers' use of trailers and other advertising customarily took advantage of their naturally elliptical form, often "promising" more risqué material than the film itself might deliver. It was feasible and common to view a trailer of a film that would have more "indecent" shots than the actual film itself. It was only after the point of purchase, after already having been ensconced in the theater, and perhaps after the film had ended, that an expectant filmgoer might realize the difference between the lure of the trailer and the actual images seen on-screen. Sexploitation distributors negotiated these contexts of institutionalized restraint and regulation, adjusting to, accommodating, and evading restrictions through creative marketing and strategies of prevarication.

One final example of conflict between sexploitation exhibitors and the impact of community groups on a film's censorship—a case that also involved the censor board in a retrospective review—was the film *Bell, Bare and Beautiful* (Lewis H. Gordon, 1963), licensed by the New York State Censor Board for exhibition in 1963. Police officers raided the Lyric Theater in Rochester in April 1964, arrested the theater manager, and confiscated the film. This action spawned a one hundred thousand dollar countersuit by the theater owners against the police department and the city for constitutional violation of their rights and for economic damages.[70] The censor board was called in to authenticate the version of the print that was being shown. Yet the motivations for the seizures and arrest, which occurred without a warrant, were brought on by somewhat misdirected energies. According to board reviewer Frank Torrell, who went to Rochester to attend the "Show Cause" trial brought on by the exhibitor,

> Chief Lombardo stated that there are many pressure groups in the city of Rochester who have initiated the action culminating in the seizure of the film at the theater mainly because manager Cooper was "hawking" Nudist Magazines during intermission priced from one to two dollars per copy, giving the impression of a burlesque type operation. Apparently several complainants had noted that many clients seemed under the age of eighteen, although, to my knowledge Cooper usually checked identification cards for proof of age at the box office.[71]

The fuzzy knowledge of obscenity law, on the part of both local police and self-appointed citizens and community groups, as well as the disparity between developments around censorship and obscenity in different cities and states and on the federal level, became a recipe for misguided confrontation with film theaters, as this divulgence of motive indicates. In Rochester, public outcry led to erroneous apprehension of theater staff, in which the accusations regarding the nudist magazines were displaced onto the film, which had been approved for public exhibition by the board in the previous year.[72] What is also interesting is that the fluidity and interchangeability between different media—between the nudist magazine and the "adult film"—could serve to incriminate the intentions of the theater owner, impugning the status of legitimacy of the theater.

The consolidation of offenses also hinged on whether the theater permitted entry to any patrons who were under age eighteen, as police officers claimed the night that they conducted the arrests.[73] Yet the claim of an age requirement was itself not a criterion that the censor board could control, owing to the lack of a state or local classification system in place for films at this time. In fact, the Board of Regents had already made a proposal in August 1963 for a film ratings system enforced by the state that could take into account the suitability of films for children. Feeling hemmed in by the erosion of the legal definition of obscenity into a narrower and narrower designation of the explicitly sexual, the Board of Regents conversely saw a widening array of problematic representations that needed to be curbed: "'the criteria governing the rating system,' they said, 'should go beyond the area of legal obscenity and should reflect the broader concern for the moral and emotional well-being of young people.' Legislation to authorize the rating plan should be drawn, said the regents, to exclude children of school age from films rated as unsuitable for them."[74] By deferring to the function of state law, the regents hoped to reinforce their power and centrality in the classification of film content in the wake of an onslaught of sexualized media and the whittling down of the usefulness of obscenity as a category for the management of films and their potential audiences. Yet previous attempts to write bills that would institute film ratings by the state had been voted down in the state senate, and this new bid was also voted down in the legislature in 1965.[75] In this context, voluntary classification had become widespread among theater owners, who often used the "adults-only" tag line as a means of caution to potential audience members and, conversely, for attracting curious adults as paying customers.

In these ongoing debates, the specificity of sexploitation films was frequently overshadowed by what the films represented on the level of culture more than textuality: their address to inappropriate audiences, their low cultural or marginal status, and their reoriented demarcation of public and private through the image of the nude female body. For the lay public at this time, as opposed to more attentive cultural and industrial insiders, sexploitation was not perceived as a differentiated genre or mode of production, and the emerging hybridity of film product in the 1960s, the perceived overlap between nudie films, independent features, Hollywood films, and foreign films, made the status of sexploitation's specific mode of production and provenance difficult to apprehend. At the same time that sexploitation films were marginal, outsider productions, they could also easily blend into the landscape of film culture in the public eye. Rather, boundaries, in terms of the age of moviegoers, the designated audiences to which films were addressed, and the content of the films, were in considerable flux, and in the absence of a rating system (instituted in 1968), the tag of "adults only" drew a rather wide swath across varying genres and modes of production. Therefore it is no wonder that public outcry against sexploitation was consonant with protests against the increasingly sexualized nature of Hollywood films. This was precisely the predicament that Frank Freeman and his ad hoc committee to curb obscenity among the nudie producers had aimed to quell a few years earlier. Thus the film theater space itself, its status neither public nor private, became both the symbolic and pragmatic site for a clash about those who might be its designated occupants and what proprieties might obtain in defining or managing that audience.

The End of Prior Restraint and Its Impact

Before moving to a discussion of the landscape of obscenity cases heard on the national and state stage, as well as to religious and community groups' activism around specific sexploitation films, it is essential to address how this landscape shifted with the waning of the power of state censorship, as the New York State Censor Board, along with the other remaining film licensing agencies in other states, were rendered obsolete, their procedural tactics deemed discriminatory and unconstitutional in 1965. This seismic shift in the state processes of censorship was facilitated and begun much earlier by an outright challenge to the practice of prior restraint in Chicago in 1961. In this case, an exhibitor refused to submit a rather innocuous movie, the opera film *Don Giovanni*, to the Chicago city censor board in 1961, to "abstractly" test the constitutionality of prior restraint. Although the U.S. Supreme Court, in hearing the case, reinforced the operations of state and city censor boards and the moral imperatives of prior censorship, the case left a wide opening for a larger fight down the road.[76] This opportunity was taken up in 1965, when Ronald Freedman, a theater owner in Maryland, contested the agency regarding the French film *Revenge at Daybreak* (Yves Allégret, 1952) and was arrested for not submitting the film to the board.[77] The agency admitted that the film, in and of itself, was not obscene, but the issue was the flouting of the rules of submission. The vigorous argument of independent entrepreneurs and foreign film exhibitors, on the other hand, was that prior restraint put the burden of proof on the accused and that the required submission of films to a board in advance of their being screened in public acted as an informal mode of censorship that interfered with the freedom of speech guarantees only recently granted to the cinema in the prior decade. Exhibitors were categorically guilty of obscenity until proven innocent through the long-standing processes of preexhibition submission of film prints and scripts to a governmental agency. Four years after the *Don Juan* decision, the U.S. Supreme Court reversed itself in 1965, stating that all such censorship systems based on prior restraint were unconstitutional.[78]

Thus the *Freedman v. Maryland* decision became the benchmark for the required revision of censorship procedures if censor boards were to continue to exist. What the legal elimination of prior restraint in part communicated was that the expansion of the permissible in film had much to do with the "catching up" of the film medium with the other constitutionally protected organs of public expression, such as literature and the press. Up through the late 1950s, the cinematic form and the industry had been built around a set of institutionally specific practices of containment and self-governance that were the ongoing legacy of the *Mutual* decision's isolation of film as an entertainment form unique and different from the other arts. The broadening of the permissible on-screen was impelled by this revision of what constituted proper restraint and management of moving images in changing times and amid seismically shifting attitudes toward sexuality. And pragmatically, it forced a sea change not only in the practices but also in the very existence of the censor board as a regulatory agency.[79]

Sexploitation Films in Court

The obscenity disputes involving sexploitation films that were argued after the demise of prior restraint often deferred to precedent established in previous cases around literature, print, and filmic works and, at times, were recapitulations of arguments made in these prior cases. But they also illuminate the place of sexploitation and its specific content as it defined or otherwise alienated its potential audience—both the intended audience of theater spectators and the "indirect" audience of juries and judges, police officers, critical observers, and the lay public.

The obscenity cases that would come before state and federal courts in the 1960s often combined or addressed two distinct categories of examination, one dealing with the concern of procedural requirements and the processes of censorship and their questionable constitutionality, and the other addressing the concern of content, that is, determining whether the text itself was obscene based ostensibly on its aesthetic, textual, sociological, or cultural merits. At the Supreme Court level, the procedural issues were easier to tackle as a means of avoiding the question of licentious film content.

The revisions of state and city censorship processes entailed shifting the onus of "proof" of obscenity onto the censor board as well as a reduction of the span of time between film submission and final judgment. If the censor board were to find the film obscene, it would itself have to initiate court proceedings against the film's producers immediately, proving how the film in question had failed the reigning "three-pronged test" modified since the *Roth* case in more recent decisions regarding *The Lovers* and *Lady Chatterley's Lover.*

One offshoot of this decision was the rise in the acquisition of expert testimony that would, above and beyond a "mere viewing" of the film, prove the text's objectionable nature or artistic value. This shift in the mid- to late 1960s would lead to the procurement of film "experts" and critics to testify both against and on behalf of a film's "redeeming social value," as evidenced most prominently in the *I Am Curious (Yellow)* Supreme Court case. This shifting of expertise and interpretive adjudication necessitated a readjustment of the processes of distinction and connoisseurship, in which the designated audience of a film was stratified and delineated by taste, pedigree, and critical experience with artistic material. As discussed earlier in the case of the *Censored* trial, the sexploitation film became embroiled in a larger cultural and political debate about the assignation of filmic connoisseurship versus vernacular understanding and the conflict between film as mass entertainment and film as art, a form of refined leisure.

In Maryland, the censor board had, instead of disbanding, revised its licensing procedures to reflect the new legal requirements of *Freedman*. Yet the burden of proving the obscenity of a film was still a task that the courts and the board were not equipped to perform, as they depended, instead, on the self-evidence of the film in question as the dominant explanatory mechanism. This was evident in a case Audubon Films brought against the Maryland Board of Censors, in which Radley Metzger's film *The Dirty Girls* (1965) was judged obscene "solely based on viewing of this film (by) a Baltimore circuit court judge" who reinforced the Maryland board's decision to suppress it. According to the judge who ruled against the censor board, the state agency "did no more to meet the burden of proof of obscenity which the statute imposed on it than to offer the picture to the city court. . . . Sex and obscenity are not synonymous. . . . The state motion picture censorship board must bear burden of proving a film is 'unprotected expression.'"[80] This need to prove the reasoning for the assignation of obscenity, as discussed earlier, necessitated the marshaling of significant experts who could attest to the film's lack of any redeeming value.

The Dirty Girls bore Metzger's trademark preoccupation with the dalliances of the European bourgeois and dealt with a set of parallel stories of two different "women of pleasure" in Munich and Paris. Quite artfully constructed and bearing an air of worldly existentialism, the film's denouement resulted in its final act of the revelation of lesbian love. It is worthwhile to question, if the procedural issues had not been so prominent, how would the erotic content of the film been handled by the court? Nevertheless, the striking down of prior restraint began to make it far more difficult for censor boards and the law to categorically argue that a film had no social value whatsoever, and we can see the ramifications of *Freedman* extending far beyond sexploitation and onward into the development of hard-core pornography in the coming years.

A similar incident occurred around the banning, again in Maryland, of the Russ Meyer film *Lorna* (1964). Although the case was filed in 1964, it was heard in October 1965, after the *Freedman* decision had come down. The Maryland State Censor Board had refused to provide a license for exhibition of the film, and again, as in the *Dirty Girls* case, had only provided the court with the film itself as evidence. Taken to the appellate court level in Maryland, the highest court ruled that although it found the film to be "tiresome, boring and cheap, often vulgar and sometimes revolting," the state did not adequately prove the obscene status of the film.[81] What the board needed to have done, according to the appellate judges, was provide "'enlightening testimony' . . . needed to determine whether a film met constitutional standards, except in the 'rare [case of] the exceptional motion picture, which not only speaks for itself, but screams for all to hear that it is obscene.'"[82] One judge dissented, however, claiming that the film was self-evidently offensive, lacking artistic, social, cultural, or any other value, and was "one of those motion pictures as to which no proof other than the viewing of it, is required to determine that it is in fact obscene."[83] According to this logic of self-evidence, *Lorna* needs no exposition; its transgressions of propriety speak for themselves. Such a refusal to engage with the film as text, and implicitly in terms of its potential to contain art or ideas, can be seen as a product of the shifting status of the discursive and legal couching of film as art as well as the conflict this notion created with the recalcitrant and confrontational content of sexploitation film as a genre. *Lorna,* a film that spawned Meyer's rural series of roughies, featured an oversexed young housewife who is raped and then falls in love with a menacing prison convict. Employing lush black-and-white cinematography and a jarring editing style, Meyer, one of the auteurs of the sexploitation industry, could certainly have mounted a defense of the film on aesthetic grounds, despite its indulgence in sadism

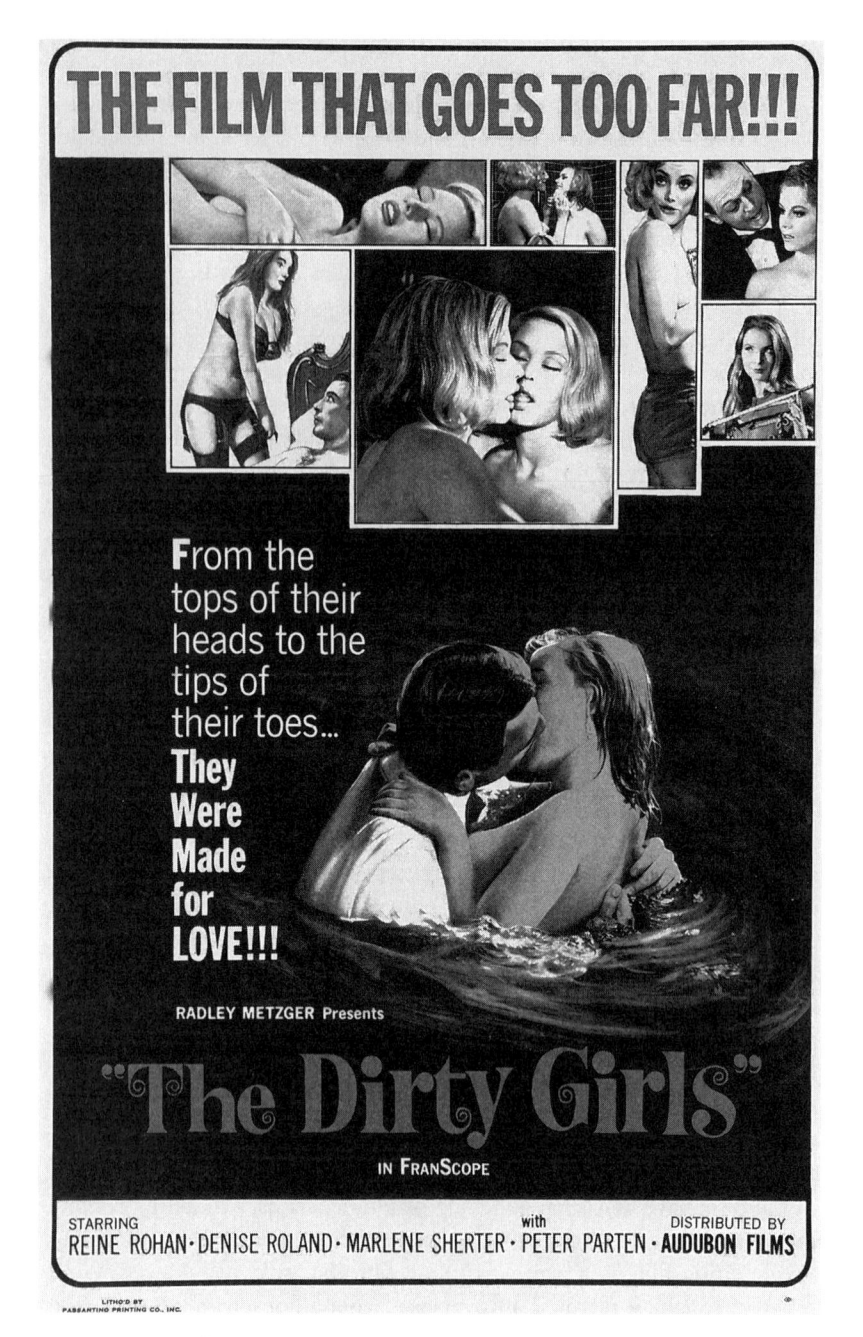

FIGURE 11. Radley Metzger's *The Dirty Girls* faced obscenity judgment in Baltimore; its poster plays on the cachet of contravening the forbidden, announcing it as the "film that goes too far."

and its stereotypes of backwoods sexuality. It seems as though the courts and the remaining censoring agencies were unable to respond to the shifting requirement of *Freedman,* nor were they able to shift gears and take a new approach to their project of film regulation within a transforming sphere of film reception.

Nonetheless, the vagaries of subjective taste and cultural valuation, whether acknowledged by the censors and the courts or not, remained the final stomping ground for aesthetic, social, or cultural evaluation of sexploitation film. A month before the state ruling that deemed the New York State Censor Board's prior censorship practices unconstitutional, Louis Pesce, board director, in responding to a question regarding how he could have passed a "salty film" like *Nature Camp Diary* (Doris Wishman, 1961) while denying a license to the Danish art film *A Stranger Knocks* (Johan Jakobsen, 1959), had proclaimed that the censor was not in fact a film critic. He went on to state that "for a censor to consider the picture's artistic value . . . would be obnoxious indeed."[84] Yet this was precisely what the flood of Supreme Court decisions defining obscenity had required. The disconnect between the law at the federal and the local levels, and between film "taken as a whole" and film as a collection of reducible, isolable parts, highlighted the irreconcilability between censorial practice and a new model of cinematic value, a value that sexploitation filmmakers became the benefactors of.

In the post-*Freedman* period, two sexploitation films became instrumental in abolishing the Chicago city censorship ordinance, again due to faulty procedural guidelines. *Body of a Female* (1964) and *Rent-a-Girl* (1965) were apprehended in Chicago in 1966, in which the city censor refused to grant a license to the films and, through the circuit court, permanently prohibited their exhibition in public.[85] When appealed to the Supreme Court of Illinois by the distributor, it ruled that "examination of these films shows that they deal not merely with sex, but with sexual deviations which can only appeal to those with a shameful and morbid interest in nudity and sex . . . and the producers have apparently spared no effort to see that the spectator searching for the erotic is not disappointed."[86] Here acknowledgment of the libidinally driven audience and of audience demand itself, which can no longer be denied, enters the discussion in the courts, as the perverse desire of the spectator is matched with the prurient intent of exploitation filmmakers. The trade and popular press had been lamenting and querying the "public's taste" throughout the early to mid-1960s, the box office figures for sexually suggestive films lending reasonable doubt to the notion of an offended or shocked audience, unveiling instead a nation of newly discovered and unsated voyeurs.[87] Both of the films under scrutiny in this case circulated around narratives of sex workers, in one a stripper, and in another a deluded girl who gets prostituted against her will, who are violently assailed or exploited by men, with morose results. Whereas the lower court depended on the assignation of obscenity to the films' content, the Supreme Court, to which the film distributor Charles Teitel appealed, chose the route of attacking the unconstitutionality of the Chicago censor ordinance in that it "failed to provide sufficient time to complete the administrative process before initiating a judicial proceeding and the ordinance did not contain a provision to assume a prompt final judicial decision."[88]

While such procedural issues about constitutionality continued to weigh down the substance of obscenity cases, other concerns also emerged. In yet another case involving Audubon, prints of the foreign import *I, a Woman* (1966), directed by Mac Ahlberg and distributed by Metzger's Audubon, were seized by police in two towns in Indiana, where the film was playing at drive-ins. The fact that the film prints were seized without any prior hearing, and that no warrants were presented as was legally required, complicated the case and forced a further clarification of the status of film in relationship to other forms of protected speech. Comparing the manner in which the prints were seized to the capture of other forms of contraband, the court ruled in favor of the film. In the court's evaluation of the case, the judge wrote, "Unlike narcotics, gambling paraphernalia or burglary tools, a motion picture film and other First Amendment material cannot be seized as contraband. . . . The legal rules governing the former are different from the latter."[89] This opinion was made in reference to *A Quantity of Copies of Books v. Kansas*, a court decision in 1964 that required an "adversary hearing" of purportedly obscene materials before seizure could take place. Although *I, a Woman* had not been detained at customs, and had played in fifty different cities, with some obscenity charges but no convictions, the seizures in this case exceeded the bounds of proper due process for a medium newly accorded constitutional protection. Interestingly, the connection between drugs and other illegal substances and immoral or obscene films or books had originally been made in U.S. Customs policy on "immoral materials."[90]

The elaborate yet broad umbrella for immoral materials created an analogy, a strange rhetorical affinity between illegal substances, such as narcotics, and obscene films, books, and magazines. This conflation links the addictive effects of drugs with the physical, corporeal drive of the obscene, placing them into one classification as tools for social (and national) harm. The implications of this customs policy do not necessarily square with obscenity law as it was being revised in these years, particularly in relation to the Kansas case. Despite the draconian implications of the preceding rules, and the threat of destruction of obscene materials as the final step in dealing with an imported obscene work, the U.S. Customs Bureau in this period was far more permissive than expected, allowing more films through customs due to this precise disparity between obscenity law and the bureau's own policies.[91]

Sexploitation films were also problematizing the definition of public space, as the films' sexual provocations were compounded by their exhibition not just at indoor theaters; they were also widely popular at drive-ins in the 1960s. The sharing of public space as constitutive of consent and willfulness is the underlying tension in a case involving Radley Metzger's 1967 sexploitation film *Carmen, Baby. Rabe v. Washington* (1969) adjudicated the legality of showing Metzger's film in a drive-in. An outline in court of the events precipitating the arrest of the exhibitor recounted that "the police officer stood outside of the fence of the Park-Y drive-in theater and watched a part of this film. . . . The picture was visible to nearby homes, to persons standing outside of the fence, and to passing motorists."[92] Also adding to the controversy was that the police officer saw preteenage children watching the film. The exhibitor was found guilty in local and state courts and was charged "with violating the Washington State obscenity statute by causing 'to be exhibited an obscene, indecent and immoral show.'"[93] In the Supreme Court in 1971, Stanley Fleishman argued the case in defense of the theater manager, and the National Association of Theater Owners (NATO) as well as the MPAA filed amici curiae on his behalf, while the anti-obscenity group Morality in Media filed a brief encouraging the previous conviction to stand. The argument of the state prosecution was that in the "context of exhibition," the film was obscene, whereas if it had been shown at an indoor theater, the film would not have been obscene. This forwarded the notion that obscenity could be variably defined by spatial context rather than social or textual context.[94] The local rulings ended up being overturned by the U.S. Supreme Court on the grounds that the original arrest was made on the basis of the context and outdoor location of its showing, and this notice was not fairly stated in the state obscenity statute as a criterion for obscenity. The high court wrote, "The statute under which petitioner was prosecuted, however, made no mention that the 'context' or location of the exhibition was an element of the offense somehow modifying the word 'obscene.'"[95] Chief Justice Burger, while concurring with his colleagues' decision, added the following comment regarding the nature of the obscene film as "public nuisance": "public displays of explicit materials such as are described in this record are not significantly different from any noxious public nuisance traditionally within the power of the States to regulate and prohibit, and, in my view, involve no significant countervailing First Amendment considerations."[96]

This instance of debate over what constitutes the public sphere and of sexploitation film's proper place within it was tendered through an idea of an *unintended spectator* whose sense of publicness is intruded upon by improper imagery of nudity and sexual license. These images became even more improper precisely by virtue of their being put out of their proper place and in public view for any person to see, irrespective of his desire or choice to see it. Additionally, the protection of private citizens, highlighted by the focus on the proximity of the drive-in to private homes, within the logic of the state court, was made in the name of individual privacy and an abstracted idea of unwitting potential audience members who might stumble upon the sight of the film screen, much like the police officer himself. This case was a remarkable instance and encapsulation of the motoring anxieties around film spectatorship in this period and, in its mapping of the coordinates of proper and improper viewing positions, in terms of public and private space, illuminated the very destabilizing force of sexual images, particularly of the sexploitation film, within the fabric of public culture in the 1960s.

The Public versus the Skin Flick

Parallel to the developments occurring in the courts, sexploitation films, alongside other "maturing" film product, were bearing the brunt of pressure from community groups and a variety of religious and political organizations that were assailing the public expansion of sexualized media in various forms. These modes of informal censorship, as mentioned earlier, held as much sway with the press and the law in advancing stringent restrictions and banning films throughout the country.

Smut cleanup campaigns had been ongoing throughout the decade, gaining force in the mid-1960s through the work of religious and civic groups such as the Catholic Legion of Decency, the National Catholic Office for Motion Pictures, and Citizens for Decent Literature, as well as through independent citizen's complaints. As early as 1960, J. Edgar Hoover, then director of the Federal Bureau of Investigation, had blasted the culture industries, particularly film, for profane advertisements and for glorifying depravity, and had encouraged stronger laws against "filth purveyors."[97]

Richard Randall and Jon Lewis have discussed how the impact of antismut campaigns and community pressure could be considerable on exhibitors and producers, at times exceeding more formal means of pressure.

In New York City circa 1963–65, religious groups and politicians had taken businesses in Times Square to task for disgracing the city and for creating a public nuisance through the sale of lascivious films, books, and magazines. Monsignor McCaffrey, one vociferous critic who held services in a church on 42nd Street, represented this view in 1963, suggesting that Times Square had become a "magnet for degenerates and criminals who 'gravitate' there to satisfy their desire for obscenity" and went on to suggest that with the upcoming World's Fair to be held in New York the following year, a cleanup was necessary to give a better impression to tourists visiting the city for the first time.[98] Indeed, the pressure of the presence of the World's Fair served as one factor in the particular instance of New York City's attempts to regulate sexually oriented businesses, such as bookstores and film theaters, in the Times Square area. By 1964, these crackdowns and anti-smut campaigns were focused largely on local bookstores and newsstands that potentially provided minors access to illicit materials and nudie magazines.[99] New York City's Mayor Wagner, by August of that year, had initiated his own "smut drive," culling together a twenty-one-member citizens' antipornography group, including members from civic, labor, and business organizations, alongside him, to serve as a steering committee for the campaign, with the attention predominantly given to newsstands and print materials. Attempting to avoid raids, book burnings, or other such "on the ground" confrontations, the committee was to address the "pornography problem" through the courts and legislation, and the mayor claimed that New York had become a "dumping ground" for these materials.[100]

This offensive seemed to have spilled over to, or dovetailed with, for a brief period, attentions given to the film exhibitors in the area. City licenses commissioner Joseph Di Carlo applied pressure on theater owners to remove suggestive and sexualized marquees and displays from the front of a number of movie houses, which the theater owners had agreed to undertake of their own volition, after complaints from religious and civic organizations as well as from pedestrians and tourists. According to the *New York Times*, the displays included "nude or semi-nude photographs to pictures about drug addiction, forced prostitution and perversion," and "some of the material has also been found to be misleading. Frames that were cut from films by state censors have on occasion been blown up into display photographs to lure customers." Community pressures could also be felt from local ethnic organizations, as Joseph Mawra's sexploitation film *White Slaves of Chinatown* was cited with igniting protests from the Chinese Consolidated Benevolent Association, which claimed that the film presented a distorted, jaundiced view of their ethnic enclave.[101] Although the theaters, including the Tivoli, the Rialto, the World, the Globe, and the Forum, had pledged compliance, by the following year, the city appeared again hamstrung by the tenor of the obscenity decisions coming down from the courts, as the marquees had inevitably returned to their lewd come-ons. Of course, these forms of dissimulation were central to the drive of sexploitation exhibitors and the marketing of the films, as has been discussed earlier in respect to trailer advertisements. Interestingly, by 1965, the complaints had come to include the Broadway Association, which was a business organization for shop owners in the area, which felt that the sexploitation marquees blighted their business image and the patina of the area in general as an appealing space for consumers. The association stated in a letter to the commissioner of licenses, "How much can a public, including as it does, thousands of children, be expected to take?" Conflating the public with the receptive innocence of children, the business owners' grievance was considered just one year later an anachronism, as the commissioner replied that the marquee titles, such as "The Rape—It Goes All the Way" and "Uncut, Uncensored Shame Dame" might have "in Victorian days made the fair damsel blush" but that, under the current rulings of the federal courts, these come-ons were no longer legal grounds for prosecution.[102]

Smut cleanup campaigns in locales outside of New York similarly focused on the relationships between film and other media. For example, a raid on the Continental theater in Phoenix, Arizona, in May 1965, in which the owner of the theater, the projectionist, and the cashier were arrested, was part of a larger sweep of bookstores and magazine shops being made by police at the urgings of county officials who wanted to adhere to a new anti-obscenity law passed by the state legislature.[103] Confiscating the sex trade "exposé" *The Sexploiters* (produced by R. W. Cresse), the "nude women around the world" Italian import *Sexy Probitissimo,* and the trailer for Wishman's *The Sex Perils of Paulette,* the police also held and interrogated "63 embarrassed stags" in a move clearly criminalizing not only the sexploitation films but also their viewers.[104]

Police raids and film seizures became common in the late 1960s, as federal definitions of obscenity chafed against local adjudications of indecent material and the very publicness of filmgoing contested the emergent sense of the spectator as a private citizen. In another instance of such incursions, seventy patrons of a screening of Andy Warhol's sexploitation-influenced *Lonesome Cowboys* (1968) in Atlanta, at the Ansley Mini Mall Theater, were photographed, in order to later be compared to possible known criminals or homosexuals, during a police seizure of the film. (The police had been tipped off by a member of the group Citizens for Decent Literature, to be discussed shortly.) The ACLU sued the police on the grounds that the spectators' rights were violated.[105] The *Atlanta Constitution* weighed in, responding to this and another recent theater raid, with an editorial stating, "The greatest obscenity involved so far was the highhanded, outrageous official behavior in photographing members of the audience viewing one allegedly obscene film, then blandly explaining that the pictures of the audience were to be compared with police records on various known criminals."[106] No doubt the specifically gay affiliations of Warhol's film raised hackles, escalating the response of law enforcement, but it also pointed to the slippery logic of the sex film's offense as also an affront of and on an idea of a film public suddenly perceived as unruly or criminal owing to their sexual or aesthetic tastes.

Charles Keating Takes on *Vixen*

The pitched battle against "smut" across media had developed into a highly politicized affair, and sexploitation films served the decency crusaders as a compelling example and easy target. The accusation that sex purveyors held affiliations with leftist politics were common in this period; however, the political orientations, not to mention aims, of sexploitation filmmakers were likely far more murky. The organization Citizens for Decent Literature (CDL) acted as a source of informal but formidable censorship pressure on film producers, and its interactions with film exhibitors and film patrons provide an interesting case of the politicization of adult film spectatorship as much as film content. The group's incredible growth in the 1960s centered squarely on the efforts of the Comstockian personality of Charles H. Keating Jr., its founder. Just as numerous anti-smut campaigns began with a focus on indecent literature, CDL shifted its focus to motion pictures as prime culprits of the nation's moral crisis. Although CDL's platform claimed not to advocate private or public censorship but rather an adherence to and optimization of existing antipornography laws, CDL's practices often involved tactics of intimidation and political and community pressure in an attempt to shame exhibitors and politicians, as well as film viewers, into submission.[107] In 1969, Charles Keating had also been newly elected President Nixon's sole appointee to the Presidential Commission on Obscenity and Pornography, replacing the previous commission member Kenneth Keating.

Based in Ohio, one of CDL's victories against sexploitation occurred in its battle with Russ Meyer and the owner of the Guild Fine Arts Theater in Cincinnati over the exhibition of Meyer's film *Vixen* in 1969. Meyer's film treated the sexual entanglements of the bored wife of a lodge owner and bush pilot in British Columbia, correlating his absence and lack of attention to her voracious nymphomania. The title character, played by Erica Gavin, proceeds to sleep with a variety of passers-by to the lodge, partaking in interracial and lesbian sex as well as an incestuous entanglement with her brother. Constitutively soft-core, Meyer's film nonetheless attempted to appeal to the youth market through a perfunctory focus on "social issues," positioning Gavin's character as a racial bigot and national protectionist who ends up in ideological conflict with a number of other, more liberal characters. The political monologue near the end of the film, as an Irish communist hijacks her husband's plane, with Vixen and a number of her sexual companions in tow, to shift his route to Cuba, could be seen as transparently inserted to make the film more topically appealing, an overt gesture toward the political turbulence of the times. One critic noted that whereas Vilgot Sjoman's *I Am Curious (Yellow)* represented the sphere of radical sexual politics, *Vixen* was made for the conservative crowd:

> To make this kind of movie the director has had to reinforce the stereotype of male and female and the weird double standards that are part of so many conventional marriages. He pushes the thought that you aren't what you do, you aren't what you feel, but that the real you, the you that counts is the role that you occupy. This is a deeply conservative idea, one right at the heart of what cultural radicalism is attacking—the tense and unhappy contradiction between the inner person and the position outer circumstances force him to occupy. Long after Vietnam is resolved, if it ever is, this struggle will continue to divide the country.[108]

Contrary to some of the previous claims made by organizations such as CDL, and as a relatively sophisticated critique of the film's marriage of sex and ideology, this reading of the film ironically distinguished *Vixen* for precisely the conservatism that moralist groups claimed it lacked. Yet, at the same time, it was perhaps Meyer's irreverent indulgence in the vagaries of screen sex, seen as an inconsequential, untroubled romp in the hay, that continued to plague groups like CDL. As critic Kenneth Turan noted regarding the faintness of *Vixen*'s social significance, drawing again the comparison to *Curious*,

> Because Meyer does not want to get entangled in censorship battles, his films are not nearly as clinical as *I Am Curious (Yellow)*. Sex is depicted as a series of contorted faces, heaving chests, ecstatic grins and banshee screams, with hands touching nothing but the side of the bed. Yet, since the sex in *Vixen* is not forced to stand duty as an allegory of the socio-political ills of our time, it ends up being what it distinctly is not in other more respectable films: a good time.[109]

The visual manifestation of the limitations of censorship, as articulated through the soft-core idiom, is discussed in terms of the film's elisions, cuts, implications, and deferral to off-screen sexual action. If explicit sex can be seen as a marker or provocation of politics, this reviewer suggests that by sustaining suggestiveness rather than veracity, Meyer skirts the potential of his film to become an allegory of contemporary life, a view at odds with the previous analysis.

In the wake of the new MPAA ratings system, Meyer voluntarily gave the film an X, presaging a strategy of rebellious self-designation and, implicitly, transgressive audience appeal that would be taken up by many other soft- and hard-core film producers in the following years.[110] However, this also meant that *Vixen* would be far more difficult to screen in mainstream, commercial theaters, relegating it to the art theater circuit.[111] Despite these factors, *Vixen* was nonetheless a resounding box office success nationally, signaling a new direction in sexploitation films toward more risqué sexual representations that inched closer to the visual approximation of the sex act. Newspaper advertisements in Ohio and Pennsylvania in 1969 blared that *Vixen* "might be the most explicit film ever made," "was a new genre of woman . . . a wild animal," and was "turning this city on." The success of *Vixen* moved Meyer closer into the orbit of the Hollywood studios, where he would soon be commissioned by Twentieth Century Fox to make the big-budget *Beyond the Valley of the Dolls* in 1969, which would further blur the boundaries between the scrappy skin flick independents and Hollywood's large-budget spectacles.

Vixen's numerous offenses to Charles Keating's sensibilities were outlined in his injunction, submitted as a private citizen, to the Ohio Common Pleas Court in September 1969. On the same day that Keating's injunction was filed, the film was seized by the Cincinnati Vice Squad. Keating relied on using the premise of a "public nuisance abatement" ordinance in effect in the state to incriminate Meyer's film. Keating's argument in the injunction cited a number of factors for the necessary banning of the picture and left no culpable stone unturned, targeting not only the motion picture and Meyer himself but also Meyer's production company, Eve Productions; Malibu Inc., the owner of the Guild Fine Arts theater where the film was showing; Clarence Gall, Malibu's president; and the film's distributor, the Tri-State Theater Service Inc. Keating argued that the film was obscene under current law, that exhibition of the film went against Ohio state law, and that the film had and would continue to cause social and moral harm to the state's citizens and thus constituted a public nuisance. As cited in Keating's injunction, the nuisance statute read, in a somewhat tautological formation, as follows, "(C) Nuisance means that which is defined and

FIGURE 12. An advertisement for *Vixen*'s run at the Hocking Drive-in, Logan, Ohio, 1969, warns spectators to leave their children at home.

declared by statutes to be such and also means any place . . . in or upon which . . . obscene films . . . are exhibited."[112] The rhetorical function of the notion of a public nuisance would serve as one of the lynchpins of Keating's argument—and his objection was in the end upheld both in Common Pleas and at the level of the Supreme Court of Ohio. Granted, this definition and reconceptualization of the public, through the rhetoric of public nuisances, put sexploitation filmmakers on shakier ground. Just as the distinction between the offending object and its watchers was questioned in the raid in Phoenix just a few years earlier, so here the public sphere as constructed by Keating went far beyond the analogy of publicness with outdoor space and privacy as indoor space, as we saw earlier in the *Carmen, Baby* drive-in prosecution. Instead, the notion of a public nuisance could contravene these more vernacular associations of spatial boundaries and was used to mobilize an idea of a permeable and contaminated national psyche. Knowledge of the potential sexual content of a film showing in a hardtop theater could therefore be as damaging as actually seeing or interacting with the film text in a more direct way as a ticket-buying audience member. In addition, Keating's claim for the film was that the representation of the mediated, fictionalized act of sex was itself tantamount to the public act itself. Through the language of Keating's legal complaint, his argument developed rhetorically and cumulatively in the following way:

> The visual and audio representations of a female as sexually available for every male and female the said female associates with, *is conduct* which degrades the sex function, which the Ohio State Legislature, in the furtherance of good morals and public decency, has confined to men and women of a certain maturity of development who are united together in a permanent sexual relationship. . . . The . . . presentations depicting incest *constitute conduct* which degrades the sex function . . . and [are] injurious to the overriding interest in a strong familial relationship, as reflected in the laws of the Ohio State Legislature and in the laws of the national community, which uniformly treat incest as a serious crime against public morality. . . . The . . . presentations depicting the perversion of lesbianism, *constitute conduct* which degrades the sex function. . . . *The acts and conduct described . . . if performed offstage and in public three dimensional form, would constitute violations of the laws of Ohio, forbidding public displays of such sexual activity, and their reproduction on the motion picture screen in public in two-dimensional form, in the manner indicated is contrary to good morals and public decency as a matter of law.* . . . That *each of the foregoing acts and the conduct of the defendants in the use of said*

property for the purposes and in the manner aforesaid interferes with the tranquility, peace, and quiet generally, of plaintiff and the nearby communities, constitutes unlawful and unwarranted and unreasonable use of defendant's property to the extreme annoyance, disturbance, discomfort and hurt of plaintiff, and is detrimental to the public good and to the common welfare; such *acts* are offensive to public decency, morals, peace and health, and constitute a nuisance which is subject to abatement under Section 3767 of the Ohio Revised Code.[113]

Keating cleverly outlines the slippery slope of association between representations of sex and the conduct of sex itself and, in the repetitive listing of the sexual crimes of this fictional film, conflates the image of sex and the act of sex, eliding the film's obvious status as fiction, while also eliding precisely the function of the *re-* in *representation* in any filmic work. The specificity of the sexual act ends up overriding the language that gestures toward this act's obvious mediation, despite the heavily parsed "audio and visual presentation" modifier. Keating's moralist agenda also claims that these representations, now transformed into live acts in the broadened public sphere (no longer limited, discursively, to the semipublic–semiprivate space of the movie theater), are equivalent to infractions against the national values of familial piety and heterosexual coupling. The privileged subjects that fall in line with these upright qualifications—normative, heterosexual, married, coupled, and therefore morally decent—in Keating's imaginary, take on the mantle of embodying the true benefactors of a national public sphere but also implicitly reclaim their own "zone of privacy" with respect to sexual acts.

As de Grazia and Newman discuss, the court's capitulation to Keating's argument and its conflations in effect "obscure(d) a difference central to free speech theory. Just as speech is protected because it is speech and not conduct, so a film should be protected because it is a filmed depiction of conduct, not the depicted conduct."[114] The mobilization of right-wing moralist anxiety around the powers of the film medium, and at the site of images of sexual simulation, is nowhere more pitched than in this case, which attests to the impact of sexploitation on the national sphere of discourse about sexuality in the realm of the moving image. Whereas Meyer's reliance on the sexual gimmick was an attempt to make *Vixen* topical and culturally "current" through his heroine's indulgence in the gamut of sexual practices, these specific acts became the site of the film's contested legality in Ohio. Yet these simulated acts induced the same kinds of conservative responses of outrage that would soon plague hard-core pornography in the coming years. Keating's home turf emerged as the territory of divergence from national standards in the playing field of obscenity law and its application. The limited victory of CDL on these grounds also attested to the ways regional legal systems could establish standards at variance from a national one with respect to the permitted and the obscene.

The Supreme Court of Ohio, in its 1971 decision, also upheld objection to the film on the faulty grounds of "pandering," using the case of *Ginzburg v. United States* as bolstering support. Reasoning that the exhibitor was primarily motivated by commercial gain, the court ruled that the film's "redeeming social value" was null and void, overridden by the theater's desire for financial gain, which was problematically equated with pandering.[115] As Dawn Sova details:

> the court also claimed that whatever social value the film might have (in its attempts to deal with contemporary issues) was negated by the evidence that "a film's exhibitor was principally motivated by the prospect of financial gain [that was] equivalent to pandering to prurient interests in sex, and so negative [sic] whatever social value or importance the film might conceivably have." The court ruled that, because *Vixen* displayed "sexual intercourse on the movie screen for commercial exploitation," not for an educational, social, scientific, moral or artistic purpose, the film was obscene.[116]

This encouragement of misreading or largely disavowing federal court decisions as guidelines for obscenity adjudication was also supported by CDL's legal strategy. Jane Friedman, an Obscenity Commission committee member, in a memo regarding her attendance of the national CDL convention in March 1969, reported on the presentation of CDL lawyers on their angle of attack not only on obscenity law as nationally written but also, by default, on sexploitation filmmakers, who were the primary culprits. CDL legal counsel James Clancy discussed the case against Audubon Film's *I, a Woman* in Kentucky, in which the prosecution was able to convince the state court *not* that the film was obscene but that the U.S. Supreme Court had failed in its responsibility to protect the average citizen from moral decay. The CDL filed amicus curiae in support of the prosecution and showed its film *Target Smut* as a persuasive device and as ancillary evidence about the cultural climate. The Kentucky state court ruled unanimously in the prosecution's and CDL's favor, against the film, stating in its brief that

> the Supreme Court has occupied itself since the [*Roth*] ruling in a somewhat futile attempt to determine what is obscene and what is not obscene.... The judicial record reflects nothing more than indecision and failure.... It seems to be universally believed everywhere, except

in the halls of the judiciary, that obscenity as such is not entitled to the constitutional protection awarded free speech.[117]

By thus sidelining the definition of obscenity as a foregone and self-evident conclusion, having a commonplace and obvious ontological identity, the CDL had begun to develop a workable strategy that would predate the U.S. Supreme Court's own reversal of its findings in 1973 in the *Miller* decision, when it would revert jurisdiction of obscenity back to the states and their "community standards." That sexploitation films were the ones often caught in the crosshairs of these politicized maneuverings on behalf of a generalized citizenry unified in purported outrage was no small coincidence, as the liminal status of sexploitation films, their riding of the boundary between the legal and the obscene, and their status as simulation rather than documentary representation further emboldened the debates at hand.

While the official party line of CDL was rather staunch, the attendees who were interviewed by Friedman were hardly as vocal about their relationship to the law of obscenity and its enforcement on the local level. One prosecutor, who was sent to the CDL convention by the mayor's office of his town in South Carolina at the behest of the local decency committee, told Friedman that he had reservations about the organization's mission and ideological stance, stating, "I would feel so silly, really, telling some soldier at Fort Jackson [South Carolina] that he can't go to a sexy movie on Saturday night, or some University student or professor that he can't read a particular book or magazine."[118] Deferring to the constitutive constitutional right of free speech as also a freedom of choice to consume what a spectator wishes, the prosecutor's reticence indicated uneasiness with treating the skin flick spectator as anything but a private citizen. This contrasted with CDL's practice of conceiving of the erotic film viewer as an inevitably public being, constituted as public at the very act of reception, as a form of willful self-designation.

The disputes over *Vixen* do not end here, with this small win on the part of community and civic pressure groups, because Keating's tactical mode of attack also took to the national stage, entering the sphere of politics, press, and reception. Keating, disappointed in the failure of the national press to cover his significant victory, shot off a letter regarding the case to Vice President Spiro Agnew.[119] Agnew, who had publicly spoken regarding the biases of news coverage, became a recipient of Keating's self-congratulations regarding the *Vixen* case and his complaints about his lack of press attention, writing, "Had the court's decision been one freeing a pornographer or declaring something to be not obscene, it would have, based upon historical probability, received nationwide coverage."[120]

Serving as both an implicit grievance against the "liberal media" and a sidling up against the offices of power, however unsubtly, Keating's letter of self-promotion also inadvertently brought the attention of Meyer's sexploitation film to one of the nation's highest offices.

The lengths to which Keating was willing to go not only to promote himself and expose perceived sexual excesses in film and print but also to assail the sex film spectator were exemplified by a complaint lodged against him to the chairman of the Presidential Obscenity Commission by one of the witnesses who testified on behalf of Meyer's film and its redeeming values. Herbert Ostrov wrote a memo to the chairman of the Presidential Commission, William B. Lockhart, informing him of Keating's persecution of him at his workplace. Ostrov was a witness on behalf of the defense in the *Vixen* trial, providing testimony as to the fact that he had seen the film outside of Cincinnati and did not consider it obscene. Keating apparently sent a letter to Ostrov's employer, drawing their attention to Ostrov's testimony, with the express intention of jeopardizing his employment there. In his letter to Lockhart, Ostrov states that he had contacted the Cincinnati Bar Association, considering Keating's act an unethical one for a lawyer, a public servant, and a commission member. In the letter to the Cincinnati Bar Association, Ostrov detailed Keating's actions:

> I was a witness in a case entitled "The State of Ohio ex rel Charles H. Keating v. A Motion Picture Film Entitled 'Vixen,' etal." . . . I testified on behalf of the defendants because I had seen such film in another city where it was playing without molestation, and having seen it determined in my honest judgment that the film was not obscene. I so testified. . . . Mr. Keating personally took it upon himself to send the excerpt of my testimony to my employer, The B'Nai B'rith. . . . I charge that with malicious intent he undertook both to invade my privacy and interfere with my contract of employment, sought both to intimidate and "punish" a witness, solely because said witness testified adversely in a cause in which Mr. Keating had a positive interest.[121]

By Keating's logic, the spectator has no claims to privacy, as his act of spectatorship creates a self-identified public identity. An arbitrary spectator is made representative through legal proceedings of all skin flick spectators. Just as Keating spoke in his injunction against *Vixen* on behalf of the protections of a generalized public, Ostrov's court testimony proved a counterexample to Keating's conviction of the skin flick's social harm. Targeting the personal life of a private citizen, who had made himself public through the act of testifying regarding his own spectatorship of a sexploitation film, Keating's action highlighted the highly politicized and as yet very fractious status of being a self-professed sexploitation viewer.

At the same time that *Vixen* was effectively banned from screening in the state of Ohio, the flurry of sexploitation product to reach screens far exceeded communities' and organizations' attempts to quell them. In smaller towns, the influx of sexploitation films to local screens presented its own unique problems, as single-theater, single-screen towns would be faced with a lack of choice as to what film to see, the decision having been made by the theater owner or manager and by the paucity of film product available. Again, Radley Metzger's films, specifically his Audubon import *I, a Woman* and his own *Therese and Isabelle* (1968), became prominent objects of dispute, as an article in *Life* magazine in 1969 detailed.[122] Residents of Chadron, a Nebraska town with a population of sixty-five hundred, were faced with Metzger's films playing at their only local theater, the Eagle. Although the films were well attended, particularly by students from Chadron State College, the mothers of Chadron remained disturbed by the fact that underage children could see the film. Local women began an educational campaign, culling together reviews of upcoming films from the MPAA mailing list, *Parents* magazine, and other sources and speaking to church groups and the PTA about the problem of sexual and violent movies. The discussions about the "sexy wave" of film product with the theater owner, with local college students, and with the mothers themselves yielded conflicting and complex discourses of the relationship of film to social change, parenting, and moral values that far exceeded in sophistication the soapbox tactics and presumptions about the mass public espoused by CDL. Responding to Metzger's highbrow lesbian sexploitation film *Therese and Isabelle,* and the paucity of "quality" film product on the local screen, the film theater owner retorted that although family-friendly activists protested the "spicy" films that showed at the Eagle, the family or general audience fare that he did screen received substantially less patronage than the sex-oriented films, which in turn drew the younger, college-aged audience to his theater. The ironies of the box office intake refuted the claims by the anti-obscenity voices that the "public," broadly defined, wanted more wholesome screen fare, while simultaneously reinforcing anxieties around the cinematic consumption of the young.

Religious organizations would take their own routes toward addressing the "sex film problem" in their communities, and in 1970, a group of priests in Detroit planned to open their own film theater to provide "parishioners an alternative to the skin flicks shown at downtown theaters—clean movies, low prices and good hot popcorn."[123] These incursions into exhibition speak to a general frustration with the dominance of the sex film in the public film market, despite mobilization otherwise.

The Federal Inquest into the Sex Film: The Obscenity Commission

It was perhaps both public complaints by "average citizens" and the force of local lawmakers' and congressmen's pleas to deal with the raging expansion of sexual media that facilitated the establishment of the Presidential Commission on Obscenity and Pornography by an act of Congress in 1967, and its work began officially in 1968. The commission was called on to examine the links between erotic media forms—including films, magazines, books, and forms of live entertainment and other sexual trades, such as prostitution—and their potential for social harm.[124] The House of Representatives explicitly stated that the commission should not serve as a censoring body but rather as a collector of information about the "smut industry." The commission was also asked to make its own determination of legislative and policy action, within constitutional restraints, of management of obscene visual material. Implicit, however, in this call to action, and call to research, was an assumption that the self-evidence of the pornographic field would yield a cautionary narrative about pornographic forms. The statement of the House went on to fault the Supreme Court in its "vacillation" over the definition of obscenity in the legal realm, making clear that the high court decisions had in some sense failed the American public.

Given a budget by the government that neared two million dollars, the commission was instituted to study the traffic in erotic materials, the audience for "adults-only" media, and the psychological and social impacts of their use. The commission was helmed by a group of sixteen presidential appointees—lawyers, sociologists, psychologists, clergy, motion picture executives, and other public officials among them—many of whom had an investment in constitutional freedoms in their private work. Approximately 40 percent of the commission's research was focused on the effects of erotic media on their audience.[125] This concern for the erotic consumer—and the unintended audiences for potentially obscene and pornographic work—extended to doing empirical research studies on a variety of topics, including a national survey of three thousand people in 150 cities asking them about their responses and attitudes to erotica; comparative analyses of sex offenders in prison and their erotic responses to other individuals in their class, gender, and ethnic categories; analyses of the returning "habitual" consumer of erotic materials in print and moving images; the potential intensity of erotic stimuli; the effect of erotica on college-aged women; and an examination of the effects of the lifting of all restrictions on the production of pornography. In a broad sense, the commission represented a full-fledged institutional apparatus for ascertaining the social attitudes and behaviors of a widening swath of the American population as it pertained to their consumption of sexually explicit products. The culmination of the decade's gradual embroilment with the obscene image, the research and findings of the commission were a highly guarded affair; the results were held from public circulation to facilitate objective research and for the purpose of avoiding public bias that might be generated by an early revelation of the work.

The Traffic and Distribution arm of the commission was dispatched to research the production and circulation of different media makers, including sexploitation film producers and exhibitors. At the head of the Traffic panel sat John Sampson, a lawyer given the difficult task of producing a report on the production history and current operations of sex media sales in print, film, and live entertainment. Sampson and his panel's hired researchers investigated and established numerous contacts with sexploitation filmmakers, including the likes of producer David Friedman, the Ohio art-sexploitation theater owner Louis Sher, producer Sam Lake, distributor Pete Kaufman, and a number of others prominent in the industry who were willing to talk with him about their business operations and the sexploitation industry as a whole. David Friedman appeared at a number of hearings, both formal and informal, and served in part as one of the primary spokespersons for the flourishing sexploitation industry. In his statement before a panel of commission members for a public hearing in Los Angeles in 1970, Friedman articulated his position regarding his small industry's relationship to censorship and obscenity and the constitution of its audience:

> Pornography dealers should not be allowed to invade the privacy of any citizen. No American should receive unrequested solicitations for the sale of pornography, nor should dealers be allowed to blatantly display their merchandise on any public street. I am not concerned that the more fanatical young liberals of the New Left have made of pornography a certain "cause celebre." What better sure-fire shocker to shake the establishment? I really believe most young people couldn't care less about the subject. They look upon sex as a participating rather than a spectator sport.
>
> I am convinced that if pornography were allowed to be openly sold in regulated outlets in the United States, it would wither and die of its own sheer ennui within a few years. However, I am realist enough to know that pornography is too juicy a political issue. Pornography, the answer to a politician's prayer.
>
> If, therefore we cannot let pornography run its own course in the United States, let someone in the Federal Government define exactly what is, and what isn't, and make this definition a standard for every

village, hamlet, town, city, county, and state. With such a standard definition, those of us in the business of producing adult communications will, at all times, know that which we are doing is legal.[126]

In asking for a concise definition of obscenity from the courts, Friedman conveyed the precarious position many sexploitation filmmakers were in by 1969–70. Friedman both attempted to uphold the juridical power of the government and simultaneously claimed that (hard-core) pornography would surely face a quick death due to audience disinterest in the coming years. His rhetorical balancing act downplayed the impact of pornography while also giving it an edge of transgression. Friedman deferred to the rights of private citizens and the constitutions of private tastes, while he himself played the proper, law-abiding citizen. Perhaps one of the most provocative things in Friedman's position was his delineation of his own films' demographic; by claiming that youth audiences are more interested in the actual act of sex than in seeing it on-screen, there is no doubt that he raised eyebrows from the more circumspect and conservative of the committee members. But this statement can also be seen as structurally consistent with the basic pretenses of sexploitation film itself as a genre—in the film's exploitation of the currency of sexual practices among the young, and in its mining of the political and public sphere for voyeuristic sights of contemporary youth culture in its imagined "decadence." Friedman's "frankness" about these issues also belied a deeper point of view regarding sexploitation films' designated audience.

As a position paper on the state of the sexploitation industry in 1970, the conservatism underlying Friedman's statement also pointed toward the impending erosion of the soft-core market and the sense of competition "skin flick" producers were feeling from more risqué film merchants, such as the 16mm filmmakers, alongside Hollywood's expanded deployment of sex in their own films. Therefore taking a more measured stance on obscenity was a means of positioning the sexploitation filmmaker defensively in relationship to a horizon of films that were potentially "more obscene" than the soft-core idiom.

The Obscenity Commission itself noted the strange logic of Friedman's and others' adherence to the letter of the law when it came to negotiating censorship and obscenity definitions. Freeman Lewis, one of the commissioners, reported on this attitude of sexploitation filmmakers and noted a certain frustration with its circular logic:

> Reduced to over-simplification they seemed to say: Censorship of almost any kind in areas of pornographic writing, art, illustration or motion pictures is good because it provides an opportunity for business

at a profit, however small. To increase our profits, we need more exact censorship laws and expanded distribution. But these laws should not be such as to make our present businesses too attractive to more powerful competitors. We could do better if we could move from the back alley into the front streets, but such opportunities, if made available, would probably destroy us.[127]

Lewis's observation was apt, gauging a view among sexploitation filmmakers that would be one of the instrumental factors in the genre's decline in the coming years. Soft-core producers in the late 1960s and early 1970s were caught in a rhetorical double bind, dependent on censorship for their business yet on the brink of losing it should content restrictions—and representational conventions of filming sex—relax enough to eclipse their specific generic trademark of leering sexuality and suggestive omission.

The Adult Film Association and the Specter of Self-Regulation

The concerns of David Friedman and other sexploitation producers, distributors, and exhibitors regarding the ways local law enforcement were handling sexploitation theaters in their neighborhoods led to the establishment of the Adult Film Association of America (AFAA). Originally called the Adult Motion Picture Association of America, or AMPAA, it had been formed in part to address the issue of "local harassment" by their members, as the post–*I Am Curious (Yellow)* period saw a precipitous rise in the uses of informal modes of pressure as well as seizure and arrests with the heightened visibility of sexploitation product on national screens.[128] The formation of the AFAA marked a double-edged moment in the arrival of adult film as a formidable player in the film industry and in the film market as well as revealing ways that sexploitation producers, despite having been making dirty movies for a decade, were nonetheless defined by a traditional and perhaps outdated set of principles with respect to their approach to film regulation. The extent to which sexploitation producers needed censorial restrictions to constitute their product was borne out in some of the formal discussion of the AFAA around self-regulation, a poignantly ironic and striking moment that articulates sexploitation film's unique aesthetic and ideological identity.

News of the first AFAA gathering in *Variety* piqued the Obscenity Commission's interest, as the news coincided with the commission's attempts to make inroads into surveying the business and economic practices of the sexploitation field. Bernard Horowitz, a commission researcher, reported on his attendance of the AFAA convention, held in Kansas City, Missouri, in January 1969. Horowitz noted that the two primary goals that AFAA designee Sam Chernoff delineated in organizing this first convention were "to form some sort of legal clearinghouse for mutual protection from legal harassment; and . . . to establish some sort of informal guidelines for film production to avoid future legal difficulties."[129] The famed free speech lawyer Stanley Fleishman, an attendee at a convention panel on legal issues facing sexploitation producers, suggested a number of ways to address issues of "exhibitor harassment" by local municipalities. These strategies included setting up an information exchange among exhibitors and producers regarding common problems faced with censorship, establishing a library of pertinent legal materials, lobbying for more amenable obscenity laws, publishing a newsletter, and taking on the task of public education about their films and the larger issues involved in local censorship and harassment.[130] George Davis, another attorney from Northern California speaking at the event, recommended a strategy in which exhibitors would offer the films up to local police in advance in order to "enjoin" them not to prosecute the work and thus to short-circuit the potential of raids and seizures.[131] Acknowledging the nature of sexploitation's identity, one contingent on courting the law yet staying just a hair on the side of legal permissibility, Davis's "pragmatic" solution ironically would have sexploitation filmmakers restaging and returning to the processes of prior restraint, albeit within the bounds of voluntary submission. Sexploitation filmmakers Steven Apostolof (who made films under the pseudonym A. C. Stephens) and Don Davis spoke negatively about uniform, across-the-board industry regulation, yet encouraged informal censorship to happen on the level of the exhibitor. They recommended that the exhibitor should use his own judgment and circumstance to make appropriate cuts as needed and then reinsert the cuts into the print before sending it along for its next screening engagement.[132] That this practice was already to some degree informally operative, in terms of the manufacture of "hot" and "cold" prints—that is, the circulation of multiple prints with different ranges of explicitness for different distribution regions—certainly didn't underplay the laborious nature of this proposed solution. The role of the exhibitor as "censor–editor" seemed to be on one level counterintuitive, and risky as well, in terms of damage done to the integrity of the print. However, as should be clear from the short-term economic modus operandi of sexploitation, the future preservation value of the films was clearly not a concern to these producers. (Interestingly, this proposed practice ceding adjudication of film content to the exhibitor also recalled the definitive role of exhibitors in cinema's earliest years.) Although Apostolof and Davis's proposal appeared to serve as an accommodation of specific localities and their standards of decency and taste, it also was a reorganization of the role of the censor and a means of "passing the buck" of decision making regarding what goes and what stays in any given film to theater personnel.

Yet perhaps the most strikingly anachronistic proposal for self-policing, which became the subject of serious discussion during the 1969 AFAA convention, was the potential for the organization to institute a code of self-regulation on film content, mirroring the by then defunct Hollywood Production Code, which had been officially deposed by Jack Valenti's CARA rating system. The welcome flyer to the 1969 convention stated that although the "fast buck" cheapie producers—designated as the 16mm hard-core filmmakers and distinguished from the soft-core old guard—were attempting to gain entry to their fledgling AFAA, the organization's goal was to establish a self-rating system for sexploitation makers to stave off legal scrutiny:

> The producers here today are ready to set up a production code that will keep our films within proper bounds and are willing to self-rate them and apply their own seal to films that are considered acceptable. They will even go as far as to determine which films do not stay within the necessary bounds and will so advise our group, which would then have the obligation to take the attitude that films that are not acceptable should be shown only at the exhibitor's own risk and will not be defended by the organization.[133]

Thus the tacit assumption was that the 16mm filmmakers would not be advocated for by the larger group of soft-core entrepreneurs and would therefore not gain legal counsel.[134] This passage also indicated the extent to which the AFAA was a means of gaining legal and aesthetic legitimacy for sexploitation films through the consolidation of the industry, mimicking the MPAA structure of the Hollywood studios. A letter from filmmaker–producer Bob Cresse to the AFAA a few days prior to the convention outlined some suggestions for a "self-imposed industry code," which are worth reproducing here in their entirety:

> Suggestions for Possible Self-Imposed Industry Code
> 1. That we not show on screen any full-front nude shots of a male or a female, revealing the genital area.
> 2. That we do not depict a male and a female together nude in any position in which there is genital contact or the remotest possibility of the actual act of copulation taking place.
> 3. No scenes depicting kissing of the breast.
> 4. That there be no scenes depicting kissing below the waist or above the knees of any individual, male or female.

5. That those words that are commonly called obscene or vulgar, referred to as the "four letter words" be deleted entirely from any scripts.
6. That scenes depicting sadism, torture, flagellation, would only be used in direct relationship to a story that specifically required the exposure of this sort of scene, and would not be used in just unrelated exploitation situations.
7. That generally we would agree to strive to avoid the blatant, graphic reproductions of sexual acts, and instead rely on suggestion rather than reality.
8. That feature motion pictures and/or short subjects released by members abiding by the Code, would cease to be one or one and a half hour exposures of just nudity without plot or purpose. That the films would indeed be based on a valid story line and would genuinely contain one or more redeeming social factors.
9. That we would not hold up to ridicule the marriage laws, the institution of marriage, parental respect, the police, city, state or federal government.
10. That within the framework of any motion picture, anyone committing a crime, immoral or unethical act would receive compensatory punishment, either from the authorities or from the results of the situation.
11. That we would in no way glorify or hold up for approval immorality as defined within the Judeo-Christian concepts of the word.[135]

Cresse was a producer of some of the most notoriously violent and sensational nudies and roughies within the sexploitation field, including the sadistic Nazi-themed torture film *Love Camp 7* (Lee Frost, 1969) as well as films such as *Hot Spur* (Lee Frost, 1968), *The Scavengers* (Lee Frost, 1969), *Love Is a Four Letter Word* (Lee Frost, 1966), *Hollywood's World of Flesh* (Lee Frost, 1963), *Mondo Freudo* (Lee Frost, 1966), and *Mondo Bizarro* (Lee Frost, 1966). Cresse's proposed "11 Commandments" appears either ironic or disingenuous in light of the extreme content of his own film product. His suggestions for a sexploitation production code bear further analysis, particularly as a document itemizing retrospective, corrective regrets about the industry and its direction in the late 1960s. In 1969, this list of prohibited scenarios was incredibly anachronistic, made obsolete by the actual representational practices of those in the industry—breast kissing; female full frontal nudity, which had been in play as early as 1966 or 1967; simulated sexual activity; and flagellation and sadism (present in roughies and their S/M variants since at least 1963) were all stocks in trade of the sexploitation film at this time. Most sexploitation directors had already been purveying these sorts of sexual images and scenarios for some years, consequently making Cresse's insistence on legislating the genre's chaste intentions read as outdated and unrealistic by this time. The layout of offensive materials to be considered off limits in its severity suggests the drawing back and retreat of many of the premises of sexploitation film *tout court*. The focus on genital visibility no doubt gestured to and wanted to distinguish sexploitation product from the prevalence of hard-core films and the rise of peepshow loops and from the short "beaver" films in urban areas around 1969–70, which provided a more overt genital "show." The designation of limits in visual content also signified a turning point, or a limit case, for the sexploitation industry's own ability to transform its aesthetic and thematic conventions in relationship to an altering obscenity standard. Additionally, the directive insisting on narrative premises and stronger story lines reflects a larger criticism regarding the direction in which the bulk of sexploitation, and notably its hard-core competitors, was moving—in which sexual action superseded dramatic conventions and plot. A number of other producers and exhibitors were beginning to stress the need for quality over sexual content or nudity. One producer stated in late 1969 that "many of the features are passing the point of no return and will have to backtrack or be in real trouble . . . heavy sex is wearing off."[136] Lee Hessel, the head of Cambist Films, also stated that with the competition from Hollywood and other independents, "adult entertainment is going to have to have a lot more entertainment value in the future to make money," while another producer insisted that the wave of the future for independents was less sex and more "social consciousness" in film narratives.[137]

These prognostications about a shift of focus, alongside Cresse's recommendations regarding more story-oriented films, also seemed responsive to critiques emerging out of the art film discourse and the decade's obscenity rulings, particularly in the nod toward redeeming social values and aesthetic merit as well as in a heightening audience sophistication with respects to screen sex. Cresse's suggestions appear to be appealing to both bluenose contingents and public pressures, as well as to the desire for larger social and industrial legitimacy for the sexploitation feature in more mainstream or conventional movie venues. Yet this maneuver of repositioning, or "backtracking," was also without a doubt a means of keeping the hard-core operators at a considerable distance. The call for a denial of immoral themes and the pious request that filmmakers not denigrate the values of church, state, and family also, at least implicitly, distinguished sexploitation filmmakers as a generational contingent that differed from the political orientations of the counterculture and the ideological affiliations of the New Left, as well as the younger producers of the 16mm films playing in shoddy storefront theaters. Just as Hollywood producers earlier in the decade had discursively negotiated an institutional mode of distanciation from nudie producers and skin flicks, as discussed earlier, here sexploitation as a consolidating industry—now branded as "adult film"—was employing a very similar tactic of distinction and product differentiation to elevate itself above the "heat artists."

Nonetheless, this "production code" initiative for the sexploitation industry did not bear fruit for a number of reasons. Horowitz, who followed up with AFAA official and producer Pete Kaufman of Texas-based Astro-Jemco on the last day of the convention, was told that the self-regulation code had not been adopted due to concerns regarding antitrust ramifications.[138] By the following year, the AFAA had reported in its newsletter that a vote of the executive committee yielded a 6–5 decision against pursuing a code for self-regulation.[139] The decision to avoid self-regulation was a telling conclusion to this possibility of censorial (and implicitly industrial) consolidation, following on the heels of its discussion at the AFAA convention the previous year. It appeared as if the divergence of opinions between exhibitors and producers indicated a larger dispute over the division of censorial labor—in terms of whom, and at what level of production, distribution, or exhibition, should take on the task of cutting, and deciding what to cut, of the potentially obscene and offensive footage.

Having come full circle from their role as marginal, scrappy independents to their position as a still small yet formidable network of players in the arena of American film production, considerations regarding the direction of the sexploitation industry also presaged their eventual decline in the coming decade. The AFAA notably became the primary organ of the adult film industry as it transitioned from the older set of soft-core sexploitation makers to the younger cast of characters who were beginning to film feature-length hard-core films and crossover instructional or marriage manual films at this time: Gerard Damiano, Alex de Renzy, Lowell Pickett, the Mitchell Brothers, and many others. In sexploitation's leering attention to the sexual practices of the young, the eclipse of soft-core skin flicks by hard-core films also signaled the end of an era of overtly moralistic pretenses conditioned by the codes of censorship and obscenity law itself. Sexploitation films of the 1960s thus can be seen as exorbitantly tied to their social, political, and regulatory contexts, not merely reflective of social changes but caught in a dynamic of accommodating prohibitions and contravening them, a fluid push-and-pull interaction.

Conclusion

While sexploitation producers continued to make and distribute soft-core films into the late 1970s, their primacy in the film market had diminished. The preceding exchanges over the future of the sexploitation mode are indicative of the more fragile circumstances these independents were facing in respect to the impact of changing obscenity standards on film content. In 1973, after significant shifts in the composition of the U.S. Supreme Court, the *Miller v. California* decision would reverse the jurisdiction of obscenity back to community standards, ending a period of the high court's intervention in interpreting and applying criteria for obscenity in film and other media. The now familiar narrative of the emergence of hard-core pornography would shortly follow in the period between 1970 and 1973, with the ascendancy of "porno chic" marked by the publicity and hype generated by the public exhibition of Gerard Damiano's *Deep Throat* in 1972, signaling a new direction in the relationship of the explicit image to the public sphere. Yet what marked sexploitation film as unique was its imbrications with its conditions of prohibition, even during the very moment when practices of regulation were being threatened and questioned and rendered obsolete by the flood of sexualized media and by changes in the field of film production. The 1970s would witness the battles against obscenity pitched more forcefully toward the producers of hard-core pornography on the local level as well as the shift toward restricting pornographic media through zoning ordinances and other regional forms of regulation. The lessons of sexploitation's battles with censors and local decency committees—in their creative accommodations to existing restrictions and their promotional courting of transgression in presentations of "barely legal" spectacle—reside in how a marginal mode of production animated and used to its own benefit larger discourses of art, social value, and erotica consumption. In the following chapters, we move to look specifically at the ways sexploitation addressed its audience, constructing stories of sexual indulgence and eroticized violence. Thematizing the figure of the illicit spectator and the act of looking at the forbidden, sexploitation films drew on a variety of popular discourses to create narratives of imagined sexual excess. The forms, themes, and textuality of sexploitation films offer a rich archive of social anxieties concerning the role of "liberated" women in the social sphere as well as the place of unbounded sexuality in public and in private spaces.

CHAPTER TWO

Peek Snatchers

Corporeal Spectacle and the Wages of Looking, 1960–1965

In their salacious come-ons and lurid promises of the heretofore unseen and the previously forbidden, sexploitation films claimed to present a window, if not a peephole, onto America's hidden desires and sexual practices. The sex films of this decade detailed the potential or fantasized outcomes of women's encroaching autonomy and self-expression. They purveyed a fascination with the rebellious youth culture, articulating the nascent visibility of nonnormative sexualities. Many of the films discussed in this book sit at odds with a notion of 1960s sexual culture as defined by a discourse of sexual liberation, as they presented a counterpoint to the emergent countercultural mantra of free love, obsessed with punitive sexual economies in a collision with the inevitable drive toward the consumption of pleasure and the quest for sensation. Sexploitation films employed a rhetoric of "guilty expenditure," in which sex is avidly desired and consumed, but not without cost: narrative resolutions run the gamut from moral, emotional, and financial ruin to death and murder.

While incredibly various in form and genre, sexploitation films in their narrative pretenses mapped a transition from "productivist" to "consumerist" models of sexuality, while visually exploiting the widening panorama of sexual practices, identities, and orientations.[1] Despite a certain crudity, the body of the spectator and the bodies within the pro-filmic scene are always in a state of negotiation, subject to the vagaries of social, economic, and cultural change. Examining the textual and cultural conditions of these scenes of looking concerns the following two chapters, as they explore the sexual ideologies and corporeal aesthetics that the films construct, in their oscillation between moralizing narrative trajectories and indulgence in highly eroticized images and performed pro-filmic acts.

Tracing a set of stylistic and thematic tendencies that emerged in the sexploitation cinema of the first half of the 1960s, this chapter examines the "nudie cuties" and "roughies" of the early to mid-1960s. The nascent sexploitation text mobilized the nude body as its material, presenting sexuality as a specular scene, and staged a specific imagination of gender roles in the 1960s caught between liberalization and risk.[2] Looking over the course of the decade, sexploitation films shift in focus from the teasing provocations of the nude female body in their first incarnations in the early 1960s (customarily defined as the "nudie cutie" film) to a combination of nudity mixed with sexual situations that emerges and persists from the mid-1960s (in the roughies) and soon to the rendering of simulated sexual acts by the late 1960s and early 1970s. Such patterns of transformation in these broad, overlapping "cycles" or subgenres are undergirded by a heightened cultural preoccupation with the social, economic, and sexual autonomy of women in the public sphere throughout the decade as well as by the intensification of what social historians John D'Emilio and Estelle Freedman have termed *sexual liberalism* in American social life and popular culture.[3] The transition from revealing the nude female body to showing the simulated sex act on-screen by the end of the decade—and its stylistic, generic, and narrative ramifications—does not follow an inevitable teleological progression. This transformation makes visible a representational field riven with conflict and ambivalence about the liberalization of sexual practices and mores.

Distinct from other forms of erotic and sexualized imagery and popular culture in this time, sexploitation bears a unique aesthetics of erotic display. Its mode of address to the film audience—and the thematization of the act of looking, of the *gawker in the text*—attests to an accidental self-consciousness that pervades the form: a quality of inadvertent cinematic reflexivity. As the "excess" of the unclothed female body comes into view, no longer a verboten element of filmic form, the very *conditions of looking* at and consuming that corporeal plenitude become the motoring engine of the sexploitation film. The paradox of sexploitation cinema is that, at the same time that sexploitation takes part in a flourishing marketplace of sexual images and products, the *consumption* of these images gets foregrounded and problematized in the films themselves. The anxious problem of "consuming sex"—with all of its gendered and cultural implications and ambivalences—becomes an organizing principle in the narrative and ideological content of the genre.[4] Thus the stories sexploitation films tell, and the fantasies they promulgate, are unique to a cultural moment in which moral panics and liberatory discourses of sexuality converge and collide.

Exploring the sexualized scripts that sexploitation films return to and restage reveals a mode of production radically preoccupied with the ambivalent status of the spectator—figured as gawkers, peepers, "peek snatchers." The needs and desires of sexploitation's "peek snatcher" spoke to the shifting conditions of the visual obscene at the turn of the decade. In 1960, American and British popular cinema both inaugurated the figure of the perverse peeper as a horrific allegory of male desire: Michael Powell's much-reviled *Peeping Tom* and Alfred Hitchcock's *Psycho*, each in its own way, inscribed the voyeur as the regnant figure of psychosexual perversion, one innocuously intertwined with the semblance of "normal" masculinity. Such figures of dangerous scopophilia would wildly flower in sexploitation cinema, in the form of the voyeuristic deviant turned rapist and torturer in the gritty, violent roughie films that would succeed the nudie cuties. The innocent gawker of the latter films would soon malignantly confuse the border between "just looking" and vicious, impulsive action. Thus the cultural concern with the libidinal nature of looking became central to sexploitation cinema's terms of possibility, providing the axiomatic figure of its erotic imagination.

Sexploitation, Soft-Core, Hard-Core

One ideological feature that characterizes sexploitation of the 1960s in contradiction to the emerging discourses of sexual freedom most directly associated with the utopic cast of the era's popular culture is that the narrative logic of sex in these films is never truly "free" but is the subject and object of a moral economy of act and mortal consequence, in which sex is perennially grounded in an unequal exchange between power and pleasure.[5] This formation relies on a diegetic structure of prohibition and ellipsis, in which the sexual act and its most explicit evidence are systematically deferred, while connotatively summoned forth—through the use of off-screen space, suggestive editing, sound, double entendre, and other forms of erotic substitution or displacement. In contrast to the naturalist, "more and better" sex ideology that emerges in hard-core pornography,[6] in sexploitation, sexual acts and the work of sustaining gender identities are bound to a morally traditionalist economy of expenditure and risk. An uneven field of social exchange proscribes the forms the implied sex act can take and how it can carry meaning in sexploitation narratives. Sex can have morbid, excessive, and often absurd consequences in these films—and the trajectory of narrative closure is tied to a sense of the dangerous mortalities and mortifications of sexual activity, particularly in its impact on female protagonists. Simultaneously, sexploitation provides an unmatched stage of brazen visibility to questions of gender identity and sexuality, giving voice to cultural anxieties regarding an emergent politicization of female desire and pleasure in the public sphere.

The contradiction central to sexploitation films of the 1960s positions the contemporaneousness of its sexual content, in its claims of the presence and "nowness" of new forms of gender and sexual relations, against the generic and narrative traditions that mark the films as contending with the historical and film historical past. Put another way, sexploitation films often reflect the generational investments of their makers, predominantly middle-aged white men who index a position between a passing moral and social order and more contemporary cultural affinities for liberationist conceptions of sex. Sexploitation films were made largely by men and for a largely male audience, yet, owing to their publicly commercial availability, opened a horizon of possibility for women to attend, particularly from the mid- to late 1960s. There are, of course, notable, though scarce, exceptions, such as sexploitation film's most prominent female director, Doris Wishman.[7] This tension makes for complex texts that traffic in the zeitgeist of cultural transformation while at the same time being bound to an anachronistic moral structure, requiring the films' viewers to shuttle between contradictory poles of identification and disidentification, pleasure and displeasure. This quality of their "datedness" emerges as much from their contemporaneous moment, in the films' bricolage of various generic markers, such as comedy, film noir, melodrama, and action films, and the residual "productivist" moral subtexts of classical exploitation traditions as it does from their retrospective reassessment.

Sexploitation films are often characterized in relationship to their generic and historical successor, the hard-core pornographic feature, and often positioned as a genre that is in some senses "deceptive," that pales in juxtaposition with hard-core's presumed verisimilitude and drive toward documentary veracity in its representation of the penetrative sex act.[8] Linda Williams, in her pathbreaking analysis of the hard-core form, implicitly makes this characterization when discussing the problematic ontology of hard-core contra soft-core. She writes:

> In contrast to both mainstream fictional narrative and soft-core indirection, hard-core tries not to play peekaboo with either its male or its female bodies. It obsessively seeks knowledge, through a voyeuristic record of confessional, involuntary paroxysm, of the "thing" itself. . . . The self conscious control and surveillance normally exercised by the "properly" socialized woman over her appearance, and so evident in the soft-core "turn-on," is what the hard core wants to circumvent. Hard core desires assurance that it is witnessing not the voluntary performance of feminine pleasure, but its involuntary confession.[9]

Williams argues that hard-core is contingent on its failure to index or make visible the female pleasure it so fervently seeks. Extending Williams's inquiry, considering sexploitation films poses the question of a potential ontology of the soft-core image. What sort of libidinal economy is entailed in the constant shunting of sexual action to off-screen space, to a position of an unmaterialized promise signified by the stylization of the nude female body and the simulation of sex? The weight of hard-core depends on a faith in indexicality and the documentary status of the image. Within these parameters, sexploitation, a form that is the progenitor for the contemporary soft-core idiom, is often attributed with characteristics of dishonesty, deception, indirection, or insincerity in its avoidance of the explicit sexual act, in its focus on voluntary female performance and the titillations of the peek-a-boo mode. Yet while sexploitation is known to traffic in diversion and deception, the films simultaneously depend on their audiences' recognition of the sensationalistic, mendacious joke, their ability to read between the lines of titillation and often its subsequent moralistic negation. Thus an element of irony frequently permeates the mode of address of sexploitation film. Linda Hutcheon defines irony broadly as the semantic product of "saying one thing and meaning another," and she further elucidates how irony is a "'weighted' mode of discourse in that it is asymmetrical, unbalanced in favor of the silent and the unsaid."[10] In sexploitation, this privileging of the unsaid, and relatedly, the unseen, that which falls between the register of the overt and covert, is produced through a set of industrial, regulatory, and cultural determinants and produces the films' unique aesthetic.

Sexploitation films are less deceptive than self-knowing and reflexive texts, functionally conscious of the limits of their own conditions of production, exhibition, and reception. The present chapter investigates this quality of reflexivity in the narratives and tropes of the sexploitation film, whose manifestations range from metatextual acknowledgments of the conditions of the film's reception to the ways in which the mode figures its own place in the marketplace of sexual commodities. For example, many films consistently thematize the social space of the "sex trade" and its various networks, such as the pinup photographer's studio, the brothel, the sex worker economy, the modeling agency, and even the "skin flick" industry itself. David James has remarked on a particular tendency in 1960s American cinema, in which the contexts of Hollywood in crisis produced a range of both mainstream and alternative films that

> frequently attempt to negotiate with surrounding social and cinematic changes, and even when they are not explicitly about a search for a satisfactory mode of production, their plots often have a metaphorical

relation to their own manufacture. Consequently, as the site of conflict or arbitration between alternative productive possibilities, they invite an allegorical reading in which a given filmic trope—a camera style or an editing pattern—is understood as the trace of a social practice. . . . Such a use of the filmic to lay bare its cinematic preconditions is especially fruitful for all kinds of sixties' films, in which the social tensions that generated them were often clearly inscribed.[11]

To the extent that sexploitation films reflect this formal inscription of their own conditions of cinematic possibility, they also differ from James's predominant focus on avant-garde and political cinema or cinema at odds with primarily commercial goals. Much more can be pursued in the relations between avant-garde, underground, independent, and sexploitation modes in the 1960s, especially geographically, stylistically, and culturally. But if James's claim that "reflexivity was a pandemic trope in sixties film"[12] can be taken as a general summation of affairs, sexploitation films clearly articulated their own generically specific manifestation of reflexivity, especially in the ways they allegorize their own conditions of reception through the trope of the *erotic spectator* caught up in the act of *consuming sex*. In contrast to a reflexivity defined through artisanal, avant-garde, or oppositional film practice, the crass commercial nature of sexploitation film and its low-budget mode of production produce a self-consciousness that reflects these unique conditions of production and its horizon of reception.

This form of reflexivity, while conditional to the contexts of changing modes of film production in the 1960s, also derives from the cinematic tradition sexploitation films emerged out of, particularly what Eric Schaefer has analyzed and termed as the classical exploitation film. Schaefer observes a comparable form of self-consciousness that exploitation films made between 1919 and 1959 exhibited, a mode of "exhibitionism" rendered through the relationship between a focus on spectacle and gap-ridden narratives. He writes:

> The centrality of spectacle in exploitation films tended to disrupt or override the traditional cause and effect chain in narrative. . . . As a result the forbidden sights stood out in relief from the shambling wreck of the diegesis. Whereas the classical Hollywood film invited the viewer to move into a voyeuristic relation with the represented events through its creation of a seamless world signaled from the shift of narration from a self-conscious to an unself-conscious mode, the exploitation film was essentially an exhibitionistic form that encouraged a different type of engagement on the part of the viewer. Classical exploitation consistently

reminded the viewer that he or she was watching a film, either through the display of spectacle or because of the crumbling continuity.[13]

Sexploitation films both extended and refined these exhibitionist tendencies so prevalent in classical exploitation films, while prioritizing specifically corporeal spectacle and setting their sights on the more explicitly sexualized body. Sexploitation films of the 1960s incorporate the very figure of the voyeur into the fabric of their films, thematizing the process and ramifications of erotic looking as both a diegetic and extradiegetic "problem," both deflecting and incorporating some of the symptoms of this awareness of their viewer within their content.

It is also important to ask whether sexploitation should only be defined in terms of what it retrospectively is not, in terms of what it is *lacking* in sexual explicitness. Sexploitation films can indeed succumb to this reading as in some sense "deceptive," but they are not reducible to it. The "compensatory" mechanisms of their style should be read as modes of excess and plenitude, in which the developing abundance in the marketplace for sexual images, which the genre takes part in promulgating as well as critiquing, is tempered by the proscriptions of their narrative ramifications and resolutions. While the charge of dishonesty certainly resonates with accounts of the kinds of hucksterism and hard-selling of these films as shock- and sensation-oriented cinematic product—for example, in producer David Friedman's consistent references to his audiences as "suckers"—it also has a negative connotation, in which the mode is inevitably eclipsed by the teleological thrust of historical change seen in the arrival of the hard-core feature.

We can productively view sexploitation films residing between the register of the implicit and explicit, in the space where seeing (enough) and knowing (the rest) commingle. Sexploitation's own syntax and play between erotic spectacle and its denial threaten the material body of the spectator, a body impacted by its own arousal. Chris Straayer, drawing on the psychosemiotics of Christian Metz, elaborates the spectatorial dynamics of watching sex, suggesting that the desire to see sex and the desire to do sex are distinct processes:

> Every shot in a film both provides what it includes and denies what it excludes, each momentary satisfaction of the viewer's desire to see also inaugurates the desire to see what isn't shown. . . . An erotic film cinematically participates in this ultimately unsatisfying chain of always offset desires and fulfillments; but it also constructs and *continually denies* a more specific desire to see *explicit* sexual imagery. . . . Both the film with erotic subject matter and the film with explicit sexual imagery can

construct a desire to *do* sex. That is, the desire to do is not dependent on actually seeing the desired act.... What is necessarily opposed in these two categories of film is their denial and fulfillment of the desire to see *sex*.... Pornography's often alleged boringness relates to its diminishment of the *desire* to see.... Sexually explicit film provides the desired sexual images but (often) doesn't construct the desire itself.[14]

Straayer suggests that erotic films both create and deflect a desire to see more explicit representations of the sex act. The spectator of sexploitation is thus called upon to fill in the gaps of what the films omit. In excessively constructing the *desire* to see sex, sexploitation films negotiate the tension of doing sex. The fear of "seeing sex" turning into "doing sex," the mimetic impulse, also becomes both a narrative discourse and an extratextual concern that gestures to the circumstances of these films' own reception.

Sexual Revolution and Sexploitation Syntax

The 1960s has long been associated with multiple manifestations of the "sexual revolution," and recent scholarship has outlined some of the most exemplary sites of this eroticization of the public sphere, with revisionist histories of the sexual revolution extending the roots of this period well back into the post–World War II era.[15] Late-1950s and early-1960s culture was saturated with images and narratives of a burgeoning sexuality—from *Playboy* magazine's emergence and the panty raids at American colleges in the 1950s to Elvis's off-screen pelvic gyrations on national television and Helen Gurley Brown's exhortation to women that they enjoy their eroticized single-girl status in *Sex and the Single Girl* (1962). Sexuality was slowly unmooring itself from reproductive obligations—the Pill became widely distributed in 1960—and becoming defined by an aspiration toward self-fulfillment and individuation. However, these cultural moments also represented a management of a tension between the visible and the not yet visible, in which the line between public and private was still being redefined.

Beth Bailey discusses the primary tension in discourses of the sexual revolution as a contestation between the *covert* and the *overt*, most clearly exemplified by the publication of Alfred Kinsey's reports on male and female sexual behavior in 1948 and 1953, respectively. Kinsey's sexological research unmasked the ways in which private behavior was at odds with public pronouncements and social rules of proper sexuality. His revelations that both men and women had far more premarital and extramarital sex than was avowed or endorsed by dominant culture were met with shock and rebuke. As Bailey asserts, Kinsey's "publicization of the private" questioned the rules governing sexual propriety, facilitating the process through which "we see the overt coming to terms with the covert"; this very process of coming to terms is what we retrospectively bracket as the myriad manifestations, cultural and social, of the sexual revolution.[16] In some sense, public culture had to catch up with the redefinition of private codes. Steven Seidman tracks this public transformation, noting that the major observable characteristic of sexual culture and courtship in the postwar period saw

> the appearance of discourses and representations carrying public authority that legitimated sex as a domain of pleasure, self-expression, and communication apart from a context of intimacy or love. . . . Sex was defined as acceptable in virtually any consensual adult context. Eros was . . . transfigured into a site of individuation and social bonding.[17]

Love, previously anchored to the heterocentric couple form and to economic structures of marriage and property ownership, was slowly being uprooted by a new culture of sexual consumerism and economic mobility, certainly facilitated by the rising affluence of America as a nation in the postwar period.[18] While this development was touted as heralding new forms of freedom, these gradual shifts also represented a new set of risks and dangers in the realm of male and female desires and identities (which were also felt and experienced unequally), trepidations which sexploitation films were prone to negotiate and map out in narratives of excessive desire and the costs and consequences of individual pleasure seeking. In the context of the gradual sexualization of the marketplace and Americans' leisure time, sexploitation as a narrative form could seize upon the fissures, tensions, and contradictions between residual and emergent gender and sexual identities. If, in the words of John D'Emilio and Estelle Freedman, "the capitalist impulse seized upon sexual desire as an unmet need that the marketplace could fill,"[19] then sexploitation filmmakers and producers dove into this profitable window of opportunity during a time of transforming sexual values and questioning of traditional social structures and institutions.

Thus the liminal status of sexploitation films—not only perched between classical exploitation and hard-core pornography but also caught amid different moral orders and between overt and covert modes of sexual ideology—reinforced their erotic mode of address, which vacillated between excess and restriction. As Thomas Waugh has noted, "the tease, an erotic enunciation orchestrated like a tantalizing power game, was still the characteristic erotic rhetoric of sixties public culture, the sexual revolution notwithstanding."[20] Sexploitation films were no strangers to, and indeed were prominent purveyors of, this form of erotic provocation. Sexploitation took up the tease as its dominant mode of spectatorial address, playing a game of one-upmanship through settings of vice and corporeal excess. The play of "exposure and concealment" that emerges from the traditions of striptease is in sexploitation film put to work on a diegetic and editorial level, which needs to balance between the contradicting terms of prohibition and exhibitionism.[21]

Whereas visual access to female nudity and sexual situations had been proscribed and cordoned off into specific sites of privatized reception—such as the pinup magazine; the much-discussed *Playboy*; and under-the-counter pornography such as stag films, mail-order blue movies, and hardcore print images—sexploitation films were unique in their unashamed publicity and their commercially mercenary tactics.[22] Consumed in the public space of the film theater, sexploitation's narratives of exposure doubled over with its exposure of its audience to sights heretofore unseen. Leon Hunt, in his discussion of British sexploitation films of the 1970s, calls this the "not meant to be seen" factor of the genre's mode of address, an intrinsic component of the "sexploitation gaze."[23] This quality of the "not meant to be seen" could be felt on multiple registers—in the come-ons of a film's press books, trailers, and marketing materials as well as in the tone of the film—be it an exposé of sex workers in the city, as in, for example, *The Sin Syndicate* (Michael Findlay, 1965) and *P.P.S. (Prostitutes Protective Society)* (Barry Mahon, 1966); the flight of the adulterous, "nymphomaniac" wife from an inept and unsatisfying husband, as in *All Women Are Bad* (Larry Crane, 1969); or the exploration of wife swapping in bucolic suburbia in films such as *Sin in the Suburbs* (Joe Sarno, 1964). Titillation was a cheap, if legally risky, resource that could be channeled to create a dynamic of viewer anticipation and deferred gratification for sexploitation's largely male audiences. Yet the "not meant to be seen" also indicated a bifurcation of allegiances and a mode of self-consciousness in which the film viewer was always made aware of the limits of seeing, with that which remained *unseen* hovering at the edges of the frame and that which was made available to be seen indelibly marked by both recognition and disavowal. The limits of the seen, one could speculate, could also return the sexploitation viewer back to the proscriptions and limitations of his own desire, in the promises of a visual satisfaction and the prospects of dissatisfaction with what the film image showed.

While textual examples of this dynamic abound throughout the history of sexploitation in the 1960s, the tension between the "not meant to be seen" and the unseen in sexploitation syntax can be illustrated through

Joe Sarno's *The Swap and How They Make It* (1966), a mid-decade narrative of partner swapping in a suburban town. Framing a scene in which an erotically bored and neglected housewife, Mona, has her first arranged illicit "swap" with a young man, Paul, in her neighbor's house, Sarno's camera remains stationary and fixed on a close-up of the two characters in the foreground, from their shoulders up. Using a minimalist, contemporary sound track consisting of a repetitive drummed beat, the new lovers kiss feverishly, as we hear the couple heaving and panting. Paul suddenly kneels down and disappears below the bottom edge of the frame, as Mona arches her neck and flutters her eyelashes in profile, remaining still in her demeanor, as ten seconds pass. Paul reappears, rising up into the frame, triumphantly wielding a pair of black lace panties. The camera has remained stationary throughout.

In a subsequent scene after the couple has made their way to the bedroom, Sarno uses comparable economy in framing via the stationary shot and long take, allowing the viewer first to see nothing but an oil painting and the surrounding wallpaper, while remaining aware that the bed lies below. A black bra lies on the frame below the painting. From this still tableau, Mona's two hands slowly emerge, rising up from below the bottom edge of the frame, her digits performing metonymically an erotic struggle mingling with erotic rapture. The hands grasp for something against the textured backdrop of the painting and then fall, disappearing from view. Mona's head and shoulder rise up entering from the bottom right edge of the frame, and we see her again in close-up, bare shoulders visible, yet sheathed by a sheet, hair out of place, as Paul follows her, beseeching her to stay. Mona wants to leave, but Paul protests and pushes her down below the prohibitive edge of the bottom frame, as Mona grabs her brassiere in faint protest. We then see her hand emerge from below the bottom edge of the screen clutching and rending the bra in another minimalist gesture of sexual tumult—an alternative to the more customary cliché of hands in close-up clutching sheets or pillows. We see first her bare leg rise slowly in the foreground and then fall, the sole of her foot close to the camera. Rather than the tumescence and detumescence of sexual organs, the rising and falling of Paul and Mona—or rather of their extremities and faces, which dramatically move in and out of the flat immobile frame established by the stationary camera—serve to manipulate both space and time through an erotic mode of temporal suspension and waiting. The bottom edge of the frame literally and figuratively bears weight as a "nether region": formal limits become the site of double entendre both visually and textually. Sarno withholds most nudity and sexual activity, while simultaneously connoting it through its absence, making

FIGURE 13. Negotiating the seductions in and outside the frame in *The Swap and How They Make It.*

the gestures of his actors carry the crux of narrative tension and erotic meaning. Formal restraint, and specifically the absence of bodies, thus gains an erotic charge through its repetitive utilization and the severity and lack of depth in the composition of the mise-en-scène. While Sarno's aesthetic techniques evoke art cinematic modes, this scene encapsulates a particular way of relating to the absences and presences in a filmic image from this highly eroticized, teasing mode of production. The overt and the covert, the seen and the unseen, were in a state of constant negotiation and renegotiation, the terms through which certain conditions and horizons of spectatorship, diegetically and extradiegetically, were being forged. Yet to understand the transformation of these horizons of aesthetic and narrative convention, we must look to their emergence from the earliest formation of the sexploitation form: the nudie cutie.

Gawk, but Don't Touch: Nudie Cuties

The development of the "sexploitation gaze" that Hunt describes is historically articulated by the nudie cutie film, which, in the early 1960s, established a market, an audience, and a textual point of view for this mode of production. Nudie cutie films featured comical or fantasy narratives that served as pretexts for presenting women in various states of undress, generally with views of women topless or with bare buttocks. Nudie cutie films are often described as analogues, motion picture versions of the pinup magazine spread, in which female nudity and its potential eroticism are framed in a naturalized, innocuous tone. The nude female appears as if a mirage, essentially passive and caught unawares of her own status of being the object of a prurient gaze. From its first representations, the nudie cutie film was marked by its dependency on and address to its newly curious audience, with advertising tag lines promising that viewers would see something that they had never caught sight of before. The self-consciousness of the nudies, rather than emanating from artistic intent, instead emerged from a permeable and productive relationship to their conditions of production, exhibition, and regulation. Such self-consciousness refracted the cultural anxieties around the potentially "prurient" moviegoing audience, making this very discomfort surrounding a newly acknowledged erotic consumer the ideological topography of the films.

Harnessing the novelty of female nudity within narratives involving the gimmick of altered sight, the act of looking at bare female flesh was thematized in the films through various narrative devices and plot twists. This ruse that allowed the male protagonist, often in or beyond middle age and connotatively infirm, to catch sight of exposed female bodies would take a number of forms, all of which could frame and mediate the nudity through some device or narrative twist, both legitimating the naked body and also distancing the audience from any direct culpability or incrimination in anything but "harmless diversion." The plot pretexts of nudie cuties consistently returned to this "scene of looking," rather than of sex, as the crux of dramatic action. Consider some of the setups: the dream sequence or fantasy structure (as in *The Immoral Mr. Teas* [Russ Meyer, 1959] and *Not Tonight Henry* [W. Merle Connell, 1960]); the use of some form of optical premise or technological device that allows women to be seen in the nude (a camera in *The Naughty Shutter* [Sammy Helm, 1963]; a taxicab as time machine in *50,000 B.C. (Before Clothing)* [Warner Rose, 1963]); the use of vanishing cream mixed with house paint that allows two painters to see through walls to the women on the other side in *Pardon My Brush* (John K. McCarthy, 1964) or more elaborate scenarios of science fiction and invisibility (*Tales of a Salesman* [Don Russell, 1965]; *Nude on the Moon* [Doris Wishman, 1961]); the voyeur's transformation into an animal or inanimate object (*Dr. Sex* [Ted Mikels, 1964]; *Mr. Peter's Pets* [Dick Crane, 1963]); or "sociologically" realist settings such as the artist's studio, in the subcycle of the artist's model film (*1,000 Shapes of a Female* [Barry Mahon, 1963]; *Nude in Charcoal* [Joe Sarno, 1961]; *Artists Studio Secrets* [J. M. Kimbrough, 1964]). In all of these films, the vision of nudity must be properly *mediated*—either by generic structure or narrative device—to cushion the visual "shock" of nudity and to quarantine the spectator from an overt acknowledgment of his own erotic intent.

This deployment of female nudity was one of the foremost defining features, and box office appeals, of early-1960s nudie films, but it also conversed with representational codes and conventions of nudity that had been broached in other media and art forms as well as in the progenitor of the nudist camp film. The construction of the male consumer can be traced back to magazines such as *Esquire* in the 1930s and 1940s, developed further in the self-determining and taste-savvy bachelor culture so lionized by *Playboy*. Featuring female nudes, in pinup drawings and cartoons, and later in photographs and foldout centerfolds (in the latter publication), these magazines produced a distinct sphere of male consumption.[24] The manifestation of the male consumer and the concomitant economic legitimation of the desires of men within the public marketplace were, by the early 1960s, well-established terrain, which the sexploitation film capitalized upon.[25] The pinup style adorning newsstands in men's "cheesecake" ⁿd girlie magazines by the late 1950s, as well as in men's interest and ⁿre magazines such as *Modern Man, Swank, Man's World, Gent,* and *Stag,* served as signposts of a popular culture inching toward the previously forbidden—in which female flesh served as a node of address to a predominantly male audience, a commodity, and a consumer good in its own right.[26]

The nudie cuties, as generic form, were preceded by the waning classical exploitation cycles of burlesque and nudist camp films in the mid- to late 1950s. Eric Schaefer details how nudist camp films presented nudity within the naturist setting and within a discourse of pastoralism (as in *The Garden of Eden* [Max Nosseck, 1954]), offering an implicit critique of modernity in their "back to basics" ethos. In contrast, the burlesque film, which featured a series of performers, such as Tempest Storm or Lili St. Cyr, on a stage, interspersed with comic skits, confronted its audience with a more transgressive thrill of aggressive female erotic performance via its direct address.[27] Both of these exploitation cycles set the stage for some of the departures that the early-1960s nudie cuties would take in respect to codes of corporeal representation, even as a number of filmmakers continued making nudist camp films well into the mid-1960s.

The nudie cuties, a departure from the nudist camp film, can also be situated in the context of Hollywood's own movement toward a more permissive cinematic standard, attesting to the aesthetic and industrial specificity of early sexploitation films. In 1960, Elizabeth Taylor's scandalous and overheated performance in *Butterfield 8* (Daniel Mann) opened with a scene that could be considered a parallel track to some of sexploitation's visual lures. Taylor, as the suggestively named Gloria Wandrous, languorously wakes up with rumpled hair in a mussed, strange bed redolent with connotations of an unbridled night of illicit sex. We see her in a shot in which her bare shoulders emerge from a wrinkled sheet, suggesting nudity but withholding it through deft editing. Slinking through a high-class New York apartment that is clearly not her own, Taylor's body is clad in a clingy, sheathlike negligee, her languid corporeality standing in for an off-screen narrative of the previous night's seduction. Discovering money left for her by her absent and evidently married lover, she leaves in a fury, scrawling "No Sale" on the hallway mirror with her crimson lipstick.

The performative labors of this scene, which bear the weight of a particular moment of struggle in the fading of the studio and, by extension, its star system, also exhibit Hollywood contending with the potentials of the cinematic future, in the demand for more risqué, "adult" screen entertainments as well as the tried-and-true narrative formulas of its own historical past, particularly the "fallen woman" film of the 1930s. It is no coincidence that the film was an adaptation of the 1935 John O'Hara novel of the same name.[28] What gave this film its draw and status, despite its very sensationalistic narrative, was not only the economics of a certain mode of production but also the box office formula of its valuable star commodity—Taylor herself, considered to be "Hollywood's last glamour girl," the highest-paid female star in that decade.[29] Alex Doty details the extent to which Taylor's scandalous and highly publicized affairs with Eddie Fisher (and soon with Richard Burton) after her widowhood by Mike Todd's death recast her 1960s persona in the public eye as an unrepentant seductress, a motif mirrored by the themes of *Butterfield 8*.[30] Parker Tyler, one of the era's keenest historiographers of Hollywood's bounded and archly stylized sexuality, noted that Taylor represented a point of transition between the classical Hollywood "sex goddess"—exemplified by the likes of Theda Bara, Greta Garbo, and Mae West—and the deflation of the mythic quality of the Hollywood star, with Taylor becoming emblematic instead of a "universal Miss Sexpot." By 1969, Tyler lamented that "sex goddessing is more a trade, than something acquired, as it were, by divine privilege.... Being a sex goddess has nothing to do with the sexual act as such. Getting laid is a strictly human, quite unglamorous occupation."[31] For Tyler, the introduction of sex, without much innuendo, in the identification and comportment of female stars signaled the end of an era of an idealized female performer who exuded eroticism through the prison bars of film industrial restraint and through the creativity of her occulted speech and performance style—for example, in Mae West's infamously cadenced jokes uttered as headily encrypted come-ons.

What sexploitation films proffered in contrast to a film like *Butterfield 8* and a star body such as Taylor's was a lack of pretense to big studio respectability in their replacement of the star with an *amateur,* unknown body that could be eroticized in new ways, while continuous with representational conventions drawn as much from cinema as from pulp novels and men's adventure magazines. Sexploitation producer David Friedman attested to this in a 1986 interview: "most of us were dead set against any star system. Our theory—Russ Meyer's, Bob Cresse's and mine—was that every week the suckers want to see a new face and a new set of tits. And before hardcore you didn't have any trouble getting a lot of very pretty girls."[32] The sexploitation film introduced to the spectator (deemed a "dupe") both the frisson of the actor's unknowability and the speed of a ceaseless variety of ever-changing faces and bodies.

As a nonunion arena of production, sexploitation producers drew their female casts from workers employed in the nude and "figure" modeling and stripping professions as well as from a pool of aspiring talent. Actors were generally paid between fifty and two hundred dollars a day for film shoots that usually lasted approximately a week. Budgets on sex films typically ran from ten to forty thousand dollars. Most sexploitation actresses, if they were not performers, were likely amateurs or unknowns who had limited prior acting experience and were aiming to gain a foothold in the acting profession through employment in sexploitation. One of the most prolific low-budget nudie producers, Barry Mahon, indicated that for around half of the women who worked for him, it was their first time in the film business: "They have no talent or it's undeveloped talent. They have a pretty face. They're young. They have a pretty figure, and we're willing to pay them more than they could make working in the dime store, so forgetting the moral aspects they are willing to work for us."[33] Given the size of the network of producers like Mahon on the New York nudie scene, one can observe the return and reappearance of until then "no-name" actresses in primary roles—Darlene Bennett, Dawn Bennett, June Roberts, Linda Boyce, Gigi Darlene, Sharon Kent, and Cherie Winters, among many others. These films became an anchoring locale, a network for their employment, perhaps even an informal "training ground," although we can only speculate the extent to which certain actresses became recognizable to the predominantly male audiences of sexploitation films. Certain actors, such as Audrey Campbell, became prominently associated with specific roles (in her case, as Madame Olga in the Olga series, discussed in chapter 3). However, the corporeal appeal of sexploitation to its audiences overwhelmingly resided in the mode's capacity to seize on the erotics of a relatively anonymous, not-yet-professionalized or trained talent base. In contrast to the studios' star system and their manufacture of polish, poise, and glamor in contemporaneous star figures such as Taylor, Audrey Hepburn, Raquel Welch, Jane Fonda, Kim Novak, and Natalie Wood, the ordinariness of sexploitation's amateur female actors without question provided a more *verité* object of male sexual fantasy, proffering the girl next door, the office girl, the shop girl.

The authenticity of sexploitation's unknown actresses derived not from the verisimilitude of a given performance and its mimetic bravado—as in Taylor's caustic rendition of Wandrous—but from the everydayness of their gait, posture, and physicality. This play between accessibility and inaccessibility could be rendered thematically, in the fabric of their narratives of visual, and implicitly sexual, availability to male enjoyment. Whereas the source of fantasy in Taylor's performance was her inaccessibility, larger-than-life glamour, and upper-class prestige, the fantasies of sexploitation's narratives could deploy the imagined accessibility of the undiscovered starlet, model, or dancer as their draw, underscoring the "variety" of the emergent sexual marketplace, particularly for the male consumer. In the transition between the burlesque mode and the nudie cutie phenomenon, certain well-known performers from the live theater, dancing, and pinup worlds would be drawn in as members of a labor pool—such as Blaze Starr, June Roberts, and Lili St. Cyr, among others. The status of these showgirls' fame was certainly not of the same order as the celebrity juggernaut of Taylor and, by extension, the studio system.

Thus the girl-next-door appeal that had catapulted *Playboy*'s centerfolds to widespread success also provided the principle of attraction for the emergent sexploitation genre. Later sexploitation films deployed the literal girl-next-door archetype and narrative—already made common by the appeals of the pinup and the girlie magazine—even more readily and transferred them into their plots through the common device of the innocent country girl as stranger to the city or the naïf inducted into dangerous sexual knowledge in films such as *Girl in Trouble* (Brandon Chase, 1963), *Bad Girls Go to Hell* (Doris Wishman, 1965), and *A Bride for Brenda* (Tommy Goetz, 1969).

But first, the nudie cuties of the early 1960s brought the corporeal quotidianness of these unknown actresses to the space of the moving, rather than the print, image. And with the moving image also came the problem of narrative, of how to create some form of a workable and saleable story to house the spectacle of uncovered female flesh. Female nudity was a central component of sexploitation cinema's box office success and promotional lure. Sexploitation's performance elements archive this quite overt commercial and production imperative to *stage* unclothed bodies for the camera. Nudity returns the performing body to a kind of fleshy documentary facticity that necessarily undermines but also exposes the conditions of working bodies and the body's work. While the spectacle of the naked and the nude has a long tradition of analysis in art history, the nudie film's engagement with the nude female body depends on a reorganization of certain principles that govern the experience of a still image, including painting, drawing, and photography. Lynda Nead, in her definitive study of the nude in art history in relation to discourses of sexuality and obscenity, establishes the set of conditions that regulate the experience of the nude in the context of high art: "One of the principal goals of the female nude has been the containment and regulation of the female sexual body. The forms, conventions and poses of art have worked metaphorically to shore up the female body—to seal orifices and to prevent marginal matter from transgressing the boundary dividing the inside of the body and the outside, the self from the space of the other."[34] Nead argues that art historical discourse has evaded the terms of representation and how they are inscribed by relations of power as well as the politicization and disciplining of both the spectator and the represented body.

Nead's observations can be directly linked to an analysis of the nudie cutie and sexploitation film. In the case of the moving image, Nead's examination suggests that the function of the nude not only circulates around the development of a discourse of form and line that manages the inside and outside of the female body but can be seen as equally wedded to a working through of the relationship and boundary between the filmed body and the spectator's body. The discourse of spectatorship, of the "gawker in the text" that sexploitation engenders, is contingent on negotiating the limits between the impermeable female body and the conditions of looking and interacting with that body, both diegetically within the film's narratives and extradiegetically in the relationships formed between the filmgoer and the film itself.

Examining the film genealogically credited with spawning the earliest sexploitation subgenre, Russ Meyer's nudie cutie *The Immoral Mr. Teas*, we can see how these motifs play out in its narrative, diagramming a mode of male voyeurism. The titular character, a hapless, bumbling denture deliveryman, is plagued with the condition of thinking he sees women naked when they are in fact fully clothed. Whether Teas is dreaming, fantasizing, or has some kind of hallucinatory malady is up to the film audience to

FIGURE 14. Mr. Teas's precarious vision of exposed epidermis in *The Immoral Mr. Teas*.

decide. The ambiguity of his condition also becomes the groundwork of the film's broadly laden irony—in which the faux-authoritative narrator's grating oration about the travails of "modern man" is juxtaposed with the denigrating daily activities of Mr. Teas. The women occupy the position of ancillary social and narrative characters—the dentist's assistant, the secretary, the soda shop waitress, the sunning girl at the beach—who transition from being "decorative," secondary players peopling the margins of the film to being reconfigured as objects of banal lust, becoming the show. Aligning the spectator both narratively and visually with Teas's leering perspective, the film presented 1960s audiences with images of women in everyday contexts posing as if unawares with breasts or buttocks exposed, in settings of fully saturated color in naturalist or work-a-day environments, often followed by shots of Teas with some kind of a perplexed response or running away in mock horror. The direct address of the burlesque dancer's or pinup model's gaze at her presumed viewer is negotiated and circumvented through the "accidental" aspect of the plot—in which Teas's visions of nakedness are an inadvertent and internalized condition to which only the audience is privy, thus allowing them to "peek" along with Teas himself. Buffering accusations of prurience and filtering them through the alibi of Teas's impotent response to these "corporeal visions," the film presented a sardonic parody of the still popular and actively exhibited nudist camp films, whose blandness presumably concealed a form of "bad faith." Ridding itself of the narrative justification around the verisimilitude and documentary veracity of the nude leisure space and the camp as an alternative way of life, *Mr. Teas* employed a new problematic regarding audience response and cultural fantasy. The film posed the question of the male erotic consumer metatextually: what happens when a male spectator is confronted with a woman in the nude? What will he do? In perhaps the first highbrow defense of a sexploitation film, American literary critic Leslie Fiedler wrote in *Show* in 1961 that the film was in fact a treatise on the conditions of its own possibility, stating:

> We realize that the joke has adapted to the conditions which make the showing of the film possible: there must be an apron; he must not touch her. It is not finally just a matter of observing certain rules of the censors, but of making those very rules the subject of the picture, the butt of its jokes. For what we are shown is not female flesh, but pin-up pictures—moving pictures of moving pin up pictures, life twice removed. . . . It is not merely like the strip-tease, the candy-box cover, the girlie calendar and the foldout nude; it is about them.[35]

Fiedler's prescient argument about the emergent sexploitation genre pinpointed a strategy and mode of address that would continue to define the generic organization of the sexploitation cycles that would follow. Fiedler's positioning of Meyer's film as a treatise on the conditions of looking was also a significant moment of recognition and convergence between high literary and low film cultures.

The film's staging of the collision between Teas's frazzled sensibilities, in his circumstantial haplessness, and the materialization of naked female flesh gave the film a metatextual self-consciousness, in which Teas becomes the model of the cinema spectator himself. These collisions manifest in the narrative as Teas literally gets bowled over by his vision. Teas's fishing expedition at a lakeside retreat is played for vaudeville laughs when a female sunbather approaches and strips off her bikini top. Teas's attraction is followed by repulsion, as he falls haphazardly and comically into the water, physically moved by his vision of naked breasts. The effects of such looking are dramatized by Meyer as ones that upset Teas's material equilibrium and so become an allegory of the shifting fields of male privilege, as conventional scopophilia turns comic, as the gawker's body careens out of control. In these farcical moments, Mr. Teas, unable to appreciate the spectacle, is himself turned into a spectacle.[36] Indeed, male autoeroticism and arousal become the textual and extratextual taboos the nudie cuties attempt to circumvent, as the male film spectator's corporeality needed to be redirected and deflected through generic, comic codes.

The ludicrously inept "failed" masculinity of Teas's character and his comical incapacity to respond with signs of aggression, sexual prowess, or arousal are proffered as the very conditions of a "look but don't touch" ethos in both the culture and under the strictures of censorious filmic conventions. Adhering to the double-edged implications of masculine impotence, this framing of Teas's character gives a certain symbolic and performative power to the female figures in the film. Meyer's later films would more hyperbolically map this dynamic in works such as *Vixen* (Russ Meyer, 1968) and *Faster Pussycat! Kill! Kill!* (Russ Meyer, 1965), in which men attempt to contend with aggressive, hypersexual figures like the nymphomaniac Vixen and the gang leader Varla—while still resonating with a functionalist model of male libido.[37] That is, a "proper" male erotic drive is derailed in service of censorial prohibitions and is framed through the generic utilization of older traditions of vaudeville comedy.

Other nudie cutie films would manage this trope of looking, thematizing the conditions of gawking at young women in states of undress in clever and sometimes strained ways. *The Adventures of Lucky Pierre*

(1961), directed by Herschell Gordon Lewis and produced by David Friedman, begins with a comic male character in a gaudy suit acting as film barker, talking directly into the camera, introducing the film "as the finest movie ever made" and featuring a "cast of thousands," and touting its budget at twenty million dollars. Each of his proclamations of the film's quality is followed by a hiccupping laugh, as the segment ends with two men in white suits dragging him away, presumably taking him to the "looney bin." This use of self-denigrating comedy, wherein the filmmakers nudge and wink at their audience through a burlesqued discourse of economically legitimate cinematic "art," sets up the ironic tone of the film as a whole. The introductory skit also establishes the serial nature of the short scenes to follow. All except the first two do not use synchronized sound, facilitating the analogy to silent film aesthetics through their episodic form and the vaudevillian nature of their performances.

The subsequent segment serves as a more overt revelation of the film's drive. We see a stationary shot of a psychiatrist, the titular Pierre (played by nightclub comedian Billy Falbo), wearing a beret and smoking a cigar, hunkered over his desk in medium long shot as the lower foreground of the frame reveals a pair of feet in black leather high heel pumps, the remainder of the legs and body of this obviously female patient cut off by the right edge of the frame. As the doctor purports to listen while writing on his notepad, the patient confesses a neurotic anxiety—that everyone in her daily life seems to be staring at her: people on the street, in the grocery store, in the elevator, even the doctor's own secretary. The doctor, unresponsive to the prattle of his patient, remains inattentive, continually looking down as an insert shot reveals that he is doodling in his notepad as the patient carries on about her self-perception. The body of the patient remains unseen until the end of the segment. Her voice is juxtaposed with her constant readjustment of her feet in the frame, as she shifts one heeled foot over the other in a parallel evocation of her off-screen talk. Her feet become a synecdoche of her body, their nervous movement indicating a kind of self-reflection and nascent eroticism that the film willfully refuses to show, saving her naked body's revelation for the comic punch line of this scene. This scene also presages the ways in which the developing softcore syntax of sexploitation would put to work the extremities of the body, parts that could signify erotics in the absence of the represented whole and the unseen sex act. The doctor abruptly claims that the session is over, and we see the fully nude patient walk from screen right to screen left wearing only a hat and a purse held before her, judiciously covering her pubic area. The doctor remains with eyes downturned, never looking up to visually match or recognize the purported psychological "affliction" of his patient with her corporeal bareness. The joke completes itself not through a form of comeuppance or responsiveness but through a comedy of unresponsiveness and in the cuing of the viewer's acknowledgment that both characters are unable to "see properly."

The malady of the doctor's patient—the perception that all are staring at her—neatly encapsulates the relations of looking that will obtain in the film itself. The comedy rests in the disconnect between the woman's misperception and inability to see her own nudity and her sense that all are staring at her, compounded by the doctor's myopic diagnosis as he proclaims her a "classic case of inferiority complex." The doctor's refusal to look at her nude body, his marked disinterest, also presents a necessary comedy of disavowal—not only within the scenario of the film but also in its extension of the perfunctory denial of the film audience's licentious interests. Seeing properly requires some recognition of the nature of the object of sight, which would also imply a logic of arousal, and the joke emerges from both the misdirection of the doctor's diagnosis and the patient's lack of self-awareness of her absence of vestments as the obvious root of her "neurosis."

This troping of myopic sight continues in the rest of the film, as Pierre—the comically geeky character who serves to link these separate nudie vignettes—is placed in situations that become consecutively more spectacular in their narrativization of the generic necessity of nudity. All of them are contingent on some context that allows the "act of looking" to be legitimated in some broad sociological sense: the artist's models in the park with Pierre working at his easel; Pierre as plumber's apprentice fixing a pipe while a woman bathes in the adjacent tub; Pierre as birdwatcher who sees not exotic birds but women sunbathing nude through his binoculars; Pierre the photographer's apprentice as he takes photos of sauntering nude models who manage to disappear completely as soon as he snaps the shutter; and Pierre as a film spectator in a nudie cutie drive-in, which brings the thematic of spectatorship full circle back to the film's opening and its ironic self-aggrandizement. As the film invites the very form of gawking that the patient in the opening scene so directly describes, the audience's credulous look is doubled over by Pierre's surrogacy for them within the diegetic world of the film. Yet, at the same time, Pierre's bumbling characteristics also operate in a position of an antisurrogate, in which the viewer can measure his own response in contrast to the protagonist. This oscillation characterizes the double mode of display and denial of the sexploitation film. Pierre, like Mr. Teas before him, acts as a buffer of sexual impulse in his haplessness in each of the narrative segments. As a plumber, he is unable to fix the pipe and then gets soaked

FIGURE 15. The nudie cutie's gawker in the promotional poster of *The Adventures of Lucky Pierre*.

by the showerhead, while a woman bathes in the tub and finally accosts him. As a painter of nude models, Pierre's abstract painting meets with a final mark of disapproval from his nude models, who proceed to beat him over the head with his own nonrealist canvas. Photographer Pierre is confounded by the disappearance of the girls he shoots as well as the final disappearing act of the camera itself. And finally, as film spectator in the drive-in, his view is gradually obstructed by newly arriving vehicles in the lot. At the same time that the film is preoccupied with the precarious conditions and impacts of looking on the male voyeur, the tableaus of female nudity contain a quality of impermanence and ephemerality, in which the erotic mirage, like the striptease that titillates with its layers of concealment and exhibitionism, threatens to disappear as quickly as it appeared to the viewer. The visual field is rendered unstable through this transience and ungraspability.

The picaresque mode and the discrete vignettes in *Lucky Pierre,* much like *Mr. Teas*'s structure, invoke silent film comedy—an association aided by the lack of synchronized sound and the comic performances of ineptitude and social embarrassment suffered by these tramplike characters. The dialogue with media that traffic in still images of the nude, such as the pinup, the nudie photograph, or the nude painting, also gives the films a certain tinge of anachronism—in which earlier forms of erotic consumption are overlaid by newer ones, transposed in the realms of the moving image. This appropriative style gives the films another layer of aesthetic referentiality, as viewers can recognize the nudie cutie within a continuum of representational conventions drawn from other sex-oriented media then circulating within the erotic marketplace.

As the nudie cutie took off, and a series of imitators flooded the American film market in the early 1960s, other means of presenting nudity without connotations of overt sexual activity emerged. One formula, implied in some of the nudie scenarios, was the "artist's model" film. Artist's model films often featured authenticating voice-over narration introducing viewers, in a faux-sociological mode, to artists or photographers as they interacted with their nude female subjects in their studios, replete with insert shots of the final art product. Because the "film as art" discourse provided an umbrella of protection from censorship, some filmmakers adopted the narrative context of the artist's studio for their nudie cutie offshoots. Explaining the necessities and exigencies of nudie film production, producer and director Barry Mahon discussed how he understood and was able to work around the legal definition of obscenity to "get away with" making films that circulated around nudity. Citing the nudist film *The Garden of Eden* as one that permitted nudity if it was represented as a "way of life," Mahon clarified that the artist's model or photographer's model film was the logical extension of a permissible and representable "lifestyle."[38] In these films, we can see another thematic motif develop that continued throughout the sexploitation cycles that would follow—a preoccupation with the "flesh peddling industry" broadly conceived, as it began to include other sex-related trades, such as modeling, sex work, and even nudie filmmaking (to be discussed below).[39] The attitudes that the films took toward these nascent industries would change, however, moving from a semidocumentary or comic disavowal of prurience to more overtly moralizing scripts that engaged with the newly "liberated" woman as a character prone either to perverse degeneration or to corruption and, finally, toward a matter-of-fact description or even parody.

In an example of such denial of the licentious, Mahon, in a statement infused by the legal proscriptions of the time, makes the point that "nudity doesn't necessarily involve sex. Perhaps we are rationalizing, and perhaps people who see our films get some great sexual thrill out of watching the girls, but I don't think so."[40] Mahon's films from this period generally avoid contravening the doctrine of obscenity law, with films such as *1,000 Shapes of a Female*, *Bunny Yeager's Nude Camera* (1963), and *Bunny Yeager's Nude Las Vegas* (1964) deploying the premise of the sociological study of the "artist at work."[41]

The film *1,000 Shapes* ratifies its content through its focus on the lives of Greenwich Village artists in New York and is narrated by an art dealer, David Green, who is arranging a show of nude paintings. The film operates in a mode Mahon himself called "semidocumentary," as it portends to bring to light a particular bohemian and geographical milieu of cultural production, one given legitimacy and popularized by the commodification of beat culture as well as the renown of abstract expressionism in the late 1950s and early 1960s. The dealer situates himself to do business in a MacDougal street café that doubles as both artist's clearinghouse and hip hangout, replete with exposed brick, carefully placed graffiti on the wall (which reads "Stamp Out ~~Mental Health~~ Conformity!"), a bulletin board for posting want ads for nude models, and a range of guitar-playing crooners. At the same time, the film aims to give audiences an art history lesson about styles of painterly figuration—using insert shots of famous paintings by Gauguin, Renoir, Rembrandt, and Ingres, interspersed with very amateur-looking canvases presumably made by the fictional artist characters. The film references the milieu of abstract expressionism and he "anthropometric" paintings of French artist Yves Klein. Klein's nts with "anthropometry" from 1958 onward involved the use bodies as "living brushes." In his *Anthropometrie de l'epoque bleue,* performed in 1960 in Paris, Klein directed naked women to apply his own blue paint to their bodies and drag each other on canvases on the floor, in front of classical musical accompanists and for a live audience. This performance was recorded by Italian directors Paola Gavara, Gualtiero Jacopetti, and Franco Prosperi in one of the first internationally distributed "shockumentary"-style exploitation films, *Mondo Cane* (1962), taking its place alongside other "strange practices" cataloged from around the world, such as tribal rituals in Africa, cannibalism, and animal cruelty. Because of the wide circulation of *Mondo Cane,* and its role in spurring on numerous sexploitation copycats in the following years in the mid-1960s (such as *Mondo Freudo* [Lee Frost, 1966], *Mondo Bizarro* [Lee Frost, 1966], and *Mondo Oscenita* [Joseph P. Mawra, 1966]), it is quite feasible that Mahon may have been aware of it in advance of filming *1,000 Shapes.*[42]

Body painting functions as both a sign of the times and as a convenient pretext for varying representations and interactions with the naked bodies of the female actors.[43] Appropriating Klein's vanguardism, the film features one painter, Doug Stewart, who begins "experimenting" with his materials, literally using the bodies of his female models as the paintbrush, or, as Klein called them, the *"femme pinceau."* A eureka moment occurs when the painter, uninspired with his traditional methods, having accidentally smudged paint on the face of his model, discovers the possibilities in applying paint directly to the bodies of his nude sitters and pressing their inky flesh against the canvas. The film takes great pains to visually indulge this tentative "solution" to the cinematic problem of *touch,* locating it within the sociological sphere of the artist's world. The art dealer narrator and Stewart the character both intone about the benefits of this new method—at one point, the narrator states that Stewart wanted to "let the texture of the skin and the line of the body be the instrument of applying the paint to the canvas." Taking pleasure in the critical description of the (obviously gendered) body in its focus on form and method, the narration negotiates double meaning and innuendo—as the art discourse simultaneously protects and provides the viewer with a dose of titillation.

Instead of a more direct scene of erotic tactility or relationality, such as a seduction scenario that might expose the implicitly prurient interest between artist and model, the surface of the female body itself is instrumentalized in the service of art. The film evades the censorial limitations on physical contact with the inaccessible female body through the resolution of the artist's formal problem. The female bodies are put to work on multiple levels, as they serve within an ethnographic mode to represent a class of willing yet low-rung laborers within this fictionalized

FIGURE 16. The artist discovers body painting and his *femme pinceau* in Barry Mahon's *1,000 Shapes of a Female*.

art world economy and are simultaneously put in service of an occulted erotics through their instrumentalization of artistic abstraction, becoming a literal aesthetic material, the embodied pliable stuff of the artwork.

Resembling the refusal of the nude models in *Lucky Pierre* to appreciate the aesthetic value of abstract form, one scene dramatizes the responses of a rather skeptical "living paintbrush." The model, who sees the dripping and orblike impressions of her own body on the canvas, begins to berate the painter for his lack of talent and his inability to employ more traditional techniques of realism to represent her nude form. She exclaims, "All I did was make a big blotch! You said so yourself that I'm just as important as you in this thing.... In my opinion that's not the way to paint a woman." When Stewart explains that the painting is not complete yet, the German-accented model retorts, "It's not even stah-ted! ... If you want a picture of a woman, then draw one!" She leaves in a huff; yet the joke remains on her. On one hand, her comments serve the film discursively as a comic derision of new, seemingly nonsensical, opaque or pretentious art practices. On the other, the model's inability to recognize the value of her own nude impression in abstracted form becomes testimony to her lack of sophistication with respect to cutting-edge, modern art and makes her the unwitting advocate tying feminine representation with realism.

1,000 Shapes of a Female thus moved the phenomenology of the filmed body closer toward a broaching of corporeal contact, transforming the "look but don't touch" ethos of films like *Teas* and *Lucky Pierre* in the direction of an encrypted physicality. Here visual and narrative access to the female body is given to the viewer through scenes of the painter directing and manipulating topless females in G-strings and panties and pressing them against the canvas, with instructions to "wiggle your hips" and "press your hips up against it, and your thighs." Erotic suggestion permeates these exchanges, undergirded and legitimated by the film's supposedly documentary transcription of scenes of innovation in artistic method.

If *1,000 Shapes* used the frame of sociological examination to explore the transforming circumstances of looking, and now formally *touching*, the naked female body on-screen, then Mahon's two features with the real-life female pinup and professional photographer Bunny Yeager allow her biographical provenance to function as a mediating buffer between the threat of prurience and the foregrounded labor, the cultural production, of eroticized aesthetic forms. In *Bunny Yeager's Nude Camera* and *Bunny Yeager's Nude Las Vegas*, Mahon employed Yeager to play herself, a photographer scouting for and photographing nude models. In the 1950s and 1960s, Yeager was widely known as pinup model turned glamour photographer and especially for her photos of Bettie Page in *Playboy* and other publications. Yeager published frequently and also produced many books of her own photographs in the 1950s and 1960s. In addition to her camera work, she was informally acknowledged as a talent scout for the men's magazine industry, having discovered Maria Stinger, Lisa Winters, and other prominent pinup models in the 1950s and 1960s. Yeager also connected aspiring actresses from her network of models with film producers visiting Miami, Florida, in the early 1960s to make nudies.[44]

In Mahon's films, Yeager's glamourous femininity justifies and reinforces the logics of male erotic consumption in the cultural sphere but also provides a measure of touristic novelty. Both films are preoccupied with Yeager's professionalism and occupational normativity, in the sense that she is a "family-oriented" woman who happens to have an unusual line of work. Yet underneath the descriptive narratives of Yeager's day-to-day life, the conflict between her roles as wife and mother and as career woman surfaces as a motivating trajectory and a peculiarly modern problem. Yeager starred in these two films, along with her husband and erstwhile sexploitation actor Bud Irwin, their real-life relationship anchoring the plots' detailing of her working life as a glamour and nudie photographer. Mahon himself also appears in the first film, acting the role of a professional friend and intermediary for acquiring new models for Bunny, whisking Bunny off to Tampa for a local pirate festival and parade on his fighter plane.

The first film, *Bunny Yeager's Nude Camera*, establishes Bunny's occupation through her own voice-over, which frames and introduces her line of work and her "daily grind." Bunny discusses the pleasures and difficulties of being a photographer of nude models. Yet, to offset the agency granted Bunny in her profession, the film departs from her narratorial point of view during the photo shoots—in which the tableaus of her nude models, interjected with inserts of Bunny's directions, are often broken to present a more fragmentary and close-up image of the model's torsos—with shots of their naked breasts drawn in closer proximity to the camera and their heads cut off. This insertion of a desiring male point of view into an all-female work space—Bunny's secretary is a woman—necessarily contradicts the sociological documentation the film purports to present. The professional demeanor of Yeager's voice and self-presentation, her narrational assertion that she runs an "above-board" business, becomes a significant plot point. When a strange man calls wanting to know about her models, Bunny ensures that her "girls" are not soliciting unwanted male attention or promising sexual favors or creating negatively prurient associations for her business. There is a tension between the film's presentation of Bunny's labor and her figuration in the image as not an agent but an object of the image. Posing shots are often presented frontally, both silhouetting Bunny in the foreground with her camera, and with reverse shots of her approving face as she directs the scene. But some moments strain at the tension between the pose for Bunny's camera and the pose for Mahon's film camera, as models look not at Bunny but at the camera, or when Bunny's face is dissolved with the posed nude image, an uncharacteristic effect used by Mahon.

In *Bunny Yeager's Nude Las Vegas*, we see Mahon using a consistent set of shot setups to relay the atmosphere of Yeager's film shoots: the shots alternate between medium shots of Yeager looking down into her 4 × 5 camera with dialogue heard of her directing the models, cutaways to the model's poses, and then shots of Yeager's head in the bottom foreground as the posed image is captured doubly for the film camera and for Yeager's photographic camera. The back of Yeager's blonde head and the camera in front of it that remains unseen obstruct the view of the model's lower body area, creating an inadvertently dense and loaded composition. Yeager's bleached-blonde hair becomes a fixture and a surrogate for the photographic camera as well as a graphical object in the frame that creates a filter between the film viewer and the topless woman posing in the background. Yeager's instrumentalization in the service of the nudie plot creates a cushion for the audience—where modeling nude, looking at

FIGURE 17. In *Bunny Yeager's Nude Camera,* the famed pinup photographer ratifies the sexploitation filmmaker's and spectator's vantage point; the posing model's affinities are split between her two "directors" in this lobby card.

nude models, and being a female photographer of nude models coalesce, a nested set of processes.

While the focus on Yeager's very visible labor personalizes and feminizes the conventions of the artist's model film and its premium on shunted male desire, allowing it to be told from a female perspective, Mahon's film necessitates the specularization of Yeager herself within this scene of looking, an act of looking at an erotic object that must still accommodate the desire of the male consumer. For example, in *Bunny Yeager's Nude Las Vegas,* Bunny consistently enforces her ironclad rule that no men should be present during her photo shoots to make her models feel at ease. The film offers numerous scenes involving her shooing away her husband's leering friend Charlie or Bud, himself leaving the hotel room for Bunny to work in peace. The film camera of course persists, allowing the film's makers to be the silent observers, underlining the double, tacit nature of sexploitation's gaze and address to its audience, as it peeks in at a "female-only" space. The focus on variety and variation allows a revolving door of aspiring models to move through the diegesis, Yeager's place of vocation a mobilized erotic marketplace. This reinforces the sense of women's availability to be seen and specularized by the film and its spectator, a function of market plenitude, a desire emboldened by both 1960s popular culture and the shifting discourses of male consumption.

Yeager's creative labor also foregrounds an inadvertent self-consciousness of the films, drawing attention to the analogous production of nudie films themselves. Yeager, while herself a celebrity whose star text is here being mobilized, also can become a diegetic extension of the nudie filmmaker; her work suggests that if a woman can take nudie photos, the act of the film's making has been normalized. This focus of Mahon's on legitimating the parallel practices of nudie filmmaking and modeling for nudie forms, such as the photographic pinup, can also be seen in the narrative of Mahon's 1964 *Nudes Inc.*, which details the slow acquiescence of a financially strapped woman to posing for pinups as she is convinced of its respectability as a line of work by the studio owner.

While Mahon's narratives sociologized the scene of looking in order to authenticate it, the later nudie cuties would take further flights of fantasy to satisfy the generic formula and its circumscription. The Texas-made *The Naughty Shutter* (Sammy Helm, 1963) would use the discovery of a magical camera that sees women in the nude at a skid row hotel as the basis for a series of hijinks in which the camera traveled like a hot potato between different residents at the motel. Ted Mikels's *Dr. Sex* took ironic nudity to a fantastical extreme in its gathering of a group of sexologists discussing the etiologies of their patients for a book they are working on together. All of the case studies share elements of absurd impossibility and the paranormal—with one patient revealing himself to be a poodle desiring to be a man to implicitly "get with" his constantly undressing female owner, and another case detailing the haunted house of a male patient who sees ghosts flitting about nightly in the nude. The sexological motif parodically references the quackery of sexology and ends with the head psychiatrist settling down in the nudie-haunted house himself.

By 1963 or so, the novelty of nudity was no longer the exclusive province of the nudie, as Hollywood was attempting to authorize its foray into this "adult" world. News accounts broadcast varied censorial and professional disputes over screen nudity. A 1963 article titled "Anatomy of Nudie Film Biz" commented that although nudie cutie exhibitors were no longer assaulted with legal injunctions, "they are running into a heightened audience sophistication. Such features now need a concocted story line, humor, special angles. The camera angle on bare epidermis alone won't suffice. The nude cultist thing itself is now a yawn."[45] Producers had been blasted for requiring actresses to do nude scenes, and the Screen Actors Guild had come to these actresses' defense, marking a distinction between the low-budget exploitation projects and the aims of mass-market cinema:

> The American producers who ask actresses to perform in the nude are making films for a mass market. They insert a short nude sequence that is used purely as audience bait, rather than for artistic reasons. The situation is more serious than the activities of fly-by-night producers, some of them unemployed cameramen, who make cheap films that deal with little else but nudity. The so-called "nudies" use strippers and photographers' models, not professional actresses.[46]

This diminution through differentiation operated through a classed marginalization of sexploitation's female performers, even if at this time, major stars, such as Marilyn Monroe, Jayne Mansfield, and Carroll Baker, represented a new willingness to bare all in studio-bankrolled productions.[47] Jane Russell, known for her fulsome Hollywood presence, announced her distaste for the nudies.[48]

Another Hollywood nudity controversy involved the film *The Americanization of Emily* (Arthur Hiller, 1964), which was threatened with the denial of a Production Code seal of approval. Producer Martin Ransohoff spoke out in "defiance" against the stringency of the Code. After being forced to cut the scenes, Ransohoff demanded that the industry begin to distinguish between lewd and vulgar nudity and nudity that is "not in bad taste."[49] Hollywood actress Carroll Baker, who had in the mid-1950s gained attention in her frank role as a "child bride" in *Baby Doll* (Elia Kazan, 1956), was in 1964 defending her own practice of doing nude scenes in films. She stated that she did "not think that movie nudity will injure the national character"[50] and spoke of her literal instrumentality at the hands of the artwork. The distinction of the art discourse seemed to reinforce the approval of a Code seal for Sidney Lumet's *The Pawnbroker* (1964), which featured a controversial scene that dramatically deployed a woman's entreaty to the pawnbroker to "look" at her bare breasts as a trigger of a past trauma, the sexual violence against his wife in the Holocaust, rendered through abrupt montage flashback. In this climate, it is widely posited that the nudie cutie producers felt a need to innovate in order to remain competitive and began to look to new genre models to maintain their product's box office appeal.

From Nudies to Roughies: Troubled Genealogies

Broadly speaking, based on the evidence of the films, from 1963 to 1965, sexploitation's generic strategies began to shift. The change from nudies to roughies tends to be narrated in fan discourse and popular accounts as a self-evident change born of economic necessity and a discreet break in style. There is without doubt a notable difference between the tone and aesthetics of the films in question. The full color, episodic scenarios and broad farce of the nudie cuties, which privilege static scenarios of the "innocent" looking, appear an extraordinary contrast to the grimy black-and-white film stock and the melodramatic, noir-inflected morality plays of the roughies and kinkies, which feast on the aggression of unleashed male sexual psychosis and female abandon. One of the few accounts of the grouping of sex film cycles from the period appeared in *Time* circa 1967: "among some *aficionados* of the nudies, the subcategories are known as 'roughies' (breasts and violence), 'ghoulies' (breasts and monsters), 'kinkies' (breasts and whips), and . . . 'mondos' (breasts around the world)."[51] But these were terms that took hold less in the film trades and more so among critics and later audiences; many of the industry papers generally referred to sexploitation broadly as "sexers" and "sex films" without these fine-tuned differentiations. Varying accounts of the passage from nudies to roughies also position different films as benchmarks, including *Scum of the Earth* (Herschell Gordon Lewis, 1963), *Lorna* (Russ Meyer, 1964), *White Slaves of Chinatown* (Joseph Mawra, 1964), and *The Defilers* (David Friedman and R. L. Frost, 1965). All of these films privilege narratives of male lust sublimated into violence or the excessive qualities of women that exhibit either socially inappropriate desires or sadistic impulses.[52]

An early historicization of this purported shift appears in Kenneth Turan and Stephen Zito's 1973 book-length study of adult film *Sinema*. They assert the end of the nudie cutie wave by 1964 in the transition to the more explicitly eroticized and violent fare of roughies and kinkies. They suggest that exhibitors were featuring double bills to attract audiences and that producers were overinvesting resources "to provide star names and glossy production values to silly, unreal stories that remained mere showcases for nudity spiced with vaudeville jokes and burlesque routines. . . . Nudity was no longer enough, not even in Eastmancolor."[53] However, the break between nudie cuties to other styles and narrative formulas such as roughies was not so clean and absolute. It might be more useful to think of this transition as a set of overlapping phases without a clear taxonomic break. We do see sexploitation cinema expand and diversify its generic strategies, focusing on sexually dramatic, often realist situations based in crime, vice, deviance, and sexual pathology.

Turan and Zito's contextualization of the changing aesthetic aspirations of sexploitation provides another factor for the proliferation of roughies in the widespread exhibition of risqué and dramatic foreign films and an expansion of sexually charged melodrama. The roughies and the hardscrabble sexual melodramas that emerged around 1964–65 clearly exhibit an aesthetic that derives from both the art house cinema and American genre films of the 1950s, such as film noir and social problem cinema. Schaefer has detailed how the rising popularity and exhibition of foreign films in art houses, as well as their adoption of "mature" themes at the time commonly associated with European art cinema, facilitated the appropriation of the art discourse by sexploitation films.[54] Mark Betz also examines how American distributors marketed European art films with a decidedly exploitation and adult thematic angle from the 1950s onward, creating, rather than taste distinction, strong affinities in the public eye between art and exploitation.[55] The lasting aesthetic impact of Italian neorealism and the diffusion of influence from the French New Wave, new realisms, and other young international film movements could be felt in many of the mid-1960s sexploitation films, with their penchant for handheld camera work, the grainy authenticity of black-and-white film stock, and plots that lingered on downtrodden realist geographies, whether urban, suburban, or rural.[56] Schaefer also links sexploitation's developing formulae to the existence on the adults-only circuit from the mid-1950s onward a genre of "grim sexually charged melodramas," made in both Europe and the United States, which focused on wayward desires and narratives of erotic dissatisfaction and betrayal.[57] The widening sphere of sexploitation's representational styles can also be attributed to the Stateside success of Bardot in Roger Vadim's *And God Created Woman* (1957) and Louis Malle's *The Lovers* (1960), as well as Radley Metzger's imports of European films, such as *The Twilight Girls* (1957/1961) and *The Fourth Sex* (1961), and art films such as *Monika* (1953) by Ingmar Bergman, which provided fodder to sexploitation producers for different ways to ground sexual content within dramatic plots.[58] Foreign imports, often sexed up or reedited with additional footage, also became a significant box office bolster for New York–based producers such as Metzger, William Mishkin, and Joseph Brenner, in titles such as *The Molesters* (Franz Schnyder, 1964), *The Skin Game* (Arnold Louis Miller, 1965), and *The Weird Lovemakers* (Koreyoshi Kuruhara, 1960/1963), which played alongside U.S.-made quickies in double bills and packaged screenings.

Both Joe Sarno's *Sin in the Suburbs* (1964), an early foray into the suburban swinger, wife-swapper narrative, and Radley Metzger's *The Dirty Girls* (1965), tracking the lives of two high-class prostitutes and shot in posh European locations, are notable films that bridge the art house aesthetic and represent a more "mature" and realist-inclined sexploitation cinema that emerges simultaneously with the proliferation of roughies. Sarno and Metzger possessed a tonier sensibility more interested in the workings of female desire and agency rather than the female's violent reprisal. Their respective aesthetics and authorial signatures must be read through a dialogue with risqué European cinema of filmmakers such as Bergman, Malle, and Fellini. Sarno's and Metzger's films also heralded a particular stylistic strain of sexploitation that extended into the later 1960s and early 1970s, as the genre altered its focus toward soft-core, simulated sex and the sexual experience of women in narratives of "self-discovery."[59]

The telos of normative generic progression from nudie cutie to roughie is also complicated by the exceptions, temporal lags, and continuities between the supposed beginning and end of these cycles. Joe Sarno's first film, *Nude in Charcoal* (1961), serves as an interesting example. Sarno wrote and codirected this film, though he is uncredited, with directing attributed to Philip Melillo. The film appeared to have played as long as through 1964 in various theaters across the country.[60] The film's press book and contemporaneous descriptions of the narrative detail a film that, while emulating the artist's model film, also seems to presage the plotlines and preoccupations of later roughie films. *Nude in Charcoal* deals with what first seems a standard artist's model formula: June Barton, the model, naively poses for her art instructor, Najlas Sarto. Yet the narrative shifts into roughie territory as the proceedings get more overtly sexualized. June is unaware that her teacher's repressed desires for her are about to turn malevolent, as he attempts to rape her on the night she is to leave his secluded estate. Sarto's possessive lover and housekeeper Elia gets wind of Sarto's affections, and the film climaxes as Elia strangles Sarto in a jealous rage, while intending to blame June for the crime. June's boyfriend arrives just in time to save her and to deflect the blame away from her.[61] While this narrative, characteristic of Sarno's style, inverts the aggression toward unrestrained female desire and directs it toward the male and a complex set of intertwining erotic relationships, here in the form of the love triangle, its elements as a thriller/melodrama ally it rather closely with the violence of the roughies. The film's press book also reveals that the producer, Premier Pictures Company, headed by New York–based Sam Lake, encouraged selling the film to exhibitors along multiple lines of interest, as the promotional suggestions bear out:

AUDIENCES WILL TALK ABOUT:

** New York at night—Greenwich Village scenes
** "MIKE"—and her wild exotic dance of love
** The lovely nudes—artist models
** The deep moving emotions of tender young love
** The violent surprise ending

YOU WILL BENEFIT FROM:

** An adult production with the "European Art Film" look
** Original "new wave" jazz score
** High budget production values—authentic locations
** A proven promotion package[62]

The press book further recommends some "Suggested Catch Lines," which indicate the multiple narrative connotations—nudie cutie, melodrama, action film, "Euro-look" art film—that the film attempted to deploy:

1. She was his student, but he was the master.
2. Artist's conflict: mistress or model.
3. Artists and models . . . nudity an everyday affair.
4. The rewards of love gone wild!
5. The breeding ground of frustrated desires.
6. Posed in innocence . . . trapped in desire.
7. Raw passions painted from the palette of life.[63]

In these proposed taglines were numerous channels of double entendre; most significant is that in its digression from the nudie cutie comedy, the tenor of the film emphasized the dramatic and tragic conclusion. Furthermore, this promotional rhetoric directly addressed the distinctly sexual contexts of the artist model scenario, so blithely glossed over in the nudie cutie films discussed earlier. The seduction of the model by the artist is actually attempted, even if deflected by the rage of a jilted woman, and the sexual desires lurking under the surface of the placid nudie come to the fore in this narrative. As one of many films, in its hybridization of sexploitation's forms, it complicates a pat genealogy of progression from nudies to roughies in one fell swoop. It also evidences sexploitation production to be a sphere of uneven development due to a variety of exigencies of budgeting, production, distribution, and regulation.[64]

Nude in Charcoal also presents the overlap of two different relationships to the screen presence of nudity and a transition from the erotic script of "just looking" to a looking that becomes an occupational and psychosexual hazard—a looking that leads toward violence or the potential manifestation of the sexual act. Another film from this purportedly "end of the nudie" period, Barry Mahon's *Confessions of a Bad Girl* (1965), offers a counterexample and complication. Mahon's film conjoins features of the nudie and artist's model film and the more violent sexual melodrama. A color film, in contrast to the fashion for black and white that took hold for shooting the downbeat roughie, *Confessions* details the working life of a newly arrived young woman, Judy Adams (Judy Adler), to New York City. Judy attempts to learn the ropes of the modeling business, only to discover that to succeed at all, one must be "cooperative," meaning erotically promiscuous and willing to get pawed or sexually propositioned to get or keep the job. Judy's episodic jobs at different venues proceed with customary come-ons and gropings and her eventual begrudging exchanges of sexual favor for work, which are treated with a certain frivolity by

Judy's narration—that is, until Judy gets attacked by a stalker who has been watching her for six months and rapes her at knifepoint, when the tone gets more dour. Extended scenes of posing are interspersed with interludes in which Judy sits at the West Village piers looking at the water and contemplating her life's path. Mahon's fusion of forms of address from the nudie mode and the introduction of sexualized violence in the last act and a melodramatic script that highlights female experience and narration thwarts a discreet taxonomy of sexploitation cycles.

As a consequence, the lineage from nudie cutie to roughie can be organized as much by a set of ruptures as by smooth transitions and commonplace logics about the substitution of violence for the scarcity and prohibitive status of sex itself. Significantly, nudies also did not disappear post 1964; they continued to be produced, albeit in smaller numbers, and to be exhibited alongside roughies and more violent or explicit sexploitation fare exhibiting on the grind house circuit and at drive-ins. These modes also overlapped considerably in their exhibition, with roughies serving to diversify the field of nudie exhibition in the mid-1960s period.[65] For example, *Nude in Charcoal* was in 1964 making its second round in Chicago, playing alongside Doris Wishman's nudist camp travelogue *Playgirls International* (1963) at the Plaza Art Theater. Therefore the vernacular narrative of a dramatic or total shift from nudies to roughies, as seen in contemporary repackagings of sexploitation by video distributors and in fan publications, is overstated. The transition is actually reflective of a broader and more gradual change in sexploitation's representational strategies in the mid-1960s, with the mode of production diversifying to capitalize on different generic formulae and aesthetic styles already circulating in the adult film market.

Sexual Scarcity, Deviant Peepers, and the Dangers of the Erotic Marketplace

The nudie cutie had characterized male desire as motivated by a form of erotic looking, an ironically feeble substitute for erotic (or autoerotic) action. Male characters were libidinally ineffective, bumbling, or impotent. The darker action-oriented films that emerged around 1964 pursued another trajectory in their transformation of male erotic desire into forms of violence, materializing the "repressive hypothesis" in its most fantasmatic forms.[66] The innocently inane male peeper, what Eric Schaefer has called the "schnook in paradise," was refashioned into a neurotic, menacing pervert, a social, criminal and sexual deviant whose response to the erotic mobility of women could only end in a violent denouement. Positing sex within an economy of either scarcity or excess, the affective capital of female sexuality could be broached as either "not enough" or "too much." What the roughie narrative framework also allowed was a focalized interest on female protagonists, introducing female subjectivity, however problematically or perfunctorily, into their stories and anchoring the concerns regarding erotic consumption within a parallel focus on the peddling itself, and locating subjectivity in the erotic female body being sold.

In the former case of the male voyeur reconfigured as deviant, certain films directly articulated this transition toward psychopathology; for example, the film *Strange Compulsion* (1964), directed by Irvin Berwick, presented a story of a frustrated voyeur, Fred (Solomon Sturges, as Preston Sturges Jr.), whose "compulsion" to spy on women was figured as a criminal pathology, for which he receives copious psychoanalysis. The introduction of sexual desire into the act of looking covertly at women in moments of privacy (and nakedness) shifted the tenor of the film toward being a noirish thriller.[67] The trailer for this film proclaimed, "Can he be satisfied with just looking . . . or must he go further with the object of his interest? . . . What is it that separates the mild deviant from a potential killer?" These stentorian assertions are set against scenes shot in high-contrast black and white, as the voyeur graduates from mere peeping to using binoculars to using a camera and, finally, to entering the homes of the women he stalks. The film's exposition posits that the "peeper as pervert's" etiology is rooted in a traumatic childhood event, providing scenes of the voyeur relating his problematic desires to a psychologist. Looking at female nudity becomes a sexual act redolent with violent ramifications, and the sexual script of the film invokes the psychology of sexual impulse drawn far more from Krafft-Ebing's *Psychopathia Sexualis* than from the dry empiricism of the Kinsey Reports.

Other films from this mid-1960s period, such as *Aroused* (Anton Holden, 1966), which detailed the acts of a serial killer who targets prostitutes, and *The Sex Killer* (Barry Mahon, 1967), about a violent peeper who works in a mannequin factory, would also take up the narrative formula of the sexually frustrated everyman turned killer of women—often prostitutes, sex workers, or promiscuous, urban women. The psychopath's crimes occur as a result of both the plenitude of the sexual marketplace and his frustrating social inability to properly gain access to it, a motif that is repeated frequently in many films throughout the decade. One excessive manifestation appears in the form of the protagonist of Michael Findlay's series of films, beginning with *The Touch of Her Flesh* (1967), in which a cuckolded, maimed husband takes sadistic revenge by torturing and killing strippers when he finds his wife in bed with another man.

The sexual marketplace itself became ripe for cinematic exploitation, in a double-edged gesture of both documenting the purported dangers of women seeking some form of economic independence and self-sufficiency and strangely reflecting on the sensationalized drives of the sexploitation industry itself, through explorations of the sex trade. Friedman and Lewis's *Scum of the Earth* took on the operations of an illegal pornography racket as its ripped-from-the-tabloids subject. The "Scum" are a group of four men: Mr. Lang the cigar-chomping boss; Harmon the alcoholic photographer, Larry the high school–aged distributor, and Ajax the resident tough. Their seedy business occurs at a photography studio as they extort and blackmail young women in need of fast cash. After first getting the young models they ensnare to tentatively pose in revealing clothing, they eventually convince them to pose topless, and under duress and manipulation, in sexual congress with the ring's strongman, Ajax. One model, Sandy, wants to get out of the business and, in exchange for being set loose, is enlisted as a "talent scout" who attracts and eases other young girls into the operation in exchange for her absence from the more lurid shoots. The innocent victim is high schooler Kim, eager to make money to be able to afford to go to Craxton College. Kim sinks into a blackmail scheme orchestrated by Mr. Lang and his cronies as the Scum extort exceedingly revealing photos of Kim and threaten to send the photos to her father. Harmon, humanized by Kim's innocence and chasteness, finally rebels, beating Ajax to death in the studio as he begins to attack Kim during a group photo shoot. Sandy pretends she is Kim, who has fled, and testifies to the police in her stead, thus not tarnishing the young girl's name. The film concludes with Mr. Lang, on the run, getting shot on the beach by the trailing cops and with a conversation between Harmon and Kim as he apologizes to her and tells her he is marrying Sandy.

David Friedman, commenting on the film and the inception of the roughies, stated that "the idea was to make them look realistic and gritty, like the old fashioned stag film."[68] Friedman's insistence on the affective associations of black-and-white film stock with stag films, in its invocation of illicit sensations, suggests an intrinsic negotiation with erotic aesthetic conventions—both from the past and contemporaneous to the genre—against which sexploitation would continually define itself. Considering how little actual nudity is presented, *Scum of the Earth* hearkened back as much to the classical exploitation period of filmmaking as to the stag film. As Eithne Johnson and Eric Schaefer have observed, roughies in fact tended to have *less* nudity than nudie cuties.[69] The film's hyping of the spectacle of innocent virgins assailed and predatory degenerates who are a menace to the social order evokes the moral outrage marshaled in the vice and sex-hygiene films of the 1920s, 1930s, and 1940s. *Scum of the Earth* functions as both a melodrama and an action film, in which betrayal and coercion lead to the advocacy of a moral lesson in the defeat of the pornography ring.

The film's anachronistic tendencies in its moralizing tone and content provide a strange synergy with its promotion of a new combination of implied unsavory sex and violence in its narrative. In the absence of nudity, which is fleeting, the film works to imply sexual misdeeds through its dialogue and use of editing. For example, in an early scene, we see Sandy, posing for Harmon, as the resident goon, Ajax, who keeps the women "in line," leers and ogles at the sidelines. Sandy is seen in bra and panties. As she takes off her bra, Harmon gives her a scarf to wear draped over her breasts. As compared with the Bunny Yeager films or any of the many nudie cuties released at this time, this film has almost no nude exposure; nipples are visible for seconds, if at all. Sandy's resistance is registered by her desire to "spill the beans" on the operation someday. Harmon suggests that, after a few "art poses," they get on to shooting the "stuff that sells." The film alternates between medium shots of Sandy and then settles on a reverse shot of Harmon directing her, after she has been presumed to take off the scarf. In the same take, the camera pans from Harmon behind the camera to Ajax's leering gaze as his desires turn aggressive. Ajax gets up and approaches the camera, his torso engulfing the shot and thus conflating Sandy's point of view with that of the film spectator. There is a cut here to a close-up shot of Sandy, seen from the bare shoulders up, as she screams, beseeching Harmon to keep Ajax away from her. Harmon mumbles and turns off the boom light behind him as the scene ends with an abrupt cut. The rape that is implied, and the documentation of it by Harmon's camera, remains in the ellipsis, in the space beyond the frame and in between cuts, filled in by the ominous chamber music that plays as accompaniment. A new formula emerges in scaling back on the nudity to suggest unsavory sexual acts through dialogue and narrative. This disputes a historical narrative of clear teleological progression between cycles toward an ever more explicit destination in screen sex and instead suggests the sexploitation mode as a complex and messy field of calculations and adjustments of its erotic and sexual expressivity.

Scum of the Earth capitalizes on the fears and anxieties regarding the sex trade, manifesting the traditional double speak of the genre in both sensationalistic and judgmental tones. The consumption of sexual images is positioned as a social problem, a problem in which the film spectator implicitly takes part. The opening scene stokes some of American culture's deepest anxieties at the time about the circulation of sexual materials. The scene is organized around a set of shots that efficiently narrate the chain of circulation of the smut ring, as we see Mr. Lang hand off a mysterious folder to a man (later recognizable to us as Ajax) in exchange for a wad of bills. Ajax walks off and peers pruriently into the folder, passing it off to another young man (Larry), who propositions a high school student at the school gate. The customer buys a single piece of "merchandise," and the shot cuts to a close-up as we see his hands open the envelope—inside is a nudie photograph, blurrily registering a topless woman posing. The film freezes its frame on this image as the opening credits roll. Unveiling the fictionalized means of distribution, *Scum of the Earth* figures the smut ring as a viral form yet also constructs a suspenseful narrative out of the concealment and final exposure of the image in the envelope.

What the film also imparts in its persistently antiquated position of the exposure and commercial exploitation of sexuality is a view of female erotic labor that is at odds with the more legitimating discourses of the artist's model films discussed earlier, and without the legal quarantine of the "nude as art" justification. Pitting young women's need for financial independence against a market that can only sufficiently employ them as a form of sexualized labor, the film posits an economy that inevitably turns women's use-value into a form of consumable pleasure for a prurient audience. This audience is largely represented as teenaged boys, as the filmmakers are able to both satisfy and give credence to cultural anxieties regarding access of sexual materials by minors—intimating the "corruption" of minors on both ends of the chain of production/consumption and mirroring the preoccupation in obscenity law with the status of the properly "adult" viewer. Unable to envision a separation of sex from the institutions that would regulate it, such as the family and marriage, the film creates an alternative, underground institution, the studio itself and its phalanx of male bosses and ruffians that attempt to keep Sandy and Kim trapped within it. The suspense generated by the tension between private and public, between the family and the independence of life outside it (college, adulthood, economic autonomy), is dramatized by the means through which Kim's virtue is threatened by her father's potential discovery of her nude photos.

The hyperbole of the film's positioning of the sex trade climaxes in a confrontation between Kim and Mr. Lang. Lang responds to Kim's desires to quit modeling with a furious diatribe as the camera cuts to closer and closer images of his sweaty upper lips and his glinting gold teeth: "All you kids make me sick . . . down inside you're dirty. You're damaged merchandise and this is a fire sale! You're a hypocrite! . . . Now little Miss Muffet, you do what I tell you!" In a sense, this barrage is a moment of direct

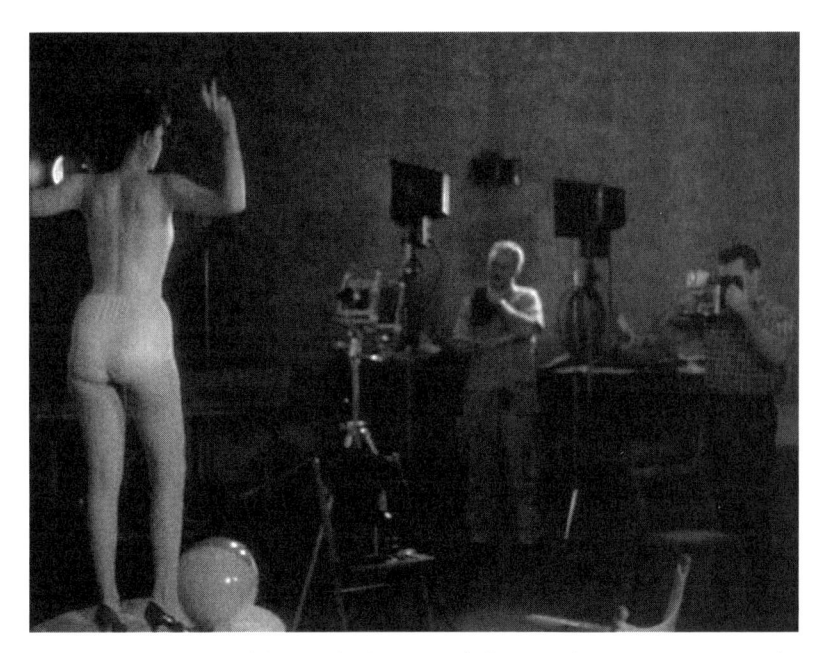

FIGURE 18. In *Scum of the Earth*, the scene of photographic capture turns on the blackmail of Kim.

address, less to Kim or the other models than to the viewer himself. The speech, which operates as an entry into the metaphoric "belly of the beast" of the smut ring, is an indictment of the audience—the implied analogues to the high school boy who in the beginning buys the erotic photograph in that first represented chain of circulation. There is a masochistic quality to *Scum of the Earth* that takes its most pointed form in this moment, as the viewer is taken to task for his inappropriate desires, desires that fuel the underground trade in the tears and fortunes of young girls' dreams, or so the film would tendentiously have it. Yet the Sturm und Drang of innocence defiled is also already positioned as an in-the-know narrative cliché by the film. The roughie, as emblematized by *Scum of the Earth*, emerges as a deeply conflicted subgenre in which the spectator is necessarily implied and indicted in a pursuit of the sexual commodity.

Rape, abduction, torture, sadism, and other forms of sexualized, violent action were the stock in trade of these dark, rough-hewn films. In their discourses on sexuality, the roughies also explicitly addressed these relations of power, dominance, and submission in the context of a cultural revaluation of conventional gender roles. Meyer's *Lorna*, made in 1964, is a film that also marked the shift toward a more brutal landscape of gender and sexual relations in sexploitation at large and in Meyer's work specifically, following on his color nudie cuties such as *Eve and the Handyman* (1961) and *Wild Gals of the Naked West* (1962). *Lorna* wove a modern-day morality tale set in a backwoods southern town. Lorna's unsatisfied and "wanton" sexual desires are put into conflict with the incapacities of her doting husband as the film becomes a tragic fable of the consequences of his failed masculinity, which lead to adultery and death. Lorna, whose eroticism is conflated discursively with her curvaceous physicality—the advertising copy for the film states she is "too much for any man!"—is a bored housewife who falls in love with an escaped convict who rapes her as she listlessly wanders the fields near her home. In the classic patriarchal fantasy of rape, Lorna's acquiescence, her transition during the rape from protest to pleasure, permits the film to present the rape as the materialization of her own unconscious wishes.[70] The convict's aggressive sexuality is visually and editorially contrasted with the soft, "sissified" demeanor of Lorna's husband Jim. The film climaxes with a violent confrontation between Jim and the convict as the husband comes home from work at the salt mines after a fight with his coworker, the grizzled, licentious, and whiskey-swilling Luther, who has impugned Lorna's marital virtue. The convict is waiting in their dilapidated shack to attack Jim. After a struggle with a large industrial hook hanging from the rafters, Lorna saves her husband yet perishes herself, along with her rapist-lover, with Jim sobbing "please forgive me!" over Lorna's impaled body.

Using a framing device to introduce the viewer to the adulterous scenario of this southern gothic melodrama, the film opens with a mobile point-of-view shot, taken from a camera mounted on a car driving down a rural town road. Its path is intercepted by a fire and brimstone–spewing preacher, who directly warns the spectator that he is entering a dangerous immoral world. The preacher invokes biblical doctrine: "Thy heart is filled with carcasses and dead men's bones! . . . Who will rise against the evildoers? Judge and so shall you be judged. . . . Pass on but there is no return." Dramatizing the spectator's oscillation between desire and discernment, the direct address inscribes a parodic religiosity into sexploitation's dynamic of display and denial. Invoking yet simultaneously mocking the faux-educational tone of classical exploitation films, this opening oratory and the return of the preacher to invoke Sodom and Gomorrah and Lot's wife are, by 1964, as much a lampooning of the hypocrisy of religious judgment as a device of narrative framing that allows the film to function as an allegorical tale removed from contemporary life. As the mobile view from the vehicle glides into town, the viewer moves into a space defined by parable, existing outside of present time.

The second framing mechanism is oriented by the commentary of the husband's two salt miner coworkers. In their overheated ogling and eventual assault of a local woman in the first minutes of the film, they instill a sense of voyeurism that threatens to abandon distanced detachment. This assault and rape serves as a prelude to both the imbrication of repressed desire and its unleashing in manifestations of violence that will follow. Luther's beating and rape of a local woman, Ruthie, after she meanders drunkenly to her meager rural home is authenticated by shots of his sidekick, Jonah, peering through the window, watching the attack in a diagram of homosocial enjoyment. Emerging from Ruthie's shack after she has been bloodied, her clothes torn off, and left clutching the mattress in despair with a bruised face, Luther announces that the woman he really wants is the unattainable Lorna. Luther and Jonah function as embodiments of a sordidly prurient masculinity, emblematizing the extremes of the confrontation with a female sexuality made visible and public, one vector of the limits of a male "desire to see" transforming into a "desire to do." Yet they also represent a homosocial model of masculinity, in which the relations between men are given primacy over those with women.

We are thus introduced to Lorna and her desires through the perspective of these male characters who embody the extremes of sexual impulse that can only be spoken through forms of debasement. The next means of framing the viewer's access to Lorna is taken from the vantage point of her insufficiently masculine, or rather improperly masculinized, husband. Jim's bodily comportment recalls that of a *Physique Pictorial* model. His tight jeans, muscled body, slicked hair, "pretty" baby face, and soft-pitched voice all signify a not-so-buried queerness, his corporeal performance signaling a concern with surface that is suspect. The characterization of Jim is central to Meyer's hierarchy of proper and improper modes of male gender identity. When Jim catches sight of Lorna settling to sleep, he approaches for a conjugal visit. He sidles up against Lorna, asking, "Lorna . . . do . . . you . . . want . . . to . . . ," yet the lack of urgency in his demeanor indicates passivity and implicit weakness. Lorna begrudgingly wakes, allowing him to have sex with her. The camera pans away from the bed and tracks slowly to the window curtain cued to the sounds of Jim's "feminized" erotic breathing. The breeze palpitating the white speckled curtain substitutes for the off-screen sex, undulating in the night's light. The domestic space is the site of Lorna's dissatisfaction as she asks, "Jim, could you . . . ?" Jim "finishes" before she is able to express her desire for erotic fulfillment. Jim's final gasping emission signals the end of sex on the sound track as Lorna rises out of bed nude and walks to the window, the lines of her darkened silhouette lit from the night illumination of the window frame.

The first sustained expression of Lorna's subjectivity is rendered through an interior monologue and flashback construction as she goes outside to contemplate the state of her married life. Lorna reflects in voice-over on how her husband is unaware of her needs: "Is it me? Why can't I tell him what's wrong? I'm a woman, not just a tool." Lorna's voice is accompanied by a montage of images as she contemplates the day Jim proposed to her and the potentiality his more ardent desire then expressed, in which their garments, Jim's military jacket and Lorna's cardigan sweater, lying on the grass, become the index of a lost sexual promise and of their proper gender roles. Lorna's eroticized physicality is associated with the pulsing rhythms of the natural world, particularly water, as she comments on the "thrilling ache inside of me" upon their first erotic encounter. Meyer uses a gelled lens and alternates between low-angle shots of Lorna standing on her porch in the moonlight and her reflection in the water. Lorna's scene concludes with her fantasy of living not in this backwater town but in a big city, in which her subjectivity is allied more overtly with the film spectator's desires and with an urban space. Lorna imagines herself as we see an extended montage of her dancing topless, shaking and jiggling like a burlesque star, superimposed over canted images of flashing marquees and bright lights.

The elucidation of Lorna's erotic needs is further extended and overlaid with a voyeuristic impulse in scenes of the following day, as Lorna "strikes" in her role as a housewife in retaliation for Jim's insensitivity in bed and refuses to wake or prepare breakfast or lunch for him. Lorna wanders into the woods and takes a swim in the nude, slowly exploring the barren fields and wooded lake around her. Lorna's naked form is shot from behind through a veil of trees as she wades in to skinny dip and her body is reflected in the water. These scenes keep a camera distance of medium to long shots, framing Lorna within this natural environment from an observer's distance. The approach of the convict who has escaped from a nearby prison is crosscut with Lorna's peaceful reverie, which sets the editorial tension and suspense of the scene through Meyer's sharp editing style. Lorna's placid relationship to her environment is thus juxtaposed with the convict's feverish and frenzied movement through reeds and across roads, as his hydraulic aggression is associated, through the parallel editing, with the eventual destination of his energies: Lorna. This scene in many ways recalls the environment of the rape scene in Ingmar Bergman's *The Virgin Spring* (1960), with a more salacious, explicitly sexual undertone.

The rape is represented both from the convict's point of view and from Lorna's as he heaves above her, linking the spectator, at least in part, with

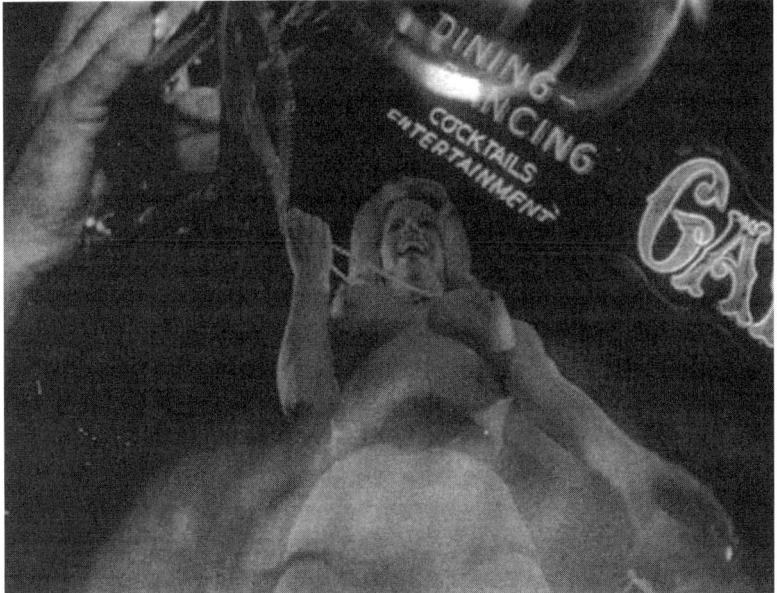

FIGURE 19. Superimpositions articulate Lorna's interiority, her longing for urban pleasures, while also presenting her as "cantilevered" spectacle in Russ Meyer's *Lorna*.

Lorna's perspective. The rape becomes the pivotal event of the film as it restructures the narrative toward a model of competing timelines allied with competing masculinities. The film becomes a parable of homosocial relations far more than male and female heterosexual relations, as Lorna perishes due to her constraints by both marriage and the discipline and subservience that the convict's needs demand. In the end, Lorna's desires, which the film certainly legitimates and visualizes metaphorically, can't be fulfilled by any single man. But narratively, she must perish, moving from a site of excess to a "scarce resource" made inaccessible, an object that eludes possession. The soothsayer/preacher returns to deliver the moral lesson at the end of the film, yet again chiding the spectator for his desires. In keeping with Meyer's characteristic mode of irony, the preacher is parodic, his entreaty to heed the call of biblical doctrine utterly at odds with the dramatic action that has transpired within the film. At the same time that the spectator is addressed through this narrational device, the mode of address is itself registered as a failure, analogous to the failure of a proper masculinity to consume female sexuality properly.

Lorna, told through the lens of a traditional story of betrayal and recompense, represents the shifting topography of sexual relations in the genre as well as introducing a female protagonist and point of view as an emerging staple. Other early roughies managed their reconfigured narrative content through devices and conventions culled from literary and filmic traditions of the past. As "consuming sex" became a problem that sexploitation films could address or solve through other variations and instantiations of "consuming sex," certain roughies attempted different means of narrating illicit sexual economies, in which sex is bought, wrested, or divested from its "owner" in more aggressive fashion.

The Defilers, like *Lorna*, established a set of framings for seeing nudity in the context of brutal situations of rape and abduction. Also produced by Friedman, the object of the film's consternation pointed as much to the ideological strains of the past as to the present. In the film, two young men who are beatnik types get tired of their affluent and leisurely lives of carousing with various willing girls and consequently hatch an abduction scheme to heighten their "kicks." *The Defilers* was a hybrid of Alfred Hitchcock's *Rope* (1948) and of John Fowles's novel *The Collector* (1963), which had been released the same year, 1965, in a film adaptation with direction by William Wyler. *The Defilers* articulated a growing skepticism and critique of an encrypted youth cultural indulgence, materializing the modern horror of youthful ennui in a plot that indicts the homosocial activities of Carl and James. The film gives primacy to the characteristic "hepcat" speech popularized by the commodification of beat culture in the late 1950s and early 1960s in films such as *The Beatniks* (Paul Frees, 1960) and *The Subterraneans* (Ranald MacDougall, 1960), and there is a way that the film presages later sexploitation film's fascination with and voyeuristic relationship to the sexuality that exuded from mid- to late-1960s youth culture.[71] Carl (Byron Mabe) is the dominant sadist and hedonist who engineers an abduction of a young hopeful starlet from Minnesota—the film slowly unveils his violent leanings as a beach excursion with a group of girls turns volatile when Carl bites a girl he is fondling.[72] Carl's first monologue on the beach establishes his distaste for "easy" pleasures as he lectures James on the benefits of seeking sensation without bounds: "Females have one function in life, to give men pleasure. . . . The only thing in this crummy square infested life that counts is KICKS!" The leaden irony of *The Defilers* counts on the (male) viewer's acknowledgment and lamentation that sexual activity is a ready "resource" that James and Carl have access to, yet is one that is supplanted, considered "not enough" for these young degenerates. Thus the dangerous appetites of Carl's sexuality are redirected toward a "blood lust" and interest in staging the scene of his own masculinist power. Figuring a misogynistic masculinity that is both deviant in a psychosociological sense and inherently insatiable (the trope of insatiability would be later deployed by sexploitation and hard-core in representations of female protagonists), the film creates a tension between Carl's sadistic drive and James's eventual moral self-reckoning. One scene in which Carl and James stalk and kidnap Jane (Mai Jansson), the innocent out-of-town girl who has come in hopes of making it in Hollywood, follows a trajectory that begins with voyeurism and ends with her abduction. James and Carl spy on Jane through the blinds of the living room window as she undresses in front of the TV for a bath. They move to peeking at her in the tub through the bathroom window (the nude bathing scene a staple of sexploitation from the nudies to the late 1960s) before they entice her the following day to come to a "real" Hollywood party. The peeping is thus "foreplay," a prelude to the "action"—kidnapping, nonconsensual sex, beatings. The "party" is in a graffitied basement warehouse owned by Carl's rich father as Carl strips and spanks Jane with his belt, exclaiming that "you belong to us, body and soul!"

The narrative of kidnapping and possession seems a return to the preoccupations of the classical exploitation film, although the individuation of perversion is divested from a larger identifiable "social problem." In the context of the mid-1960s and the emergent challenges proto-feminist discourses were posing to a misogynist order, the narrative of sexual ownership, the wresting of possession of female desire back into the hands of men, seemed "a return of the (barely) repressed" within an imagined masculine subjectivity.[73] This is not to say that a roughie like *The Defilers* was an "accurate" depiction of male psychology but that the cycle permitted the articulation of a fantasy of resistance to the rising independence of women in the public sphere. The film, while offering spectacles of female degradation—signaled by Jane's sullied and puffy face, streaked with makeup—is simultaneously contemptuous of Carl and James's luxury of free time and their malignant plethora of erotic boredom, and in that sense an older "productivist" economy of sexuality leaves a trace on the film's resolution, in which Carl is killed by James, his better conscience. Carl's pathological sexuality is linked with his failed identity as a productive worker as he leeches off the privileges of his family fortune.[74] Carl's perversion, at the same time that it models a traditionally patriarchal relationship between men and women, also has a residue of homosexual etiology, in which, much like *Lorna*'s male characters, the "problem" of the narrative is one that resides in the failures of masculine identity to make sense of a new arena of heterosexual relations and a changing landscape of sexual commodity. Carl and James, bored with the "free sex" they are getting from numerous willing female partners, must return and restage a drama of sexuality that is contingent on their reinstated power, a drama that depends on sexuality as a scarce resource that must be seized and re-possessed.

The Defilers, in visualizing the sexual psychopath, treads across the criminological discourses about sex crimes in postwar America. Estelle Freedman explains that changing social and legal responses to the category of the sex offender expressed less a concern for the guarding of female virtue than a renegotiation of the object of male sexual "perversions." She writes regarding public discourses in the 1950s that

> the response to the sexual psychopath was not then, a movement to protect female purity; its central concerns was male sexuality and the fear that without the guardianship of women, either men's most beast-like sexual desires might run amok, or men might turn their sexual energies away from women entirely. Adult women were now suitable objects for "normal" male sexual desire, even normal male aggression, but the discourses on the psychopath mapped out two new forbidden boundaries for men: sex with children or with other men.[75]

The homosocial bond between Carl and James resonates with Freedman's contextualization as the connotations of the beatnik, bachelor, and rich spoiled young man—each with its own historically specific implications—return to the specter of gay desire, a sentiment best expressed between these two characters in their final fight to the death.[76] The film wants to have it both ways. It explicitly details the newly legitimated aggression then claimed to be at the root of male sexuality when defined by a heterosexual sphere of desire, in which rape is a less heinous problem than child molestation. But it also mobilizes shock and outrage in the "defilement" of female purity itself as one of its contradictory lures.

The refigured "bachelors" Carl and James represent the utmost extreme of a consumerist economy of erotic self-fulfillment, in which individual gratification inevitably transforms into a death drive. This motif both intersects with contemporaneous generic developments in figuring masculinity in the teenpic of the 1950s, the biker film, made emblematic by Marlon Brando and James Dean, and which will soon take on countercultural affiliations with the biker exploitation cycle, as well as through the articulations of masculine identity, sadomasochistic violence, and gender performance then emerging in avant-garde films such as Kenneth Anger's *Scorpio Rising* (1963). By framing Carl and James's pathological detour into kidnapping, rape, and torture as the aftermath of a dissatisfaction with the free availability of hetero sex in the frolicking scenes on the beach and in their apartments, the film posits their pathology as a potential "aftermath" of sexual liberalization, in which a new economy of sexual access and the loosening of erotic restraints lead to violence, a moral unraveling that also provides spectatorial pleasure from a distance. The film also sets the stage for a paranoid fantasy of the erotic future in which such economistic models of sexual availability ricochet—in which "free" sex in one form necessitates "enslaved" sex in another.

The Defilers posters and promotional materials combined the promise of sex with shock horror tactics, with taglines blaring, "Everything they touch is stained!" "A Shattering Study of the Shameless Sick Set for Shock-Proof Adults!" and "Seen! Savored! Snatched! Strapped . . . !" with a stark drawing of a dismembered hand superimposed over a variety of images of Mai Jansson in states of sullied degradation and dishabille.[77] This disembodied hand, which graphically becomes the metonym for defilement, also articulates a logic of substitution that governs the roughie in the mid-1960s—the hand a vehicle for touch and erotic contact (as well as for labor) is mobilized as a Frankensteinian motif of a horrific leisure class, an agent of violent molestation severed from an accountable body. The image of the creeping hand thus allows defilement to stand in for the sense of a forbidden erotic tactility.

These roughie narrative premises of masculinity's fundamental malfeasance in the face of sexual liberalization had a long tail well into the late 1960s. But it is interesting to consider the perspective of a female

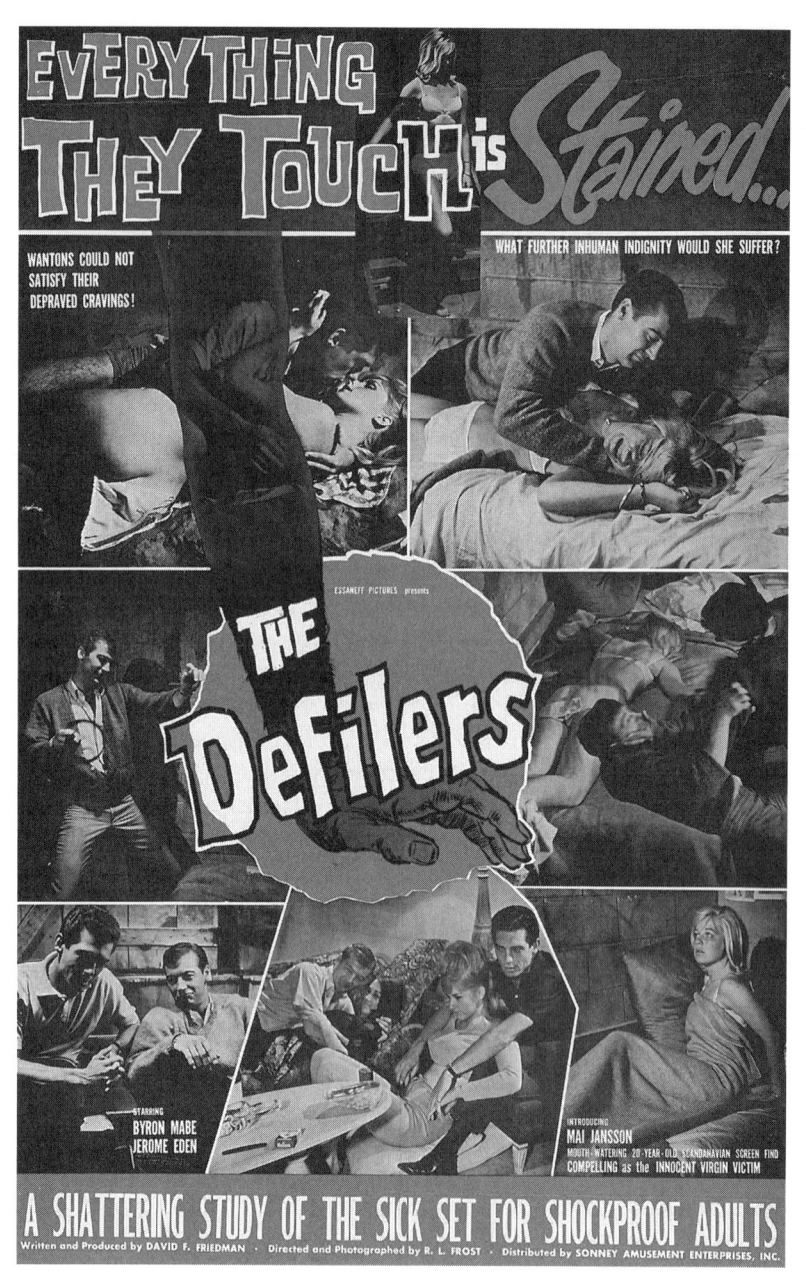

FIGURE 20. In *The Defilers* poster, the horrific severed arm dramatizes the violent, psychopathic potential of a homosocial leisure class.

directorial voice on the emergent narrative forms of the transforming sexploitation film. Doris Wishman was one of the only women directing sexploitation films in the 1960s; she began her career making nudist camp films and nudies, later becoming one of the most prolific American female filmmakers of the postwar period.[78] Her roughie *Bad Girls Go to Hell* offers an alternative mapping of the "rape script" so prevalent in these formative roughies, of violence rendered as specifically sexual violation so readily employed as a narrative arc in *Scum of the Earth, Lorna*, and *The Defilers*.[79] *Bad Girls Go to Hell*, like *The Defilers*, also centers on a young woman's flight to the city, yet without the glimmer of promised fame implied by Mai Jansson's dashed Hollywood dreams. Wishman's mid-1960s films reflect a counterpoint to the male-authored narratives of betrayal and recompense so popular in the early roughies made by men, with the rape occurring as the catalyst rather than the outcome of narrative action. In this sense, the logic of plotting upends some of the characteristic structures of suspense's sexualization in the mid-1960s sex films. In *Bad Girls*, Wishman's heroine, listless Boston housewife Meg Kelton (Gigi Darlene), is sexually assaulted by the janitor in her apartment building and kills him in self-defense, then runs away to New York City, ashamed and afraid of the consequences of her actions. What Meg encounters in New York is no different from what she has escaped as a cyclical pattern of come-ons and attempted sexual engagements ensue with each person, male or female, who takes her in—the nice man in the park turned abusive alcoholic in private, the amorous lesbian bohemian, the married couple whose husband attempts to rape Meg. The only relationship that yields genuine feeling is Meg's brief encounter with the arty Della, whom she admits to loving but insists on leaving the next morning.

The twist of Wishman's conclusion reinforces the sexual repetitions that Meg cannot escape—she wakes just before she is caught by a detective in New York to realize that it was all a bad dream, yet the exact sequence of events that led to her flight recur, as Meg's husband leaves for work and she gets attacked by the janitor again, returning the viewer in spiraling formation to the opening of the film. Here Wishman's authorial signature is inscribed in the way that the world's sexual exploitation creates a tautological vacuum, a modern horror from which Meg—and implicitly women of the 1960s, both married and single, in public and private spheres—is unable to break out of. In Wishman's rendering, all places, suburban and urban, contain the same threats to female subjectivity and desire. Space and time are reorganized through structural repetition, in which all diegetic locations lead back to the originary site of trauma and sexualized betrayal. The notable exception is the case of

FIGURE 21. Meg's spiraling nightmare of sexual assault captured by Doris Wishman's vertiginous camera, complicating sexploitation's point-of-view structures in *Bad Girls Go to Hell*.

the lesbian encounter with Della; yet Meg's rejection of her hostess here makes Della's solicitation of affection yet another in a series of unwanted advances that threaten her corporeal integrity.

That Wishman prioritizes a female protagonist as the anchor of action—or entrapment and inaction—is also significant, as it shifted its narrative investments toward the experience of temporal traction, seemingly moving forward only to look back. There is an irony and wistfulness in the ways her films articulate the double bind of women's limited agency. Wishman's filmic structure gives Meg the features of both subject and object through this spiraling structure of the dream sequence. Meg sees herself, and we see her, in retrospect, through each repetition, but only too late—as her subjectivity gets split between past and present. In presenting the rape as the structuring violation of the plot, instead of leading up to it, as *The Defilers* or *Lorna* does, Wishman deracinates the reliance of sexploitation on erotic spectacle, even though she too capitalizes on the sexualized exposed body. *Bad Girls Go to Hell* articulates the narrative universe of violation so redolent in the roughie through the pointed, disjunctive perspective of the victim, whose self-exile to the city becomes an inversion of the emergent naïf in the urban paradigm of many other sexploitation films. The absurdist logic of the dream sequence only serves to reinforce the futility of any attempt to escape, a retort, if not for the location of this filmic object, akin to the looping, reflexive structures and grim paradigms of an existentialist modernism on evidence in Bergman's *Persona* (1966) or the identity games of John Frankenheimer's *Seconds* (1966).

Bad Girls Go to Hell and many of Wishman's films from this period, such as *The Sex Perils of Paulette* (1965), *Another Day, Another Man* (1966), *My Brother's Wife* (1966), and *Indecent Desires* (1968), explored the plight of women in social systems they could not entirely gain control of and sought the articulation of a female voice.[80] While Wishman was an exception in a predominantly male industry, sexploitation films of the mid-1960s as a whole did become more preoccupied with female experience in contemporary American life, shifting gears from the nudie's pinup aesthetic and diversifying away from narratives of merely sexual violence at the hands of deranged males. The mode's construction of sexual melodrama derived in large part from the predicaments of women in quandaries of suburban ennui, on one hand, and challenges of urban life and work, on the other. In the latter half of the 1960s, sexploitation films' tone begins to shift toward a less burdened moral economy—a reflection of industrial necessities and forms of competition in the film marketplace—and the lifting of some prohibitions on content. The following chapter considers this transformation and the directions sexploitation films take in exploring these subjects, along with sexual "deviations" and "perversions," as they simultaneously give way to a soft-core ethos of simulation and give more diegetic space to the sex act itself.[81]

CHAPTER THREE

Girls with Hungry Eyes
Consuming Sensation, Figuring Female Lust, 1965–1970

Early- to mid-1960s sexploitation cinema established an economy of looking organized around male desire, articulated through a dialectic of prohibition and license. The innocuous and comic nature of the nudies introduced the novelty of the erotic marketplace's new "freedom to look," which, within a few years, transitioned into a more violent sublimation of sexual energy with the production of the art cinema–inflected black-and-white roughies and sex melodramas. A growing market for adult fare was emboldened by high court decisions such as *Jacobellis v. Ohio* (1964), which involved Louis Malle's *The Lovers* (1958) and circumscribed the truly obscene within the domain of "hard-core pornography." In the wake of the retreat of state censorship practices and the striking down of prior restraint (1965), sexploitation films inched further from covert to overt sexual representation. This chapter considers the representational politics of the cinema of the mid- to late 1960s as the films' sexual ideologies moved from an economy of "seeing sex" closer to an ethos of "doing sex," expanding their representational repertoire.

Although emboldened by a liberalizing trajectory in American culture, sexploitation films expressed deep ambivalence about social change. Representationally, women were introduced as agents into the economy of erotic exchange in the evolving film cycles of the mid- to late 1960s. As the previous chapter's discussion of *Lorna* (Russ Meyer, 1964) and *Bad Girls Go to Hell* (Doris Wishman, 1965) makes clear, sexploitation cinema imagined the experience of women as they contended with the possibility of erotic and economic autonomy. The films began to rely on melodramatic narrative formulas, mixed with action, to track women's psychological and physical ensnarement in vice syndicates and systems of underground exploitation, yet they also refracted changing imaginaries around female desire and independence. While the nudies and early roughies prioritized the facilitation and production of male erotic frustration as a condition of their status as consumers in a changing sexual marketplace and social order, the development of characters such as Lorna, in the film's suggestion of her nagging desire for greater erotic fulfillment, or in the listless energy of the bored Meg, left to her own devices after her husband goes to work, indicates an altering representational horizon as sexploitation began to contend with, rather than merely capitalize upon, its sensational female bodies. Taking a more explicitly sexualized cast in the latter half of the decade, sexploitation films shifted the problem of "consuming sex" more forcefully into the province of female desire and social experience, complicating the dynamics of the gawker and voyeur seen in the early-1960s nudies and bestowing the mantle of sexual interest and curiosity to female protagonists and observers. Encounters with eroticized "others"—particularly with the figure of the lesbian, brothel madam, or sex worker, as well as with alternative social and cultural formations and spaces—could serve to initiate the female naïf so central to the diegetic formulas of sexploitation into the pleasures, profits, and risks of carnality outside of the institutional bonds of marriage and family. But she would nevertheless remain embedded in the conditions of a mercantile capitalism.

Working It / Sex Hunger

The sexploitation film took up wider discourses surrounding women's experience in American life, particularly in love and in labor, and their narratives reflected a sustained consideration of the double binds of female sexual subjectivity. These elements were already clearly in place in a number of the films that established early hallmarks of the sex melodrama variant of mid-1960s sexploitation, including the earlier mentioned *The Dirty Girls* (Radley Metzger, 1965) and Joe Sarno's *Sin in the Suburbs* (1964). Diagramming on one hand a cosmopolitan erotics organized by a trade in female erotic labor—in Metzger's examination of the lives of two call girls, one in Paris and one in Munich—and on the other a script of suburban erotic boredom that leads to an alternative economy of sexual commerce in the form of the anonymous, masked sex swap, exemplified in Sarno's sultry Long Island minimalism, these films' dramatic investment in the conditions of women's erotic identity was notable, expressing a psychological sensitivity largely unseen in other sexploitation films. Suggesting two routes toward this new thematic terrain, and two distinct strata of budgeting, with Metzger working on the higher and Sarno on the lower end, both filmmakers sought to titillate by presenting previously hidden, illicit sexual activities exposed to the light of day by their brands of sexual realism and melodrama. At the same time, these films elaborated the inner lives of their female protagonists, not just the material trappings of their sexual and social bondage. For example, in *Sin in the Suburbs,* Geraldine (Audrey Campbell), a suburban mother, begins to dip her toe into swinging and adultery with her fellow lonely and bored neighbor Lisa. Geraldine entertains neighborhood men at home, while her husband, like Lisa's, perennially works late in the office. Her adolescent daughter Kathi (Alice Linville) walks in on one of her mother's indiscretions, running off into the arms of divorcée neighbor Yvette (Dyanne Thorne), who seduces her. Female sexual ennui and self-discovery motivate mother's and daughter's entanglements. The housewives are easy prey to a masked swapping ring engineered by Yvette and her creepy "brother" Louis, who acts as the master of ceremonies. Sarno layers the suburban women's intersecting stories of desire, lust, and boredom upon the mutual discovery of mother and daughter participating in the sex club ritual. Despite the sensationalist plot, Sarno's steady pacing, attentive focus on the performative affects of dissatisfaction and longing, and dramatic emphasis prioritize female characters, their spaces, and their desires amid the stifling climate of postwar repression and the limiting avenues of suburban domesticity.

In this sense, Sarno's and Metzger's films point to two pervasive trajectories of female subjectivity and personification we see emerge in 1960s sexploitation, the urban working girl or sex worker and the nymphomaniac wife or suburban woman who, in the absence of paid work, generates alternative affective currencies and systems of exchange—adultery, swinging, swapping. These two directions often intersected, for example, in Sarno's *Moonlighting Wives* (1966) and *Anything for Money* (1967) and in varied films, such as *One Naked Night* (Albert T. Viola, 1963), that trace the itinerary of women moving from small towns and suburbs to the city, one of the most common tropes in sexploitation narratives. We see it too in Mahon's *Confessions of a Bad Girl* (1965), discussed earlier, in which Judy Adams must come to understand what "cooperation" as a working nude model means, in yet another reflexive rendering of the modeling industry as a form of erotic labor. That film indulged the spectator with "documentary" scenes of nude posing but tempered it with Judy's voice. After a stalker rapes Judy, she sits by the piers on the West Side, a mise-en-scène of dereliction and abandonment. Her voice-over laments an equivalence between her posing work, its demands for sexual favors, and its dangers: "He only did by force what others did with their promises or their money. . . . I got what I deserved."

Sexploitation films deployed and were no doubt impacted by a perv

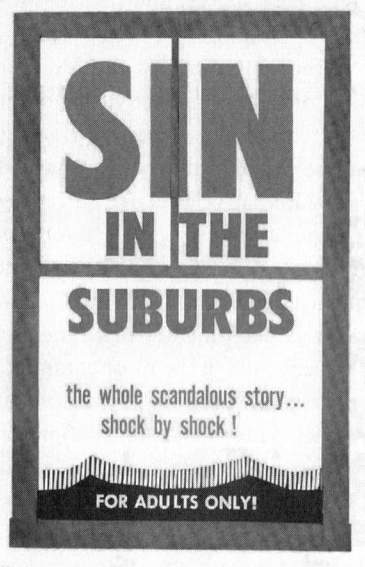

FIGURE 22. Joe Sarno's *Sin in the Suburbs,* in its story of suburban women's erotic boredom and an illicit sex club, highlighted relationships and exchanges between women.

model of female subjectivity in the 1960s: the figure of the single working girl. Helen Gurley Brown's *Sex and the Single Girl* (1962) was instrumental in this regard—a best-selling advice book written for young professional women who were seeking economic, sexual, and romantic fulfillment.[1] Brown exhorted women to embrace their status as sexual beings, to use the office as a place to date and to flaunt their assets, to consider sex as a province of female pleasure, and to treat relationships with often flawed men (be they married or known Don Juans) with equal measures of functional pragmatism as well as with genuine ardor—to sustain their sexiness. In her guidebook and call to arms for average women, whom she called "mouseburgers," Brown encouraged both an industrious practice of the female self and a refusal of sanctimony that would demand that women be arbiters or keepers of sexual morality. Acquiring romantic and sexual experiences, much like acquiring skills for a job, provided the requisite "training" as well as hedonic practice that would prepare the single girl for finding a romantic mate and, later, marriage, if not in her twenties, then surely by the late thirties, as it had for Brown.[2] Hilary Radner suggests that Brown's Single Girl "emerged as the new feminine ideal of consumerism."[3] As a working girl whose identity was defined by the workplace and pursuit of a career rather than by an exclusive interest in reproduction and family, Radner posits the Single Girl as a figure who could put sex itself "to work" as a means toward attaining pleasure. The Single Girl could use a "technology of sexiness" to further a potential, though not inevitable, "marriageability," in which

> sexual expertise replaces virginity as the privileged object of exchange outside the law of the family. The seeming contradiction between sex as pleasure and sex as capital is not addressed. For the Single Girl, sex as pleasure, her practice, is her capital.[4]

While similarly conflating the function of pleasure and the necessity of independent capital, sexploitation films negotiated the figure of the single girl as one still connected to, or at odds with, patriarchal institutions, particularly in the cosmopolitan urban sphere. For sexploitation films, the distinction between the working girl and the sex worker was a permeable zone as the former edged into the latter with great alacrity in their narratives. The expanding range of roughies often placed the single girl, aspiring to be a legitimate working girl, on an incontrovertible path to becoming a sex worker, ensnared by cynically exploitive systems of labor. In this formula of aspirations deflected, female desire for psychic and economic autonomy is rerouted, as the only capital that a woman could employ was her body, her only currency her sexuality. This was sexploitation's iteration of the double binds and ambivalences that inhered in the sexual revolution, the films luridly giving voice to the conflict, expressed by other means in Brown, between pleasure and capital, liberation and entrapment.

The mid-1960s sexploitation film thus treated the character of the working girl—usually the average woman turned unwitting prostitute or escort or shuttled into some other form of erotic labor—with certain ambivalence. This figure was perennially negotiating between normative male heterosexual desire, as a sexual object and locus of spectacle, and a budding self-determination, as a sexual subject that activated the narrative drive of the films. The complexity of that sovereignty was also tensed between her emergent erotic needs and economic self-sufficiency. Many films from the mid-1960s onward would take up this imagination of female sexual hunger as narrative driver, pursuing the consequences of desire unrepressed, at times with ritualistic or sadomasochistic inflections.

What thus emerged was the problem of a specifically female sexual dissatisfaction, rendered through the characterization of women's voraciousness and "mounting sex hunger," as described by Betty Friedan's 1963 feminist text *The Feminine Mystique*—another watershed for understanding the contemporary specificity of women's daily lives in this moment. Giving voice to sentiments seen in comparable form in Brown's advice book, *The Feminine Mystique* instead focused on women who were negotiating their dissatisfaction as a condition of their roles as child rearers and homemakers.[5] Friedan observed that, for these women, sexuality was the grounds upon which female identity was necessarily forged and the metric of their primary value. Her trenchant critique unveiled a popular culture in which "the image of males lusting after women gave way to new images of women lusting after males."[6] This hyperbolic imaginary of an overwhelming female lust was being borne out quite manifestly in the alteration of sexploitation's representational practices—Friedan could just as easily have been talking about any number of sexploitation films when she wrote of women's pressured status and their image as "aggressive sex seekers, sex creatures."[7] As sexploitation cycles and styles developed and proliferated in the mid-1960s, in concert with changing obscenity standards, films began to place more emphasis on the nature of female desire, its unlimited potential for deviance, disruption, and excess, with titles themselves articulating this dynamic—*My Body Hungers* (Joe Sarno, 1967), *I Crave Your Body* (Abe Lutz, 1967), *The Pleasure Lovers* (Charles Saunders, 1959/1964), *Nympho* (Nick Millard, 1965), *Good Time with a Bad Girl* (Barry Mahon, 1967), *Motel Wives* (Adam Clay, 1968), *How* (Don Walters, 1969), and many others. The wildly varied .id- to late 1960s thus witness a broadening of concerns from y male site of perverse aggression, as seen in the degenerate peepers, to renegotiating the relations of *seeing*—and soon, of *doing*—sex and, in the process, challenging the very conditions of sexual visibility.

Indecent Desires: Kink, Sadomasochism, Vice

Rent-a-Girl (William Rose, 1965) (subject of a 1966 Supreme Court of Illinois case discussed in chapter 1) provides one interesting example of a bridge between the general arc of *Scum of the Earth* (Herschell Gordon Lewis, 1963) or *The Defilers* (David Friedman and R. L. Frost, 1965) and a more sexually "modern" narrative that treats the female experience of erotic labor and its exploitation. In it, a young woman, Karen (Barbara Wood), appears relating her tale to a doddering but kindly police officer through an extended flashback. After her boyfriend rejects her sexual advances, Karen, bored and lonely, is lured into posing for nude photographs by her shady neighbors, brother and sister team Adam and Evelyn, who run a modeling agency. Karen is quickly solicited into their organization as their wealthy clients with kinky tastes employ the procured girls, who are in fact call girls, in various fetishistic and sadistic scenarios—we see one woman who works for the service gets sprayed with a water hose by a lecherous old client. Harriet Grant, another wealthy client of the agency, is a noted sadomasochist with a penchant for flagellating her victims. In a climactic party scene, Harriet brands Karen with a hot poker. Soon the tables get turned on the sadist as she is blackmailed and whipped by Evelyn and her lover, Kitten. The film's modification of perspective, through Karen's voice-over, gives narrational authority to the female character, yet at the same time, the film evokes earlier exploitation films that use the defiled young woman as a device, as she recounts her gullible descent into victimization at the hands of an under-the-radar sex trade. Karen's desire for pleasure, which she originally seeks with her disinterested sexually unresponsive boyfriend, leads to punitive consequences by her involvement with her sleazy, exploitative neighbors. Harriet, the sadomasochist character, and Evelyn, the devious neighbor and procurer of girls, indicate sexploitation film's imaginary beginning to identify the locus of perversion within femininity itself, in the intertwinement of the seeking of carnal knowledge and the desire for self-sufficiency, if not profit.

Rent-a-Girl was not the first sexploitation film to feature sadomasochism and scenarios of torture. The thread of these practices and the admixture of cruelty and sexual exploitation saturated many different cycles and subcycles of sexploitation, a common variant and "episode" that could be applied liberally in sexploitation narratives. More generally, the element of violent reprisal and the structuring of narratives around rape were prevalent in roughies like *The Defilers* and *Lorna* and pervaded the entirety of sexploitation cinema—the threshold of consent a permeable and profitable border that could yield great dramatic energy. It also laid the groundwork for the sublimation of sexual energy into scenes of violation and torture. It was in a variation of the roughie form, in what has, largely retrospectively, been termed the "kinky" subcycle, that this sadomasochistic tendency was most prominent. Whereas roughies and kinkies were relatively continuous in terms of their cycles of production in the 1960s, kinkies highlighted sadomasochistic themes, often focusing on perverse or nonnormative sexuality and displacing the sex act onto underground institutions of sexual exploitation. Fetishistic scenarios of submission and dominance further extended the imbrication of sexuality within a marketplace of illicit goods and *occulted* the terms of sexual consumption. The rhetoric of the tabloid exposé, the framework of deviance theory, and the pseudo-scientific examination of the psychosexual all coalesced in kinkies' styles of narration and in their aesthetic imaginaries. Sexual tendencies, tastes, and orientations emerged as a subject problematized in relation to other forms of criminalized, or pathologized, activity—such as prostitution, the drug trade, mob activity, and labor exploitation. Underwriting the kinky was a tone of sober sociological investigation, which bestowed some modicum of defense of its subject matter for bearing some "socially redeeming value," in line with the language of *Roth v. United States* and subsequent obscenity decisions.

White Slaves of Chinatown (1964), directed by Joseph Mawra and written and produced by George Weiss (Weiss was producer of Ed Wood's *Glen or Glenda* [1953]), is an exemplary and definitive film in this regard. It spawned a group of Olga sequels, which resembled episodes in a series, highlighting the primary appeal of the titular dominating brothel madam and drug dealer who runs a dungeon of submissive, opium-addicted girls—*Olga's Girls* (Mawra, 1964), *Olga's House of Shame* (Mawra, 1964), *Madame Olga's Massage Parlor* (Mawra, 1965), and the later *Olga's Dance Hall Girls* (dir. unknown, 1969), made with a different producer, director, and crew.

White Slaves of Chinatown revived the white slavery plot from exploitation films and plays of the teens, such as *Traffic in Souls* (George Loane Tucker, 1913), combining this with a drugs-and-vice angle also culled from classical exploitation films and inflected by the 1930s fallen woman film. The film staged a confrontation between the sexual and political culture of the mid-1960s and an orientalist, moral panic narrative drawn from earlier historical moments. Shot on the streets of New York City, the film often provides a repetitive loop of footage of East Chinatown, particularly around the Bowery, Canal Street, and East Broadway, images scored with "Night on Bald Mountain" by Mussorgsky as well as bombastic kitsch stock "Chinese" music. Replete with opium dens and ethnic hideaways, and peppered with dubious statistics regarding drug consumption, the film exuded Cold War paranoia.[8] The film also drew heavily on the imagery and fantasies resident in 1950s and 1960s fetish magazines, photographs, and pulp novels and their iconic scenarios of submission and dominance, such as the work of bookseller, photographer, and filmmaker Irving Klaw, known for his pinup and bondage photos of Bettie Page, and John Willie, publisher of postwar fetish magazine *Bizarre*. Thus the amalgamation of sexual contemporaneity in the form of the consumer market for kink and sadomasochistic images joined with a willful anachronism deriving from Progressive-era urban vice reform in a heady stew of forceful imagery.

The film opens with images of newspaper headlines, which appear to be from 1930s exploitation road show films, announcing a drug wave sweeping the youth of the nation: "1,000 TEENAGE ADDICTS HERE." Shot silent, using post-synch sound, which was common among the low-budget sexploitation films produced in New York, the film employs fast-paced voice-over narration. The narrator, in classical exploitation mode, warns of the dangers of the opium ring; expounds on captor Olga Saglo's (Audrey Campbell) iron grip on her female captives, who also work as prostitutes; and describes Olga's involvement with the "Syndicate," which has Communist affiliations, as they supply her with drugs in exchange for the money that she makes off the street from her harem. The male narrator is supplemented by Olga's own voice-over articulating her desires and discussing her relationships with her captives. These intimate moments of interiority, shot in her bedroom, position Olga as both hypnotic erotic object and subject, as her narration complements her changing garb for meetings or undressing to go to bed.

As the generic problem of consuming sex had embedded itself in the sexploitation form, *White Slaves* narrated a world in which erotic consumption intertwined with other illegal economies of exchange and forms of corporeal abandon. New York sexploitation regular Campbell (also the lead in *Sin in the Suburbs*), performs Olga with an undemonstrative, icy, and severe style; the role cemented the actress's lifelong association with the character. Regal and reticent, Olga hooks her captives on opium, marijuana, and heroin and pimps them on the streets, taking pleasure in her own empowerment at the expense of her simpering female minions. David Andrews suggests that *White Slaves* transposes the male exploiter of older drug and vice films into a female figure "whose monstrous 'otherness' is a function of her transgressive gender identity."[9] Olga's bisexuality is continuous with this male fantasy of female dominance, and it is one tempered by moments of relative tenderness and intimacy. Such moments serve as interludes from the work of torturing and disciplining her "girls," while also being suggested as one of the strategies for sloughing off her captives' resistance. Many scenes occur indoors in the "dungeon," a dank basement lair with crumbling walls and bare rooms. The expressionistic, Grand Guignol scenes of torture feature sparse, minimally dressed chiaroscuro tableaus, resembling the expressivity of late silent cinema as much as the 1960s present. New girls are punished in the solitary and dank basement of Olga's lair or constrained by various implements—such as stocks, ropes, and hanging devices—their bodies often ornamented by background-cast shadows. In one scene, the camera occupies the point of view of the victim as Olga reaches in to burn her with a cigarette, collapsing the spectacle of the female body's submission with the punishing address to the film spectator caught between erotic relish and dread.

In the subsequent *Olga's Girls*, which spends even more of its screen time in Olga's hideout, the expressionistic capacity of the set and the bare practices of brutalization in the torture devices, including a chastity belt, become forms of corporeal supplication as well as vibratory implements, extracting involuntary convulsions from the bodies of Olga's captives. The British film critic Raymond Durgnat described the scenes in *White Slaves* and *Olga's Girls* with a relish of distaste:

> A nude girl is trussed astride a chair, facing its back, with her wrists handcuffed between her thighs and flogged. Her position possesses certain erotic overtones, but other sequences are even less amiable, notably those on which breasts or ribs are accorded treatment with a spiked vice, or that in which a girl with neck and wrists jammed in a portable pillory device is burned about the breasts with an oxy-acetylene torch. . . . One scene in particular in which a girl is gagged with taffeta, has electrodes affixed to her thighs, and quivers under the electric shock until her ripe breasts are shaken loose from their brassiere, seems to cross whatever frontier exists between libertarian sado-masochism and the pleasures of the OAS.[10]

Highlighting the threshold between sexual connotation and a fiendish interest in screening torture, Durgnat found it difficult to rescue an erotic supplement from these images, even if he recognized their potential to affect a woebegotten, pathetic audience. In his exploration of these films' brand of sadism, Durgnat thus concluded:

FIGURE 23. *White Slaves of Chinatown*'s imperious Madame Olga in an expressionistic composition, torturing a captive.

Olga's Girls will undoubtedly attract not only those spectators that lack the opportunity, but not the will, to actualize their fantasies, but the shy and henpecked, compensating for their plight, or those who see these tortures as expressionistic paraphrase of female sexual response (just as one suspects female spectators saw Errol Flynn's plight on the rack in pirate films as displays of the male physique in sexual tension).[11]

As Durgnat's observations reveal, sexploitation films like *White Slaves* and *Olga's Girls* were negotiating the tricky boundary of indirect forms of using flesh as erotic material, perversely using the as yet prohibitive terms of sexual acts to create images that suggested the paroxysms of sexual pleasure and quivering release unable to be seen through other means and well in advance of the involuntary paroxysms of orgasm as pictured by hard-core pornography.

While detailing the conflicts between the captor and her slaves, *White Slaves* presents Olga's severity of character in mythic, oneiric proportions, primarily through the use of facial close-ups and low-key lighting schemes. Olga alternates between being a mediating figure and an object of desire herself for the addressed spectator, close-ups of her face gazing at the suffering of her girls, punctuating the high-contrast scenes of dungeon torture. These aesthetics orient the viewer in alignment with Olga's gaze, a decided shift from the orientation of other roughies and nudie cuties to a male erotic observer. Olga is also discursively positioned as an insurmountable drive, analogous to the somatic pull of addiction itself—the narrator (Joel Holt) hyperbolizes that "to refuse Olga was to lose your soul!" and that "Olga was not something you could fight!" Shot construction often highlights the fascination the camera has with Olga's staged diabolics, close-ups of her face framed with a brio that could rival a minimalist Josef von Sternberg.

The affiliation with the tantalizing nature of addiction is highlighted by a compensatory logic in which the film supplants the sex act, not only through the torture scenes, but also by substituting the imputed gestures of sexual slackening with the bodily ecstasies of the white slaves' drug highs. In a party scene, introduced as if via diorama framed by a bamboo rolling screen blind, pulled up, the women under Olga's discipline are seen in states of opium- and marijuana-induced rapture, their languid postures and facial expressions suffused with redirected eroticism as they puff cigarettes, roll their eyes, and exhale bounties of smoke. The camera lingers on one actress's legs, clad in black fishnets, as Olga's only male subordinate, a heroin addict named Jimmy, encroaches upon the stockinged woman and begins to kiss her. The cramped space of the drug orgy is described by narration as a space of capture; the narrator's voice intones that all of the girls have "acknowledged Olga as their master," as we see their faces with eyes rolling back and smoke veiling the room and snaking from their half-open, agog mouths. A much later scene with one of the captives, Elaine, after her submission, shows her smoking opium (in cigarette form) in front of a small vanity mirror, the medium close-up on her face reframed by camera movement to expose her partially exposed breasts underneath a cardigan sweater. Elaine's facial laxity and stupefaction are cinematically linked with her erotic pliancy through the shift from her face to her breasts. In another scene, a captive shoots up and then lies down on a basement floor mat, exposing her breasts for the camera. (This is also a strategy taken up in later Olga films, such as *Olga's Girls*.) Addiction and the slack gestures in the body produced by its highs associatively hint at the postures of sexualized arousal.

White Slaves has a disorienting, hallucinatory quality that is facilitated by a disjunction between sound and image, a product of the use of post-synch sound. This financially expedient and circumstantial tech-

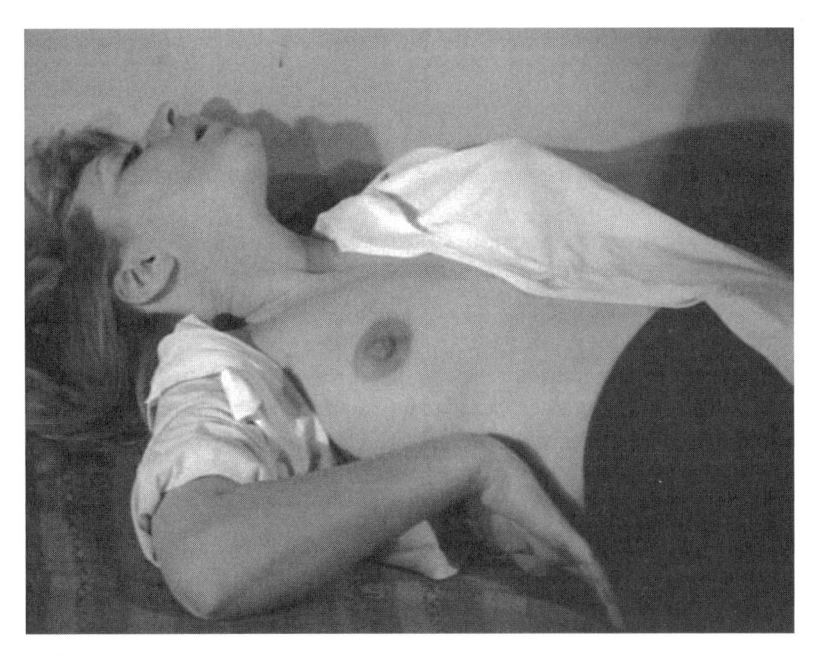

FIGURE 24. A drugged captive convulses, her exposed body insinuating erotic rapture, in *White Slaves of Chinatown*.

nological choice yields an aesthetic depth and element of reflexivity. The visual image does not directly correspond to the details of either mode of narration, creating a conflict between the film's direct address to a pretense of a "citizen-viewer," however makeshift—like the one appealed to in Mahon's *Censored* and many in the pseudo-documentary, sex exposé mode—and the viewer who has come to the theater to see plentiful images of illicit bodies. This willful textual ambiguity, a consequence of budgeting exigency, bifurcates the film's opposing impulses. Akin to the preacher's presence in *Lorna*, the film's pretext of an "aim to educate" ends up as unconcealed irony, producing a gap within which erotic impulse can reside. Such dialectics between pretense and audience desire are hard not to read as the tongue-in-cheek gesture of recognition between filmmaker and audience.

The primacy of sparse mise-en-scène and the shadowy, high-contrast nature of the black-and-white cinematography overwhelm the details of the voice-over narration. *White Slaves* is emblematic of the thin line between aesthetic impoverishment and fevered inspiration. Despite its heavy-handed narration, the film creates a diegetic space of discontinuities and disjunctions between what is heard and what is seen through its lax observance of continuity rules. For example, the narrator's description of the captives' states of feeling sharply conflicts with the actresses' awkward, sometimes amateur performance styles. Such disjunction creates a looseness of description through the overlaps and gaps between image and sound tracks as well as in the at times abrupt transitions between one shot and the next. *White Slaves* exemplifies a problem of visibility that sexploitation, as a narrative form structured around the problem of *seeing sex,* created but also challenged. The contradictory visibility of sexploitation cinema presented a fissure between word and image, between explicitness and innuendo, and between an overweening ideology of residual moral crisis and the excessive visualization of the bodies of sexual "others" (lesbians, women of color, gay men, sexually active women, sex workers, etc.), in the recalcitrance of the bodies that exceeded these discursive frames.

White Slaves, and the Olga films that followed, capitalized as well on the work of exoticism, using ethnic and racial associations to mark off perversion as something linked with an inscrutable foreignness. The anxiety about whiteness in the sexual purity plot of early exploitation cinema was diffused, anachronistically, within a hybrid space—in *White Slaves,* the space of Chinatown coded and overloaded with early-twentieth-century moral panics, but also infused by contemporaneous struggles over racial emancipation. We can understand the film set against a cultural backdrop in which the struggle over racial equality among African Americans was reaching a critical turning point—1964 saw the passage of the Civil Rights Act, born out of the late President Kennedy's policies and also critiqued as insufficient by black civil rights activists. *White Slaves* and the subsequent Olga films, with their retreat to orientalist tropes of the past and their insistence on white women's possible bondage in sexual debt and addiction, seemed to process the contemporaneity of racial relations (and the centrality of an anxiety regarding miscegenation as a key tool in racial segregation) through an anachronistic impulse and a regressive investment in protecting sexual purity. Yet, at the same time, the films spoke to their own moment through a form of redirection, positioning the license and sensation seeking of the youth culture in familiarly moralist terms. In *Olga's Girls,* Olga's lust boils over for a young African American woman named Bunny (Loloni Nocolo), one of her captives, who works double duty as the madam's servant and lover. Bunny suffers some of her greatest tortures, including an extended scene where she waits in a basement cage in a chastity belt. Olga's sexual taste also marks her perversion and her implied "weakness," while allowing a spectatorial voyeurism upon racialized bodies.

In the final shots of *White Slaves,* Olga has managed to subordinate and train all of her recruits into pliant subjects, and as she primes them for what seems a benign photo shoot, fully clothed, the implication is that she is dispatching them to become spies across the globe. The narrator tells us that this is not a film about Chinatown per se but about a situation that can fester if certain conditions are given to exist. The final credo invokes Cold War fears and resorts to jingoistic patriotism, stating that this is a problem "we" need to be vigilant of to protect "our communities, our children, and our country," just as the documentary city images show a Chinese restaurant window with workers behind a counter and roast ducks hanging aloft.

Sexology, Deviance, and the Sex Exposé

The contradictoriness seen in *White Slaves* between word and image, between a residually moralist discourse and the fleshly, sensational body, was also central to the sex exposé subgenre of sexploitation films, pseudo-documentaries regarding social problems. In many of these films, a male narrator purported to be an expert tells a story of evidentiary deviance, erotically charged criminality, or sexual pathology that accompanies illustrative footage that claims a documentary facticity—seen in *White Slaves of Chinatown* as well as in films such as *Chained Girls* (also directed by Joseph Mawra, 1965) and *File X for Sex* (C. Davis Smith, 1967). *Chained Girls,* for example, is a complex pseudo-documentary on the private practices of lesbian subcultures in Greenwich Village, peppering its narration with manufactured statistics in intertitles listing the number of women who have had lesbian experiences, the number of women charged with sodomy, and so on.[12] The claims made for lesbian life and its customs—that same-sex relationships last four months at best, that women "slip into" lesbianism without even knowing it—are juxtaposed with highly performative images, a diorama of sexual practice. The film suggests sexual activity through a developing filmic syntax, as sex acts are suggested through the use of ecstatic faces and extremities, bare legs, shoes and clothes strewn on the floor. The point of view of the lascivious butch as she observes and evaluates the femme is collapsed with the film's point of view, as the camera often tracks up and down the bodies of the women, establishing a touristic, heterosexual male gaze under the auspices of the same-sex desire of lesbian pickups and "cruising." In one scene, a dominant lesbian photographer uses her sessions to ogle the spectacle of posing female bodies, en route to their seduction. The obvious pedagogical alibi of social authority is set slapdash against the erotic pull of the images themselves, with their focus on the resistant corporeality of female bodies performing for the camera, in a world apart, a fantasy world of women's-only rituals, including a lesbian wedding ceremony.

In *File X for Sex*, subtitled *Story of the Perverted*, a doctor seated at a desk introduces a set of case studies of female nymphomania, male satyriasis, erotic narcissism, and homosexuality. The style of filmed sex scenes often cleaves apart from the narrative voice-over. For example, in the satyr scene, in which the doctor tells us that the male is really "frigid"—and in which his hydraulic drive for sex with women is thus feminized through a discourse of female sexual dysfunction—the actual sex scene, in its use of a swirling, unhinged mobile camera, follows the entwined body of the satyr and his female companion. This aesthetic device plunges the viewer into a closeness and intimacy with the bodies that otherwise belie the perfunctory voice-over. The handheld camera moves, reframing the sexual action from the waist up, fading into a close-up of the man's back on top of his sexual partner (played by Darlene Bennett). The aesthetic techniques Smith used aimed to mimic, through mobility, the raptures of erotic corporeality, defeating the very premise of a sexological case study in its claims to objective, pedagogical, or distanced discernment.[13] The mode of address of the social or scientific authority acts as a veil for the articulation of spectacle, a loose membrane that holds the episodically discrete scenes of perverse sexual etiology together. The housing mechanism of a psychological narrative is challenged by the visual images and the syntactical organization of represented sex acts, a move to represent the erotic body at closer range.

Chuck Kleinhans, writing on the narration in mondo sexploitation and other "sleazy" 1960s pseudo-documentaries, examines the function of the narrator as a fundamentally cynical operative and mediator between the film's aim of profit and the lewd desire of the naive or curious filmgoer. Kleinhans argues that the viewer of the sensationalist mondo takes on an attitude of "reverse disavowal," of knowing very well that the narrator is a put-on, but accepting his address if it permits an ironic form of voyeurism. Kleinhans argues that "the narrator, even in his cynicism, pretends to address an impossibly naïve viewer . . . an absent viewer who would actually fall prey to the narrator's absurd claims."[14] This is, of course, a viewer who never existed but is nevertheless a placeholder in sexploitation's mode of address in these faux documentary films that allows the conjunction of fraudulent pedagogy and hitches it to corporeal spectacle, a pretext discussed in chapter 1 with respect to Barry Mahon's *Censored*.

Sexploitation films employed the discursive framework of sexological or sociological exposition and such pseudo-authoritative narration, rec-

GIRLS WITH HUNGRY EYES 169

FIGURE 25. *File X for Sex*'s poster catalogs characters' psychosexual case studies, using the language of sexology and psychology.

ognizing and capitalizing on the ways that audiences, confronted with the scientific and scholarly challenges to commonplaces regarding sexual practice after Kinsey, used these forms of knowledge as a means of cultural voyeurism. The boom in sexual science and attendant reportage in the mid- to late 1960s, particularly energized by the release of William

Masters and Victoria Johnson's *Human Sexual Response* in 1966, and surrounded by a developing literature of sex-help, provided a frame through which the private sphere of sexuality could be accessed and become an object of consumption.[15] The move of sexuality out from a marital context into a sphere of consumption and nonreproductive possibility, with the wide availability of the birth control pill along with other factors, was crucial in both giving legitimacy to sexology's claims and founding a market for the dissemination of sexual knowledge. Janice Irvine examines how the "sexual marketplace" colluded with and facilitated the "development of sexual science" through a "shift of sexual discourse into the public arena . . . an increasingly public vision of erotic satisfaction has generated a willing group of consumers readily enticed by promises of more and better sex."[16] Therefore the tension in sexology's claims regarding sexuality was drawn between the ideological demands of its market and its aim for scientific objectivity. The faux-documentary, sex exposé, in which case studies of "perversion" could provide pretext for an omnibus narrative—such as *The Abnormal Female* (George Rodgers, 1969), *File X for Sex*, and *Strange Rampage* (Harry Kerwin, 1967)—profitably used the narrative frame of sexology, benefiting from the assumptions regarding its interest to a larger consumer public who might take furtive pleasure in images and explorations of sociosexual deviance. Comparably, sexploitation also discursively poached from other social sciences, such as the sociology of deviance, criminology, psychology, and anthropology, disciplines that had in these years set their sights on social groups deemed nonnormative or "perverse" as objects of study.[17]

Whereas sexploitation film of the 1960s prominently utilized plots that exploited lesbianism and bisexuality, male homosexuality was more scarcely featured, even as sexploitation was often associated with the filmic "underground."[18] An industry and a market directed by and addressed primarily to straight males did little to make grist of emerging gay identity and sexual practices, with some notable exceptions, including Barry Mahon's *I Was a Man* (1967), which featured the transgendered Ansa Kansas playing herself as well as reenacting her past male self in a fictionalized recounting of her transition between genders. Another exception was Andy Milligan, a gay, New York–based exploitation filmmaker who shot a groundbreaking and extremely low budget film, *Vapors* (1965), that detailed the pathos and realism of an afternoon among gay males in a bathhouse. The film ended with one of the unclothed characters walking, with his penis exposed, directly toward the camera, contravening a clear prohibition not just in the law but also in sexploitation conventions against full frontal, and especially male, nudity. As Jimmy McDonough details in his critical biography of Milligan, *Vapors*, at the level of exhibition and affiliation, drew closer association to the underground and gay experimental film scene, screening first at experimental film venue The Bridge in the East Village, New York, alongside a film by Storm De Hirsch, among others, before being blown up to 35mm and circulating in grind house venues and in the sexploitation market and playing alongside films such as Shirley Clark's *Portrait of Jason* (1967) and being compared to Kenneth Anger's *Fireworks* (1947).[19] The gay male sex film market developed in large part in separate, though at times geographically proximate, exhibition venues from sexploitation. The films differed to some degree critically and aesthetically, although there were notable overlaps or proximities, for example, in the distribution of Andy Warhol's *Chelsea Girls* (1966) by Sherpix, an art house and sex film distribution company run by Lou Sher. Other representations of gay male sexuality, figured as sexually aberrant examples in the "case study" format, appear in films such as John and Lem Amero's *The Lusting Hours* (1967), which details the practices of prostitution, transvestism, sadomasochism, and male hustling. One notable scene involves a male hustler cruising in the Port Authority bathroom, filmed through what appear to be the hatches of a screen, likely just the reinforced window of the bathroom door, which adds a layer of surreptitious voyeurism, as if the spectator and/or camera is the lookout in the "tearoom trade." By the late 1960s, some minor appearances of gay male sexuality would provide comic relief or a foil of emphasis, especially as these films moved toward a lighter, more jocose tone. But sexploitation films were largely fixated on the spectacle of female sexuality for a heterosexual, primarily male viewer, and thus gay male desire remained anathema to its generic transmutations. However, the subject of lesbian sex, as evident in pseudo-docs like *Chained Girls* (Joseph P. Mawra, 1965) as well as in more melodramatic and romantic variants, such as the high-gloss *Therese and Isabelle* (Radley Metzger, 1968), provided fruitful and open territory for the form.

Remapping the Voyeur: Bisexuality, Lesbianism, and the Female Observer

The contradictory identity and address of sexploitation films espoused a conservative worldview regarding sexuality, implicitly yearning for a golden age of more constrained sexual roles and a desire for fixed meaning. Alternatively, the films opened onto a domain of the heretofore unseen sphere of minority sexual subjects, figured through a strategy of visual excess and erotic spectacle. These opposing impulses and the contradictoriness of the films are often perceived as a form of textual incoherence but were produced by a tension between legitimating discourses and narratives that might provide an alibi or buffer sexual license and the primacy of visual spectacle. But it might be wise to view such contradiction as a site of productive ambivalence, a space seeded by all kinds of strange, preposterous, but also compelling representations of an emergent female erotic subjectivity.

By the late 1960s, sexploitation films came to be dominated more and more by a "descriptive" quality, with increasing sexual explicitness, a move toward greater simulation, and, by the late 1960s, a return, in some sectors and for particular cycles, such as the swinger and swapping films and larger-budgeted genre send-ups, to utilizing color film.[20] Craig Fischer posits "description" as distinct from narrative to explain the formal operations of exploitation cinema as a mode perched at the border between classical Hollywood narration and hard-core pornography. Description is defined by Fischer as a pausing of narrative flow in favor of an elaboration of the "properties of things;" for sexploitation films, this means the approximation of bodies in some form of sexual activity.[21] The visualization of simulated sex acts, as well as sexual spectacles like dancing, stripteases, or extended scenes of models "posing," or women lounging in states of undress, would come to overwhelm plot-driven elements in the creation of films that more directly treated sexual subjects and sexual acts as the crux of dramatic action. Inching closer from "seeing" to "doing," sexploitation films established a set of conventions that maintained certain elements of evasion while exposing more of the sexed body, in this middle ground between the explicit and implicit.

In his discussion of classical exploitation's mode of production and style, Eric Schaefer explains how exploitation's lack of tight narrative continuity, its often shoddy construction and reliance on forbidden spectacle over and above plot structure, created a condition of reception that he describes as a form of "delirium."[22] In 1960s sexploitation films, as we have seen, this kind of constitutive "madness" becomes a more sustained process of schizophrenic arousal, in which the delirious is taken up as specifically erotic through the disjunction between narrative pretexts and the visual field. By iterating this delirium through a discourse of sexual perversion and excess in the figures of sociosexual Others, straight male desire could be mollified while also deflected.

The roughies and kinkies brought into a conflicted field of visibility dramatizations of nonnormative sexuality that point to the margins of heterosexual identities and practices. In this they bear a striking parallel to the similarly low-cultural and suggestively erotic pulp paperbacks that, in the 1940s, 1950s, and into the mid-1960s, titillated readers with stories of forbidden affections and violent reprisals and gave a popular cultural visibility to gay and lesbian life. In a sense, sexploitation films of the mid-1960s took up where the pulp paperback had left off, transposing the narratives and discourses of "wayward sexuality" onto the moving image. As Susan Stryker describes, the pulp novel allowed a space for the articulation of as yet taboo subjects and inchoate desires:

> Mid-twentieth century paperbacks mapped a world of loose women and lost men who wandered in a moral twilight, a world of sin and sex and drugs and booze and every ugly thing human beings could conspire to do to one another. It was a world in which bisexual experimentation, like a single puff from a marijuana cigarette, often served as a first step on a long and sordid journey that tended toward heroin addiction, murder, homosexuality, the breakdown of gender distinctions, and the certain madness that lay beyond.[23]

The ambulatory world here invoked, with its inflections of a nascent queer identity and its negotiation of the stirrings and anxieties of alternative sexualities, can certainly be seen in the roughies, kinkies, and other mid- to late-1960s sexploitation cycles—a time in which private sexual behavior was being measured against transforming public standards. *White Slaves*, of course, took up this vernacular analogue quite literally, between sexual nonconformity and drug addiction, in its anachronistic qualities, reversing the causality between them—in which sexual deviance is interwoven within a network of larger "social problems."

Pulp scholar Yvonne Keller, in her discussion of the lesbian pulp novels she calls "virile adventures," notes a distinct management of voyeurism in their narratives, a structuring of the function of vision that, even in the more conservative strain of the 1950s novels written by men for a presumably male readership, is ultimately mutable and ambivalent.[24] She locates the twin poles of voyeurism and surveillance as prevalent cultural discourses of the postwar period that make their way into this erotic and sensationalist genre of popular literature. Keller concludes that even in the male-authored narratives of lesbian pulp, the function of voyeurism is not so simple; in its preoccupation with the crossing of boundaries, from heterosexuality to homosexuality, from self to other, voyeurism allows for a space of identification. She writes,

> Voyeurism in 1950s culture served as a safe method for dominant culture to control, but also to desire and identify with the Other, while simultaneously guarding the rigidity of the boundary between self and Other. The voyeurism of the ideologically blatant pulps is a form of

titillation that reaffirms the dominant. Yet the discourses about the invisibility of this object of sight—whether homosexual or communist—serve to raise the level of anxiety, to heighten the need for surveillance, and in some cases provoke identification with the Other. Voyeurism in the fifties thus becomes an attempt to see the invisible, to control the Other, a voyeurism that must be repeated again and again because it simultaneously breaks down the boundaries of sight and of self.[25]

The voyeuristic trope in sexploitation, too, was negotiating a balancing act between identification and disavowal. Just as the lesbian pulp novels often deployed a budding lesbian character's point of view to mediate between the desires of the male (presumably hetero) reader and the desires of the lesbianism described in the text, so too did sexploitation films of the mid-1960s begin to introduce female observers into their narratives as modes of authenticating stories of sexual initiation, plots of induction that often parlayed bisexuality as a polysemic practice and route women could take in their foray into the public sphere and modes of sexual exchange.

While the male voyeur and the peeper turned psychopath certainly did not disappear, the emergence of the female observer as a narrative figure and the thematization of female erotic looking could serve as node for the recasting of male desire, as well as offering a wider articulation of female erotic subjectivity. By allowing the emergence of female protagonists whose subjectivity and narratorial points of view could anchor the narrative action, the problem of *seeing sex* was transforming into a closeness and proximity with *doing sex,* just as on the visual track, "nudity with sexual situations" was transitioning to representations of simulated sex acts. If, in earlier sexploitation films, we see nudity as an adjunct to scenarios that do not represent sexual acts but indicate sexual situations, in the latter half of the 1960s, particularly from 1968 onward, the *event* of sexual activity begins to take up more screen duration, but also begins to challenge or test the bounds of narrative cohesion as plots grow looser and more episodic in their construction, built around extended scenes of simulated rutting.

This transformation, born from a more permissive cultural and legal climate and the end of prior restraint, is most evident in sexploitation films from the mid-1960s onward, as filmmakers created exceedingly and explicitly sexual scenarios as sites for dramatic conflict. Andrews observes that the later-1960s sexploitation films would incorporate an autoerotic female observer into the diegesis, supplanting the nudie cutie's male observer with a figure that could reinforce the focus on female bodily display. He further suggests that, "given the widespread assumption that the observer represented the audience, this autoerotic woman implied that sexploitation's audience was at least potentially female."[26] Andrews diagrams the appearance of the female voyeur and feminine identification in the late 1960s as part of the emergence of what he calls a "feminized," "classical soft-core" mode within sexploitation cinema. Whether this female observer represented the potential of a female audience, as Andrews claims, is more complicated than a one-to-one correspondence. For a mode of production contingent on the patronage of primarily male viewers, it seems that the emergence of a diegetic female observer, along with sexploitation cycles' interest in perversion and deviant sexuality, appeared more a "solution" to the problem of erotic consumption in its frame narratives, a novel variation that might prove profitable and diegetically expedient. I don't want to suggest a simple displacement argument—in which male desire is foisted onto female figures of sexual difference that "act out" in lieu of the viewer—which also seems too simplistic. But in the conjunction between what was legally permissible and defensible, what could be justified on the level of narrative or social value, and what could quarantine the film from a presumption of overt male prurience, as well as potentially invite a wider, gender-variant audience, the shift from a repressed male gawker to a *desiring female observer* defined by deviant, voracious insatiability is an incontrovertible development.

The prevalence of the female watcher, the "girl with hungry eyes" (eponymously inscribed in the 1967 film by William Rotsler), too comes precisely in a moment when female sexual agency and expressivity are being negotiated in new and diverse forms, across varied modes of production, from Roger Vadim's *Barbarella* (1967) to Mike Nichols's *The Graduate* (1967) to Luis Bunuel's *Belle du Jour* (1967) to Russ Meyer's *Vixen* (1968). Sexploitation film at this time was also gaining a much broader audience base as sex film exhibition spread from downscale urban grind houses to suburban and bigger chain theaters.[27] The crossover success of Radley Metzger's Audubon Films import of Mac Ahlberg's *I, a Woman* in 1966–67 was widely seen as a significant benchmark of attitudinal and industrial change. The film featured the fresh face of the Swedish Essy Persson in her debut role, portraying a young nurse who, in her sexual and romantic choices and refusals, among them in jettisoning her boring fiancé and other inadequate lovers, pursues the terms of her own pleasure. The film "opened up" the sexploitation market to wider audiences and to gender-diverse spectatorship. Vincent Canby, reporting on the unexpected success of the Swedish–Danish production, began his article with the testimony of a "Brooklyn housewife" telling her son-in-law to see *I, a Woman* but to leave his wife at home because the film was "too dirty."[28]

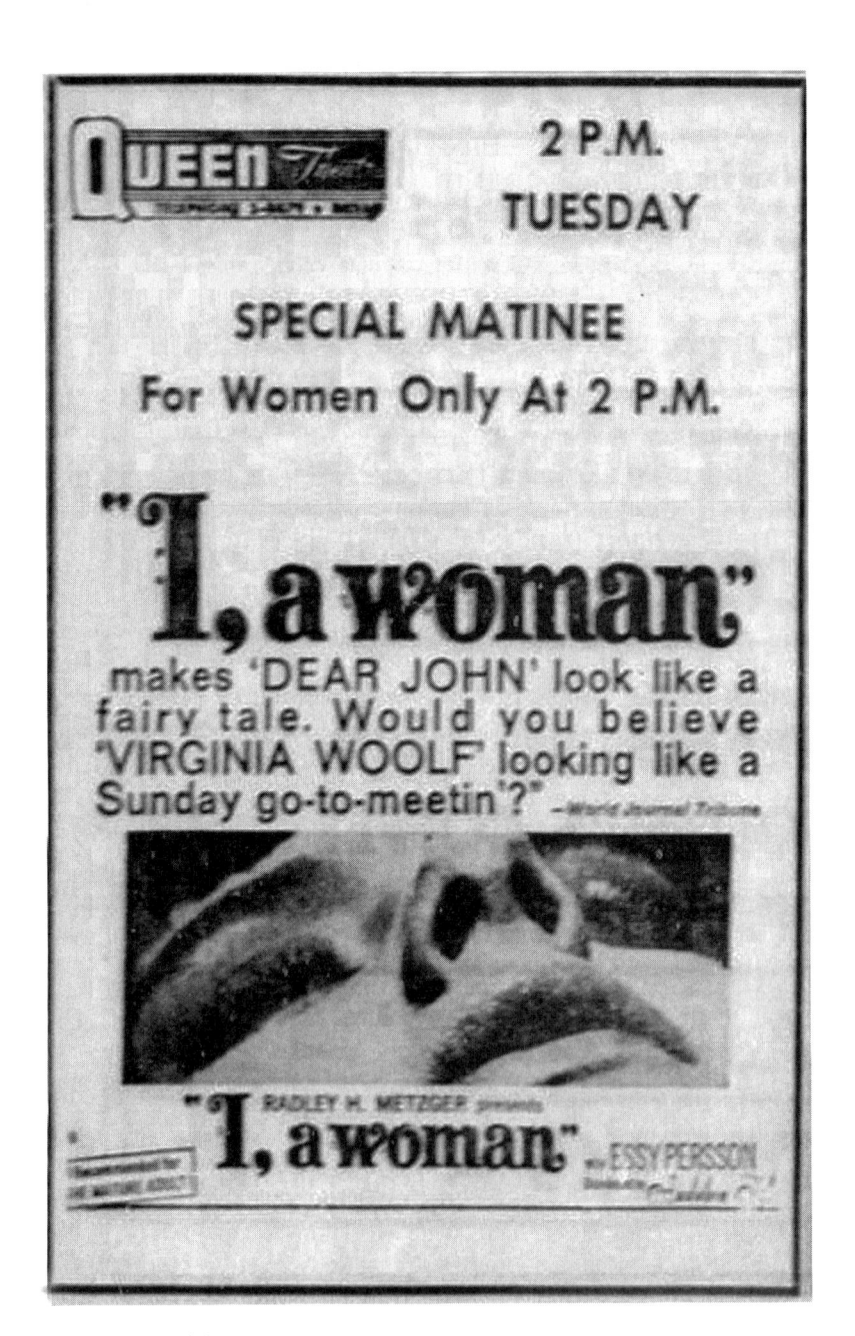

FIGURE 26. Audubon's breakout sexploitation import *I, a Woman*, with its iconic promotional image of Essy Persson's upturned face, exhibited for a women-only matinee in Bryan, Texas, in April 1967. Advertisement from the *Daily Eagle*, April 3, 1967.

Another reporter testified in the *Rolling Meadows Herald*, from a suburb north of Chicago, to seeing the film with his wife and her two married female friends, "none of whom were offended." The article ran alongside a report of the film being pulled by police from a local theater after community complaints by a women's group.[29] And in the town of Bryan, Texas, the Queen Theater, in a special promotional ploy, reserved a Tuesday at 2:00 P.M. for a women-only matinee to further the film's address to female audiences, who could screen it unperturbed, presumably, by lasciviously minded male company.[30] Metzger's films and his imports, with their particular strains of aestheticism and stylistic extravagance, as well as those of the bawdy, punchy Russ Meyer, were instrumental in this regard of popularizing the sexploitation film and facilitating the expansion of the "couples" audience, demographically linked to the suburban and exurban locations where adult films were more frequently playing by around 1967.

At the level of narrative, the female observer was often figured through an eroticized narcissism, inflected by a pop-Freudian reading of homosexuality as explicit self-love. Metzger's *Dirty Girls* (1965) introduced the

FIGURE 27. The female (and couples) audience: a female adult film spectator meeting a date in front of the window and one-sheet displays of Mawra's own *Olga's Girls* at the Victory Theater, in *Chained Girls*.

trope of the aroused female character, Monique, suggestively masturbating in the mirror as she kisses her own reflection, her face in close-up and the condensation of her breath in the mirror signifying the manipulation below the frame. This motif of narcissistic arousal and reflexive specularity would be appropriated in later sexploitation films, posed as an unraveling continuum between visualized self-love and a trajectory toward bisexual tendencies. The autoerotic gesture could speak to both a developing elaboration of subjectivity and simultaneously a collapsed notion of female sexuality as coextensive with, fluidly proximate to, other forms of "deviant" sexual practice. In the image of the woman "consuming herself" in the mirror, the female not only observes but takes part in sexual action. Thus the autoerotic female subject could become an optic of sorts, a medium through which sexual spectacle could be sustained, and one where *seeing sex and doing sex began to converge.*

The advent of the autoerotic and sexually goal-oriented female protagonist was abetted by the revelation of clitoral orgasm as independent of the mythical vaginal orgasm, research forwarded most prominently in William Masters and Virginia Johnson's 1966 publication of *Human Sexual Response*. The medical clarification of female sexual function had radical implications for straight sex and, in its most extreme form, hinted that both the penis and, by implication, heterosexual intercourse were no longer necessary for female sexual fulfillment.[31] As the popularization of sexual science introduced the possibilities of autonomous female pleasure into the public sphere and into a national lexicon, sexploitation films engaged with the notion of women's "mounting sex hunger" as a force of hyperbolic narrative energy. *Barbarella* (Roger Vadim, 1968), for example, portrayed a sexual future in which Jane Fonda's character's inexhaustible capacity for orgasm vanquishes the start of an interplanetary war. Barbarella's orgasmic short-circuiting of Duran Duran's stimulation machine—designed to overwhelm and kill its victim through pleasure—is, as Linda Williams suggests, an actualization of a feminist interpretation of the discovery of clitoral orgasm, in which female biological capacity exceeds the finitude of a male orgasm and its puny metrics. Barbarella's sexual future gives cinematic shape, in Williams's account, to the words of feminist psychoanalyst Mary Jane Sherfey that "theoretically a woman could go on having orgasms indefinitely."[32]

Following on such sexological revelations, sexual pleasure was beginning to be treated as a mode of egalitarian exchange or equivalency, in which the orgasm became a unit of measurement or a currency in pleasure. The capital of the body, as discussed by Hilary Radner, is equalized in its free exchange, as sexual autonomy and the measurability of female orgasmic response divests female pleasure from its association with sexual object choice. The orgasm signifies pleasure, and pleasure becomes a currency, yet one still inevitably grounded in sexual difference. Radner writes regarding the practices of the self of the single/working girl:

> Within a paradigm in which woman bartered her participation in the sexual act for material goods of one sort or another, her pleasure was irrelevant to the act itself. A different system of exchange was inaugurated in which the woman was the agent rather than the object of exchange, in that she exchanged orgasms as pleasure in a system of equivalence in which her pleasure was measured against his pleasure, or against her pleasure, as the case may be.[33]

Sexploitation films echoed this sea change in the understanding of the mechanics of sexual function, in many films' preoccupation with female characters set adrift in landscape of polymorphous pleasures, in which autoeroticism blended with a naturalized attraction toward sexual encounters between women, for example, in films such as *Her Odd Tastes* (Don Davis, 1969), *The Layout* (Joe Sarno, 1969), and *Vibrations* (Joe Sarno, 1969). As a result, bisexuality and lesbianism became an expedient way to present sexual content without the incriminations associated with full frontal male nudity, which remained for sexploitation films a forbidden zone of exposure. Turan and Zito, in their journalistic survey of sex cinema written in 1973, *Sinema,* claimed that lesbian sex scenes became a legal loophole useful for sexploitation's representational strategies, writing that "there is a great deal more explicit activity in the lesbian scenes than in the heterosexual ones, because it is much easier to fake sex between two women than between a woman and a man."[34] Despite the spurious assumptions in their analogy between sexual visibility and simulated sex, their statement reinforces how lesbian sexuality became a staple of the late-1960s sex film, a token benchmark in the "progress" of sexual liberalism in the adult marketplace. The lesbian or bisexual female character became an axiomatic figure in sexploitation, offering the female protagonist an avenue for sexual adventure and discovery, while also portending the dangerous potentials of a female erotic self-fulfillment loosening from patriarchal regimes of regulation and control—and potentially from coupledom altogether.[35]

The lesbian character mediates heterosexual relationships, becoming a shadowy agent of erotic self-discovery and exploration for other female characters. In Metzger's *The Dirty Girls,* lesbianism is the surprise ending that reveals that the prostitute Monique's affection rests with a woman, named Lawrence. An American john who has just had a sexual encounter with Monique mediates this revelation. A shower scene in which the lesbian lovers are reunited is intercut with an image of the john on the train reminiscing about Monique, with a recurring male voice-over questioning, "Who is a dirty girl?" The customer becomes analogous to the film spectator, the voyeur who is haunted by the "mystery" of Monique's erotic essence. Yet unlike the film spectator, the client does not know Monique's "true desires" as does the film's viewer. In the juxtaposition between the male client's reverie on the train, in his recollection of Monique and her elusive charms and the revelation of the true object of Monique's desire, a woman, the certitude of his erotic knowledge of Monique is questioned, made unstable. Thus the vision of Monique, tempered by a male consumerist fantasy, is fractured and instilled with doubt.

A few later 1960s films bear out the instantiation of bisexual directionality, positing female protagonists as erotic consumers and as bearers of erotic vision, allowing the female observer to supplant the complications of male voyeurism expressed in early- to mid-1960s nudie cuties and roughies. *A Bride for Brenda* (Tommy Goetz, 1968), produced and distributed by New York–based Distribpix, headed by Arthur Morowitz, details the sexual awakening of young Brenda through the voice-over of the desiring landlady, who vaguely witnesses Brenda's descent into same-sex carnality. The narrator herself never appears in the diegesis as a character, giving her voice a plaintive immateriality. Brenda's arrival in New York City from a rural elsewhere is doubled with her sexual self-exploration as she loses her virginity with the first man she meets, Nick. Returning to her apartment, which she shares with two female roommates, Jane and Millie, Brenda's overflowing erotic energies are literally associated with cinematic projection, as her masturbation is framed in the bottom left foreground of the image against a cinematic projection of her roommates tussling on a bed in the right top background of the frame. The framing of the film is explained by the overwrought narrator as a strategy of corruption on the part of her roommates and not just a fantasy. The following night, Brenda consummates her curiosity with Jane and Millie, after a day wandering about Central Park with a parasol and questioning her sexuality—the narrator asks us, "How could she know if she was a lesbian? She had never seen one or known one." The female narrator, whose omniscience is justified by her residence adjacent to the girls' apartment, explains alongside the unfolding images that Brenda has been fully corrupted. The film ends with a "marriage ceremony" in which four women, including the three roommates, paint each other's naked bodies with a marker on a bed, as Nick, the virginity-claiming one-night stand, is strung up and "tortured" and then finally released to join the women on the bed. The narrator's regret that she should have done more to "warn" Brenda couches the lesbian thematic loosely within a pathology of underworldly deviance, despite the trilling nature of the voice-over, which pauses and indulges in every sexual description. Brenda's nascent sexual subjectivity is thus voiced through the invisible neighbor, who tells her story through a soft-core mode of overheated, baroque description. The film manufactures a relay of female erotic looking between the narrator's diegetic claims of eavesdropping and Brenda's own voyeurism, which materializes in her pursuit of sex with Jane and Millie.

Monique, My Love (Peter Woodcock, pseud., 1969) also uses the device of the female narrator, no doubt for both films a function of economic necessity in that the films could be shot without sound and have the voice-over added in postproduction. Rita, Monique's roommate, is writing an eponymous book about Monique's sexual exploits. Monique is an aspiring skin flick actress and divulges everything to Rita. The rapt fascination of the narrator/writer eroticizes her secondhand experience of Monique's modeling jobs and visually materialized sexual plenitude. The function of observation is doubled over, as the pretext of the novel about Monique is overlayed with scenes of Monique and other models acting and posing for the diegetic "camera" on the job, as we hear Rita telling us about Monique's states of feeling. The excess of observation is justified through both Rita's vicarious desire "to be and to have" Monique and the thematization of the vocation of Monique's starlet aspirations through the diegetic ploy of the vague machinations of the sex industry, which provide the "stage" for Monique's exhibitionism. The film's loosely episodic scenarios of stripping and posed nudity conclude in a scene between Monique and Rita, who consummate their relationship as the observation is given over to the spectator through various mediating devices, including a shot through a mirror. The final scene, representative of sexploitation's expanding repertoire of showing sexual activity, shows Monique and Rita caressing each other on the couch, revealing Monique's exposed pubic hair as she and Rita embrace. In the final take, the camera pans over their entwined bodies, bush and all, the shadow of the camera faintly visible on their pale legs.

Lesbian desire could also be seen as a socially disruptive force, one that more openly and violently upended the place of men in the sexual marketplace and the social order—as in Michael and Roberta Findlay's *A Thousand Pleasures* (1969). In it, a psychopath, who has just axed his wife and locked the body in the trunk of his car, is ensnared by a lesbian couple who live in a suburban hideaway. Among its inhabitants is a young woman, Baby, who lives in a crib and who fondles and stimulates herself with a carrot. In a preposterous turn of events, the lesbians proceed to torture him and plot to use his sperm to create a baby. (One wonders if this is one of the films John Waters saw in his time in New York in the late 1960s.) In the Texas-made *She Mob* (Harry Wuest, 1968), a lesbian gang abducts the male lover of a wealthy woman. Common to many narratives regarding lesbianism or bisexual communities, as well as sexual nonnormativity more broadly, was a tendency to turn nonhetero activity from a subcultural mode to an occult mode, as in the halfhearted gesture toward occult practices in the ending to *A Bride for Brenda*. Jeffrey Sconce observes the concordance between sexual practices, the occult, and altered states in the sexploitation film and adult print culture of the late 1960s, a conjuncture of taboos given material shape in the intersection of sexual, physical, and religious experimentation and extreme forms of perceptual experience.[36]

Vibrations might represent the apex of sexploitation's aesthetic aspirations within the lower-budgeted class of New York sex dramas, and another representation of lesbian exploration that edges into another arena of perverse sexuality, that of incest (a common Sarno theme). Sarno's attention to space and frame glories in the productive material limitations of shooting. *Vibrations*'s plot treats the too-intimate, incestuous relationship between two estranged sisters. The "wild," sexualized sister Julia (Maria Lease) shows up at her younger sibling Barbara's (Marianne Prevost) New York apartment, having tracked her down from finding her poem in a magazine. Barbara, serious but uptight, works freelance as a typist of others' manuscripts from home. Insinuating her way back into her sister's life and home, Julia discovers through overhearing sex sounds at night that the "storage room" next door is being used for polymorphous sex trysts, led by a woman named Georgia who yields a large body massager for self-pleasuring. Georgia is often joined by another couple, and we see Julia lying awake at night in stark lighting listening and pleasuring herself. Julia's voraciousness, both for her sister's affections and any kind of sexual experience, comes into conflict with Barbara's sense of propriety and her need for boundaries. Julia wanders the streets of New York in the day, returns in the evening, and attempts to seduce her sister, recovering some exploratory bliss alluded to as an earlier element of their filial and erotic connection. As their relationship grows more strained, Julia both betrays her sister by bedding one of her clients and begins to partake in the sexual activities next door. Soon Barbara, seduced and drawn magnetically by her sister, joins in on the next-door carousing, and an extended scene details Barbara watching as Julia is plied with the vibrations of the sex machine. Barbara ends up running off with one of the orgy participants, a man, as Julia succumbs to a bottomless pit of pleasure, drowning herself in the ministrations of the woman with the vibrator in the storage closet next door. The film, shot in a cramped New York apartment, deploys spatial limitations to create a unique aesthetic that makes the most of the small ensemble of actors, primarily the two female leads, their monadic faces, breasts, and torsos sculpted by the cleaved light, their bodies pliable material reducible to the substantiality of light and shadow. Sarno's characteristic expressive economy in medium shots above the waist and copious two shots and close-ups in long takes utilizes his principals' bodies as architecturally central to the mise-en-scène. The pull of sexual pleasure, flouting taboos of both sexual orientation and family, becomes an end unto itself for Julia, as Sarno jettisons any moralistic framework, leaving only the endurance of her body in the face of sexual exhaustion in the film's closing images.

Monique, A Bride for Brenda, and *Vibrations,* among many other films of this time, exhibit a transformation of representational strategies within sexploitation film, particularly of lower-budgeted films at this time, moving away from elaborately plot-driven scenarios of dramatic action and toward a performative soft-core erotic tableau that maximizes the spectacle

FIGURE 28. Joe Sarno's *Vibrations* utilizes stark, expressive lighting to cleave pictorial space in his incestuous chamber drama of estranged, bisexual sisters Julia and Barbara.

of nudity and simulated sex, becoming looser and more episodic, in an erotic picaresque mode. The main characters spend exorbitant amounts of time lounging around, waking up and stretching, getting dressed and getting undressed, and languidly writhing on beds, couches, and chairs, caressing themselves either for a camera or for their own pleasure. Concomitantly, the duration of scenes with simulated sexual activity grew longer. Sexualized body-to-body contact was broached through scenes of extended fondling and groping, gyrating and rubbing, with the expansion to full frontal female nudity, but one that continued to keep explicit genitality and penetration at bay.

Pleasure and Profit: Working Girls, Swingers, Free Love

With the transforming focus on the female as erotic consumer and participant in the late 1960s, the tension between being an object of consumption, being an agent in the act of selling oneself, and becoming a sexual consumer seeking her own pleasures was manifested in sexploitation narratives that conflated sexual trajectories between sex for money and sex for pleasure. A number of films placed female characters within an explicit economy of sex work; these narratives often overlapped with narratives of urban debauchery or with other pseudo-sociological, primarily fictional analyses of alternating sexual practices, such as wife swapping, swinging, and other forms of sexual exchange or subcultural or countercultural initiation. Sarno's *Sin in the Suburbs,* and his many subsequent films, established this narrative trope—in which the "key club" members became masked, anonymous players, reducible to faceless numbers, sexual participants who could be exchanged and rearranged. This motif of the swap also gave great valence to the sense of sexual acts as a sphere of exchange and currency, mobilized and loosened by a new market of not only male but also female desire.

In a post–prior restraint era, and in a moment when social protest and countercultural movements were beginning to flourish, the politicized charge of sexuality became more directly linked to radical culture as youth cultures seized on the liberatory possibilities of erotic expression en masse and in more overt ways. Beth Bailey elucidates how expressions of transgressive sexuality began to gain force in the counterculture: "transgressive sexuality offered a visual and verbal language, shocking vulgarity, sex served as a weapon against 'straight' or non-hip culture. And within the counterculture, the sex = freedom equation had become such an overdetermined convention that it was sometimes hard to find another language in which to explain the superiority of the hip to the straight."[37]

Sexploitation's mode of address also began to change in the late 1960s, responsive to industrial necessity, to a diversification of the sex film field, and to accommodate the widening permissiveness of American cultural life as well as the radicalization of young people and rising social protest movements. Consuming sex and seeing sex, as one aggregate of such wider social and political revolutions, were being heralded as a pandemic national problem by an older moral order as young people began to embrace the rebellious potentialities of an eroticized public culture. Although youth had always been a site of titillation for sexploitation producers, the explicit link between youth culture and sexual freedom forced sexploitation strategies to shift to accommodate this changing cultural landscape. Films such as *Mondo Mod* (Peter Perry, 1967), *The Hippie Revolt* (Edgar Beatty, 1967), and *Like It Is* (William Rotsler, 1968) found sexploitation filmmakers attempting to capitalize on their audiences' curiosity regarding the roiling counterculture and youth cultural refusal of traditional mores, but these films always marked their own "outsiderness," positioned clearly with their older generationally distinct audience. Similarly, the drug scene and experimentation with psychedelics among the counterculture were also featured in films like *Smoke and Flesh* (Joe Mangine, 1968), *The Acid Eaters* (Byron Mabe, 1968), *Blonde on a Bum Trip* (Ralph Mauro, 1968), and *Mantis in Lace* (William Rotsler, 1968). Other independents, such as American International Pictures and Fanfare Films, had embraced the youth market appeal of the updated mold of the biker film with films such as *The Wild Angels* (Roger Corman, 1966) and *Hells Angels on Wheels* (Richard Rush, 1967), which also had a considerable quotient of sex and violence.

Some films also attempted to conjoin their earlier preoccupations, such as the bored and oversexed housewife, as made prominent in the early-1960s Sarno films, with this new landscape of perceived bohemian excess. Swinging and swapping were important zones of investigation, as they provided novel, modular plot construction as well as structuring the seriality of sexual encounters, but they also spoke to a moment in which sexual experimentation and the questioning of marriage and the monogamous couple form were permeating popular culture. Consider the pretexts of *Free Love Confidential,* a 1967 film (directed by Gordon Heller, produced by Harry Novak in Los Angeles) that seemed caught in the crosshairs between an emerging sexual liberationist discourse and the insistence on the dangers and risks of the sexual marketplace, here keyed as a site of bohemian, proto-hippie self-indulgence. Kaye, a bored suburban housewife, finds her husband sexually unresponsive to her overtures and more concerned with his work. Kaye's friend Giselle convinces her that they should answer an ad in the *Free Press,* placed by a photographer who seeks "groovy chicks" for a photo shoot. Kaye and Giselle, pretending to be hipper than they are, venture into the bohemian lair of Robin the photographer. He plies them with marijuana and conducts a shoot very derivative of the mod stylings of Michelangelo Antonioni's Code-challenging *Blow-Up* (1966). An "orgy" ensues in which Robin, Giselle, and Kaye loll and wrestle in bed, taking turns photographing each other with Robin.

Counter to his promise to hand over the negatives, Robin gives them a blank roll of film. Kaye and Giselle panic and go back over to his apartment to retrieve the incriminating evidence, only to find that there is a stern, suited, dandyish gentleman named Mickey there. After Mickey, in his gruff voice, begins to seduce Kaye and Giselle, they discover that Mickey is really a butch lesbian in drag. They struggle as Mickey demands that they either have sex with her or produce five hundred dollars for the return of the roll of film. After procuring the money, Giselle and Kaye are sent to a hippie hot spot, the Mojo Club, where they are told to deliver it. Instead, they find Mickey in femme garb onstage doing an elaborate performance and cracking her whip as beatniks play bongos and heads and freaks mill about drinking LSD-laced punch, offered by a toga-wearing master of ceremonies whose white shift bears the slogan "LOVE." Of course, Giselle and Kaye fall prey to a harrowing drug trip, which allows the filmmakers an extended stroboscopic, distortion-laden extended montage scene, in which pulsating eroticism, a gamut of stylistic effects, and youth cultural debauchery coalesce—we see the girls go-go dancing shot in canted angles, teeming undulating crowds, grotesque faces shadowed by patterned lights, dancing limbs fragmented in mirrors. In the midst of her drug high, Kaye imagines strangling Mickey in revenge. The girls wake up the morning after in the club, realizing it was only a bad trip. On their way home, they run into Robin, who gives them the film back but wants to take more photos with them. The friends run off as Robin raises his camera, signaling their provisional education by their previous exploits. A bohemian type walks by them and offers them a copy of the *Free Press*, and Giselle and Kaye keep running knowingly down the street as the film ends.

Kaye and Giselle's pursuit of hip "modern" pleasures—exhibitionism, drugs, erotic adventure—is a temporary escape from their suburban ennui. A descent into the new sexual economy of "free love," their interactions with the freewheeling world of "loose pleasures" still come at a cost: the threat of the disruption of the women's private lives through the circulation of sexual images of them. *Free Love Confidential* cordons off its own imagined representation of the counterculture and drug culture, as did

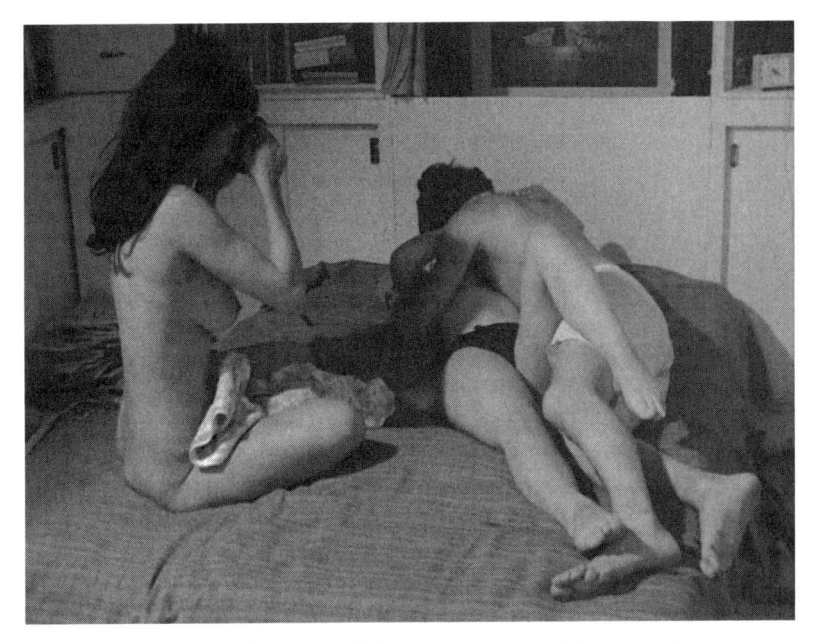

FIGURE 29. *Free Love Confidential*'s bored housewives dally with a bohemian photographer in a *Blow-up*–inflected threesome.

many other films of its time, within an imbalanced economy that broadcasts the risks these subcultural spaces of bohemia pose to the integrity and coherence of a feminine self still allied with the private, domestic sphere, with marriage and the patriarchal demarcation of property ownership. Thus the moral corrective model of earlier sexploitation still inheres in its narrative, in which sexual license and experimentation breed ill consequences, although offering some temporary sphere of self-exploration.

Contending with the premises of sexual liberation in the larger culture, other narratives attempted to imagine a more permissive social world overwhelmingly connected with the sexual practices of the urban and the young, with greater equanimity. Films revolving around "working girls," as discussed earlier, are traceable to the early nudie cutie cycles, particularly the artist's model films. If, in those films, the woman as pinup photographer or the aspiring model was still bound to a system of exchange defined by men, in the later 1960s films, female characters began to establish their own terms of sale or exchange.

From the mid-1960s onward, the articulation of female labor in a public marketplace often blurred the boundaries between sex for pleasure and sex for profit. In the mid-1960s, sex for profit was seen as an economic necessity that indelibly marked the sex worker as deviant but also gestured toward a bevy of larger social problems, as in *The Hookers* (Jalo Miklos Horthy, 1967), in which three women's entrance into prostitution is elaborated through psychologically inflected character studies that posit past traumas. One segment, starring Fleurette Carter as Callie Sue, an African American secretary in an urban office, quite strikingly posits a correlate between southern racism, racial sexualization, and sex work. Offering flashbacks to Callie Sue's youth and her rape by two racist brutalizers, shot from her perspective in a rural field, the film connects the melodrama of racial violence to the violence of sexual valuation and exploitation in the racial, sexual, and class hierarchies of the urban office. Callie Sue, now a lowly but diligent office worker, is doggedly harassed by a white male coworker who wants to bed her, sans romance or any overtures of a date. Callie Sue tries to claim her value as a woman and makes him pay, literally, for something the creep expects for free. In *Hot Skin, Cold Cash* (Barry Mahon, 1965), a woman works the Times Square beat for legal fees for her imprisoned husband, encountering various johns and peculiar types along the way, including a priest who wants to convert her. And in *Agony of Love* (William Rotsler, 1966), marital sexual frustration causes housewife Barbara (Pat Barrington) to consign herself into an inexplicable circuit of sexual labor on the side to feel something in excess of her suburban malaise.

As the decade inched forward, more conventional and less socially marginalized spaces of work also became repositories of sexual engagement. Although Joe Sarno was one of the key architects of the exploration of the languishing climate of the American middle-class wife in the suburbs, and many films explored the fate of the young working girl getting by in the city, many other films began to move toward everyday scenarios of workaday life and leisure. *Office Love-In, White Collar Style* (Stephen Apostolof, 1968) exemplified this trajectory, detailing the workplace and extracurricular erotic exploits of Stephanie Morris, a secretary who is employed at a computer dating service. The computer dating service as workplace invites a blurring of boundaries just as it signals a new era of sexual coupling and technologically aided romance. With affable sexual voraciousness, Stephanie sleeps her way through the entire firm, moving from boss to boss's wife to boss's son and his brother-in-law. Economic autonomy and sexual mobility are thus rendered mutually constitutive. Stephanie's status as a single working girl depends on her circulation through the sexual economy of the office, in which the principles of "democratization" and egalitarianism rest in her choice of sexual partners. Stephanie's willingness and sexual availability come to represent her work ethic, an ethic meted out by the pursuit of sexual encounter as work, at work, and after work as well.

Stephanie is promoted to being the boss's executive secretary; this is clearly a reward, played for knowing laughs, of her sexual diligence. As a function of conflating the boundaries between sex as work and work as sex through an ascendant cultural logic of free exchange, the film posits an ideology in which pleasure becomes an equalizing unit of currency but, paradoxically, still implicitly requires a form of recompense "on the side." Diverging from the rather grim economies of earlier roughies and kinkies, *Office Love-In* approached a more liberatory or naturalist sensibility in its treatment of sexuality. This is most aptly represented in the blithe acrobatics of its main character, Stephanie, and the lack of plotted comeuppance for her promiscuous "sins." Rather than a scarce resource, the principle of Stephanie's sexual mobility requires her free circulation as a shared asset that accumulates erotic capital in its distribution. As an early model of a "free love" discourse entering sexploitation narratives, the film reinforces the ways that the structures of competitive capitalism, embodied in the "swinging" office setting, were conducive to a logic of ambulatory sexuality in the marketplace of pleasure.

As part of this changing tide of sexploitation's sexual ideology, female erotic looking in the film operates to facilitate sexual activity, to authorize its enactment. In one scenario, Stephanie pairs off on a double date with one of the boss's sons, a bank teller. The couples retreat to the son's apartment to watch a "stag film" (the footage is drawn from an earlier A. C. Stephens film, *Suburbia Confidential* [1967]) featuring soft-core bondage: a woman being tied to the posts of a bed and tickled with a feather. The incredulous and bemused faces of the couples are highlighted in close-up as they watch the film in the darkened room. After the final reel runs through the projector and the lights come on again, the couples engage in campy, tongue-in-cheek dialogue about how credible or believable the film was. "Can you believe it? Do people actually do that?" one of the men exclaims, while Stephanie's friend retorts, "I believe, I believe!" as they retreat into separate rooms to try out the positions and techniques they have learned from the stag film.

This scene doubles over the viewing scenario, incorporating the specter of the (fake) 16mm stag film in a trajectory of erotic pedagogy. In this way, the film echoes a process that Robert Eberwein has discussed in the self-reflexive devices of sex education films. Eberwein argues that the film within a film structure of many sex education films allows the thematization of vision and for the conditions of the films' reception to be modeled.

This incorporation of the "scene of instruction" in sex ed films both mediates and buffers the viewed act, in which distance and objectivity are staged in relation to spectacles of the "effects of sex on the body."[38] Yet, in the context of *Office Love-In*'s fictional narrative about the erotic circuit and "free" sexual exchange, within the diegesis, the scene of *seeing sex*, in the form of the stag film, is overlaid with the potentiality of *doing sex*. Toying with the possibility of the arousal of its audience, *Office Love-In* more directly addresses its viewer through the diegetic staging of its own "couples audience," the double-dating coworkers, within the film. Stephanie and her female compatriot are the spectators who bridge the gap between seeing and doing sex, using what they've "learned" in the stag film as a framework for its reenactment with their one-night stands. Stephanie is of course the first to "try out" in the bedroom the bondage practices she's just seen, deflecting cultural (and extradiegetic) anxiety regarding male desire onto her plucky sexual initiative and status as industrious "go-getter" in the collapsed universe of work and/as sex.

The manifestation of this new sexual ethos of free exchange is treated with far less anxiety than rendered in earlier films, in which the distinction between seeing sex and doing sex, as we have seen, was more rigidly enforced. This acknowledgment of the uses of sexual media is ratified through the contexts of sexual liberationist discourse, with which the film allies its characters and social milieu. The "new woman," the "liberated" working girl, becomes the model of enactment of a new moral order of sexual availability and sexual consumption, as she embodies the voracious (and soon to be "insatiable") consumer far more than the consumed. The aggressively sexual antiheroine became a key figure for late-1960s sexploitation cinema, in line with its heightening explicitness, forwarded as much by the buxom pneumatic energies of Russ Meyer's roughie and biker-themed films, from *Faster Pussycat! Kill! Kill!* (1965) and *Mudhoney* (1965) onward to the previously discussed *Vixen* (1968). Female desire, no longer merely suggested or implied, became an unleashed force, with women as voracious agents and seekers of sexual pleasure.

Another extreme of sexual liberation, imagined as a farcical potentiality, was on display in Manuel S. Conde's *Nymphs Anonymous* (1968), in which women organize a new sexual economy. *Nymphs* posits a somewhat preposterous implication for the possibility of female sexual freedom. A proto-feminist federation of oversexed women subordinates the "feeble" male sex through sexual submission. An application-based, members-only secret sex society is created by the anarchic anonymous sex hunger of nymphomaniacs. Male bodies are a resource that is farmed and traded, harvested for nude bartending and sexual servicing. *Nymphs*'s ludicrousness centers on an imagined sexual "meantime" that contemplates the feminist future as a disorganized utopia and dystopia at once, riddled by desertion and sexual exhaustion—the plenitude of a liberated female future foretold. An angry husband who has been abandoned by his newly inducted wife goes rogue and attacks some of the men in the employ of the federation. He is soon captured and made a sex slave himself. Here Betty Friedan's critique of women's "sex hunger" comically meets the militancy of a newly incendiary class of women, no longer satisfied with consumer goods and suburban split levels and now emboldened to make men their captive property and sexual servants.

Industrial and Aesthetic Reflexivity

Late-1960s sexploitation films underwent a transformation and expansion marked by the widening of permissible sexual content, with more films being made on the high and low ends of the budget spectrum. The volume of small-budget films, many made in New York City by producers such as Distribpix and American Film Distributors, sizably expanded, as did the production of mid-range product (budgeted at around one hundred thousand dollars), such as the work of Meyer, Metzger, and producers like Friedman and Harry Novak. The successes of art distributor theater chain Sherpix and the Pussycat theater chain in California also indicated a "sex exploitation explosion," as a 1969 article in the *Independent Film Journal* announced. Industrially speaking, this growth can be seen as stemming in part from the reduced output of the Hollywood studios as well as their ventures into more competitively "mature" fare in these years, with films such as *Who's Afraid of Virginia Woolf?* (Mike Nichols, 1966), *The Fox* (Mark Rydell, 1967), *Midnight Cowboy* (John Schlesinger, 1969), *Point Blank* (John Boorman, 1967), *The Killing of Sister George* (Robert Aldrich, 1968), and *Bob & Carol & Ted & Alice* (Paul Mazursky, 1969). The sexploitation market expanded to a wider range of rural, drive-in, and suburban theaters. In general, the widening market for adult independent or crossover films merged sexploitation and art film devices, for example, Milton Moses Ginsberg's *Coming Apart* (1969), which fused a sexploitation gambit figured on a male psychiatrist hiding out in his bachelor pad as a stream of women wander through, with the premise of a hidden camera recording a faux-diary in real time, a structure drawn from Jim McBride's *David Holzman's Diary* (1968).

The impact of foreign films' sexual content on American films continued, as the imported films themselves challenged legal and regulatory precedents and posed obscenity quandaries for their exhibitors. This was most dramatically visible in the case of Michelangelo Antonioni's tale of ennui in swinging London in *Blow-Up,* which was refused a Code seal but released anyway by MGM under the auspices of its subsidiary, Premier Films, to great critical success. This scuffle was widely seen to reinforce the need for the establishment of the CARA ratings system.[39] It was also evident in the flurry of trials, court and obscenity cases involving the exhibition of Vilgot Sjoman's Swedish import *I Am Curious (Yellow)* (1967) in U.S. theaters from 1968 to 1971. *Yellow*'s coupling of documentary aesthetics, political critique, frank and full frontal male and female nudity, and character study of its young questioning main character, Lena, polarized courts, publics, and critics. It also made apparent that a new niche market for a hybrid adult art house film had arrived, making $6.6 million by 1969.[40] No longer the "only game in town" with respect to nudity, sexual situations, and adult content, sexploitation film producers were in a considerable bind—between competing with Hollywood's more daring approach and being pressed upon by more explicit fare showing in storefronts and more low-rent venues, in the form of 16mm simulation films, beaver films, and hard-core peep loops. Pressured as well from within by competition over exhibition, sexploitation's strategies in its "boom period" reflected a diversification of generic formulae and an amping up of sexually overt content. While threatened by the encroaching power of explicit screen sex, for recognizable-name filmmakers such as Russ Meyer, such convergence of content had benefits. Meyer's *Beyond the Valley of the Dolls* (1969) was bankrolled by Twentieth Century Fox, one of many studios looking to exploitation product to diversify its market share and appeal to a hipper audience. Fox signed Meyer on a three-picture deal. *Dolls,* scripted by young film critic Roger Ebert, a grab bag of late-1960s youth culture tropes, rock numbers, Hollywood allegory, and freakoutery that sensationally aped the Manson murders, was a box office hit, making a close to tenfold profit and signaling the first collaboration of the sexploitation industry and Hollywood.

Some observers saw this moment of saturation and tension in less copacetic terms. Richard Corliss illuminated the change in product as the sex film reached a crossroads: "The sexploiters has only two choices: either move to the center, and share the largesse of middle-American prurience with the majors by once again making substantially the same kind of films, only more so, or move to the left, and make pornography. . . . The result of this polarization has been a steep decline in quality."[41] Corliss went on to complain that the prevalence of hard-core sex had eradicated the "romance of the narrative form" of the sexploitation film and instead elevated the documentary aesthetics of the beaver and stag film, as "artistry was giving way to science, and a critical appreciation of the genre was forgotten for a new field of study, pornology, with its male and female subdivisions, penology and vaginology. The films were becoming tough, desperate, sadistic sloppy, depraved and dull."[42] Highlighting the retreat of diegesis, the triumph of the sexual organs, and the documentation of intercourse in the transforming sex film scene, Corliss identified a central aspect of the uniqueness of sexploitation as a historical form: its demand, however strained, for a suspension of disbelief and its assertion of a narrative universe.

Corliss reserved praise for some producers who continued to hold a true investment in narrative, including Meyer and Metzger, for their abilities to remain above the fray, as well as the films *Hot Spur* (sex western; Lee Frost, 1968), *The Curious Female* (sci-fi sex fantasy; Paul Rapp, 1969), or *The Spy Who Came* (sex spoof; Ron Werthheim, 1969). At the height of the sexploitation boom as well as this crucial moment of change, producers such as David Friedman's Entertainment Ventures Incorporated and Harry Novak's Boxoffice International were producing full-color features. Their two studios represented some of the mid-range and higher-budgeted films being made within the sexploitation circuit, with costs closer to the hundred thousand dollar range.[43] Friedman's production of *Starlet!* (Richard Kanter, 1969) brought the self-consciousness and circumstantial reflexivity of sexploitation films full circle in its treatment of the behind-the-scenes operations of exploitation and skin flick production. Spotlighting the EVI studios themselves, with Friedman appearing in a cameo role, the film was a fictionalized treatise on the state of the adult film industry at the time, as the trailer blared: at last "an adult film about the adult film industry!"

In the tradition of Hollywood's backstage melodramas, such as *All about Eve* (Joseph Mankiewicz, 1950), with its tale of the sparkling ingenue set against the aging star, *Starlet!* positioned the emergent competition of the hard-core 16mm producers contra the legitimated product of soft-core sexploitation through the figures of its two dueling stars—the young Carol Yates, who is discovered through a stag film (and is renamed Starliss Knight by the EVI studio bosses as an attempt to break her into soft-core), and Maxine Henning, an aging sexploitation star who has been relegated to spaghetti westerns. "Breaking into the business" for Carol Yates is marked by her being discovered by the soft-core producers. Soft-core sexploitation in the film is positioned as a more financially stable and viable production venue than hard-core stags, in which the stag is both the stepping-stone and the hidden illegitimate mode that must be kept secret. David Andrews, following an argument made by Eric Schaefer regarding

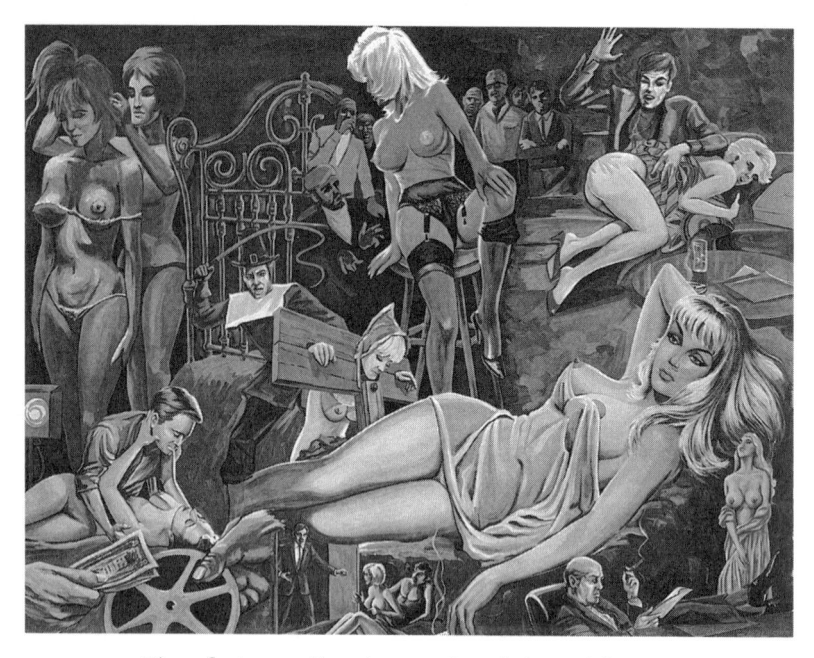

FIGURE 30. The reflexive motifs and seamy degradations of the casting couch for a sexploitation starlet, as illustrated in the interior of *Starlet*'s press book. Painting by Rudy Escalera. Courtesy of Something Weird Video.

classical exploitation, reads this film as indicative of the ways that sexploitation in its full-fledged soft-core period aimed to "displace its abjection" onto stags, claiming its higher cultural legitimacy, but with limited results.[44] *Starlet!* is significant in its thematizing of its own conditions of production, placing sexploitation film on the map as a valid and economically established mode of cultural production, a self-validating gesture of asserting stature by performing it formally and thematically. By analogizing the operations of a soft-core sexploitation studio with the prestige and industrial professionalism of major studio practice, and through the representational codes of Hollywood's own traditions of self-conscious films about themselves, *Starlet!* deploys a sardonic hubris about its own place in the film market, and it constantly references the accomplishments of its producers through inside jokes as well as its stilted dialogue. *Starlet!*'s inscription and reflexivity about its own means of production signals a divergence from dramatizations of the genre's conditions of reception as well as marking one distinction between the Los Angeles and the New York styles of sexploitation production. The West Coast filmmakers, much closer to the orbit of Hollywood and working on soundstages and studios, as did the EVI production, bore much greater allegiance formally to the large-scale modes of production of the mainstream film industry. The studio set becomes itself a space of enactment, aspiration, possibility, and irony—sending up certain trends within the late 1960s, including the competing exploitation formula of the biker film. The reflexive gesture, if seen in a continuum from the earliest sexploitation films discussed in the previous chapter, has moved from the fantastical imagined space of comedy to industrial generic modes.

In the context of the expansion of sexploitation's reach and exhibition in the late 1960s, the self-importance of *Starlet!* indexed the currency of this mode of production's rising fortunes, extending the preoccupations of earlier films with the exploitative nature of the sex trade into a more comic, rather than melodramatic or tragic, mode. The apotheosis of sexploitation's self-reflexive tendencies, the film's discourse with itself about itself, revealed an industry both in a paradoxical period of market prominence and under threat by more explicit, and more culturally derided, cinematic forms.[45] These threats, proffered by a more competitive market, as Corliss's complaints suggested, came from varied locations, including the aforementioned beaver films and 16mm features. By 1970, the sex film market had changed irrevocably with the introduction of the spectacle of hard-core sex onto the scene, through both the infiltration of loops and "Frisco" films, short films showing women exposing their genitals, seen in storefront theaters and peepshows, and also the emergence of feature films that framed the explicit sex act through a variety of frames. The sex documentaries, such as *Sexual Freedom in Denmark* (M. C. Von Hellen, 1970) and *A History of the Blue Movie* (Alex de Renzy, 1970), took as their claimed goal the exposition of contemporary sexual practices as well as the historicization of sexual representation, in the latter case. Much as *Starlet!* inscribed its own legitimacy through the assertion of a diegetic universe furnished by the adult film studio, so, too, did *A History of the Blue Movie* assert the importance and social value of sex cinema through a historicist impulse. Using the reflexive frame of historicity, de Renzy's film curated a series of sex films, from the earliest stags, such as *A Grass Sandwich* and *Buried Treasure,* on to latter-day productions, including de Renzy's own, in a self-reflexive loop back to the present. De Renzy asserted these films' cultural significance *as historical* through their instantiation within a continuum of explicit representation. The utility of a pedagogical framing of explicit sex had also facilitated the production of varied marriage manual, or "white coater," films, such as *Man and Wife*

(Marv Miller, 1969) and *The Language of Love* (Torgny Wickman, 1969), which presented explicit sexual positions within a discourse of marital improvement and sexological instruction. But the biggest intervention and challenge to the sexploitation form came in the form of the hard-core narrative feature, forwarded by 16mm practitioners such as Michael Benveniste and Howard Ziehm, who produced, in advance of *Deep Throat* (Gerard Damiano, 1972), the first widely distributed hard-core feature, *Mona* (alternately *Mona, the Virgin Nymph*), in 1970—much like *Deep Throat*, the film that would in two years eclipse it, a treatise on the liminal status of fellatio as a sex act.

Thus, formal, discursive, and historical reflexivity served this moment as a protective gesture, an authenticating device, and an entry point into a set of new representational possibilities. The transformation of the sex film scene and of the nature of filmic obscenity in these years was incontrovertibly intertwined with the fate of sexploitation as a form and with the constitution of a new, expanded horizon of erotic consumption. The terms of these negotiations are the concern of the following chapter, which treats the self-awareness of the sex film critic and spectator in the latter half of the 1960s as the "problem" of adult film reception became a subject not only of film critical but also of national, federal, and popular concern.

CHAPTER FOUR

Watching an "Audience of Voyeurs"
Adult Film Reception

The previous two chapters have elaborated how sexploitation films consistently allegorized their conditions of reception. But what anxieties, crises of legitimacy, and modes of projection were entailed in the public imaginary that produced such fictions, and out of what cultural conditions did they emerge? Here I turn to examine cultural discourses surrounding watching simulated sex in the public space of the film theater by pursuing the historical reception of sexploitation films in the 1960s and the troubled and elusive nature of the "skin flick" audience. The encounters chronicled here illuminate the negotiation of the novelties, pleasures, dissatisfactions, and discomforts of sexploitation consumption by empirical and imagined audiences.

From a retrospective vantage point, it may be easy to view the audiences for sexploitation films categorically as "rubes," "dupes," or "dirty old men," lured into the theater by salacious promises of fleshy excess. Indeed, this is also an attitude that sexploitation producers themselves perpetuated, creating a notion of a gullible spectator whose naïveté, loneliness, and sexual need or curiosity could be the formula for box office profit. In his analysis of the construction of the sexploitation audience through film advertising, Eric Schaefer has detailed how the textual and promotional strategies of sexploitation producers, by characterizing their viewers as degenerate, lewd, or desperate loners, proved both efficacious but later also costly, as the mode was unable to evade the unsavory aspects of its association with the "lecherous."[1] So no doubt a measure of skepticism or wariness with respect to this characterization of actual viewers is necessary.[2] But this discourse of the "dupe" and "rube" itself is also, as we will see, thus embedded in the experience of the sexploitation film as a commodity form and its complex address of evasion and subterfuge, as it relies on the disjunction between the promise of *too much* and the reality of *not enough* and on the boundaries between the implicit and explicit image.

Thus parsing the evidence of sexploitation's filmgoer—both as historical subject and discursive manifestation—undoubtedly treads a tricky terrain. On one hand, one must negotiate the vernacular stereotypes and imaging of the reprobate, malingering, dissolute deviant—the "dirty old man," who plays into alarmist readings of the film spectator as the aroused, mimetic pervert. And on the other hand, one has to acknowledge that the historical reception sphere for sexploitation cinema was a predominantly heterosexual male one, even though it began to transform toward a more mixed audience and couples crowd by the late 1960s, as confirmed by the Obscenity Commission reports of 1970.[3] The narrative of the sexploitation audience—in the window between the emergence of the mode in the form of the nudie cutie and the arrival of the hard-core pornographic feature (roughly 1960–72)—is a narrative of male desire and heterocentric spectatorship, even as it opens out onto and abuts alternatives. Queer implications lurked at the margins in many sexploitation narratives, as seen in films such as *The Defilers* (David Friedman and R. L. Frost, 1965) and *Lorna* (Russ Meyer, 1964). More explicitly, the corporeal proximity of men to each other in the sexualized, public space of the film theater is a significant condition for homosociality and male contact that sexploitation film exhibition historically generated, as discussed by Jeffrey Escoffier, Jose Capino, and Samuel Delany, among others. The production of gay adult film in the late 1960s, contemporaneous to sexploitation but in distinct, if not proximate, locations, also attests to these potential elsewheres.[4] Moreover, the later 1960s preoccupation with female sexual desire further complicates questions of identification and reception. These points, regarding a slavishly heterosexual masculine culture and the contradictions and countervailing tendencies that lurk below it, seem obvious but also necessary to acknowledge. The kind of filmic experience offered by sexploitation film—its simulated soft-core sexual scenarios, female nudity, the tactics of tease and deferral as well as titillating appeals to spectacle, and its leering at guilty pleasures—identifies a cinema constituted through a horizon of prohibition, in a calculus of sensational display and moral and formal denial. Therefore narratives of sexploitation's spectatorial experience negotiate the often-uneven historical trajectory from concealment to revelation—giving frequently sardonic voice to sexploitation's incessant potentials for disappointment and ambivalence.

Industry preconceptions regarding the demographics of the American film audience were being reconfigured in the 1960s, seen in what Paul Monaco describes as the phenomenon of the "runaway audience."[5] The

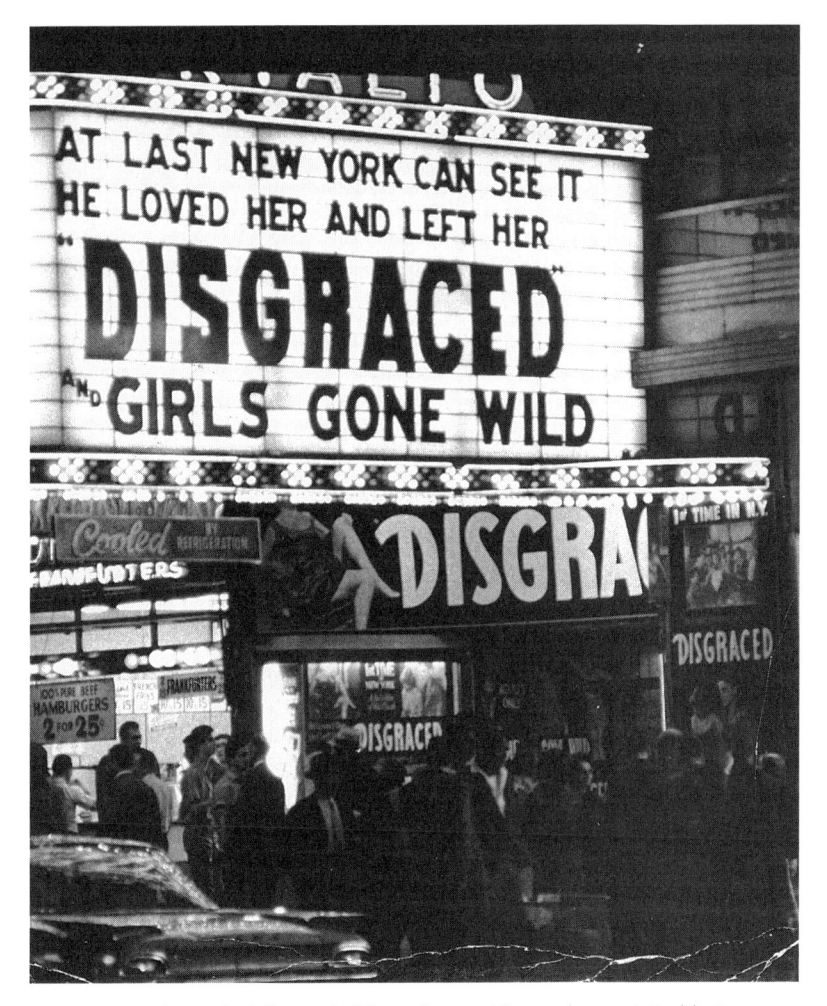

FIGURE 31. The Rialto Theater in Times Square (date unknown), its blaring marquee and posters attracting a crowd. Photograph by D. Jordan Wilson. Collection of Michael Bowen.

discourses around sexploitation film and its dubious viewers introduce a set of knotty questions regarding art, obscenity and aesthetics, youth and adult markets, boredom and arousal, and class and taste designations. The reception of sexploitation films across a range of locations—from the film critical establishment; in the popular press and industry press; from underground, literary, and countercultural sources; in anonymous newsletters; and in sociological and federal investigations of the empirical audience of adult films—reveals a wide range of ways in which the "erotica consumer" emerged as a public figure within an arena of debate about sexual representations, screen permissiveness, and the changing nature of filmgoing in the 1960s. In 1960s film culture, the reorientation of the film as art discourse, the influx of foreign films with sexual content, and the redefinitions of Hollywood product in relationship to the independents all facilitated a venue within which sexploitation would begin to be taken seriously, both industrially and aesthetically, by a critical establishment. The development of a viable market for specifically "adult" film by the late 1960s was thus inextricable from and perpetuated by the widening exhibition of sexploitation—the mode in fact was instrumental in shifting the notion of adults-only cinema to its association with primarily sexual material.

The varying accounts of spectators and spectatorship here indicate the extent to which the identity of the erotica consumer was a fluctuating one, caught between the commonplace of distinctly middle-class, middle-aged masculinity and the potential of an "in-the-know," youth-affiliated, and more diverse—in terms of gender and sexual orientation—group of spectators. The adult filmgoer as a figure was also characterized, as we will see, by certain affects and behaviors: boredom, arousal, stillness, dissatisfaction, frustration, self-awareness, and skepticism—rhetorical tropes of viewer response. As this chapter argues, the sexploitation spectator, both an imagined figure and a material, actual one, makes visible an emergent mercurial market for male desire and articulates consumer subjectivity centered on and through adult media. This element of consumerism and the articulation of consumer choice as an expressive right is itself a consequence of the shifting legal and cultural discourse around adult film spectatorship. As Leigh Anne Wheeler has demonstrated, and as chapter 1 touched on, organizations such as the American Civil Liberties Union that defended adult media reconfigured a reading of the First Amendment to account more broadly for the rights of consumers as well as producers, signaling a sea change in the public imaginary regarding the *right* and *freedom to look*, a right and freedom newly linked with contemporary sexual subjectivity.[6] This chapter contends that adult film spectatorship was negotiated precisely in this wider context and through the terms and ambivalences of an emergent consumer discourse around sexploitation cinema. This exploration is not interested in reclaiming the transgressive or resistant nature of a group of historical spectators or moments of reception, or in extending the overwrought debates in audience research and cultural studies regarding "passive" and "active" viewers.[7] Rather, the aim here is to complicate a history of adult film reception, sketching out some areas in which sexploitation films, their spectators, and their exhibition contexts began to be discussed in diverse critical and social scientific arenas. Historically and methodologically, the use-value of a reception study of sexploitation films can help fill out a history of filmgoing in the 1960s.[8]

Critical Reception: "Deception" and the Problem of Aesthetics

In the mid-1960s, in light of the deployment of nudity not only by sexploitation cinema but also by Hollywood and art house cinema within the competitive vagaries of the film market, the criteria of filmic taste flowered into an alibi for altering audience demographics and the capacious accommodation of ever more explicit film fare by the general moviegoing public. An article in *Time* magazine in 1964 characterized the cultural sweep of a new era, the "second sexual revolution," which was being inaugurated by a condition called "Spectator Sex":

> For now it sometimes seems that all America is one big Orgone Box. . . . With today's model, it is no longer necessary to sit in cramped quarters for a specific time. Improved and enlarged to encompass the entire continent, the big machine works on its subjects continuously, day and night. From innumerable screens and stages, posters and pages, it flashes the larger-than-lifesize images of sex. From countless racks and shelves it pushes the books which a few years ago were considered pornography. From a myriad loudspeakers it broadcasts the words and rhythms of pop-music erotica. And constantly, over the intellectual Muzak, comes the message that sex will save you and libido make you free. . . . The cult of pop hedonism and sexual sophistication grows apace.[9]

The industry press and the film critical establishment were beginning to take notice of sexploitation films and makers as industrial players and competitors in their own right, prominent purveyors of this brand of "pop hedonism." A *Variety* article in early 1965 would exclaim, "Wider Public for Sexy Films: Folks 'Tsk-Tsk' but Buy Tickets." In it, Radley Metzger's business partner in Audubon Films, Ava Leighton, states that, "despite the talk of censorship and so-called public outrage, more and more theaters are playing this (sexploitation) product all the time."[10] As sexploitation films began to establish a stronger foothold with wider exhibition through the imports and productions of Audubon and other New York– and Los Angeles–based outfits, the developing marketplace for erotic imagery would create a range of responses to sexploitation as a social and cultural phenomenon as well as an as yet denigrated, yet nonetheless aesthetic, experience.

The success of art houses in the 1950s established a viewing public that was at odds with Hollywood's now antiquated notion of a mass audience.

Ironically, the art house reception sphere was conceived of as both a site of more mature, adults-only product and an emergent venue for younger viewers.[11] Eric Schaefer has described how sexploitation filmmakers capitalized on the patina of the film as art discourse to bolster their box office returns, suggesting that "by the early 1960s, the terms art theater and art film had become synonymous with nudity."[12] The overlap between the film as art discourse and the developing venues for sexploitation film is evident in the publication *Art Films International,* ostensibly a magazine for the art house connoisseur. On further examination, however, it reveals itself as a venue for the linkage of high- and lowbrow forms through their shared preoccupations with screen eroticism and nude exposure, be it of no-name American starlets or European bombshells such as Sophia Loren. Initially titled *Adult Art Films* in its first issue in 1963, the magazine featured articles with titles such as "Starlets: Is the Bust a Must?" and "Where Will They Kiss Next?"[13] The text would be accompanied by large black-and-white stills from salacious scenes in a variety of imported films playing in art houses as well as from classic and contemporary Hollywood films, ranging from *The Carpetbaggers* (Edward Dmytryk, 1964) to *Women of the World* (Gualtiero Jacopetti, 1963) to *The Silence* (Ingmar Bergman, 1963) to the latest Brigitte Bardot vehicle.

Art Films International serves an example of early- to mid-1960s affiliations of adult cinema with a discourse of connoisseurship, while also allowing a more prurient aim, a direct mingling of the "cold beer and greaseburger" and "white wine and canapes" crowds David Friedman diagrammed as respective audiences for exploitation and art cinema.[14] It is also a predecessor of the sex film magazines that would begin to circulate in the mid-1960s, such as *Wicked Films, Torrid Films, Shocking Reels,* and *Banned,* that cross-promoted soon-to-be-released films by sexploitation producers but also did double duty as pinup magazines.[15] Yet in the early 1960s, *Art Films* clung closely to an aesthetic appreciation model more allied with the art house mode of reception, while coyly handling its main subject—the eroticization of the screen. Addressing its potential readership, an advertisement for the magazine within its own pages features a spotlight on a director's chair, the back of the chair emblazoned with the publication's logo and a copy of the magazine on the seat, with a tagline at the top of the page stating, "The naked symbol for today's adult film audience . . ." The minimalism of the advertisement underscores the project of legitimation at work, in which the "Art" of cinema is marshaled through a signifier that collapses authorial direction and spectatorial refinement; the word "naked" suggests the more lewd aspects of the magazine's character in its appeals via the ribaldry of the film stills.

NUDERAMA

by David Moller

As an itinerant lecher, I have travelled the world over and have found in all big cities a "Times Square" of some sort. All such honky-tonk sections — wherever they are, however they may differ — have in common a half-dozen or so movie-houses exhibiting films calculated solely to—how shall I put it—titillate our libidinous impulses. These are the nudist films, the girlie films, the Z-budget backstage melodramas featuring barebosomed, over-ripe chorines. Occasionally, an honest anthropological documentary finds its way to such screens, and the trick is to wait patiently for those few long shots of bronzed beauties sporting stichless in the surf. Occasionally, too, a quality foreign film is booked, e.g., the Italian *Love in the City*, and stills therefrom are selected for their suggestive content and posted outside with provocative text. But the nudist films are the staple, and these are endlessly re-titled, re-issued, and re-exhibited within that strange circuit that unites the Times Squares of this world.

All that flesh. And even for itinerant lechers, such a bore ... like the last such movie-house I visited, along Forty-Second Street. It was a hot day in August, the pavement baking through your shoes, the dark, air-conditioned recesses beckoning you from beyond the cashier (admission $1.50), the odor of lobby popcorn like trade winds from a pagan, bare-bosomed isle.

But once inside, you begin to feel a growing disenchantment.

FIGURE 32. David Moller's essay "Nuderama" in *Art Films International*, illustrated with an image of female passersby outside a sexploitation theater.

Grouping together a wide range of films across classical and contemporary Hollywood, European productions, and independent sexploitation films under the elevating rubric of art, *Art Films International* linked itself with another newly minted magazine of more serious film criticism, *Film Comment*, which took advertising space amid *Art Films'* pages. An *Art Films* article from 1964, titled "Nuderama" (originally published in 1962 in *Vision* magazine, the direct predecessor of *Film Comment*), would survey the scene of the nudie film market. The writer, David Moller, reflected an ethnographic style that would become, as I will show, customary among film critics turned "participant observers" peeking in on the cultural phenomenon of sexploitation film and its attendant spaces of reception. Characterizing himself as an "itinerant lecher," Moller remarked that Times Square had become an archetype of a particular kind of urban space, in which the films were

> calculated solely to—how shall I put it—titillate our libidinous impulses. These are the nudist films, the girlie films, the Z-budget backstage melodramas featuring bare bosomed overripe chorines. . . . Occasionally a quality foreign film is booked. . . . But the nudist films are the staple, and these are endlessly re-titled, re-issued and re-exhibited within that strange circuit that unites the Times Squares of the world. All that flesh. And even for itinerant lechers, such a bore.[16]

His feint of weariness tempered the connoisseur's knowledge of the repackaging tactics of exploitation distributors. This manifestation of the discourse of boredom in response to sexually implicit and erotic media forms in the 1960s represented a new means of negotiating the field of aesthetic taste and distinction, as the interpretive deflection of boredom would in this period become an alibi of a disinterested, distanced gaze in relationship to the panoply of erotic entertainments and thus draw recourse to forms of aesthetic valuation or, more specifically, devaluation. Patrice Petro links the etiology of boredom to the defining conditions of media in twentieth-century modernity, stating that "boredom reemerges as both an aesthetic and phenomenological problem. . . . Boredom seems to be about too much and too little, sensory overload and sensory deprivation, anxieties of excess and anxieties of loss. . . . The term boredom thus anticipates a visual economy of repetition notably absent from ennui, and a displeasure in being seen while looking that simultaneously evokes the experience of the classic male voyeur as well as the ostensible (feminine) object of his gaze."[17] Thus the efficacy of the discursive regime of boredom works as a means to make sense of as well as position oneself in relationship to a new horizon of erotic entertainments. Boredom, an affect that accompanies the perception of novelty, as Petro reminds us, becomes here a strategy of disidentification in the nudie film reception context.

Writing about the predominantly nudist films showing in the early 1960s, Moller characterized the audience's expectations as follows:

> Once inside you begin to feel a growing sense of disenchantment. You feel taken, because the lobby advertisements and the $1.50 had led you to expect something special. The all-male audience of the cinema I went to was not made up of sexual deviates and perverts in the final throes of sexual crescendo, and one had only to be seated in front of the screen for a few minutes to see why. There is something rather sexless about a nudist film, once one has got over the initial shock of seeing a little more of the female torso than usual. After all, once there is nothing more to hint at, or to infer, or to expose gradually, a great deal of excitement is taken out of the nude female bosom. The sheer fact of the lady's nudity inhibits rather than enhances the salacious elements of the film.

After the "shock of the new," nudity, has been naturalized, erotic stimulation turns into a form of understimulation that characterizes the affect of the bored spectator. Reinforcing Leslie Fiedler's lament regarding the sexlessness and reflexive deficiencies of *Mr. Teas,* Moller's elucidation of the resonant disappointment undergirding nudie film spectatorship would become an ongoing means of both spectatorial justification and sociological, if not aesthetic, legitimation. According to Moller's argument, the audience's sexual intent is deflected by the unerotic nature of the films on display, and thus the characterization of male desire is by default shaped precisely by the failures of the film to "properly" arouse. Therefore the film's failures allow it to be written about. Moller hopes to normalize the male audience's "natural curiosity" regarding female nudity. He goes on to discuss the failed virtues of Doris Wishman's nudist camp film *Hideout in the Sun* (1960) as well as the recycled B movie *Love Island* (Bud Pollard, 1952), featuring Eva Gabor in an island epic narrative, into which a number of scenes of documentary nudity and exposed breasts were spliced in this recirculated print. Moller details the bisected narrative of *Hideout,* which joins an action caper with a nudist melodrama, suggesting that the film would have been better served as a ten-minute short, whereas "spread over seventy minutes, it was like a slow death . . . dramatic urgency, such as it is comes to a grinding halt once we hit the nudist colony, and thereafter we are treated to an orgy of interminable games of handball, women setting picnic tables, people swimming and sun-worshippers reclining in deckchairs."[18] Moller, and the other critics who followed him, would tread a tricky ground of admitting to the indulgence of these films and thus potentially courting the shaming brand of social "deviate." Therefore, in evaluating the nudie films as subpar aesthetic products, the films' aesthetic failures could guarantee the audience's faculties of judgment and capacity for discernment apart from the films' erotic lures. Moller thus concludes his argument with a defense of the film audience:

> That was the program, monotonous and more than a little pathetic. Contrary to prevailing myth, we of the audience at these flesh shows do not spend the whole of our day there. I emphatically did not stay for a second showing. Nor do we hide under our seats when the intermission lights go on. Instead, we glare at one another sulkily, feeling cheated. I left without a single snigger, chuckle, bead of sweat, or tingle of excitement, reconciled to returning to the outside world, perhaps relatively more exciting—the world of clothes and reality.[19]

Moller's need to identify himself as part of a nascent group of anonymous spectators is significant in its recognition of the construction of the sociological and commonplace characteristics of this group in a popular imaginary. The nudie audience, positioned as yet another "special interest" group, alongside art cinema patrons, would begin to fracture the previously held imagining of a mass audience ruled by Hollywood fare.[20] The nudie film public was thus becoming distinct from the art house's clientele, while retaining the art house audience's presumably steely resolve in the face of corporeal revelations on-screen. Admitting to having been willingly "cheated"—that is, paradoxically succumbing to the role of, at least in terms of money spent, a "sucker" or "dupe"—Moller's autoethnography takes part in a developing pattern of writing about the emerging reception culture of adults-only cinema. To avoid being characterized as "pathetic," Moller and other critics would need to mark off the films as monotonous, boring, and aesthetically insufficient. A later critic, writing in 1968 regarding his trawl through the 16mm and sexploitation houses, would query, "Are seven or eight minutes of sex worth the 60 or 70 of painfully amateur boredom?"[21] The tension that would develop in writings such as Moller's regarding the nudie film experience would vacillate between the poles of articulating positions of interest and disinterest, between a ribald curiosity and rapt erotic attention, and a disaffiliating move of boredom, a disassociation with the salacious reputation of the sexploitation film market as a whole. The trajectory from disinterest to a justified interest or investment in the genre or specific films was of course underwritten by an acknowledgment of an embarrassing and not yet fully socially mandated marketplace for male desire.

Other critical moments of reception would begin by the mid-1960s to evidence an interest in aesthetic analysis, even if only through a framework of negation, in terms of what the films tended to lack. Michael Valenti, writing for Paul Krassner's countercultural, underground paper *The Realist* in 1965, managed to venture into the grind house strip in Times Square for a similar experiment in participant observation. Valenti's tale from the "front" signaled an emerging trend and cultural curiosity with what went on inside the confines of the skin flick house, from the vantage point of a younger and more hip audience, and with a seriousness of interest in what the films actually looked (and sounded) like.[22] Valenti's mission was to find out if the films "cheated" their audience, asking, "was it true that they promised more outside than they delivered inside? And parallelly [sic], was anything inside *really* sexy?"[23] By foregrounding the question of the dupe, of the gullibility of the nudie film regular, Valenti engaged in a discourse of erotic consumption that would robustly emerge in the adult film market just a few years later. His cinephile orientation was also revealed in one of his primary complaints about the practices of sexploitation exhibition—in the unannounced use of dubbing in many nudie imports repurposed for American distribution.[24] Throughout his article, there is a concern over how to make sense of sexploitation in relation to operative conventions of cinematic taste and in terms of filmic aesthetics. Discussing an exceptional moment of poolside seduction in Radley Metzger's *The Dirty Girls* (1965), he wrote:

> It is that rare and wonderful thing again, art accidentally intruding itself. Unable to show what is happening in the pool, the director has no alternative but to leave it to the imagination, to suggest it through the faces of the onlookers. Never has voyeurism triumphed so gloriously over the sordidness of reality.[25]

This reading of accidental artfulness that could emerge from the viewing of sexploitation films was extended in Valenti's discussion of the climate of indirection and the specter of censorial limitations that characterized sexploitation films of the mid-1960s, still operating within the purview of prior restraint. Attending to the virtues of the American-made nudie film, as opposed to the imported European "art film," Valenti noted that

> where the American made nudies are superior (using the criteria of the aficionado, now) is in suggesting the explosive climate of the frankly pornographic film: in the domestic ones, it's always three seconds before strip-down. This of course, is solely aura, a kind of bachannalian ambiance created by the pulsating jazz, the nervous camera, the girls in

easy-to-shed clothing. But the clothes stay on, or if they come off the camera finds something else to explore, maybe a lace curtain caught in a light spring zephyr. If you have 15–15 vision, maybe you can catch a subliminal patch of breast just before the camera swings away.[26]

Acknowledging the illicit nature of sexploitation in its visual manifestations of a certain ambiance, this critic's sardonic recognition of the devices of the soft-core tease, recalling specifically the curtain-blowing scene in Russ Meyer's *Lorna,* speaks to the recognized conditions of erotic suggestion and necessary restraint in the elucidation of screen sex. Valenti, deploying a cineaste discourse, singled out a British film (originally titled *Naked Fury,* 1959) rereleased by Joseph Brenner Associates on the exploitation market in 1964 as *The Pleasure Lovers,* calling attention to the exemplary aesthetics of its rape scene:

> Crass commerce aside, the one area where the nudies are threatening to do something new is in the use of the camera. . . . Best example . . . rape scene in *The Pleasure Lovers.* . . . In that one fascinating scene, artistry fights for recognition. A moaning musical score neatly cleaves the scene from the rest of the movie as the gang leader enters the captive girl's room. . . . The rest of the action has a chiaroscuro underwater quality, undulating waves of flesh and fantasy enveloping each other. Suddenly he's standing over her muttering, "You're not so pure baby . . ." Here the camera becomes a hydra-headed voyeur that sees all. The brassiere is torn away, first backview, as the victim whimpers. Then swiftly the camera backtracks, the brassiere is magically replaced and once more torn away, this time in front view. This is a new kind of voyeurism, as though the act is so important, so electrifying that it can't be seen too often or from too many different angles. Finally another male fantasy fulfilled, victim submits to her rapist.[27]

Valenti's observations of this film, articulating the motif of voyeurism so prominent within the public culture of this time, attest to a developing appreciation of the lures of the sexploitation film and its unique mode of address. The fracturing and temporal repetitions of the described scene seem to fuse a New Wave aesthetics of disjunction, which had so enchanted cosmopolitan film audiences, with the stark economic bottom line of sexploitation's mode of production. Fiscal necessity merges with formal devices, thus repeating licentious action and reduplicating the spectator's desire. This scene, fractured, in this film critical interpretation, from the cohesiveness of narrative, is put to work as a mobilizing, cinephiliac fragment, unmoored from the humdrum nature of the rest of the film.

Yet Valenti would reserve his most smugly clever insights for the elusive qualities of the skin flick audience itself, yet without Moller's defensive self-consciousness regarding his own perceived social status as "lecher." Valenti described his anonymous viewing companions through the terms of a stilted fascination regarding their in-house behavior, commenting as follows on their characteristic stoicism and seeming indifference to some of the "dishonest" disparities between the promise of the trailer and the content of the films:

> Perhaps *expecting* to be cheated, the audiences seem to have no particular reaction to this cynical practice. As to that audience, regardless of time of day or night, weekday or weekend, it is composed of lone men who sit passively and patiently, as far apart as possible in a geometric mosaic worthy of 9th Century Arab architects. (It is considered bad form to sit either directly behind, or behind and one seat to the side, of an earlier arriver. And in five of six trips, I never heard a patron address a single word to another patron.) There are very few women, generally escorted—except the few Golden Agers—and always seated in the last three rows. (I haven't figured out why—unless it's simply that women have better eyesight than men.) There is no talking, no coughing, no complaining—even when, as occurred one night, a feathery centipede seemed to have swum into the projection stream. It took the projectionist ten minutes to spot the trouble—ten of the most silent minutes I've ever spent in a movie house. And this in Times Square. . . . What this disciplined audience does permit itself is breathing.[28]

This observation regarding the disavowed homosocial architectonics and geometric organization of adult film theater seating became a common refrain among critical "interlopers," attesting to a heightened preoccupation with the physical comportment of the skin flick regular. Valenti's impressions of this group of viewers, whether or not they are accurate or embellished, nevertheless exhibit a recurring and persistent fixation on the bodily and visceral response of the nudie-going public. The irony of the discussion of heavy breathing was likely not lost on *Realist* readers, in that the very act of breathing, which was deployed quite often in sexploitation films themselves as a marker of specifically female arousal, is constructed into an extratextual index of male bodily response in the space of the darkened film theater. Valenti's incredulity serves as an alibi, makes him an outsider observing the regular audience's lack of physical response as a symptom of repressed autoerotic desires. It also confirmed the sense in which the audience, collectively imagined and figured, could only be made to materialize through a "confessional" gesture of self-abnegation, which signifies a desire toward invisibility and anonymity. At the same time, their group (in)activity is recognized as an emblem of collective desire and the prohibition on embodied sexuality in the public space of the film theater, a sensibility or practice of reading that pervades other accounts of the sexploitation audience from this time.

Set against this projected drama of (predominantly) male embarrassment, Valenti's sardonic acknowledgment of the presence of a small coterie of female viewers indicated the broadening appeal of the sexploitation film for the couples audience by the mid-1960s. Yet it also deflected the possible danger and discomfort implicit in women's visitation of a predominantly male space of erotic consumption. Certainly sitting in the back row implies a reticence to be seen by other theater patrons as well as allowing for the potential of a quick exit if necessary, a pragmatic fact that Valenti scarcely deigned to register beneath the veil of his somewhat dismissive "with-it" humor.

Finally, noting the spreading cultural pervasiveness and acceptability of seeing sexually tinged drama in public, Valenti observed that the nudies were migrating from the grind house ghettoes to tonier art houses, prognosticating that "in an increasingly alienated world, the hard-breathers may ultimately be sharing the delectations of the flesh and the cleansing stroke of the whip with Vassar girls in pony tails and young men with beards, and wondering what ever happened to their lonely private world of dirty movies."[29]

By 1967, sexploitation films had entered the cultural lexicon, and the trade press was speculating on their influence on aboveground filmmakers. *Variety* compared the radical change in content from the comparatively chaste *Orgy at Lil's Place* (Jerald Intrator, 1964) to the more direct depiction of bare breasts and "sexual episodes" in the 1966 release of Radley Metzger's *The Alley Cats*.[30] Their impact could be felt in the claims of *Los Angeles Times* film critic Kevin Thomas, who would attribute to the "majority of pictures currently playing around town" the generic characteristics of exploitation, from Otto Preminger's *Hurry Sundown* (1967) to the mondo film *Africa Addio* (Gualtiero Jacopettie and Franco Prosperi, 1966) to Andy Warhol's *Chelsea Girls* (1966).[31] By reversing the operative assumption that lowbrow forms have the capacity to move up in status, whereas highbrow cultural forms rarely get demoted to lowbrow assignations, Thomas laments the creeping influence of exploitation's strategies of sensation, shock, and exoticism on the larger film industry, from Hollywood to foreign imports to the avant-garde. This blurring of aesthetic registers and acknowledgment of the mutual interplay between high and low forms could be seen in an emergent aesthetic criticism of the sexploitation film—in which literary allusions and high art comparison could be set against the perceptual experience and disorientation offered by the sex film.

Valenti was thus not alone in his exploration of some of the phenomenological aesthetics of the sexploitation film amid the overwhelming ambiance of heavy breathing; the poet Fred Chappell would pen an aphoristic essay, "Twenty-Six Propositions about Skin Flicks," in the film appreciation book *Man and the Movies* (1967), employing a baroquely associative style of analysis. His prose most directly recalls surrealist writings on dejected forms of popular cinema, such as Ado Kyrou's essay "The Marvelous Is Popular," as well as the ecstatic classical film theory of Bela Balazs and Jean Epstein, in their attentiveness to corporeal realism and *photogenie*.[32] Chappell's style of engagement with sexploitation's imaginary enumerates the counterintuitive virtues of the nudie film, in which the recalcitrant corporeality of the filmed body ultimately resists any exegetic framework or distanced analysis. But Chappell begins with the premise of the cheap, addressing implicitly the accusations of sexploitation's aesthetic, as well as moral, poverty:

> That *cheapness* as an aesthetic judgment is purely literary and applies only to the psychological work in hand. That no movie is properly called cheap, because all are: mere depthless images which flicker one over another over a darkened surface. *Cheapness*: nothing to do with subject matter. . . . How many fine novels are sordid at heart! . . . To expect a "great movie" is to insult the eye. The business of the eye is to suck the surface images off all its objects, to skewer them, to glut the brain. The business of the eye is to suspend critical judgment. . . . The question the nudie movie broaches is, why isn't the eye satisfied with these images?[33]

From the failures and disappointments of Moller and Valenti, we come to another form of aesthetic dissatisfaction, but one more attuned to the ephemerality of the cinematic medium. Proclaiming the democratization of the notion of art that had so motivated Susan Sontag's essay "One Culture and the New Sensibility," Chappell performs an "erotics of art" in which he attempts to follow the terms of the nudie films' most basic presumptions, reducing them to their most fundamental substrate.[34] Allying the nude female body with an accidental innocence, Chappell claims that innocence is not a "literary property" that can only be "chanced upon" but whose "use lies in its obscurity, an obscurity not produced by modesty, for surely innocence is neither modest nor immodest."[35]

Chappell attends to the filmed body, highlighting the ways in which the underlying moral code of sexploitation is set in conflict with the ineffability of corporeal flesh:

> In almost all nudie films there is a true but unarticulated idea . . . that physical nature itself is corrupt, has in itself the possibilities for its destruction; and is always unwittingly shown corrupted, flimsy under the grasp of society. But the human body, often exhibited as sadistically and masochistically degraded, as soiled and contemptible, burns through whatever attitudes the film tries to enclose it in. It maintains its integrity. Veins, pores, blemishes, follicles are stoutly independent and inform us that this kind of indignity is temporary, that the nonchalance of merely being defeats a superficial morality. . . . Does that girl's body . . . also resist the imagination? It's not malleable material for the camera, cannot be moralized or attitudinized. But it can be placed. It cannot be made shocking, nor more interesting than it already is. But it can invest its surroundings with some measure of stateliness or, at the least, with the brassy taste of the incongruous.[36]

Here Chappell comes to the crux of his reading of the disjunction between the flesh and the narratives that encase it, in which the screened body, in its materiality, is irreducible to an ideological purpose. A certain kind of purist formalism flowers in Chappell's prose, as he sees in sexploitation films a resistance of the structural features of the flesh to the impermanence of any given moral posture or narrative pretense. The female body thus becomes both a liberatory template that deflects social codes of propriety in its mere existential heft and also a site of irreducible physicality, weighted down by its own phenomenological features that implicate the cinema as an indexical form of realist representation. The novelty of nude exposure is here worked over into a kind of existential paradigm that naturalizes or diffuses taboo through the deployment of the ordinary. The mute facticity of the exposed body seen in unflinching close-up, its pores, follicles, and imperfections, signifies a pull toward the sublime through the banal.

The tension between the indexicality of the cinematic signifier as manifested in the body is placed next against the formalism of accidental filmic caprice, that is, in the films' often haphazard editorial organization. He continues:

> The single most salient element of skin flicks is poverty of the imagination. Obvious enough. But sometimes it operates as a curious virtue. In a great many skin flicks there is absolutely no way to tell what image will be thrown on the screen next. Cocteau—who had imagination— would have envied the skin movie this quality. It gives the audience

a restive apprehension. One emerges from the theater exhausted and exasperated, not because of the pictures of simple bodies, but because of uncontrolled tension.[37]

Thus the privileged realist object is transmuted into a surrealist one, in which the misdirected and impoverished energies of the films' limited means of production produce an experience of derangement, at least through Chappell's creative *detournement* of the coded and constrained erotics of nudie film spectatorship. *Uncontrolled tension* becomes a migratory term, moving from the lower body to the upper body—from arousal to discernment—a deflection of arousal into an experience of disjointed narrative and cinematographic structure, manifesting in exhaustion and confusion. The anticipation and erotic waiting that the sexploitation film structurally produces are mined by Chappell for aesthetic revelation, musings that both look back toward the avant-garde spectatorial practices of Kyrou and forward, presaging the camp aesthetics and cultist appreciations of latter-day audiences who delight in the revivified fragment. The body in the end, however, triumphs over form: in Chappell's estimation, the flesh is the site, the "raw material that worship is exercised upon,"[38] without the intervention of the personal vision of a creative author. What allows Chappell's interpretation to work is a certain obviation of the function of the sexploitation director—whose seemingly anonymous and no-name status provides a text without a functional or recognizable *source*. In the same year that Roland Barthes wrote "The Death of the Author,"[39] Chappell's engagement with the sexploitation film experience privileges the moment, space, and climate of reception and the quality of the images unmoored from any narrative or necessary knowledge of their production, its own form of "automatic writing." For these cinematic images and dislocated fragments to retain their power, they appear as abstracted from a system of production or from the intertext of a directorial oeuvre. Chappell's postsurrealist interpretive style imbues the aesthetic features of the sexploitation film circa the mid-1960s with the frisson of chance encounter, in which artistry again "accidentally" intrudes through a form of alchemical happenstance.

"King Leer" and the "Ophuls of Orgasm": Meyer, Metzger, and Authorial Distinction

Whereas the notion of an absent author facilitated Chappell's reading of the skin flick experience, the place of an authorial discourse in reception of the sexploitation film was not entirely absent. Because sexploitation was critically discussed far more as a cultural and economic phenomenon that signaled a larger transformation in filmic tastes and permissiveness, rather than as a rarefied art cinema, the discourse of authorship was usually less readily employed, despite the inroads that Andrew Sarris's popularization of the *politique de auteurs* of the Cahiers du Cinema school had made in the United States.[40] For example, Roger Ebert, in distinguishing the varieties of exploitation films currently on the film market in 1967—between the American International Pictures biker and youth culture model and the gritty sex and violence model of the sexploitation film—would pan the welter of skin flick currently circulating. Characterizing sexploitation films as subpar products within the rubric of film art, he would write:

> Turned out on starvation budgets by anonymous outfits in Miami Beach and New York City, they play to a loyal clientele in big cities, college towns and county seats. They are wretchedly bad. Many of them are not even real sound movies; to save money the makers don't buy sound synchronized film. Instead they shoot one character's face while the other is talking or use narration.[41]

Ebert notably claims that Russ Meyer is the "only competent cameraman and director making skin flicks" yet, in the end, despairs that "exploitation films have brought forth a great mountain of trash and no new Antonioni or Fellini. And in the meantime they continue to degrade the cinema taste of countless exploited moviegoers, who may wake up one day to discover that they thought *Riot on the Sunset Strip* was a pretty good movie."[42] Ebert's observation regarding the paucity of directorial talent, while lauding Meyer, seemed a dismissal of the genre whole cloth precisely because of the constraints imposed by sexploitation's means of production. Nonetheless, his highlighting of Meyer's talent reflected a broader critical recognition occurring as sexploitation films entered their most lucrative period in the late 1960s. Meyer and Radley Metzger would in these years come to be seen as the dominant authorial voices of sexploitation; the two would consistently garner the lion's share of critical attention when it came to distinguishing their "exceptional" talents or aesthetic graces from the rest of the entrepreneurial, and lower-budgeted, "rabble." So, their ability to move outside of the quarters of the grind house and gain crossover appeal to larger audiences allowed their films and their works to be discussed through the lens of authorship.

Polar opposites in film thematics and style, the two R.M.s represented the bifurcated impulses of sexploitation film more broadly. Whereas Meyer reveled in the inept physicality of his spectator and the boorishness of a stereotypical underclass, Metzger promoted an aspirational project, both in terms of genre and narrative, classing his films in terms of the already available upper-middlebrow tenets of the art house patron. Owing to Meyer's reputation within the trade press as innovator of the sex film genre both in the nudie and roughie modes, he would get the primacy of recognition in accounts of the boom of the sexploitation market in the mid- to late 1960s. However, it is around 1966 that Meyer's auteur status begins to take off, as a review of his mid-period roughie *Mudhoney* by Kevin Thomas would crown him the best visual stylist of male desire.[43] Cementing Meyer's lowbrow American gothic approach to sexuality, Thomas posited the possible gratifications his films provided to a film audience: "nice middle-class Americans have always loved to view low-life from the safety and comfort of a movie theater seat, and the appeal of *Mudhoney*'s authentic locales and gallery of grotesques is, ironically, the same as in serious pictures from *Freaks* to *Mickey One*."[44] Here Meyer's films work in bridging different tastes, exposing the parallels between middle- and lowbrow cultural forms. Meyer's talent implicitly lies, in this assessment, in his facility for cutting down to size the pretensions of a middle-class consumer. By 1968, the assessment of Meyer's filmic artistry was competing with a contrary discomfort with the baldness of his thematic fixation on his "pneumatic" heroines. One unnamed Warner Bros. director commented, "A lot of people are just plain confused by Russ Meyer, me included. . . . Everything he shoots is filled with all those incredibly overdeveloped babes prancing around without their clothes, right in the middle of what is sometimes powerful drama and brilliant use of the camera. You just don't know how to react to that incongruity."[45]

If Meyer's cinema was beginning to be taken account of as one of jarring disjunction in which form militated against content, and in which his montage style and dramatic pacing confronted the spectator with an excessive female morphology, then Metzger's critical reception treated him more as an impresario, even though his mastery of art house stylistics and the aspirational tone of his films paradoxically created a deeper suspicion about his authorial intention and his economic bottom line. Metzger could become "the envy of this [exploitation] film trade," using the classed status of his films to parlay his creative distribution strategies into theaters otherwise not prone to playing sex films. Vincent Canby would propose in 1968 that Metzger's productions, both of his own direction and his imports, were "breaking down the distinction between sex-violence films and conventional films."[46] Similarly, Kevin Thomas commented that Metzger's enviable formula involved giving a sexploitation film a patina of art house legitimacy, claiming that Metzger had made the lucrative discovery that "if you give a sexploitation picture the arty, respectable look of a foreign

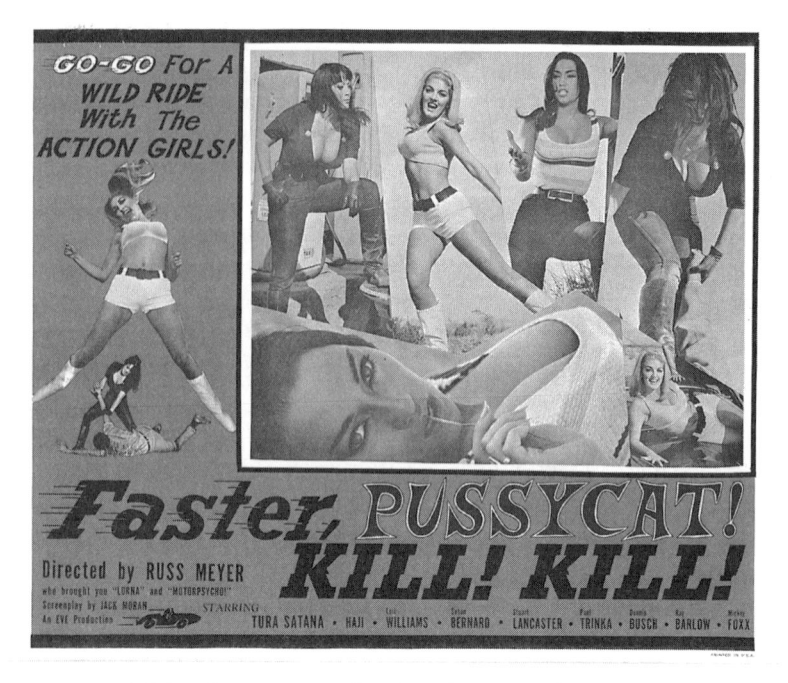

FIGURE 33. Critics often commented on Russ Meyer's stylistic preoccupation with aggressively pneumatic females, as in his roughie *Faster Pussycat! Kill! Kill!*

film, complete with subtitles, you can reach all those people who wouldn't be caught dead in a Russ Meyer nudie."[47] In Thomas's estimation, then, Metzger was operating within a new model of exploitative dishonesty, whereas Meyer was at least being direct about his prurient aims and preoccupations. Metzger's craft was seen as conditional to his business acumen, and other reviews of his films would take a circumspect and suspicious tone about his films and their notable style. Metzger replied to these accusations with a defense of his creative choices, distinguishing them from the standard sexploitation film: "If you were going to make just another sex film, you wouldn't have to go to Paris, you wouldn't have to buy a novel by Violette Leduc, you wouldn't get Georges Auric to do the score, you wouldn't have to hire an Essy Persson to play the lead."[48]

By positing a classed hierarchy between his own features and the sexploitation market, Metzger made a claim for a larger audience for his films and purportedly deflected the more "prurient" viewer who was out to see flesh regardless of the finer points of story, sentiment, and ambience. Metzger preferred not to term his films sexploitation films but rather "class specialty films"[49] or "class sex" and tried to "'appeal to the sophisticated filmgoer, not to the skinflick audience' . . . he conceive(d) of his audience as consisting of 'sophisticated married couples in the mid-30s' rather than of aging insurance salesmen with their finger poised behind their suitcases."[50] These intentional modes of address to a particularly classed audience produced a speculative, if not successful, alibi of a middlebrow spectator who wants to be educated and edified as much as entertained or aroused.

Many reviewers remained unconvinced by Metzger's aims of elevation. Thomas, again, would pan *Carmen, Baby,* stating that "in these days of loosened censorship, a filmmaker can promise lots more, but this picture is pretty much the same old cheat. (Shooting through a deep purple brandy snifter will blur the most explicit love making.)"[51] Referring to Metzger's mise-en-scène of occlusion and his characteristic interest in filtering sexual activity through foregrounded decorative objects, the reviewer's aside implied that Metzger had merely repackaged the same obviation of the sexual act seen in more lowbrow and low-budget sexploitation films in more sophisticated, and thus more disingenuous, cinematic finery. Renata Adler also raised a specter of skepticism in her review of Metzger's *Therese and Isabelle* (1968), worrying that although the film attempted to be sincere, it nevertheless succumbed to "us[ing] the screen as a confessional" and "more often . . . seem[ed] an attempt by the producer-director Radley Metzger . . . to make a mint out of a growing audience of specialized sex watchers."[52] Vincent Canby was far more generous in his treatment of Meyer's work, and in an essay on the charms of the Swedish actress Essy Persson, who had starred in the crossover import hit *I, a Woman* (Mac Ahlberg, 1965/1966) and in Metzger's own *Therese and Isabelle,* he claimed that these two films, "compared to the technically sloppy, leering and pointless melodrama of *Johnny Whip's Women* . . . look like Ingmar Bergman productions, even with their great swatches of sex and patches of flesh."[53] Noting that Metzger took "filmmaking seriously," Canby's affiliation of his style with Bergman was a significant move toward the acceptance of Metzger's terms of elevation, rather than degradation, through cinematic eroticism. Such an aspirational trajectory was often deployed through use of the term *erotic* to describe Metzger's work—in various articles by the early 1970s, Metzger would be termed "aristocrat of the erotic," "auteur of the erotic," and most creatively, by Richard Corliss, the "Ophuls of orgasm, the Cukor of concupiscence."[54]

Even in the economically successful import of *I, a Woman,* which Metzger did not direct but promoted and distributed, Metzger's curatorial mode of authorship was still strongly felt. There is a way in which the appropriative, hybrid nature of Metzger's style and his sensitivity to the aesthetics of art house cinema's existential *gravitas* gave even the films he bought the rights to and distributed an inflection of his own directorial signature. For example, the Audubon release *The Laughing Woman*

"THERESE AND ISABELLE"

FIGURE 34. The lush art cinema–influenced style of Metzger's works, here on display in the stately mise-en-scène of *Therese and Isabelle*, earned him serious critical attention throughout the late 1960s.

(1970), an Italian production written and directed by Piero Schivazappa, bore a comparable style to Metzger's own films and would be attributed to Metzger by Thomas.[55] Thus Metzger's "direction" could extend to an understanding of Audubon as a curatorial project in which the production and distribution outfit attained a recognizable "house style."

Despite these prominent film critics' qualifications of their films' quality, both Meyer and Metzger would accrue an acclaim and name recognition in the late 1960s and into the 1970s. Meyer was courted by Richard Zanuck and made two films for Twentieth Century Fox, the most notable being *Beyond the Valley of the Dolls* (1969) (the script cowritten with the previously favorable Ebert). Metzger continued his economic success in managing his own directorial ventures and imports such as *Camille 2000* (1969) and *The Libertine* (Pasquale Festa, 1969).[56] Meyer was also the guest of honor at a film festival devoted to his work at Yale University; additional fetes followed at other colleges.[57] Both Meyer's and Metzger's films also made their way by the early 1970s into the film archives of the Museum of Modern Art, where Metzger's *The Lickerish Quartet* was shown with an accompanying talk in January 1971. Meyer soon after made an invited lecture appearance alongside a screening of *Beyond the Valley of the Dolls* and on a separate panel on censorship in July and October 1971.[58] Although the Metzger screening received little notice beyond the bounds of short mention in *Film Comment*, the Meyer appearance was the object of wider popular press discussion. Perhaps Meyer's presumably more brazen and crass films were seen as a surprising stretch for MoMA. Apparently, the audience at the screening became uncharacteristically rowdy, at least in the context of the gentility of a high art space. A local reviewer described the scene:

> They hooted like Indians on the warpath, hollered like SDS'ers at a George Wallace rally, cheered like Mets fans on a particularly good day. And as the 109 minute motion picture drew to an end, a stout woman toward the front was sending forth sound waves which can best be described as a cross between a hiss and Bronx cheer. Someone behind her told her to shut up, and she shouted caustically, "Whatsammatta—the movie's so intellectual you can't understand it if I talk?"[59]

The relocation of the sexploitation genre, and particularly Meyer's films, from their customary and lower-middlebrow exhibition spaces into a highbrow space seemed to create an unexpected spectatorial energy—and what seemed to have been a collision between differing cinematic taste publics. Laurence Kardish, then assistant curator of film programming for the museum, confirmed for the reporter that such noise and audience ballyhoo was a "rare" occurrence at the museum. When asked why MoMA had decided to screen Meyer's films, associate film programming curator Adrienne Mancia rationalized, "He does use sex and sordid aspects of life, but there's a lusty air to his films, vitality, energy and a sense of humor. He knows his craft very well. And we feel his films should be discussed in some more serious place than a 42nd Street movie house."[60]

The discursive incorporation of Meyer and Metzger into a contemporaneous narrative of cinematic development represented the heightened cultural legitimacy and accessibility of sexploitation films, as the genre was no longer seen as a marginal or underground form but a thriving industry, even if, paradoxically, those very terms of legitimation were used to debate the merits, or lack thereof, of the two directors' artistic contributions to film culture. At the same time, Metzger's and Meyer's films were, in terms of finances and production values, a cut above, clearly operating within a higher scale of production than most sexploitation producers. Thus the slickness and polish of their films made them more amenable to wider consideration by the mainstream and trade press. This discourse of authorship, however troubled, nevertheless represented a heightening sophistication about and around sexploitation filmmaking, as the differentiation necessitated by the cinematic marketplace overlapped with the developing market in sexually oriented materials across media.

"A Guide for the Discriminating Voyeur": The Late 1960s Market, Connoisseurship, and Consumerism

Aside from the treatment of Meyer and Metzger, critical responses to sexploitation films in the late 1960s as art, or as aesthetically valid, tended toward the derogatory and dismissive. Margot Hentoff, observing the wave of soft- and emerging hard-core pornographies, spun the "uses and gratifications" model of sociology into a declaration of sexploitation's outdated morality:

> Flesh on the screen is another matter. Since the actors are not really there we are not really there either. To go from the theater to the tenderloin grind-houses is to create even more distance, moving back in time and down in class. I have heard that some skin flicks are good, but it seems unlikely. It is their function, after all, to complement the ordinary fantasies of somewhat witless horny men; if they become too bizarre, too special in taste, they lose their broad appeal. Skin-flicks, therefore, reflect the standards of the community they serve and tend to be humorless and hypocritical, still making use of shame as titillation in the old pre-liberation fashion, rather like a filmed confessions magazine story. A little soft whipping. A little rape. The convention: "I didn't want to do it—but I went crazy with lust." . . . "Go East," one wants to tell the audience. "In the art houses it is happening in focus." But the eroticism in serious films is perhaps no more attractive to this businesslike audience than reading Genet is to those who share Rex Reed's esteem for the work of Jacqueline Susann.[61]

Tracking a trajectory of middlebrow erotic alienation in the face of an emerging cornucopia of erotic commodities, Hentoff defined sexploitation films as already outdated, reflecting the sex-negative mores of an older generation and a different class. The grind house films reflected a "preliberation" moment, yet they also are registered as denigrated products, which couldn't match the aesthetic values and more esoteric erotics of the art film. Suggesting that sexploitation films were defined by and simultaneously defined their audiences, Hentoff's critique of the insufficiencies of the films in rendering complex fantasies also flagged the gendered orientations and proscribed, deficient aesthetic tastes of their viewing public.

Despite their purported insufficiencies, sexploitation films played into a larger imaginary in which America had become an "audience of voyeurs," as a 1969 article in *Time* magazine proclaimed. The national magazine lamented that sex was now a "spectator sport" and that distinguishing between the avant-garde and the crassly commercial sexploitation film was no longer an easy task, especially in light of the loosening laws on obscenity. Observing that the puerile 16mm shorts playing in storefronts as well as the "sophisticated voyeurism" of directors Meyer and Metzger had now moved from the "tenderloin to midtown," the writers hoped in their conclusion that the integrity of "public taste would act as the best censor" in distinguishing the gutter trash from the aesthetic gold.[62]

The period from roughly 1967 to 1970 coincided with the consolidation of sexploitation as a formidable competitor in the film market, represented most overtly by the name recognition and expanded budgets of Meyer and Metzger but also signaled by the larger numbers of new filmmakers and producers dipping their toes into the skin flick waters. In this short time frame, the economic fortunes of sexploitation were on the rise at the same time that studio Hollywood was struggling with its own solvency.[63] The raging local and national debates about obscenity, the introduction of the CARA film ratings system in 1968, and the stratification and segmentation of the American film audience all contributed to a climate of rapid transformation and unease about the future of the film industry as it was intertwined with sexual content and screen permissiveness. Hollywood, in the lead-up to the unveiling of the ratings system, had in 1967 commissioned a survey of filmgoers, canvassing their age demographics and their attitudes toward sexual content, an initiative that in part was responsive to the creeping growth of sexploitation films into areas that had been the studio's strongholds just a few years prior.[64]

Sexploitation films had expanded their reach from inner-city, urban theaters to suburban, rural, and drive-in theaters in the latter half of the 1960s. The notable crossover success of Meyer's *Vixen* (1968) and Metzger's import *I, a Woman* (1967), as well as his *Carmen, Baby* (1968) and *Therese and Isabelle* (1969), overlapped with the influx of continental sexuality from European shores. The censorship hype generated from Sjoman's *I Am Curious (Yellow)* (1967), for example, served as a significant benchmark in that it facilitated the escalation of production of sexually oriented films and heightened their attendant local regulation.[65] Sexploitation producers were feeling vulnerable from the heat of local law enforcement far more directly, as local community groups and religious organizations would actively lobby their municipal politicians to clean up their local theaters, as we saw in chapter 1. Production went up from around 50 films released a year in 1967 to between 135 and 150 by the end of 1969.[66] Between 1967 and 1970, the number of theaters showing sexploitation films full- and part-time grew from approximately four hundred theaters nationally to figures ranging roughly between five hundred and seven hundred, when including theaters that were not exploitation houses per se but often played such product.[67] Many small art houses were converting from showing imports to screening entirely adult films, partly due to failure to compete with larger art theaters.

By 1969, sexploitation films had collected a certain status of fragile legitimacy, as more explicit films were being made outside of its borders, and the challenge faced by sexploitation producers was either to make more explicit films to vie with its competitors or to expand outward toward sturdier plotlines and higher budgets, thus being able to play in a wider range of first-run theaters, as Meyer and Metzger were doing, in order to remain viable.[68] The ratings system, while introduced as a palliative measure in 1968, had also heightened confusion as sexploitation filmmakers began to voluntarily brand their films with an X rating to avoid skirmishes with the MPAA but also as a means of free advertising—the studios had failed to copyright the X, and the use of it by intrepid producers and exhibitors showed a canny recognition of its marketing potential as a beacon of salacity.[69]

The tastes and preferences of this relatively new and suddenly very public erotic consumer, accounted for by popular and underground criticism, is most explicitly archived and documented in the unique newsletter called *Artisex*. Anonymously produced by Larry Klar under the pseudonym Art E. Sechs, it was published first out of a post office box in Arlington, Virginia, and, from 1969 on, from a post office box in Tallahassee, Florida. It was distributed privately by mail subscription, with its first issue appearing in February 1968. Starting in a biweekly format of four to six pages, and transitioning into longer monthly issues on legal-sized paper, *Artisex* was published through 1971. As its editorial identity developed, its format and its content also expanded. The newsletter, in its minimalist, typewritten form, presented itself as a place where avid sexploitation viewers could find "honest" ratings and evaluations of sexploitation films currently in distribution and exhibition in various U.S. theaters. Later issues of *Artisex* began to feature ad-mat images from films, personal ads, reviews of red-light districts and adult entertainment venues in various U.S. cities for the traveling erotic consumer, classifieds, sexual enhancement products such as flavored douches and vibrators, and other propositions for sexually related services. What is striking from a retrospective viewpoint is how much these documents resembled a prototype for more contemporary DIY cult film fanzines, written not by interlopers but by "regulars."

The historical specificity and conditions of the sexploitation film market are constitutive of *Artisex*'s identity and are embedded throughout its pages, beginning with its self-defined raison d'être. In 1968, its announced editorial policy employed the legitimating discourse of anticensorship and freedom of expression and the appreciation of sexploitation films as an art, although one with unrealized potential and in need of improvement. The editor asked his audience, "Are you as frustrated as we are at the poor quality of the sexy movies of this somewhat enlightened age? Some are so incredibly dull, so badly done, that they do not deserve an audience; others are not sexy; a few are OK; very few are excellent."[70] Mobilizing a more engaged consumer of sexploitation films, the editor addressed his public: "YOU are getting rooked at the box office because you have no way of predicting ahead of time what you are going to see."[71] *Artisex* reviewed and meticulously rated films, via a numerical percentage system, using a broad set of criteria that each had its own weight in points—"Direction," "Plot," "Technical," "Nudity and Looks," and "Sexiness" (a seventh criterion that fell away quickly was "Interest")—with a total cumulative score (50 for form, 50 for sex, totaling up to a possible 100) assigned to the film. *Artisex* would subsequently provide explanations of its rating criteria for specific categories in subsequent issues and would collate all the ratings of previous films reviewed in a master index published at the end of each year.

An archive of sexploitation film reception, a proscriptive discourse of filmic evaluation, and a device for delineating cinematic tastes for adult film, the content of *Artisex*'s reviews is eye-opening. The specific focus on the aesthetics and structure of many sexploitation films is notable in its focus on generic expertise—particularly in the primacy given to narrative continuity, cinematography, and editing. Reviews would express disappointment and frustration with the limitations on the extent of sexual display and the sexiness of erotic scenarios, particularly in the failures of a film in integrating these elements into a coherent plot. For example, reviewing the 1967 Joe Sarno film *Deep Inside*, the reviewer states:

> This production is a poorly contrived series of love scenes, with girls stripping to bikini pants and lots of huffing and puffing with different males. The love scenes are less graphic and not so well done as most others today. The story line, all about the evil machinations of the frigid hostess . . . is comparatively dull. There are too many discontinuities and irrelevant situations. The short lesbian love scene is bland and seems to be an afterthought thrown in. On balance, not very good.[72]

This review fuses contradictory discourses resonant with the status of sexploitation film in the cinematic marketplace in the late 1960s—it articulates,

FIGURE 35. The anonymous sex film consumer report *Artisex* features its mission statement "What is Artisex?" on the front page of the May 1969 issue. Courtesy of the Kinsey Institute for Research in Sex, Gender, and Reproduction.

at once, *both* a desire for quality of aesthetics and narrative value and a need for more explicit sexual scenarios. *Artisex*'s rating criteria indicate that the factor of "Sexiness," given 30 points, numerically trumps all other categories of judgment. This contradictoriness indexed the shift occurring in film production and film content more broadly, as sexploitation's livelihood was being threatened by 16mm storefront merchants showing hard-core shorts and the Hollywood studios who had entered the market with films that exploited sex much more directly than before.[73] Reviews in *Artisex* would often highlight when a film had been merely repackaged and re-released under another title (termed a "rerun"), demonstrating a heightened consciousness about the rapidly changing conventions of screen sexuality in this period and the capacity of sexploitation films to appear "outdated" if recirculated. As one ad would assertively announce, "Hello Sucker! Are You getting Gypped at the box office . . . Are you fed up with shelling out $4.00 for—A 1964 nudie? A 1966 rerun? No Plot? Lousy Acting? Bland Sex?"[74] This doubled interest in narrative consistency and overall production value and in explicitness of sexual content also highlighted the quandary sexploitation filmmakers were in at the time, as some predicted that they would need to invest more money and resources to create solid narrative features that could compete with the minor "cheapie artists" and the majors.[75] Films that tended to rate highly combined sizable production values, directed by name producers (Friedman, Metzger), and also featured a quotient of sex or nudity that was considered intense or effective. We also see a significant change between 1968–69 and 1970 in which the films that rate the highest shift from the glossy and bigger-budgeted soft-core style of films like *Therese and Isabelle* and *Thar She Blows* (Richard Kanter, 1968) to films that begin to push the boundaries of depicting the actual sex act—such as the Danish film *Without a Stitch* (Annelise Meineche, 1968) and the marriage manual film *Man and Wife* (Marv Miller, 1969), and fully explicit 16mm films such as *The Voyeur* (dir. unknown, 1970).

A different mode of cinephile engagement, *Artisex* provides historical evidence of the consolidation of a particular audience base, collectively oriented around a taste and preference for adult films. *Artisex* addressed the problem of the disparity between the extratextual and the textual through the corrective of film criticism and the initial alibi of an investment in anticensorship and art, all as a means of protecting the audience, now designated more broadly as educated erotic consumers or "sex fans," from becoming "dupes," a hybrid *Consumer Reports* of sort for the furtive sexploitation fan.

A mini-marketplace and sedimented reception sphere, *Artisex* also began to solicit film and book reviews from its readers in exchange for free issues of the publication, thus incorporating its subscribers' tastes into its accumulating archive of ratings—most writing with pseudonyms like "Robert Salacious." Owing to its anonymity, we can only speculate about the range or diversity of its reading audience, but based on the expansion of the issue and the broadening of the services it offered in its pages, one can suspect that the numbers were respectable. The archives in which I found the newsletter, the Kinsey Institute, the Labadie Collection at the University of Michigan, and the Museum of Modern Art Film Study Center, as well as advertisements in the publication for the Sexual Freedom League, also provide additional speculation about the range of publics—countercultural, politicized, artistic, and dissident—to whom it might have been circulating. The anonymity of the newsletter and the pseudonymous editor "Art E. Sechs" also reinforced the nature of the desired anonymity of viewing an adult film at this time, still a somewhat illegitimate and embarrassing leisure activity to publicly profess, as the critical accounts often also supported.

The publication's intense, insider-status connoisseurship, and its focus on the films' production details and names of producers, directors, and actors, might have gone unnoticed by less frequent audiences or the customary interloper (nonregulars like Moller or Valenti). Later issues stated that the major distributors of sexploitation subscribed to *Artisex* and that it implicitly worked as a check, a form of accountability on the quality of the films for their makers. Lodged somewhere between the overt confrontation of male pleasure represented by the "peter meter" trademarked by Al Goldstein in the pages of *Screw* magazine and the social invisibility and comportment of shame manifested by the patrons of adult film screening spaces of the period, *Artisex*'s amalgam of sexual liberationist tendencies, its discourse of connoisseurship, and its insistence on anonymity represented the conflicting poles that organized the parameters of sexploitation spectatorship in the late 1960s.

Ethnographies of Reception: Sexploitation and the Adult Film Audience under the Sociological Lens

Whereas *Artisex*'s anonymous evaluation of the quality of sexploitation testified to the widening audience and their negotiation of adult film taste, the focus on the sexploitation industry had also expanded and widened in the popular press, among community activists, and in federal quarters, as the "scourge" of skin flicks in local theaters became one of the most visible signs of a transformation in public mores. The image of blazing adult film marquees would often be used as a metonym of a culture of careening sexual excess, even when the content of the reportage might have little to do with sexploitation films specifically.[76]

An area of continued interest was the sexploitation film audience itself, which had shifted from being seen as a shadowy mass to a formidable box office public and a sociological curiosity of national interest. In the wake

FIGURE 36. The Globe Theater on 42nd Street in New York City circa 1969, advertising *Detention Girls* alongside more explicit flicks. Collection of Michael Bowen.

of moralist claims, by organizations such as Keating's Citizens for Decent Literature and other religious groups, of the harm done to minors and other "weak-minded" individuals by purportedly obscene media, the need to assess the skin flick audience from a socially scientific and objective viewpoint was viewed as a civic imperative by politicians and legislators.

Thus the adult film audience became an empirical and sociological entity, a newly visible site of broader cultural changes in attitude toward erotic media forms. Rather than remaining an object of sniggering and speculation, the late 1960s saw the preoccupation with the behavioral comportment of the sexploitation and adult film audience being taken up as a national problem by the institution of the Presidential Commission on Obscenity and Pornography in 1968.[77] A number of the studies solicited by this federal committee examined the patrons of sex shops, erotic bookstores, and adult films, yielding primary data that had never before been accumulated about the derogated "erotic consumer."[78] On the level of demographics, the commission's research was intent to reveal that, rather than an "undesirable type" or a low Other, the adult theater clientele was resoundingly normative in its social status, consisting of "predominantly white, middle-class, middle-aged, married males who attend alone."[79]

Charles Winick, a sociologist at City University of New York, whose research included the study of desexualization in American life as well as addiction and prostitution, produced one of the accounts that contributed to the final report of the commission. As an analysis of adult film patrons in the cities of New York, Atlanta, Kansas City, Chicago, and Los Angeles circa 1969–70, Winick's study launched an ethnographic approach to adults-only audiences grounded in participant observation fieldwork.[80] Winick engaged in conversations with adult moviegoers after they had left the theater, never identifying himself as a researcher, and thus using their consumption as empirical evidence of their investment in the films, at the point of purchase. When taken from a film historical perspective, despite their considerable ethical complications, his findings were rich and complex primary documents. Although the larger focus of many of these commission studies was underwritten by an interest in the influence of pornography on criminal behavior, and Winick's own methodology was invested in the "social interactionist," "uses and gratifications," and sociology of deviance schools of social scientific thought, the more mundane details drawn from adult film audiences' engagements was unique, particularly in the firsthand accounts of viewers' relationships to sexploitation and emergent hard-core genres.

On the basis of his interviews, Winick uncovered a set of generic expectations regarding sex films from his research pool. Close to one-third of the attendees, who were predominantly male, stated that they had started to frequent adult films around 1967, as sexploitation films had flooded the cinematic marketplace.[81] Many regulars did not take much notice of directors and actors, who were usually unknowns, but instead oriented their choices around specific theaters and the *experience* of seeing an adult film more generally.[82] Some respondents reflected that the trailers were indeed better than the films themselves and provided the most appealing part of the show—suggesting that audiences had in fact "gotten wise" to the dissimulating tactics of the soft-core film and were willing to accept this factor as a customary part of the skin flick experience.[83]

The generic expertise of the audience studied by Winick was constituted around similar factors to those noted in the *Artisex* newsletter. One defining feature of many of the adult film patrons Winick surveyed was what he termed a discourse of consumerism, consonant with the connoisseurship highlighted by *Artisex*. Many of Winick's interviewees, while rarely using the mantle of art, took pleasure in noting inconsistencies in plot, the film print's quality, the reappearance of objects in the mise-en-scène, the dishonest retitling and rescreening of the same films, the differential splicing of the same films at different periods of their short runs, trying to ascertain which films were made at the same time with the same cast and crew, and observing other markers of the economic limitations on the production quality of the films.[84]

Other consumer-oriented preferences that disclosed the vagaries of the exhibition space included stated choices of *when* to go see the film, preferences that illuminated generational differences between younger and older filmgoers that reflected the changing climate of reception and exhibition. One fifty-five-year-old patron stated that he preferred to see the films during the weekdays, because on weekends, the snickering and talking younger crowds were distracting and disruptive to his filmgoing experience.[85] As other box office studies had indeed revealed, the best business hours for adult film theaters in urban areas were between 9:00 A.M. and 5:00 P.M. on weekdays, reinforcing the assessment that male working viewers would stop in to see these films on their way to, or on break from, their day jobs, and in fact many of the interviewed were salesmen.[86] Winick's observations about time of attendance would provide an interesting counterpoint to the MPAA's surveys, which noted that young audiences would see films primarily on evenings and weekends, reinforcing their patterns of filmgoing as an adjunct to courtship and socializing.[87] This comment also echoed Michael Valenti's sardonic prediction just a few years prior that soon enough the "interloper" youth audience—"hippies with goatees and Vassar girls with pony tails"—would invade the solitary space of the diehard older crowd. Such a confrontation or disparity of reception between youth and older audiences highlighted the generation gap manifested by sexploitation's own content—which capitalized on the spectacle of youthful sex and young bodies. Additionally, it signaled the differential investments in seeing adult films—for the younger audiences, popping in to see a skin flick seemed a recreational novelty, a campy group experience, or a form of rebellion, and for the older patrons, a solitary exercise in seriousness, dependent on anonymity and invisibility. Hentoff in 1969 observed such an implicitly generational confrontation at the Hudson Theater, then a Times Square grind house with "edgy" fare. The Hudson, bought by the Avon chain of adult film theaters in 1968, was known for having shown a stream of Andy Warhol's films, such as *I, a Man* (1967), *Bike Boy* (1967), and *Nude Restaurant* (1967). Hentoff wrote, "The laughing people have taken up the Hudson—a source of distraction for the heavy viewers, who occasionally turn and threaten to maim the next person who snickers."[88] And another youth culture–oriented critic, writing for the music magazine *Fusion* circa 1969, would expound on his own exploration of the skin flick theaters on Washington Street at the heart of Boston's "Combat Zone."[89] In his estimation, sexploitation films could only be healthily viewed through the filter of humor:

> When the flicks are approached with a certain predisposition and attitude, they can be absolutely hilarious—enough material to keep a gifted earbender going for two weeks. Seen in a different perspective, of course, they are sad, pathetic, obscene, exploitative, perhaps even sinful in the way they take advantage of human frailty. But their inherent unconscious humor is perhaps the best (the only?) element to dwell on if one wishes to retain whatever emotional health one has left. Any humor in them is a result of interaction between the films' basic purpose (to make you horny) and the inordinately low budgets used to achieve this end.[90]

This treatment reinforced the generational differences between different reception publics for sexploitation as well as the changing constituencies that frequented the adult film marketplace as it diversified.[91] Winick's study also outlined the aversion of some adult film patrons to uses of humor, either in the theater space itself or, at times, in the tenor of the films on-screen.

Whereas the moribund nature of many sexploitation films, their indulgence in moralizing narrative denouements encouraged a disjunctive reading practice on the part of younger viewers "slumming it" and enjoying the novelty and illegitimacy of these theater spaces, "just for kicks," Winick's informal interviews in contrast attested to how the older audience for adult films had accepted the moralizing crux of sexploitation films. While seeking out sexual excess, respondents raised concern over countercultural films, such as the Danish film *Without a Stitch* or the art house/ sexploitation hybrid *Coming Apart* (Milton Moses Ginsberg, 1969), for their normalization of on-screen sexual practices through explorations of character psychology and dramatic realism. As one interviewee noted regarding the sexploitation film, "for kids, it's very educational. Boys and girls should see these movies. They don't try to peddle any point of view. *Without a Stitch* is immoral because it tries to tell you that everything is OK. These movies are educational because they show you a lot but don't promote it as good."[92] *Without a Stitch,* with its liberal and permissive approach to female sexual exploration—a young woman seeking greater sexual satisfaction travels in pursuit of carnal experience—sat at odds with this respondent's perception of the tenor of much sexploitation product.

Thus the ideological alibi of sexploitation films of the 1960s, in which sex could only be treated in moralistic and negative terms, had inhered in the taste and aesthetic distinctions between different generational constituencies. Sexploitation producers themselves frequently denied that the youth audience in any way provided their economic base. David Friedman stated before a hearing of the Presidential Commission on Obscenity and Pornography that young people were "participants, not spectators,"[93] and therefore, owing to their sexual activity, had no need for adult film. Yet the widening viability and presence of sexploitation films on the national sphere of film exhibition staged a particular confrontation between differing audience tastes and generational sensibilities around filmic sexuality. As Eric Schaefer has shown, the emergence of 16mm adult film production as a form of competition for 35mm sexploitation exemplified a rift in both the function and orientation of adult movies tendered along the lines of generational conflict. During a cultural moment in which social protest, antiwar activism, and the antiauthoritarianism of youth movements intersected with the uses of sexuality as a form of liberation as well as resistance to the "old" order, the changing terrain of adult film production would often map these divergences, with the generic tenor of sexploitation and its moralizing conclusions giving way to the more loosely organized acts of sexual concupiscence in the simulation and hard-core films.

The period in which the commission studies were conducted composed a unique moment in American film history in terms of the convergence of various genres and categories of adult film within a booming, albeit volatile, erotic marketplace. Justin Wyatt details this transformation, charting the relationship between the film product of the major studios, art house imports, underground films, and sexploitation independents, explaining that while the adult film became a legitimate form of entertainment, it also was viewed, particularly between 1969 and 1971, through a discourse of contagion.[94] Wyatt further explains how the adult market split into three segments, adult, soft, and hard: "adult dramas, which incorporated increasingly explicit sex scenes and subject matter; soft-core pornography, which often utilized X as a ratings attraction; and hard which was limited to large cities and linked to hard-core bookstores and stripclubs."[95] The corner that sexploitation films, as a distinct market, may have had on the representation of screen sex would ironically begin to fray by 1970, as discussion of a product shortage that year indicated that general release and "hybrid and new genre" films were eating into sexploitation's profits.[96] Hollywood majors, with more capital to invest in bigger-budgeted pictures, began to dominate the adult market. Younger 16mm producers would begin to make films that quickly progressed from striptease to explicit intercourse, while still sustaining a narrative element, thus introducing cheaper hard-core entertainment to a public already oversaturated by a plethora of adults-only product.[97] Bookstores, massage parlors, nude theater and live sex shows, body painting, sex clubs, and sex services would all flourish in big cities, legitimating the market desire of a male public previously "bumping the grinds" in the relative dark.[98] A number of sexually oriented papers, such as *SCREW, Pleasure, Kiss,* and the *New York Review of Sex,* also gained an eager audience, as they combined the sensibility of political insurgency—many of the editors having left a variety of New Left underground publications for which they previously worked—with an aesthetic and ethos of explicit sexual expression, thus melding the interests of the radicalized youth culture with a more sexually mercantile impulse.[99]

Although male desire and the commodities that would appease it, including the soft-core sexploitation film, would by 1970 emerge into the light of day and extraordinarily public scrutiny, the conditions of that visibility remained rather fragile. In the Commission Technical Reports and other sociological surveys, the homosociality of the exhibition space would rarely be directly anatomized, although patterns of seating and desire for privacy, isolation, and the potentiality of autoerotic behavior were matter-of-factly described. A doctoral dissertation by sociologist David Allen Karp most overtly explored the furtive dynamic in adult bookstores and movie theaters in Times Square, using the notion of "deviance disavowal" as a way to explain the behavioral patterns and clandestine social relationships that would develop in the context of this urban "sexual community."[100]

Conducting his research in early 1971, Karp was seeing firsthand the transformation and segmentation of the adult film market. Karp laid out a pattern of actions that he called "hiding behavior," behavior on the part of adult business clientele that was paradoxically utilized as a strategy to deflect or buffer scrutiny in a sexualized public space. Most of Karp's observational work was done in the Capri Cinema—one of the four movie theaters owned and run by sexploitation film producer

FIGURE 37. The expansion of the adult media marketplace, visible here in the varied sexual entertainment on offer in Tucson, Arizona, in 1970, including *Mona*, the first hard-core narrative feature, as well as adult print materials and multiple "stag" and "Swedish" films. From the *Tucson Daily Citizen*, November 25, 1970.

Chelly Wilson—in which he observed that patrons tended to maximize privacy through patterns of establishing a perimeter of personal space. Karp's elaborate recording of seating with indexes and charts ultimately reinforced the paradox at the heart of his study, of the contentious relationship between privacy and publicity in a space that forces the collision of the two through the potential of sexual activity. Karp implied that such "hiding behavior" was in part a presumed deflection of being cruised as well as a tacit acknowledgment of the possibility of masturbation. Richard Corliss, among the few commentators to openly admit to masturbating in sex films, announced in 1971 that although he went to sexploitation films to get off, of late, "movie masturbation has left its classical period . . . as the ultimate voyeur became the penultimate exhibitionist," as cinema onanists came out more into the open. Corliss's flourish aside, in many cases, the discourses of the autoerotics of the movie theater space were often studiously circumvented and circuitously talked around.[101]

In Karp's attempted conversations with moviegoers, there was a distinct reluctance to share expertise regarding films and a deferral to answers of "I don't know" if asked if a film was "any good" or worth watching. Karp also characterized the audience at this theater by their absence of affective expression—echoing numerous other vernacular critics and observers regarding the statuesque silent composure of the skin flick audience.[102] The act of moviegoing, of spectatorship itself, within this public context of legal and social scrutiny, became a loaded proposition—either a privilege of wishfully invisible consumption (normative straight masculinity) or a threat of vulnerable consumption (gay, queer, "deviant" sexuality). The anxiety around sexploitation and other sexualized media forms develops precisely out of this slippage between the act of viewing sex and the act of doing sex, which was localized and made visible by virtue of its placement in public. As both Philip Brian Harper and Gertrud Koch argue, albeit in different contexts, the threat and displeasure of being seen looking in a sex theater is one of the defining features of adult film spectatorship.[103] Thus the heralded claims of the surprising "normativity" of the adult film patron were tendered through a disavowal of the evident homosocial and homosexual potential uses of the theater space. The public image of the sexploitation audience, the catatonic mass audience in a clandestine swath of heavy breathing, would soon migrate to characterize the moviegoing public of the hard-core pornographic feature.

Boredom, Obsolescence, and the Waning of Sexploitation

Sexploitation's fortunes in the climate of this approaching hard-core horizon were no doubt rocky, and the adult film market had strikingly changed in just two short years. The sexploitation mode now occupied a crowded place among many other sexual entertainments that were becoming exceedingly explicit. Looking back again at *Artisex*, we can ascertain how their own shifting critical purview from 1970 to 1971 indexed some of these changes in the sexploitation field. The newsletter in this time began covering 16mm films as well as red-light districts in various cities, with a "Report on the Undergrounds" detailing the emergence of 16mm shorts and fifty- to sixty-minute "quickies" in cities such as San Francisco, Indianapolis, Dallas, and Houston.[104] The specific form of connoisseurship that *Artisex* constructed, which in 1967 and 1968 issues was more embedded in the ostensible quality and continuity of sexploitation, was in some ways being undermined by its prioritization of explicit sexual representation in its recommendation of many sexually explicit 16mm films to its readership, and its privileging of the criteria of "sexiness" above all. Along with the changing focus of the reviews in their preferential treatment of the modernized "stags," the newsletter's advertising and layout changes, which shifted toward more ad-mat images from films, as well as promotions for sexual products and services, suggested the ways in which *Artisex,* as a microcosm of the sexploitation film world, also became a map of the adult entertainment market multimedially defined. *Artisex* enthusiastically diversified and incorporated other sexual commodities into its array of offerings, becoming a clearinghouse of sorts for the clandestine but curious "sex fan." This transformation also exhibits how the sexploitation audience was being redirected toward more explicit screen fare and other forms of visual media within the proliferating marketplace.

The renegotiation of the terms of the sex films' "aesthetic appreciation" that *Artisex* seemed to champion was a product of the ways that, in Justin Wyatt's words, "hard core did erode the soft-core audience."[105] In the case of its rating criteria, the January 1970 issue professed a change in the terms of its "Sexiness" policy, which reflected the wider range of representations being promulgated in films. In the attribution of numbers for different scales of "sexiness," the highest number 29–30 was matched with "stag stuff, with close-ups." The sidebar explanatory text stated, "Dramatic modification of the 'Sexiness' criteria has been necessary at this time due to the unusual progress made in sexual permissiveness on our screens during 1969. . . . As formerly rated films are given a new look in updated digests, the previously assigned figures will be adjusted."[106] This form of hyperattunement to the changing codes of sexual explicitness, yoked to a discourse of taste and connoisseurship, provides an interesting paradigm for thinking about erotic spectatorship, particularly in its self-consciousness regarding the temporal instability of categories of the obscene and the "explicit." Attentive to "oldies" that were being recirculated by canny sexploitation distributors, *Artisex* often flagged scenes that were read as racy in 1967 and were just dull or dissatisfying in 1970—one such example is William Rotsler's *Agony of Love* (1966), in which Pat Barrington's body survives the cut but the film's now outdated presentation of sex acts fails. Suggesting that, just a few years prior, audiences were more willing to withstand boredom to see a few short minutes of erotic activity, the later issues articulate its connoisseurship through the lens of altering standard of sexual explicitness, in which boredom—coded as erotic dissatisfaction or frustration—was no longer tolerable. The last issue of

12

Excited by R. Salacious

B&W, a G.J. Prod., Canyon Distr Release, wr & dir by Adkov Telmig, w/Ellyn Donalson, Evan Richter, Kim O'Hara, Candi Carson.

Two working girls have quite a weekend! They get home from work on Friday, and, while one takes a bath and masturbates, the other spots a peeping tom at the window. She lies on the bed facing him and spreads her legs to give him a show.

A little later a neighbor comes in to borrow something. He is queer and not interested in girls, but they take off his pants and rape him. Still later they go out and pick up a couple of guys, have sex in the car, in a park, and go home. Then they trade partners. The boys leave, stealing their money and car, so the girls hitchhike, leading to similar sexy encounters. So there's no plot really, but who cares? The girls are pretty and often naked, there's a lot of humor, and the acting isn't bad. There is a very funny scene of a car on a freeway while the driver is, supposedly, getting blown. When the two guys get to the girls' apartment, one of them asks if they have any Perry Como records. So, even though it's a year or more old and the sex is not as explicit as later films, it is pretty good, definitely recommended in spite of its age.

BEYOND HUMAN SEXUAL RESPONSIBILITY

EXCITED
ADULTS
A CANYON DISTRIBUTING RELEASE

SEXUAL FREEDOM LEAGUE

The SFL is going through CHANGES! Read about them in SEXUAL FREEDOM Magazine #3

$1.00 • SFL, Box 14034
San Francisco 94114

A UNIQUE CLUB DEVOTED TO SWINGING GUYS & DOLLS
* MODERN   * BROADMINDED
* PEN PALS * BIZARRE

BROCHURE & SAMPLE ISSUE $1.00
Profusely Illustrated
* PHOTOS
* PERSONAL ADS * OFFERS GALORE
One Year Subscription........$5.00
Gals & Couples...join for one year and get the following things FREE!
1. All new members receive 1 free ad.
2. 12 big issues filled with new ads.
3. Letters to men forwarded free.
4. A personalized introductory system.
THE GROUP
601 S. Vermont Avenue Los Angeles, Calif. 90005

SWINGERS!
BROADMINDED SOPHISTICATES!
OVER 350 Gals & Couples listed! Two new up-to-date SPECIAL issues LOADED with photos & descriptions of lovlies. PLUS complete details about "The Club for ACTION". ADULTS ONLY! Give age. RUSHED 1st Class Mail. LADIES LISTED FREE!
ALL FOR $1.00. CONFIDENTIAL, Dept. 4
P.O. Box 1290, Seattle, Wash. 98114

FIGURE 38. The changing consumerist discourse of *Artisex* in 1970, as the newsletter embraces the potential of a wider sexual market for erotic services, such as swinging exchanges, and mail-order products such as sex aids and douches. Courtesy of the Kinsey Institute for Research in Sex, Gender, and Reproduction.

Artisex in 1971 announced that, in the wake of the radical transformation in adult film content toward a hard-core idiom, the publication was being suspended to make way for a biweekly glossy review, claiming that "we've arrived at an important turning point in sexploitation, art films, stag films and the reporting of the sexual renaissance. . . . The original purpose of ARTISEX—to influence filmmakers and distributors to upgrade the quality of their productions—has in a sense been realized. . . . The hardest core stag films are now being shown commercially in almost every major metropolitan area. Tasteful, artistic, realistic and explicit sequences of intimate sex are relevantly woven into scenarios that compete favorably with major studio products."[107]

Boredom of course seems to be the other side of connoisseurship, and as already mentioned, it often became a viewing hazard in discussion of the welter of adult films in the late 1960s and early 1970s. Richard Corliss, writing in *National Review* in 1969 on the opening of the Andy Warhol film *Fuck* (1969; alternately titled *Blue Movie*), outlined the spectatorial predicament that bridges desensitization and boredom among the sex film audience:

> Exposure breeds sophistication, and sophistication distance. Though we may be charmed and, in a sad way (mourning our lost innocence), moved by the fairy tales of our youth, we can no longer believe in them. . . . When two people begin the sex act in a sexploitation film, we know it's just an act. We're very sophisticated, and a little bored. So much of the magic disappeared with our gullibility.[108]

The common trope of audience boredom was a pragmatic articulation of the limits of spectator patience in the public sphere of sexploitation, in which the economic constraints of repetition and generic formulas presumably restricted experimentation and aesthetic innovation. But what Corliss also points to is the ways in which expanding sexual knowledge is yoked to nostalgia or melancholy for a lost sense of earnest or "gullible" reception. Boredom emerges as a complex index of both heightened connoisseurship and critical distancing as well as excessive, repetitive, or serialized consumption. In the case of sexploitation, the decline of the genre gets linked to its failure to adequately update itself. Another reviewer, scanning the skin flick scene, suggests that if "man's nature is his true intelligence," then "boredom will save the human race."[109] Here boredom serves as a system of embodied checks on the denigration of spectatorship into the dregs of indulgence and bad art. Yet, by 1971, a *New York Post* article headline, referencing the catatonia of the skin flick patron and positing the corporeal exteriority of boredom, sardonically observed, "Adults Only: And They Sit Like Granite."[110]

Some sexploitation filmmakers shifted to making hard-core pornography—such as Radley Metzger and Joe Sarno, who both transitioned to working under porn pseudonyms—and according to David Friedman, as cited by Eric Schaefer, roughly half the members of the AFAA were making hard-core by 1974. Others attempted to adjust to the competition posed by hard-core features in the early 1970s, first in 16mm, then in 35mm. In this context, a discourse of obsolescence pervaded some of the critical responses to the glut of erotic entertainments clogging the marketplace. The appeal of soft-core was claimed to be wearing off by late in 1970, with some theaters in Los Angeles reverting back to playing general release or foreign films due to lack of audience interest.[111] The reporter "optimistically" prognosticated the future of adult films within this climate: "There will continue to be audiences, mostly middle aged and sad, for the plotless depersonalized sex stuff; and an occasional film may command the attention of a larger audience. . . . But it would seem harder than ever now to make a case for restricting the freedom of the screen for an audience of consenting adults. The spectators have found, as Cecil Smith famously remarked, that sex isn't a spectator sport."[112] Similarly, in mid-1971, the *Daily News* was reporting that even what they called the "stag movie houses," meaning the 16mm hard-core feature-length films that had developed from the beaver films and simulation films in a very short span, were suffering financially. A theater owner was quoted stating that "there's nothing new for us to show anymore." According to this account, the 16mm hard-core acrobatics had become a throwaway novelty, and the blue movie slump was directly caused by audience boredom, market saturation, and the economic recession.[113] Nevertheless, within the following two years, hard-core images would reinstate their novelty in a theatrical mode, proving to be an adaptable form, for a time.

In 1971, American auteurist and *Village Voice* film critic Andrew Sarris wrote the following homage to the waning of sexploitation:

> Even if hardcore pornography were driven underground once more, it is doubtful that movies would ever return to their original state of coy leericism, to their sexless satyrs and hardboiled virgins, in short, to their infinite hypocrisy. The road back from porn to corn is effectively blocked by a society bumping and grinding to the tune of manipulative advertising and clinical journalism . . . "Sin in the Suburbs!" Those were the days when the doity movie seemed on the verge of becoming a stimulating subgenre.[114]

Sarris lamented the speedy end of the soft-core skin flick, simultaneously finding artistry in the fading form. Speaking in a moment just prior to the emergence of the hard-core narrative feature, and in which hard-core cinema had already become available through the 16mm theaters, Sarris sensed the import of such a transformation of the horizons of cinema-going, evincing a nostalgia for the mid- to late 1960s. He accorded the sexploitation film with a much-vaunted place within the development of conventions of erotic representation, a set of codes contingent on censorial limitations and a different moral order. Identifying and reclaiming sexploitation director Joe Sarno as an overlooked auteur, Sarris used his case to bookend the period from 1962 to 1968 as a window for innovation and diversification of the sexploitation feature:

> Sarno's cramped compositions and flat perspective were the ideal stylistic expressions of a charmingly naive satanism. The typical Sarno shot consisted of two people in the background talking about two people in the foreground talking about two people in the background. The very congestion of the intrigue contributed to its expressive economy.[115]

What is interesting is the extent to which Sarris enveloped the appeal of the skin flick within a concern for filmic form, exploring an occulted aesthetic of small means and economic limitations during its seeming twilight period. The overloaded mise-en-scène of Sarno's films provided an ample opportunity to employ an auteurist reading strategy, distinguishing Sarno from the more known success of soft-core auteurs Radley Metzger and Russ Meyer. That Sarris was charmed by the compacted, densely laden, and multivalent uses of Sarno's "economy" of visual and narrative elements speaks to the extent that aesthetic criteria became intertwined with understandings of the films' fiscal and censorial conditions of existence, yet seen as a part of recent historical past. A small budget and the specific prohibitions on screen sex transmuted into a set of admirable techniques of making do, where redemption could be wrought from aesthetic challenges. Sarno became significant to Sarris only through a retrospective, somewhat nostalgic frame, appreciable as a bittersweet discovery after the prognosticated and prospective decline of the fortunes of sexploitation as a distinct set of industrial strategies. Sarris concluded:

> For whatever reasons, there was a period between 1962 and 1968 when there seemed to be a noteworthy diversification of the doity movie. . . . The patrons of doity movies . . . expect little and for a long time they received less. Then gradually they were receiving more, and then suddenly too much. But that is perhaps the way of all revolutions.

> The point I want to make is that doity movies were for a very short time a bit more fun than anyone had any right to expect. Why? Because all sorts of marginal people chose to be gratuitously ambitious under the most discouraging conditions.[116]

The narrative of occlusion and innovation that Sarris constructed resembles the Cahiers du Cinema's lionization of B-grade filmmakers such as Samuel Fuller under the pretexts of a formally enriching set of studio limitations. The delayed assessment of the cultural work of sexploitation is historically narrated by Sarris as one of a revelatory gift within the continuum of historical change, a retrospective discovery rendered by the obsolescence of cinematic conventions and the emergence of hardcore sex on film screens. Voicing a cinephile response, Sarris found treasure through the terms of an altered landscape of admittedly diminished spectatorial expectations of sexual representations in the cinema.

Less than one year after Sarris's elegy for 1960s sexploitation, hard-core film exhibition metastasized around Gerard Damiano's *Deep Throat* in June 1972. Although other sexually explicit 35mm features, such as Howard Ziehm's *Mona* (1970) and the educational sex documentaries such as *Sexual Freedom in Denmark* (John Lamb, 1970), had preceded it, *Deep Throat* captured the public imagination through its economic success, viral notoriety, and legal confrontations.[117] Shot partly in Miami by former hairdresser and film producer Gerard Damiano on twenty-five thousand dollars, the film's national screening drew more than three million dollars in profit in six months and seemed to mark a new moment for sexually explicit entertainment—a cultural acceptance intertwined with the legitimacy of box office boffo. Linda Lovelace stars as "herself." She enjoys sex but cannot orgasm, until she visits a doctor (Harry Reems) and discovers that her clitoris has been misplaced in her throat. Fellatio provides Linda with the "dams bursting and bells ringing" feeling she has been missing, and she goes to work for the doctor as a nurse "aiding" his patients through oral therapy. Laden with zingy jokes—as when Linda's roommate asks the man giving her cunnilingus, "Do you mind if I smoke while you eat?"—and a relaxed colloquial feel, *Deep Throat* represented the fusion of sexploitation's narrative organization and the "beaver" film's explicitness. Indeed, the trope of female sexual self-discovery that had become so pervasive in late-1960s sexploitation films, in its psychological inflections, had shape-shifted into a lighthearted yet explicit literalization, in the film's assertion of the physiognomic structuring of gratification. Despite the fact that cunnilingus appears in four of the film's eleven sexual "numbers," the genital site of female pleasure, the clitoris, for Linda remained obscured, primarily off-scene, imbued with an inaccessible interiority, supplanted by coincidence in a reinforcement of male pleasure.

The cultural phenomenon of the film's success compelled *New York Times* reporter Ralph Blumenthal to coin the term *porno chic* to describe the adult film zeitgeist, one defined in large part by the constitution and breadth of the film's curious and copious audience, no longer restricted to the skin flick regulars, and which included the oft mentioned luminaries Jackie Onassis, Truman Capote, and Marlene Dietrich. Blumenthal wrote, "It has drawn approximately 5000 people weekly to the New Mature World Theater on West 49th street here, including celebrities, diplomats, critics, businessmen, women alone and dating couples, few of whom, it might be presumed, would have previously gone to see a film of sexual intercourse, fellatio and cunnilingus."[118] Although sexploitation films had made considerable inroads into this wider audience, as discussed earlier and in the previous chapter, the effects of *Deep Throat* on a public imaginary were incontrovertible. Discussion of *Deep Throat* as an emblem of sexual mores and the state of pornography in the United States ran the gamut. Vincent Canby expressed a studied ambivalence, if not sheer dislike, while acknowledging the film's historical if not historicist importance: "the film is a piece of junk, at best only a souvenir of a time and place."[119] Canby suggested reflexively that the only way one could review a pornographic film was through an autobiographical approach, documenting "every little quiver" the critic felt, perhaps reinforcing inadvertently André Bazin's claims about the ontological challenges real sex poses to cinematic representation. Collapsing aroused, sensate experience with the idealist detachment of film criticism was not something Canby could abide, for ethical and aesthetic reasons, dissatisfied as he was with the paltry confessionals *Deep Throat* had inspired among his journalist colleagues. The film trades devoted quite a bit of ink to subsequently covering the film's

FIGURE 39. A 1973 ad in the *Fresno Bee*, California, for *Deep Throat*—programmed with its predecessor *Mona*—announces the exact tabulation of the film's audience popularity.

legal cases in various cities, including in New York shortly after its first run in 1973, in which Manhattan judge Joel Tyler ruled it obscene, "a feast of carrion and squalor," a "nadir of decadence."[120] Rendered obscene for a time in New York State and faced with similar charges, seizures, and convictions in cities across the country for both its exhibitors and its actors and producers, *Deep Throat*'s legal notoriety as an obscene text snaked well into the 1980s.

Consequently, sexploitation film's sphere of reception, in the advent of porno chic, would be eclipsed by the more explicit appeals of a wave of subsequent hard-core features, even as the looming death knell of hard-core would continue to be sung by many on the sidelines. For a brief time, the cinematic future was painted as a place that might productively merge hard-core sexual content with sophisticated narrative techniques, a feeling no doubt emboldened by Hollywood R and X fare in films like *Carnal Knowledge* (Mike Nichols, 1971) and more daring and explicit European imports like Bernardo Bertolucci's *Last Tango in Paris* (1972). *Tango* was avidly championed by critics Pauline Kael and Charles Champlin, who wrote that the latter film measures the former as a "mountain measures a swamp."[121]

However, the optimism of this narrative was dampened by the 1973 Supreme Court decision in *Miller v. California*, which declared that adjudication of obscenity would revert back to the states and their "community standards," complicating any broad national definition of obscenity, a project handed over to the definition of localities. The *Miller* case decreed that obscenity did not warrant constitutional speech protection and applied a three-part test to determine whether a work was obscene but proscribed it definitively to "patently offensive sexual conduct." This landmark decision caused a wave of panic and trepidation among adult filmmakers, mainstream producers, and free speech advocates, who anticipated a "chilling effect" that would impact what filmmakers would feel they could or couldn't make and what exhibitors could or could not screen, for fear of local regulation. As Wyatt remarks, the success of *Deep Throat* and its successors, such as *Behind the Green Door* (Artie Mitchell and Jim Mitchell, 1972), *The Devil in Miss Jones* (Gerard Damiano, 1973), and *The Opening of Misty Beethoven* (1975; directed by Metzger under his "nom de porn," Henry Paris), was consequently tempered by the news of the high court decision and its implications.[122] *Miller* no doubt impacted producers and exhibitors of X material inordinately, as it redirected the onus of regulation to local authorities and thus put the burden on exhibitors, theater owners, and film producers to handle costs incurred from legal proceedings and arrests.

The soft-core strategies central to sexploitation syntax in the 1960s were also quickly incorporated into Hollywood film and by other larger-budgeted independent producers such as Roger Corman in the early to mid-1970s. Columbia's release of *Emmanuelle* in the United States in 1974 indicated the studios' relative comfort in dealing with soft-core product.[123] Soft-core sexploitation films continued to be made into the late 1970s and gained continued distribution in the drive-in circuit and in the southern states, where exhibitors were more wary of hard-core. But the moment of sexploitation film's cultural primacy and uniqueness as a purveyor of the forbidden or virtually obscene in the public space of the film theater had passed on to its hard-core successors. Ironically enough, despite the sense of a wholesale shift in sexual representation, the hard-core narrative feature boom itself proved temporary, as the theatrical potential of films with explicit sex was soon overshadowed by the draw of the domestic viewing market and the economic and technological appeal of home video.[124] As Schaefer has noted, the hard-core narrative feature could thus be viewed as a divergence rather than as emblematic of the conventions of hard-core porn; he states that "what has become increasingly evident is that the feature-length hardcore narrative was merely an *entr'acte* between reels of essentially plotless underground stag movies in the years 1908 to 1967 and the similarly plotless ruttings of porn in the video age (emerging in the mid-1980s and continuing to the present)."[125]

Sarris's ode to the "golden days" of sexploitation as a unique node of 1960s filmgoing experience and Corliss's lament for the fundamentally romantic and narratively driven experience of sexploitation would both prove prognostic, setting the stage for the kinds of retrospective rediscoveries of sexploitation film production as a finite form in the following decades within contemporary cinephile and cult venues, particularly in the discourse of the cult auteur. The conditions of sexploitation film reception, in their articulation of and concern with the problem of an adults-only film audience and in their negotiation of the aesthetic features of the sex film, can be seen as complex instances of the changing horizon of expectations regarding adult film product. The reception contexts described here and the terms through which sexploitation were talked about illuminate the ways that sexploitation as a mode of production and a distinct form of erotic commodity took part in the increasing liberalization of the screen and the adult film industry's continual struggle with aesthetic and cultural legitimacy. The erotic consumer, who would become a figure of denigration and speculation in discussions of hard-core films, was being constructed throughout the 1960s as a figure that encapsulated the conditions of self-consciousness that obtained in watching sex and its approximations on the big screen. Aesthetic connoisseurship transitioned into a model of erotic consumerism informed by the proliferation of sexuality in the public sphere, in which the side effects of boredom and alienation were means of militating against the accusations of naïveté or, even worse, an embodied arousal.

These particular case studies are reflective of a number of sites where the reception of sexploitation films provides a core sample of a set of oppositions between the insider and the outsider, the youth audience and older viewers, lowbrow dead-seriousness and highbrow detachment motored through aestheticism, cinephile leanings, or camp humor. Yet the variegated responses to sexploitation speak not only to the complexity of the films' reception in this period but also to the rapid shifts occurring in the cinematic marketplace in respect to audience demographics, changing screen content, sexual politics, and altering filmic tastes. An initial retrospective viewpoint on sexploitation films might find the pleasure of the films tendered through a triangulation of the film text, the contemporary viewer, and the historical spectator, at whose expense and presumed gullibility we may laugh and find charm in these obsolete, "dated" artifacts. However, the actual historical archive of confrontation between the film texts, the contexts of screening, and the historical audience for sexploitation should give pause—as these very discourses of occlusion and obsolescence and the negotiation and awareness of the films' purported "deceptiveness" were at play in the films' original contexts of reception.

Conclusion

Skin Flicks without a Future?

There is no better place to end than in the desires for the future of the past, of sexploitation cinema's febrile imaginary, materialized by a sex film and reflexively about the sex film as a waning form. In the year 2427, a futuristic culture lives on in what remains of Los Angeles, which was ravaged by an earthquake in 1969. The society is ruled by "Master Computer" and a secret group of cult film viewers gathers each week to view cherished "underground" films from the film historical past, "decadent films which have been outlawed in these enlightened times." These covert rebels, led by Liana and Jorel, screen sex films from 1969; they espouse the beauty and allure of an extinct film culture that appears to be the "last hope for our civilization." Our fearless cinephile, Liana, acts as the master of ceremonies, informing her polyamourous congregants—who lie about a mod white set in gold and silver metallic garments—that before censorship was outlawed by Master Computer, such "highly moral films" still existed and circulated freely, artifacts of a culture invested in love and romance.

This speculative fiction opens *The Curious Female* (1969), directed by Paul Rapp.[1] The film uses the framework of science fiction to tell a story about the sexual future through the lens of the retrospective "present" of 1969—resembling the styling of *Barbarella* and *Logan's Run*. Liana's pupils are stupefied as she shows them a short "stag" film, "The Vacuum Salesman," which (clearly made for the purposes of Rapp's film) mimics the playful piano score, ornate credits, and black-and-white grainy stock of stags from mid-century. The reel ends rather chastely with a moment of toe sucking, after the vacuum man and his prospective "customer" unclothe, in scenes that show bare buttocks and breasts. We return to the frame narrative, and one of the spectators exclaims, "Only two people!"

FIGURE 40. The sci-fi sex film future with Liana and Jorel as subterranean cinephiles screening a film for their polyamorous congregants in Paul Rapp's *The Curious Female*.

as Liana pronounces, "This form of relationship which was considered beautiful became extinct in 2004."

Liana proceeds to show her secret film society the feature for the evening, a film made in 1969 called "The Three Virgins," a purportedly full-length soft-core sexploitation film that returns us back to the present through a narrative regarding the last remaining virgins on a college campus circa 1969. A computer dating service is the staging ground for the search for and discovery of these sexually anachronistic women, as a gay businessman requests of the agency that they find him some virgins to interview for a job he is offering. The computer dating agency yields only three women out of its vast database. The three virgins, in full 1960s period detail, become friends, and each searches for her own truth of erotic fulfillment through the shedding of the stigma of her virginity—Susan becomes liberated through her adoption of a free love philosophy, Joan through finally getting married to her recalcitrant fiancé; Pearl discovers after her dissatisfying first time with a man that she is really a lesbian.

The Curious Female alternates between the science fiction frame narra- ιd the skin flick past through the pretext of the changing of the film reel, as Liana explains various obsolete customs represented in the film. On the subject of virginity, it is revealed that every woman in the future society has her virginity systematically "removed" at the age of thirteen. When marriage is mentioned, one of her audience members doesn't fully understand, asking whether men and men can get married, or women and women. Liana, the sex film historian, clarifies that same-sex relations were considered "unnatural" in the late 1960s past. This shuttling back and forth in time through the device of the film screening cleverly allows the legitimation of the sexploitation film, and the relatively chaste morality it represents, through an imagining of the immoral-as-amoral sexual future. The imagined hedonistic permissive society of 2427, in which polymorphous perversion, homosexuality, and polyamory—rather than the heterosexual couple form—are the coin of the realm, is posed as a farcical, tongue-in-cheek potentiality, against which the film's present of 1969 utterly pales in comparison. As a "nostalgia for the present" as well as an allegory for the future, the skin flick, rendered a time capsule, has already in 1969 become "historical," much as a fever of historicity spread through the films that buttressed the transition from soft- to hard-core circa 1969–70. Alex de Renzy's transitional *History of the Blue Movie* (1970), albeit in a different register, could present hard-core sexual acts through the frame of a documentary history of sex in cinema. Similarly, the flight of fancy of *The Curious Female* archives a particular moment in which sexploitation as a form was being mobilized as an index of the present as well as being treated as already past. Sexploitation's status as cultural object was thus made a meta-reflexive site of negotiation with the cultural changes wrought by political unrest and the manifestations of the sexual revolution. These details are especially poignant for how specifically it imagines the sexual future—as a female-led rebellion through the instrumentality of sex cinema, resuscitated as a romantic, moral, humanistic cultural form. The sex films of 2427's past ameliorate and offer a corrective to the too queer and too egalitarian sexual future, one that has been reduced to nonsensual and too liberal modes of reproduction and stimulation. Sexploitation films thus contain a history that needs to be recovered for their documentation of social, moral, human values. The film imagines 1969, in its contemporaneity as distant past—it is a moment of debauchery and jadedness not far removed from its diegetic sci-fi future, in which the only remaining virgins are a statistical impossibility and a scarce resource. The computer dating service of the 1969 story is the prototype for the Master Computer of 2427 and highlights a technological horizon in which contact is always mediated and measured by nonhuman means, a supplanting of contingency, authenticity, and sincere feeling. The film ends on the discovery and raiding of the film screening as Master Computer interrupts the scene of the screening, directing his armed guards to evacuate the premises. The cinephiles are faced with prison and punishment, and we are given their image now from Master Computer's perspective, as his voice scolds them for nonconformity. After the underground film club members are rounded up, Master Computer asks his guard to project the last reel of the skin flick—the guard demurs, confused, as the technological supreme being explains, "I may be a computer, but I'm only human." Thus the insistent materiality of sexual desire trumps and permeates the bounds between human and nonhuman, concrete and abstract realms, the body not a remainder to be sloughed but the animating ghost in and of the machine.

These ideas are of a piece with the discourses around sexual media accounted for in the previous chapter, as in Margot Hentoff's suspicion that new sexual forms might cordon off each spectator in his own technical cocoon of self-stimulation, a view that today's sexually saturated digital media environment of portable screens and the radical availability of the

FIGURE 41. The anachronistic "three virgins" discovered at the computer dating in the 1969 film within a film in *The Curious Female*.

mediated sex act only magnifies. But these notions also articulate a very specific stake for the study of sexploitation films and other adult media as a location in which sexual experience, identity, and subjectivity are organized and made to mean as a measure and an inscription of history and change, the repressive alongside the reflexive. Seeing sex in the world of *The Curious Female*'s future is rendered obsolete, just as doing sex is rendered so efficient as to divest its actants of identity or uniqueness, trapping them in a melting jumble of deindividuated, numbered bodies. In some sense a treatise on the enabling and limiting condition of sexploitation spectatorship, as one bound to the conditions of female sexual autonomy, *The Curious Female* encounters the sexploitation film's value in its modesty, in the skin flick's tendency toward a repressive drive. The covert film society, a reconstituted underground, forecasts the resuscitation of sexploitation film's historical value with the distance of time and hindsight, through the processes of cinephilia and cultification.

The film invites and tasks the female spectator, film historian, cinephile, with recovering the sex film's history and giving it new life, much as Liana does and much as later sexploitation films summon the female observer as a central figure. It is not surprising, then, that the loss-of-virginity narrative in "The Three Virgins" is also steeped in a discourse of wistful obsolescence, in a countervailing gesture, bemoaning something at the cusp of extinction, a dramatization of the social changes wrought by the sexual revolution and the adult film's part within it. Such a dramatization of "loss of innocence" thus operates in multiple registers, as it inscribes the moment both of extinction of that logic of tease, prohibition, and restriction and of recovery, in which one could hope to encounter a sexual image, to reconstruct the time in which it felt "new."

Extinction, of course, haunts sexploitation cinema and very sharply defines its latter-day identity, one filtered through precisely this kind of distanced and historically detached observation, in which the conventions of screen sex seem both near enough but also alien and alienated. Watching a sexploitation film, one can't help but be struck by the weight and gravity of quotidian flesh, the ragged historicity of erotic comportment, the frisson of banalized erotic spectacle, even as one strains to experience its elements of novelty, its shocks of the unforeseen. One cannot help but imagine a historical spectator's first encounter with it, the horizon of expectation that framed these contradictory, simultaneously transgressive and regressive works. Everyday female bodies pose and fall out of poise in a resolutely placed, smudged, imperfect mise-en-scène. The low-boil erotics of revelation and display, seediness and unseemliness, sneer out a come-on, a taunt, a dare to look and an injunction to look away. These relations, like a magnetic relay of pushes and pulls, are collected and inscribed in a range of gestures, narrative insistences, and generic formulae. The shower scene; the photo studio posing; the mistresses' dungeon; the heaving, grappling, and entangled evasions of implied bed sex; the swinger party; and the naive single girl new to the city all articulate the cultural and ideological preoccupations of the sexploitation cinema with sex in public, female autonomy, and a sexual spectacle that inevitably imbricates the spectator in a seamy, illicit mode of address.

The anarchic energies of these films speak to an alternate understanding of the 1960s, one that counters the optimism of a rosy liberationism with a spoiled cynicism and pervasive anxiety about the newly public status of sex and the changing nature of gender identities and newly public sexual practices. Sexploitation films indexed the zeitgeist of sexual liberation and its discontents and were aesthetically marked by an American independent scrappiness, a sub-B-movie vérité, and varieties of commercial ingenuity. Constraint and erotic surplus converged in the American sexploitation cinema, inextricable components of the mode's cultural and industrial positioning between restrictive representational politics and their eventual erosion in favor of an oncoming, now seemingly inevitable tide of permissiveness. Yet, despite the association of 1960s sexual culture with an emergent utopic mode, shame, displeasure, pain, and embarrassment, negative affects, ambivalences, and forms of spectatorial self-abnegation pervade the films, even at their most comic, bawdy, silly, or irreverent. As *Lewd Looks* has detailed, sexploitation's contradictoriness was constituted through and by both these repressive and reflexive drives, much as it can be sustained by a cinephile interest in the curious sex film imaginaries of a collective historical past.

The Curious Female also highlights how sexploitation films were permeated with a sense of untimeliness, anachronism—both hearkening in their moment to more innocent, less "depraved," more conservative values and exploiting the currency of and curiosity in sexuality as an index of 1960s contemporaneity. If anything, they exhibit the ineffable if unspoken fact that cinematic sexuality represents a fractious, vernacular index of historicity; it exposes—doubly—the very fragility of sociopolitical codes as well as the provisional nature of representational conventions. The sex film archive, as many have remarked, is one that has not "aged well." These "skin flicks" exist both in their time and out of it—in which delayed and deferred moments of corporeal display, of tease and innuendo, of outré excess and acting out, mark the tentativeness and brazenness of ⁻⁰⁻ cultural polis, acted on by industrial and social forces. Sexual- somewhere between sickness and seduction, is made to exist narratively, aesthetically, in a netherworld of moribund fictional conceits, switch and bait timed and syncopated to the beat of a strip show. A painfully self-conscious cinema—sexploitation films were aware of what they promised their spectators and what they could not deliver.

This self-consciousness, this stance of circumstantial reflexivity, traces back to the contexts and discursive locations of sexploitation as a newly public form of sexual expression. The concerns with the modes' status in relation to the sexual forms that would supersede it, particularly hardcore porn, are also reflexively mapped in reception contexts of the time, as the previous chapter has shown. Such contexts also reflexively telescope an untimely future for sexploitation. William Wolf would complain in 1968 in the pages of *Cue* magazine regarding the fundamental hypocrisy of the late-1960s sex film:

> In 1980 or thereabouts it may be that one will look back nostalgically at movies of the mid-sixties and smile condescendingly at those quaint old films in which there are cuts, fadeouts, blankets, frames showing only ecstasy on female faces while the males were busy off camera, on shots of breasts, entwined legs and moving buttocks. People may laugh at us for not having depicted *everything*. Well the time isn't far off when we will, and then what toppers will the exploitation outfits dream up?[2]

Wolf constructs a futuristic scene of spectatorial incredulity quite distinct from the science fiction fantasy of *The Curious Female*, with its mod polyamorous cinephiles and a future use value for the sex film. For Wolf, sexploitation has already become an inadequate and outdated mode, and its styles, forms, and conventions are recognizably passé, moving toward a state of exhaustion fueled by its core dishonesty in withholding representations of "real" sex. Wolf assails the aesthetic pretense of "class" sexploitation films, such as Radley Metzger's *Therese and Isabelle* (1967) as well as adult art imports such as Vilgot Sjoman's *I Am Curious (Yellow)* (1967). He suggests that what movie houses need is less tease, pronouncing that "one more expressionistic montage in a sex movie may force me to the point of invading the projection booth and putting on an old-fashioned stag film."[3] Associating the index of sexual contemporaneity with the relative "honesty" of on-screen sex, even as he hearkens back to the hard-core history of stags, Wolf calls for a more direct approach, one without hypocrisy and "charade."

In contrast to *The Curious Female*'s recuperation of the soft-core film's quaintness as a site for future nostalgia and fascination, Wolf's imagining of the futurity of sexploitation film is one of obsolescence and belated embarrassment. The telos of hard-core pornography's drive toward ever more explicit representation is both reinforced and contested by the nagging sense of sexploitation's multivalent inadequacy. For Wolf's speculative spectator watching these films in "1980," the purported shocks of sexploitation would be resident as much in the imagining of past audiences' gullibility and naïveté as in the "quaint" sense of their styles of ellipsis and avoidance. Both too much and not enough, sexploitation films' very historicity is articulated in their own moment as their peculiar legacy to future audiences, an at once excessive, embarrassing, if not just disappointing archive of an era's sexual subterfuge.

No doubt Wolf's view is stilted toward an investment in moving past simulation toward the "real thing." But what can we learn in the present from the aesthetics of this derided subterfuge and the discourses of spectatorship, scenes of looking and modes of consumption that sexploitation films generated? This book has aimed to show how the sexploitation film emerged out of a context of industrial change and sociocultural transformation, a significant and constitutive cultural force in the period's sexualization of the screen. The conditions of looking that obtained within this cinema speak to the tensions and conflicts that pervade the sexualized image and the eroticized body in the 1960s, caught between the regnant moral codes of postwar propriety and the emergence of more liberationist ideals. The sensational bodies of sexploitation film's imaginary connect the body of the spectator and the body on-screen in a tight couplet, as each provokes, arouses, frustrates, and constitutes the other in a constant oscillation.

Wolf's assessment of the skin flick's possible future emerges from sexploitation's historical contexts of reception and connects to the contemporary moment of sexploitation films' recirculation and redistribution and their legacy for film culture and film spectatorship. Even within their own moment, sexploitation films were being conceived of as *of* their time and simultaneously out of step with it, already obsolete—as Wolf and the many accounts of the previous chapter have shown. That sense of sex films' historicity, its nature as a fading form whose conventions were rapidly mutating, pervades much of the writing about them in the late 1960s and early 1970s, threatened by the widening sphere of the permissible and the rising sense of explicitness in cinema, theater, art, and cultural life.

Watching sexploitation from our contemporary vantage point, we might wonder whether sexploitation films have begun to resignify this very process of historical disjunction, in the shifting expectations about and radical transformations of the meanings of adult spectatorship in our digitally mediated present of *on/scenity*, or what Eric Schaefer has discussed as the gradual shift of private sex into public spectacle that characterizes the sexual revolution.[4] Was Wolf correct that audiences would find quaint charm in the constitutive omissions of sexploitation and the body of films that shuttle from the mid-1960s to its multiple generations of contemporary audiences through specialty collectors, VHS rentals, DVD rereleases, file sharing, Netflix, BitTorrent, on-demand, and digital streaming? It was indeed in the "thereabouts" of the 1980s, as Wolf prognosticated, that sexploitation's second life began. First resurrected on videotape, and later in the 1990s and 2000s by DVD and digital downloads and on online forums and fan review sites, an effusive amateur, fan literature on the cultist values of sexploitation has spawned within a larger canon of trash cinemas and discarded or low-cultural popular forms such as the educational scare film and the shlock horror of Troma. This new generation of audiences has had recourse to both romanticize and historicize, albeit in amateur modes, the conditions of sexploitation's existence. This valuation extends from the diegesis to the extradiegetic worlds that subtend the films, a point provocatively made by Jeffrey Sconce in his discussion of cult fans and the epistemic margins of the "paracinematic."[5]

These subsequent generations have found in what I have elsewhere discussed as the "dated sexuality" of the genre considerable aesthetic and cultural value, and it is in the presaging gesture of *The Curious Female*'s Liana, that we might see corollaries to contemporary film and media practices. Anna Biller's meticulous reconstruction of the late 1960s and early 1970s universe of sexploitation film in her 2007 film *Viva* testifies to the pathos of the sex film for contemporary female cinephiles, those much speculated upon, and speculative audiences and largely undesignated addressees who situated sexploitation's aspirations in wider popularity and legitimacy. The artisanally made and meticulously crafted *Viva* offers a hothouse pastiche of tropes from sexploitation's nymphomaniac wife and swinger film variants. It presents a story of a bored suburban woman whose disinterested lover spurs her on to a set of adventures with her friend and neighbor. Barbi, who renames herself "Viva," after the adult magazine of the time, literally "plunges" into the sexual revolution, concatenated as an episodic series of sexploitation scenarios in which Barbi is both watchful observer and hesitant participant—the nudist colony, the perverse photographer, the brothel, the orgy. Biller, an Asian American, plays Barbi as a searching ingenue turned *belle de jour*. Taking up a devotional approach to sexploitation's aesthetic that acknowledges the fascinations of the repressive and reflexive elements of 1960s culture and its impact on women in its very material forms, from interior design to cooking to undergarments, Biller configures an entire world that speaks to the place of a sexually curious woman in the space of a market of commodities and consumer goods. Mise-en-scène equates the thingly quality of the body in a continuum with the film's thrifted, early 1970s decor, and Biller's own labor is multiplied in her countless roles creating and constructing this diegetic universe, now with a tinge of retrospective fantasy and longing. Staging her sexploitation cinephilia as her aesthetic practice and the "work" of the film, Biller's engagement with sexploitation as an archive points to future modes of creative historiography in both the reconstruction of sexploitation's past lives and its reenactment as a coherent generic world within which female subjectivity and the pursuit of corporeal pleasures could be explored in precisely a more rather than less utopian mode.[6]

Sexploitation films offer challenges to the practices of film scholarship. They contest both the ways in which cinematic value, contingent on the merits of aesthetic exceptionalism, is distributed and theories and histories of sexual representation in popular media. Using a framework that binds the historical materiality of the films to historiographic concerns about the nature of viewing sexuality in the expanding public sphere of the 1960s, *Lewd Looks* has pursued a consideration of the contingencies of the obscene image in recent history and that image's entwinement with the construction of new modes of spectatorship, novel scenes of looking at bodies and at the social bodies that look.

One might treat these works as artifacts, texts, traces of cultural praxis, that emerge from a universe that is incontrovertibly identifiable with an era now so commonly reconstructed and restaged by a retrospective culture—more pop cultural and mainstream than Biller's *Viva*. The longing, nostalgia, and sometimes condescension toward the sexualized media of the 1960s extend from the Austin Powers franchise to the rapt fascination of the hit television series *Mad Men*'s revival of everything pertaining to the 1960s and its popular and material culture. Television has also partaken in the fascinations with the prohibitions, myopias, and mid-century sexual subjectivities dredged up by the Masters and Johnson–inspired show *Masters of Sex*. This desire for the patina of the 1960s spans from indie director Wes Anderson's vintage collector aesthetic to websites, such as Retronaut, that peddle in the archival, material stuff of the decade. The 1960s and the legacies and materialities of its sexual culture are not even barely "over" in our own millennial cultural imaginary but rather are in a constant state of return. For example, high-profile exploitation enthusiast filmmaker Nicholas Winding Refn has brought wider attention to the form in his publication of the exploitation poster collection of

FIGURE 42. Anna Biller's *Viva* reconstructs sexploitation films' preoccupations with suburban sin and reworks its melodramatic mise-en-scène. Still from *Viva*, courtesy of Anna Biller. Photograph by Steve Dietl.

Jimmy McDonough as a lavish coffee table book, *The Act of Seeing*, continuing the popular "grind house nostalgia."[7] Recent documentaries have taken an especial interest in sexploitation filmmakers, with *The Sarnos: A Life in Dirty Movies* garnering wide international exhibition. On the horizon is also a planned Hollywood biopic about Russ Meyer and Roger Ebert, *Russ and Roger Go Beyond*, with art house filmmaker Michael Winterbottom slated to direct. And David Simon, creator of the acclaimed TV show *The Wire*, has completed production of the new HBO show *The Deuce* (2017–), which explores the advent of hard-core in New York City's Times Square scene in the 1970s and into the 1980s.[8] These recent remediations and archivally inflected projects attest to the significance and continued fascination that sexploitation, the era of sex films, and the adult film industry it spawned hold for contemporary viewers and publics.

The objective of this book has been to account for the culture that produced these films and the culture these films in turn gave rise to. The contradictoriness of sexploitation cinema, in its dialectic between indulgence and illicitness, between the freedom to look and the expressive constraint of the tease, speaks to how we apprehend sexual change through aesthetic conventions and how we aggregate sexual transformation as an index of social and political subjectivity. Even if that "coy leericism" that Andrew Sarris lovingly eulogized has waned and given way to more direct modes of sexual address and more documentary registrations of the sexual act in our contemporary moment of overexposure, constant access, and exhibitionist-oriented media, sexploitation's legacy of innuendo persists. It persists not least of all in the desire that mobilizes our contemporary media culture's retrospective, historical imaginary regarding 1960s erotic forms.

ACKNOWLEDGMENTS

This book began, as many do, as a doctoral dissertation in the Department of Cinema Studies at New York University. I owe immense thanks to my advisor, Chris Straayer, who took me and this project on with boundless energy and generously guided me through numerous thickets and false starts, providing dazzling insights and steady reassurance throughout. Robert Sklar gave his unwavering support and asked the keenest questions; the memory of his skepticism will always animate my thinking about film history. Anna McCarthy's enthusiasm and advice gave me great motivation over the course of writing. Eric Schaefer and Linda Williams, whose work's imprint is seen throughout these pages, deserve special gratitude, both for inspiring the ideas and paths taken here and for providing a horizon of possibility for the study of adult film history.

I received assistance from staff at various institutions and archives where research for this book took place: Bob Tissing and the staff of the Lyndon Baines Johnson Library were incredibly kind and helpful, and my visit to view the Commission on Obscenity and Pornography files was made possible by an LBJ Library Moody Research Grant. Thanks are due to the staff of the New York State Archives and its Motion Picture Division, where the New York State Censor Board materials are housed; to Ron Magliozzi at the Museum of Modern Art Film Study Center; to the New York Public and Performing Arts Libraries; to Ann Harris, Catherine Holter, and Mai Kiang of the NYU Cinema Studies Department's Study Center; and to Charles Leary, who alerted me to relevant materials in the William K. Everson Collection at NYU. Materials from the Kinsey Institute of Research on Sex, Gender, and Reproduction and from the University of Michigan Labadie Collection provided crucial material for chapter 4.

The writing of this project was supported at the University of Wisconsin–Milwaukee through a range of Humanities Research Travel grants, a Graduate School Research Committee grant in 2011, and fellowships held at the Center of International Education and the Center for 21st Century Studies. I am grateful to have met Doris Wishman and Joe Sarno, David Friedman, Chuck Smith, and Audrey Campbell largely through the unflagging efforts of film historian Michael Bowen, who shared his enthusiasm for adult cinema with me while I was at NYU. Michael was also kind enough to provide the book some rare images. I continue to learn from him a great deal. I must also thank Radley Metzger for his kindness and willingness to answer my questions and Lisa Petrucci and Something Weird Video for making images available at a moment's notice and with unflagging generosity. This project would have been inconceivable without the indefatigable efforts of Lisa and Mike Vraney at Something Weird Video in bringing sexploitation cinema to a wider audience. Some of this research benefited from invited presentations at the International House in Philadelphia, the University of Michigan, the Chicago Film Seminar, the Australian Center for the Moving Image, Concordia University, the University of California, Irvine, and the Offscreen Festival—many thanks to my hosts and audiences at all of these events for their engagement and insight.

Friends and colleagues at UWM and elsewhere provided guidance, critical engagement, and pep talks along the way. The incomparable Patrice Petro deserves profuse gratitude for pushing me at a critical moment in the process. My colleagues at UWM Film Studies have been exceptional boosters, incredible friends, and conspirators: thanks to the special community that is Gilberto Blasini, Tasha Oren, Tami Williams, Jocelyn Szczepaniak-Gillece, Peter Paik, and Andy Martin. In the Department of Art History, I must thank my terrific colleagues Jennifer Johung, Richard Leson, Tanya Tiffany, Derek Counts, Ying Wang, Kay Wells, and the inimitable Kenneth Bendiner, Emeritus. I could not have continued this work in an art history department without the warm collegiality and encouragement of the exemplary Andrea Stone and Jeffrey Hayes. Kennan Ferguson, Carolyn Eichner, Jennifer Jordan, Marcus Filippello, Shelleen Greene, Erica Bornstein, Aneesh Aneesh, Richard Grusin, Ivan Ascher, and Carl Bogner must be thanked for their dialogue and conviviality.

I also owe great debts to friends, colleagues, collaborators, and readers in many places who engaged with parts of this work or otherwise cheerleaded over many years. Damon Young read early and late drafts and was my key interlocutor on all things sex cinema. Lucas Hilderbrand, over years of joking, dancing, rehashing, and dirty movie watching, helped me reconceptualize the project and see its lightness. Carla Marcantonio's years of comradeship always enlivened me across many phases of this project.

Karl Schoonover was a careful, eloquent, and astute reader of earlier drafts and a wonderful ally. Lazaro Lima, Patricia White, and Ivone Margulies were astonishing mentors and supported this project in direct and indirect ways. Homay King, Ryan Powell, Marc Siegel, Ara Osterweil, Amy Herzog, Juan Suarez, Mark Betz, Hoang Tan Nguyen, Kevin Heffernan, and many others were also crucial in their conversation and motivation. Other friends provided intellectual, cinephilic, and creative stimuli at vital moments: thank you Marina Zurkow, Abigail Simon, Doug Dibbern, Agustin Zarzosa, Lauren Steimer, Adrian Martin, Girish Shambu, Kay Dickinson, Zach Campbell, Alex Tisman, Liz Helfgott, Henriette Huldisch, Sudhir Mahadevan, Peggy Ahwesh, M. M. Serra, Drake Stutesman, Jonathan Buchsbaum, Whitney Strub, Peter Alilunas, and Federico Windhausen.

I must thank my editors and the staff at the University of Minnesota Press. I couldn't have asked for a more savvy editor and steward for this project than Danielle Kasprzak—her commitment helped this book in countless ways. I am also grateful to Jason Weidemann and Doug Armato for their early enthusiasm for the project and for the guidance of Anne Carter. Thanks to Allain Daigle for the superb index. I must also thank Jeffrey Sconce and Constance Penley for the largesse of their thoughtful, energetic feedback on the manuscript.

Thanks to my parents, Mikhail and Bella Gorfinkel, and to my sister Suzan Gorfinkel for believing in me and for the example of their work ethic, their humor, and their sense of possibility. This book is dedicated to my *babushka,* Roza Gornshteyn (1921–2014). She surprised me when I came to visit her for tea one day by revealing that she was reading a biography of the Marquis de Sade; I am grateful for the lessons of her intellectual curiosity, survivor's spirit, and lust for life, which continue to sustain me.

This book would not have materialized at all were it not for certain instrumental partners in crime. I owe incalculable debts to John David Rhodes and Michael Lawrence—whose company and friendship always signal home. John David supplied brilliant advice from start to finish as well as the book's final title; our years of spirited conversation and collaboration are an ongoing joy. Michael was at the ready to crack me up and tackle problems, miniscule and major, at any time. My enormous gratitude must also go to Jennifer Johung for her unyielding loyalty and care and for talking me off many ledges, over many whiskeys. I would be bereft, and this book the poorer, without the intellectual vitality and warmth that her friendship bestows. Finally, I am most grateful to Alex Pickett, whose love and even-headedness kept me sane through the wager with oneself that is the writing process; I'm humbled in the face of the gift of a life shared with you.

NOTES

Introduction

1. Williams writes that on/scenity is the "gesture by which a culture brings on to its cultural arena the very organs, acts, bodies and pleasure that have heretofore been designated as obscene and therefore literally kept off-scene." Linda Williams, "Proliferating Pornographies On/scene: An Introduction," in *Porn Studies* (Durham, N.C.: Duke University Press, 2004), 3. See also Williams, *Screening Sex* (Durham, N.C.: Duke University Press, 2008).

2. Paul Monaco, *The Sixties: 1960–1969,* History of the American Cinema 8 (New York: Scribner's, 2001).

3. Laura Wittern Keller and Raymond Haberski Jr., *The Miracle Case: Film Censorship and the Supreme Court* (Lawrence: University Press of Kansas, 2010); Robert Sklar, *Movie Made America: A Cultural History of American Movies* (New York: Vintage Books, 1994), 269–74.

4. On the development of the art house market and its attendant exhibition practices in the postwar period, see Barbara Wilinsky, *The Emergence of Art House Cinema* (Minneapolis: University of Minnesota Press, 2001), and Tino Balio, *The Foreign Film Renaissance on American Screens, 1946–1973* (Madison: University of Wisconsin Press, 2010).

5. On the relation between the product shortage and the emergence of the exploitation market, see Kevin Heffernan, *Ghouls Gimmicks and Gold: Horror Films and the American Movie Business* (Durham, N.C.: Duke University Press, 2003).

6. Eric Schaefer, "Adults Only: Low Budget Exploitation Films," in *Wiley Blackwell History of American Film,* ed. Cynthia Lucia, Roy Grundmann, and Art Simon (London: Blackwell, 2012), 9.

7. While space here does not allow it, the very constitution of the category of adult cinema, in its branding of both audiences and film texts, is worth further exploration, as it is linked to the development of sexploitation as a mode of production. See, on adult film as a category of new mature family melodrama in the

1950s, Barbara Klinger, "'Local Genres,' The Hollywood Adult Film in the 1950s," in *Melodrama: Stage Picture Screen,* ed. Jacky Bratton, Jim Cook, and Christine Gledhill, 134–46 (London: BFI, 1994).

8. The definitive text on American avant-garde cinema of the 1960s remains David James, *Allegories of Cinema: American Cinema in the 1960s* (Princeton, N.J.: Princeton University Press, 1989). On the importance of sexuality to the underground cinema of the 1960s, see Juan Suarez, *Bike Boys, Drag Queens, and Superstars: Avant Garde, Mass Culture, and Gay Identities in the 1960s Underground Cinema* (Bloomington: Indiana University Press, 1996), and Ara Osterweil, *Flesh Cinema: The Corporeal Turn in American Avant-Garde Film* (Manchester, UK: Manchester University Press, 2014).

9. Eric Schaefer, *Bold! Daring! Shocking! True! A History of Exploitation Film, 1919–1959* (Durham, N.C.: Duke University Press, 1999).

10. Ibid., 69–72.

11. Edward de Grazia and Roger Newman, *Banned Films: Movies, Censors, and the First Amendment* (New York: R. R. Bowker, 1982); Richard Randall, *Censorship of the Movies: The Social and Political Control of a Mass Medium* (Madison: University of Wisconsin Press, 1968), 64.

12. By some less verifiable accounts, these numbers of films produced reach into the thousands. Kenneth Turan and Stephen Zito, in *Sinema: American Pornographic Films and the People Who Make Them* (New York: Praeger, 1974), give two conflicting figures: one estimates that approximately one thousand exploitation films were produced in the decade (55). The second figure cites William Rotsler, who claimed that there were approximately five thousand films made between 1959 and 1973, two thousand of which were categorized as soft-core, and that, in the period between 1970 and 1973, there were three thousand hard-core sex films produced (228).

13. See David Allyn, *Make Love Not War: The Sexual Revolution, an Unfettered History* (New York: Taylor and Francis, 2001); Clayborne Carson, *In Struggle: SNCC and the Black Awakening of the 1960s* (Cambridge, Mass.: Harvard University Press, 1995); Todd Gitlin, *The Sixties: Years of Hope, Days of Rage* (New York: Bantam, 1993); Peter Braunstein and Michael William Doyle, eds., *Imagine Nation: The American Counterculture of the 1960s and 1970s* (New York: Routledge, 2001); John D'Emilio, *Sexual Politics, Sexual Communities: The Making of a Homosexual Minority in the United States, 1940–1970* (Chicago: University of Chicago Press, 1983); Martin Duberman, *Stonewall* (New York: Plume, 1994).

14. Hayden White, "The Substance of the Sixties," in *Revisiting the Sixties: Interdisciplinary Perspectives on America's Longest Decade,* ed. Laura Bieger and Christian Lammert, 13–26 (Frankfurt: Campus, 2013).

15. Despite the white-centric narratives of sexploitation, occasionally story lines around African American or racially or ethnically "other" characters or protagonists materialized. Sexploitation also provided a certain, if limited, amount of employment to nonwhite women, as is evident in the casting of Haji and Tura Satana in Russ

Meyer's *Faster Pussycat! Kill! Kill!* as one prominent example. However, racially diverse protagonists were relatively scarce, with some exceptions, for example, in Jalo Miklos Horthy's *The Hookers*. In this regard, sexploitation is distinct from the development of a blaxploitation cinema in the late 1960s and early 1970s, which represented different strata of production and different conditions of emergence and which appealed to a different audience demographic. Amy Abugo Ongiri points to the shared ideological terrain of the rural sexploitation film and the blaxploitation film in terms of how they manage the relationship between space, sexuality, and perceived degeneracy in American culture; see her "Hillbilly Hustle: The Thin Line between Hillbilly Sexploitation and Blaxploitation in Trash Cinema," *Bright Lights Film Journal*, January 31, 2008, http://brightlightsfilm.com/hillbilly-hustle-the-thin-line-between-hillbilly-sexploitation-and-blaxploitation-in-trash-cinema/#.Vgt4nBNViko.

16. Hilary Radner, "Queering the Girl," in *Swinging Single: Representing Sexuality in the 1960s,* ed. Hilary Radner and Moya Luckett (Minneapolis: University of Minnesota Press, 1999), 2; Eric Schaefer, "Sex Seen: 1968 and the Rise of Public Sex," in *Sex Scene: Media and the Sexual Revolution,* ed. Eric Schaefer (Durham, N.C.: Duke University Press, 2014), 2. On the instrumentality of media images in producing a sense of the sexual revolution, see Steven Seidman, *Romantic Longings: Love in America, 1830–1980* (New York: Routledge, 1991), 121–56; John D'Emilio and Estelle Freedman, *Intimate Matters: A History of Sexuality in America* (New York: Harper and Row, 1988), 275–301; and Beth Bailey, "Sexual Revolution(s)," in *The Sixties: From Memory to History,* ed. David Farber, 235–62 (Chapel Hill: University of North Carolina Press, 1994).

17. The contracting of Russ Meyer to make two films for Twentieth Century Fox is an example of such attempts by Hollywood to mime the strategies of sexploitation in the late 1960s.

18. Schaefer, *Bold! Daring! Shocking! True!*, 56–75.

19. Coppola made the nudie western *Tonight for Sure* (1962), and De Palma made a number of forays as observer and director into the nudie world, specifically with his feature *Murder a la Mod* (1967). Cinematographers László Kovács and Vilmos Zsigmond worked as directors of photography on a number of mid-1960s sexploitation films, including *A Smell of Honey, a Swallow of Brine* (Byron Mabe, 1966) and *Kiss Me Quick!* (Peter Perry Jr., 1964). Maitland McDonagh details the connections of the New Hollywood directors to the world of exploitation, specifically that of Roger Corman, but she does not mention sexploitation. McDonagh, "The Exploitation Generation," in *The Last Great American Picture Show,* ed. Thomas Elsaesser, Alexander Horwath, and Noel King, 107–30 (Amsterdam: Amsterdam University Press, 2004).

20. Sarris, "Ethos of the 'Doity Movie,'" *Village Voice,* October 7, 1971, 59, 76.

21. Paul Watson, "There's No Accounting for Taste: Exploitation Cinema and the Limits of Film Theory," in *Trash Aesthetics: Popular Culture and Its Audiences,*

ed. Deborah Cartmell, I. Q. Hunter, Heidi Kaye, and Imelda Whelan (London: Pluto Press, 1997), 79.

22. Tom Waugh, "Cockteaser," in *Pop Out: Queer Warhol*, ed. Jennifer Doyle, Jonathan Flatley, and Jose Munoz (Durham, N.C.: Duke University Press, 1996), 61.

23. Karl Schoonover, *Brutal Vision: The Neorealist Body in Postwar Italian Cinema* (Minneapolis: University of Minnesota Press, 2012).

24. Robert Sklar, *Movie Made America: A Cultural History of American Movies* (New York: Vintage Books, 1994), 286–304.

25. Mark Betz, "Art, Exploitation, Underground," in *Defining Cult Movies: The Cultural Politics of Oppositional Taste*, ed. Marc Jancovich, Antonio Lazaro Reboll, Julian Stringer, and Andy Willis, 202–22 (Manchester, UK: Manchester University Press, 2003); Schoonover, *Brutal Vision*, 69–108.

26. Wilinsky also historicizes the practice of art house cinemas in the 1940s and 1950s in how they advertised and framed their films as "for adults only." Barbara Wilinsky, *Sure Seaters: The Emergence of Art House Cinema* (Minneapolis: University of Minnesota Press, 2001), 104–28.

27. *Report of the Commission on Obscenity and Pornography* (New York: Bantam Books, 1970).

28. On the history of the stag film and some aspects of its style and conditions of reception, see Al Di Lauro and Gerald Rabkin, *Dirty Movies: An Illustrated History of the Stag Film* (New York: Chelsea House, 1976); Linda Williams, "Stag Film Genital Show and Genital Event," in *Hard Core: Power, Pleasure, and the "Frenzy of the Visible,"* 58–92 (Berkeley: University of California Press, 1999); Thomas Waugh, "Homosociality in the Classical American Stag Film: Off-screen, On-screen," *Sexualities* 4, no. 3 (2001): 275–91.

29. Steven Marcus, *The Other Victorians: A Study of Sexuality and Pornography in Mid-Nineteenth Century England* (New York: W. W. Norton, 1964), 266–86. Linda Williams also discusses Marcus's notion of the pornotopia in relationship to categories of utopic space in hard-core film in *Hard Core*, 153–83.

30. Marc Jancovich, ed., *Defining Cult Movies: The Cultural Politics of Oppositional Taste* (Manchester, UK: Manchester University Press, 2004); David Andrews, *Soft in the Middle: The Contemporary Softcore Feature in Its Contexts* (Columbus: Ohio University Press, 2006).

31. Linda Williams, "Film Bodies: Gender, Genre, Excess," *Film Quarterly* 44, no. 4 (1991): 2–13.

32. Jeffrey Sconce, ed., *Sleaze Artists: Cinema at the Margins of Taste, Style, Value* (Durham, N.C.: Duke University Press, 2007), 4.

33. Eric Schaefer cogently describes the contingencies and difficulties of studying "adult film," attending particularly to issues of archival access and preservation, in "Dirty Little Secrets: Scholars, Archivists, and Dirty Movies," *The Moving Image* 2, no. 2 (2005): 79–105.

34. See Eric Schaefer, "The Orgy at Lil's Place Pressbook," *Film History: An International Journal* 28, no. 2 (2016): 173–95; *Orgy at Lil's Place* event announcement,

screening as part of the Orphans Midwest Conference, Indiana University Cinema, September 27, 2013, http://www.cinema.indiana.edu/?post_type=film&p=4782.

35. Andrea Juno and V. Vale, *Incredibly Strange Films* (San Francisco: RE: Search, 1986); Michael J. Weldon, *The Psychotronic Video Guide* (New York: St. Martin's Griffin, 1996); Weldon, *The Psychotronic Encyclopedia of Film* (New York: Ballantine Books, 1983).

36. Jeffrey Sconce, "Trashing the Academy: Taste, Excess, and an Emerging Politics of Cinematic Style," *Screen* 36, no. 4 (1995): 371–93.

37. Eddie Muller and Daniel Faris, *Grindhouse: The Forbidden World of Adults Only Cinema* (New York: St. Martin's Griffin, 1996).

38. Schaefer, "Dirty Little Secrets," 82–83.

39. Josh Alan Friedman, *Tales of Times Square* (Portland, Oreg.: Feral House, 1993); Bill Landis and Michelle Clifford, *Sleazoid Express: A Mind Twisting Tour through the Grindhouse Cinema of Times Square* (New York: Fireside/Simon and Schuster, 2000); The Deuce, http://www.nitehawkcinema.com/series/the-deuce/; *The Rialto Report: Documentary Archives for Adult Film*, http://www.therialto report.com/.

40. "This Is Softcore: The Art Cinema Erotica of Radley Metzger," program, Film Society of Lincoln Center, http://www.filmlinc.org/series/this-is-softcore-the-art-cinema-erotica-of-radley-metzger/. For a reading of Sarno's documentary, see Mariah Larsson, "Joe Sarno and Historiography: Some Thoughts on *The Sarnos: A Life in Dirty Movies*," *Journal of Scandinavian Cinema* 3, no. 2 (2013): 101–5.

41. On this film, see Elena Gorfinkel, "The Body as Apparatus: Chesty Morgan Takes on the Academy," in *Unruly Pleasures: The Cult Film and Its Critics*, ed. Xavier Mendik and Graeme Harper, 156–69 (Guildford, UK: FAB Press, 2000).

42. On Mike Vraney's legacy and the archival implications of Something Weird Video, see David Church, "Something Weird This Way Comes: Mike Vraney 1957–2014," *The Moving Image* 14, no. 2 (2014): 51–67.

43. Robert Eberwein, *Sex Ed: Film Video and the Framework of Desire* (New Brunswick, N.J.: Rutgers University Press, 1999); Jon Lewis, *Hollywood v. Hard Core: How the Battle over Censorship Saved the Modern Film Industry* (New York: NYU Press, 2000); Joan Hawkins, *Cutting Edge: Art Horror and the Horrific Avant Garde* (Minneapolis: University of Minnesota Press, 2000); D'Emilio and Freedman, *Intimate Matters*; Barbara Ehrenreich, *The Hearts of Men: American Dreams and the Flight from Commitment* (New York: Anchor, 1987); Hilary Radner and Moya Luckett, eds., *Swinging Single: Representing Sexuality in the 1960s* (Minneapolis: University of Minnesota Press, 1999).

44. David Cook, *Lost Illusions: American Cinema in the Shadow of Watergate and Vietnam, 1970–1979* (New York: Scribner's, 2001).

45. Barbara Klinger, "Film History Terminable and Interminable: Recovering the Past in Reception Studies," *Screen* 38, no. 2 (1997): 107–28.

46. Barbara Klinger, *Melodrama and Meaning: History, Culture, and the Films of Douglas Sirk* (Bloomington: Indiana University Press, 1994), xx.

47. A term used in an article referring to the skin flick audiences of Russ Meyer, in Steven Lovelady, "King Leer: Top Nudie Filmmaker Scrambles to Outshock Big Studios," *Wall Street Journal,* April 24, 1968, 1.

1. Producing Permissiveness

1. For wide-ranging accounts of film censorship, see Randall, *Censorship of the Movies*; Ira Carmen, *Movies, Censorship, and the Law* (Ann Arbor: University of Michigan Press, 1966); Harry Clor, ed., *Censorship and Freedom of Expression: Essays on Obscenity and the Law* (Chicago: Rand McNally, 1971); Matthew Bernstein, ed., *Controlling Hollywood: Censorship and Regulation in the Studio Era* (Rutgers, N.J.: Rutgers University Press, 1999); Frances Couvares, ed., *Movie Censorship and American Culture* (Washington, D.C.: Smithsonian Press, 1996); Murray Schumach, *The Face on the Cutting Room Floor* (New York: Morrow, 1964).

2. Michel Foucault, *The History of Sexuality, Vol 1,* trans. Robert Hurley (New York: Vintage Books, 1980).

3. This film was alternately titled *This Picture Is Censored* and *Banned* in different screening contexts by the distributor. Richard Krafsur, ed., *American Film Institute Catalog of Motion Pictures, 1961–1970* (New York: R. R. Bowker, 1976).

4. This decision, involving the film *A Stranger Knocks,* will be discussed in more detail later in this chapter. "Film Censorship Hit in Maryland: 48-Year-Old Law Attacked in Legislature and Courts," *New York Times,* February 16, 1964, 96. This practice was upheld in a previous Supreme Court decision in a case involving the Chicago censor board in 1961, which reversed its own decision here.

5. Vincent Canby, "Films Exploiting Interest in Sex and Violence Find Growing Audience Here," *New York Times,* January 24, 1968, 38.

6. Robert Metz, "Marketplace: A Risky Sector of Movie Field," *New York Times,* May 8, 1969, 66; "Marketplace: Sale of Nudies to Cover Lien," *New York Times,* November 27, 1969, 62.

7. The *American Film Institute Catalog of Feature Films Released in the United States, 1961–1970,* ed. Richard Krafsur (AFI, 1976), classified pseudo-documentary films such as *Censored* as "compilation films" (160).

8. Roth v. United States, 354 U.S. 476 (1957).

9. For a contemporaneous legal critique of the rhetoric of the "average person" clause and the "audience problem" in the series of Supreme Court decisions spanning from *Roth* onward, see Richard Funston, "Pornography and Politics: The Court, the Constitution, and the Commission," *Western Political Quarterly* 24, no. 4 (1971): 643.

10. De Grazia and Newman, *Banned Films,* 289–90.

11. Ibid., 289–91.

12. Susan Sontag, "The Pornographic Imagination," in *Styles of Radical Will,*

35–73 (New York: Farrar, Straus, and Giroux, 1969); Paul Goodman, "Pornography, Art, and Censorship," *Commentary* 32, no. 2 (1961): 203–12.

13. U.S. v. Paramount Pictures, Inc., 334 U.S. 131 (1948). See also Sklar, *Movie Made America*; Thomas Schatz, *Boom and Bust: American Cinema in the 1940s* (Berkeley: University of California Press, 1999).

14. De Grazia and Newman, *Banned Films*, 77–86.

15. Garth Jowett, "'A Significant Medium for the Communication of Ideas': *The Miracle* Decision and the Decline of Motion Picture Censorship, 1952–68," in Couvares, *Movie Censorship and American Culture*, 258–76; Ellen Draper, "'Controversy Has Probably Destroyed Forever the Context': *The Miracle* and Movie Censorship in America in the Fifties," *The Velvet Light Trap* 25 (Spring 1990): 69–79.

16. Garth Jowett, "'A Capacity for Evil': The 1915 Supreme Court Mutual Decision," *Historical Journal of Film, Radio, and Television* 9 (1989): 59–78; Miriam Hansen, *Babel and Babylon: Spectatorship in American Silent Film* (Cambridge, Mass.: Harvard University Press, 1991); Janet Staiger, *Interpreting Films: Studies in the Historical Reception of American Cinema* (Princeton, N.J.: Princeton University Press, 1992).

17. Douglas Gomery, *Shared Pleasures: A History of Moviegoing* (Madison: University of Wisconsin Press, 1992), 180–95.

18. Roth v. United States, 354 U.S. 476 (1957).

19. Ibid.

20. Randall, *Censorship of the Movies*, 52–53.

21. De Grazia and Newman, *Banned Films*, 98.

22. Jon Lewis, *Hollywood v. Hardcore: How the Struggle over Censorship Created the Modern Film Industry* (New York: New York University Press, 2000), 105–15.

23. Murray Schumach, "Adult Hollywood: Moral Responsibilities of Industry Increase as Censorship Relaxes," *New York Times*, October 29, 1961, X7.

24. Arthur Mayer, "How Much Can the Movies Say?," *Saturday Review*, November 3, 1962, 18–20, 53.

25. William Fadiman, "In This Corner—Hollywood," *Saturday Review*, December 19, 1959, 9.

26. Marjorie Heins discusses the implications of this appeal to the protection of youth in her cultural and legal history of censorship. Heins, *Not in Front of the Children: Indecency, Censorship, and the Innocence of Youth* (New York: Hill and Wang, 2001), 60–88.

27. Excelsior Pictures Corp. v. Regents of the University of the State of New York, 144 N.E. 2d 31, 165 N.Y.S. 2d 42, 3 N.Y. 2d 37 (1957); "Nudist Film Gains in Censor Battle," *New York Times*, July 4, 1957, 16.

28. Dawn B. Sova, *Forbidden Films: Censorship Histories of 125 Motion Pictures* (New York: Checkmark Books, 2001), 144.

29. Samuel Klafter, "Education Law—Censorship of Motion Pictures—N.Y. Licensing Statute—Indecency," *Albany Law Review* 22 (1958): 189–90.

30. Ibid., 191.

31. De Grazia and Newman, *Banned Films*, 248.

32. Keith Werhan, "The Tie That Binds: Constitutional Law and Culture, Obscenity and Child Pornography," *South Atlantic Quarterly* 100, no. 4 (2001): 902.

33. Even in the case of *The Garden of Eden*, different states would react variedly to the exhibition of the film in their localities—with a response of boredom in Boston and sustained censorship in Kansas, where the film was forbidden from being shown. "Nude Films Dull, Boston Judges Find," *Washington Post*, January 23, 1959, A3; "Judge Upholds Ban on Movie," *Washington Post*, November 4, 1959, A6.

34. De Grazia and Newman, *Banned Films*, 275–76; also see Fanfare Films v. Motion Picture Censor Board, 197 A. 2d 839 (1964).

35. Frederick Guidry, "Suppression of Rubbish," *Christian Science Monitor*, June 3, 1964, 5.

36. Bill Becker, "Movie Industry in Drive on Smut," *New York Times*, September 8, 1961, 35.

37. Michael Fessier Jr., "Anatomy of Nude Film Biz: Chary Theaters as Main Hurdle," *Variety*, June 19, 1963, 19.

38. "Maryland's Movies," *Washington Post*, November 25, 1962, E6.

39. Richard Randall relates that according to the testimony of the New York censors, the rate of appeal and negotiation by all producers or distributors who submitted films during this time was estimated at 50 percent, but in the last few years of the existence of the board, it doubled. This partial information has to be weighed against my relative sample of sexploitation films and distinguished in relationship to available resources and time for appeals. Randall, *Censorship of the Movies*, 114.

40. This discussion of New York State censoring practice is drawn from an examination of approximately seventy-five case files of sexploitation films submitted to the New York State Censor Board between 1960 and 1965. Although I have identified that there were approximately 150–200 sexploitation films submitted for review during this time frame, I strove to choose some representative examples of sexploitation films for a cross-sectional analysis. It should be stated that although this analysis accounts for how sexploitation distributors managed conflicts with the censor board in New York, it is important to note that many distributors may not have ventured to submit films for a license to New York State and might have opted to exhibit in other states instead. As the New York State Censor Board was operated through the rubric of the New York Board of Regents, this material is housed at the Film Scripts Division of the New York State Board of Education Archives in Albany (hereinafter NYS Archives).

41. A representative letter outlining this policy was sent to exhibitor William

Mishkin for the revised version of *The Immoral Mr. Teas*. Letter from NY State Censor Board to William Mishkin, February 21, 1961, *Immoral Mr. Teas* (Revised) file, box 68544-2229, NYS Archives.

42. Eliminations and Licensing Letter, March 8, 1965, 2, *Sex Perils of Paulette* file, box 73278-2541, NYS Archives.

43. Eliminations letter, NYS Censor Board to William Mishkin, February 21, 1961, *Immoral Mr. Teas* (Revised) file, box 68544-2229, NYS Archives. See also Jimmy McDonough, *Big Bosoms and Square Jaws: The Biography of Russ Meyer, King of the Sex Film* (New York: Three Rivers Press, 2005), 120.

44. See Carmen, *Movies, Censorship, and the Law*, 153–83, for further examination of licensing practice in these states.

45. Myron Feinsilber, "Cry Heard in the Land: Movies Earthier Than Ever," *Los Angeles Times*, May 2, 1965, N11.

46. For a broad overview of Radley Metzger's place in 1960s sexploitation and his films' aesthetic strategies, see Elena Gorfinkel, "Radley Metzger's 'Elegant Arousal': Taste, Aesthetic Distinction and Sexploitation," in *Underground USA: Filmmaking beyond the Hollywood Canon*, ed. Xavier Mendik and Steven Jay Schneider, 26–39 (New York: Wallflower, 2002).

47. Eliminations letter, October 19, 1961, *The Twilight Girls* file, box 73186-2536, NYS Archives.

48. Affidavit of Radley Metzger, December 20, 1961, 4, *The Twilight Girls* file, box 73186-2536, NYS Archives.

49. Metzger's sentiment was mirrored by Murray Schumach in 1961, writing in light of a recent decision upholding prior restraint in Chicago. "The Censor as Movie Director," *New York Times*, February 12, 1961, B1.

50. Randall, *Censorship of the Movies*, 116–18.

51. Ibid., 121–122.

52. "Appellate Court Overrules Regents on Film Obscenity," *New York Times*, July 4, 1964, 8.

53. Also on this topic of the pros and cons of resistance to censorial order for film distributors and producers, see Randall, *Censorship of the Movies*, 116–18.

54. Randall states that the board required so many eliminations that the seventy-minute film would have been reduced to only twelve minutes in running time and that the credits were also required to be cut. Ibid., 93.

55. John Sinor, "Modesto's Obscenity Trial's 4th Week," *Variety*, February 14, 1962.

56. Julian Miranda to Louis Pesce, memo, April 12, 1962, *Not Tonight Henry* file, box 70264-2371, NYS Archives.

57. Louis Pesce to Charles Brind, Esq., May 8, 1962, *Not Tonight Henry* file, box 70264-2371, NYS Archives.

58. Stanley Fleishman to NYS Board of Regents, legal memo, May 1962, *Not Tonight Henry* file, box 70264-2371, NYS Archives.

59. Sinor, "Modesto Obscenity Trial's 4th Week."

60. Affidavit of Ted Paramore, May 18, 1962, 2, *Not Tonight Henry* file, box 70264-2371, NYS Archives.

61. Ibid., 3.

62. Ibid., 5.

63. Turan and Zito, *Sinema*, 14–15; "The Trade: Nude Wave," *Time*, October 20, 1967, 101.

64. Louis Pesce, Review Report notes, April 30, 1964, *Nudes Inc.* file, box 73463-2548, NYS Archives.

65. Review report, June 5, 1964, *Nudes Inc.* file, box 73463-2548, NYS Archives.

66. Louis Pesce, memo, "Deletions in Advertising Trailer," July 24, 1964, *White Slaves of Chinatown* file, box 72407-2494, NYS Archives.

67. Ira Carmen, "Appendix II: Interview with Mr. Louis Pesce," in *Movies, Censorship, and the Law*, 271–73.

68. Henry A. Wise to Mrs. Wachenauer, "Re: Motion Picture Entitled *Blood Feast*," February 11, 1964, *Blood Feast* file, box 71423-2436, NYS Archives.

69. Trailer exam report, A. Mack to L. Pesce, February 10, 1965, box 72107, NYS Archives.

70. Jack Turner, "Theater Sues City for Smut Charges," *Democrat and Chronicle* (Rochester, N.Y.), April 23, 1964, B1.

71. Frank Torrell to Louis Pesce, memo, April 28, 1964, *Bell, Bare and Beautiful* file, box 71465-2438, NYS Archives.

72. An article in *Variety* noted this tendency of outraged private citizens to sound the alarms based on seeing merely the trailers or marquee advertisements at a theater as grounds for contacting local authorities. "Didn't See Film, Hated the Ads," *Variety*, June 19, 1963, 5.

73. Turner, "Theater Sues City for Smut Charges," B1.

74. "Regents Propose Rating of Movies: State Law Revisions Urged to Protect School Children," *New York Times*, August 2, 1963, 16.

75. A. H. Welles, "Hearings to Open on Movies Today: State Officials to Consider What Children Should See," *New York Times*, September 23, 1963, 34; "Admissions Bill for Youth Loses: Would Allow Entry to 'Adult' Films Only If with Parents," *New York Times*, March 18, 1965, 26.

76. Anthony Lewis, "High Court Backs Movie Censoring," *New York Times*, January 24, 1961, 1; Anthony Lewis, "Censor Upheld: Court Rules Pre-submission of Films Can Be Required," *New York Times*, January 29, 1961, E8; Sam Pope Brewer, "Company to Fight Virginia Film Ban: Plans to Renew Challenge to Censorship—Others Press Earlier Case," *New York Times*, February 26, 1961, 54; Eugene Archer, "Rehearing Asked on Censored Film," *New York Times*, February 28, 1961, 37; "Johnston Sees End to Film Censorship," *New York Times*, April 11, 1961, 41. See also *Times Film Corp. v. City of Chicago*, 365 U.S. 43 (1961).

77. Murray Schumach, "Maryland Tests Film Censorship: Movie Industry Joins Case Involving Prior Restraint," *New York Times,* December 24, 1963, 11.

78. "Film Censorship Hit in Maryland," *New York Times,* February 16, 1964, 96; A. H. Weiler, "Movie Censorship Seen in New Light; but Supreme Court Decision Draws Mixed Response," *New York Times,* March 3, 1965, 35.

79. John D. Pomfret, "Film Censorship in State Is Upset," *New York Times,* March 16, 1965, 1; Fred P. Graham, "Movies and the Court: State Must Streamline Its Procedure if Censorship of Films Is to Continue," *New York Times,* March 16, 1965, 43; Howard Thompson, "State Reassesses Film Censorship," *New York Times,* March 17, 1965, 52; Murray Schumach, "Film Censorship Shifted by State: Regents Vote to Withdraw and Transfer Jurisdiction," *New York Times,* March 27, 1965, 14; John Sibley, "Film Censorship Is Upset by Court," *New York Times,* June 11, 1965, 33; Bosley Crowther, "Goodbye to the Censor," *New York Times,* June 20, 1965, X1.

80. Quoted in de Grazia and Newman, *Banned Films,* 285. See also Leighton v. Maryland State Board of Censors, 218 A. 2d 179 (1966).

81. "Court Upsets Censors on 'Lorna,'" *Washington Post,* October 21, 1965, A33.

82. De Grazia and Newman, *Banned Films,* 276; Dunn v. Maryland State Board of Censors, 213 A. 2d 751 (1965).

83. "Court Upsets Censors on 'Lorna,'" A33.

84. Feinsilber, "Cry Heard in the Land," N11.

85. "Judge Bans Showing of 5 Films in City," *Chicago Tribune,* August 4, 1966, B4.

86. Quoted in de Grazia and Newman, *Banned Films,* 295. See also Cusack v. Teitel Film Corp., 230 N.E. 2d 241 (1967).

87. Vincent Canby, "Naughty Films' Nice Grosses: Public Taste Calls the Shots," *Variety,* October 28, 1964, 1; "Public: No Taste or Voyeurs?," *Variety,* November 4, 1964, 5.

88. Sova, *Forbidden Films,* 61. See also Lewis, *Hollywood v. Hardcore,* 148–49.

89. De Grazia and Newman, *Banned Films,* 297.

90. The passage is here quoted at length for its full clarity and effect: "a) Prohibition of Importation: All persons are prohibited from importing into the United States from any foreign country any book, pamphlet, paper writing advertisement, circular, print, picture or drawing containing any matter advocating or urging treason or insurrection against the United States, or forcible resistance to any law of the United States, or containing any threat to take the life of or inflict bodily harm upon any person in the United States, any obscene book, pamphlet, paper, writing, advertisement, circular, print, picture, drawing, or other representation, figure, or image on or of paper or any other material, or any case, instrument or article which is obscene or immoral or any drug or any medicine or any article whatever for the prevention of conception or for causing unlawful abortion, or any lottery ticket,

or any printed paper that may be used as a lottery ticket or any advertisement of any lottery. No such articles, whether imported separately or contained in packages with other goods entitled to entry, shall be admitted to entry; and all such articles and, unless it appears to the satisfaction of the collector that the obscene or other prohibited articles contained in the packages were inclosed therein without the knowledge or consent of the importer, owner, agent, or consignee, the entire contents of the package in which such articles are contained, shall be subject to seizure and forfeiture as hereinafter provided: Provided, that the drugs herein before mentioned, when imported in bulk and not put up for any of the purposes hereinbefore specified, are excepted from the operation of this subdivision: Provided further, that the Secretary of the Treasury may, in his discretion, admit the so-called classics or books of recognized and established literary or scientific merit, but may, in his discretion, admit such classics or books only when imported for noncommercial purposes." Tariff Department, Bureau of Customs, Region II, New York, "Tariff Act Section 305—Immoral Articles—Prohibited," March 1967, Customs Documents file, box 63, Presidential Commission on Obscenity and Pornography Records, LBJ Library.

91. Randall, *Censorship of the Movies*, 137–43.
92. De Grazia and Newman, *Banned Films*, 307.
93. Sova, *Forbidden Films*, 73.
94. State v. Rabe 484 P 2d 917, 79, Wash 2d254 (1971).
95. Rabe v. Washington, 405 US 313 (1971).
96. Ibid.
97. "FBI Hoover Urges Crackdown on Smut Salesmen," *Chicago Daily Tribune*, January 2, 1960, 5.
98. George Dugan, "Priest Denounces Smut in Times Square," *New York Times*, May 6, 1963, 32.
99. "Crackdown Hits Smut Specialists: Most Times Square Shops Now Sell No Banned Material," *New York Times*, February 26, 1964, 39.
100. Charles G. Bennett, "New Smut Drive Planned by City," *New York Times*, August 7, 1964, 31.
101. "Film Houses Plan Display Clean-Up: City Receives Pledge from Times Square Theaters," *New York Times*, September 15, 1964, 32.
102. "City Seen Powerless on Movie Marquees," *New York Times*, October 28, 1965, 46.
103. "Phoenix Smut-Chasers: From Books to Seizure of Three Sexploitation Pix," *Variety*, May 19, 1965, 19.
104. Ibid. See also "Crackdown to Continue: Theater Raided, Sex Film Seized," *Phoenix Gazette*, May 15, 1965, 13.
105. "Raid Warhol *Cowboys*, Photo Patrons (Who Scram Fast) for Photo File," *Variety*, August 13, 1969; this case is discussed in Maurice Yacowar, *The Films of Paul Morrissey* (Cambridge: Cambridge University Press, 1993), 21–22.

106. "Obscenity and the Law," editorial, *Atlanta Constitution,* August 28, 1969, 4A.

107. For more on the importance of Keating and CDL in the development of new right-wing anti-obscenity strategies, see Whitney Strub, "Perversion for Profit: Citizens for Decent Literature and the Arousal of an Antiporn Public in the 1960s," *Journal of the History of Sexuality* 14, no. 2 (2006): 258–91.

108. Nicholas von Hoffman, "Radical Sex and Politics," *Washington Post,* April 2, 1969, B1, B9.

109. Kenneth Turan, "*Vixen*: Top of the 'Skin Flick' Heap," *Washington Post,* August 13, 1969, D8.

110. McDonough, *Big Bosoms and Square Jaws,* 224.

111. Sova, *Forbidden Films,* 303–4.

112. Petition, "State of Ohio, ex rel Charles H. Keating Jr. vs. A Motion Picture Entitled 'Vixen', etal," September 22, 1969, Commission Correspondence file, box 43, President's Commission on Obscenity and Pornography Collection, LBJ Library.

113. Ibid., 4–6, emphasis added.

114. De Grazia and Newman, *Banned Films,* 332.

115. Ibid., 333.

116. Sova, *Forbidden Films,* 304.

117. Jane Friedman, "Report on the National Convention of the Citizens for Decent Literature," March 14–15, 1969, 3, Anti Obscenity Organizations, file 1, box 2, President's Commission on Obscenity and Pornography Collection, LBJ Library.

118. Ibid., 4.

119. "Dear Mr. Agnew . . . Press Ignores Me, He Says," *Post and Times Star* (Cincinnati), November 27, 1969, 20.

120. Charles Keating to Vice President Spiro T. Agnew, November 25, 1969, Commission Correspondence file, box 43, President's Commission on Obscenity and Pornography Collection, LBJ Library.

121. Herbert Ostrov to Cincinnati Bar Association, December 18, 1969, Commission Material file, box 26, President's Commission on Obscenity and Pornography Collection, LBJ Library.

122. Hugh Moffett, "Sexy Movies? Chadron, Neb. Tries Gentle Persuasion," *Life,* May 30, 1969, 52C.

123. "Detroit Priests to Open 'Clean' Movie Theater," *Washington Post,* May 2, 1970, C10.

124. William Kling, "House OK's Panel to Study Obscenity," *Chicago Tribune,* August 8, 1967, 1.

125. Jules Witcover, "The Secret Study of Sex: Battle behind the Scenes," *Los Angeles Times,* March 23, 1970, 14.

126. David Friedman statement, April 29, 1970, "Los Angeles Hearings, May 4

& 5, 1970" file, box 28, Presidential Committee on Obscenity and Pornography Collection, LBJ Library.

127. Memo by Freeman Lewis, January 13, 1970, Memorandum file, box 50, Presidential Commission on Obscenity and Pornography Collection, LBJ Library.

128. David Isaacson, "The Need for an Adult Film Association," *Independent Film Journal*, October 14, 1969, 20; "Green: 'Curious' Reception Harms Rest of Market," *Independent Film Journal*, October 14, 1969, 24.

129. Bernard Horowitz, "The Adult Motion Picture Association of America: A Case History," 4, AFAA file, box 62, Presidential Commission on Obscenity and Pornography Collection, LBJ Library.

130. Ibid, 5.

131. Ibid, 7.

132. Ibid, 9.

133. Welcome letter, AFAA Convention, January 13, 1969, AFAA file, box 62, Presidential Commission on Obscenity and Pornography Collection, LBJ Library.

134. Sam Chernoff, "AFAA Formed to Check Irresponsible 'Heat Artists,'" *Independent Film Journal*, October 14, 1969; and Sam Lake, "Sexploiteer Calls Cheapies Harmful to 'Quality Conscious' Distributors," *Independent Film Journal*, October 14, 1969, 18. For a discussion of the relationship between the emergence of 16mm hard-core features and sexploitation and the arrival of hard-core, see Eric Schaefer, "Gauging a Revolution: 16mm Film and the Rise of the Pornographic Feature," *Cinema Journal* 41, no. 3 (2002): 3–26.

135. Robert Cresse to AFAA, January 10, 1969, AFAA file, box 62, Presidential Commission on Obscenity and Pornography Collection, LBJ Library.

136. "Pioneer's Borden: Many Films Pass No Return Point," *Independent Film Journal*, October 14, 1969, 22.

137. "Ticket Sales Need More Than Sex and Nudity: Hessel," and "Social Consciousness Is Pebble's Direction for Low-Budgeters," *Independent Film Journal*, October 14, 1969, 24.

138. Horowitz, "Adult Motion Picture Association of America," 12.

139. *AFAA Newsletter*, May 15, 1970, 2, AFAA file, box 62, Presidential Commission on Obscenity and Pornography Collection, LBJ Library.

2. Peek Snatchers

1. Schaefer discusses the management of this shift in the classical exploitation film in *Bold! Daring! Shocking! True!*, 15. He draws on the work of Lawrence Birken in his analysis of the changing structure of modern identity, spanning the late nineteenth century to the early twentieth century, from a productivist model of sexuality oriented around work, reproduction, and family toward a consumerist model that serves a democratizing function stressing pleasure, individuation, and a move away from rigid gender roles. Schaefer argues that exploitation films invoked a productivist skepticism regarding sexuality and vice, thus quarantining their

narratives from legal and moral scrutiny while still capitalizing on illicit spectacle. The productivist–consumerist framework has also been substantiated in a variety of social and cultural histories of twentieth-century sexuality, including D'Emilio and Freedman, *Intimate Matters,* and Jeffrey Weeks, *Sexuality and Its Discontents* (London: Routledge, 1985); it has also been critiqued in John Levi Martin, "The Myth of the Consumption Oriented Economy and the Rise of the Desiring Subject," *Theory and Society* 28 (1999): 425–53. Also see Lawrence Birken, *Consuming Desire: Sexual Science and the Emergence of a Culture of Abundance 1871–1914* (Ithaca, N.Y.: Cornell University Press, 1989).

2. While this chapter and the next aim to be expansive in their scope and coverage of the variety of sexploitation films made in the period between 1960 and 1971, every film selected necessarily involves numerous films left out. The historiographic problem of what counts as "representative" is particularly fractious with the sexploitation mode, as their historical marginality seems to necessitate an approach of global comprehensiveness. Such strategy obviously has its limits in that close analysis of individual films is shuttled in exchange for broader patterns, but this might also imply that no single film within this low-cultural genre deserves the attention accorded to more legitimate "film art." Therefore, in chapters 2 and 3, I aim to balance between a larger picture of the mode's transformation and the specificities of individual film texts, with the awareness that every inclusion depends on the exclusion of many other films worthwhile for the historical record.

3. D'Emilio and Freedman, *Intimate Matters,* 239–360.

4. This structuring notion of a generic "problem" is derived from Linda Williams's essay, "Film Bodies," on the "body genres" of melodrama, horror, and pornography. Williams states, "The deployment of sex, violence, and emotion is thus in no way gratuitous and in no way strictly limited to these genres, it is instead a cultural form of problem solving. . . . Pornographic films now tend to present sex as a problem, to which the performance of more, different or better sex is posed as the solution. In horror, a violence related to sexual difference is the problem, more violence related to sexual difference is the solution. In women's films, the pathos of loss is the problem, repetitions and variations of this loss are the solution" (9). Notably, sexploitation film, as a liminal mode of production, employs elements of all of these body genres in different variations across its history—incorporating aspects of shocking violence, melodramatic affect, and pornographic impulses in a hybridized narrative mode.

5. That sex could ever be "liberated" from its repressive constraints is precisely the myth that Michel Foucault challenged in *History of Sexuality, Vol. 1.*

6. Williams, *Hard Core,* 91.

7. Of course, there were also notable exceptions to the domination of the field of production by men. Roberta Findlay, cinematographer, actor, and sometime director, collaborated with her husband, Michael Findlay, and continued on to make her own porn and horror films in the 1970s and 1980s. Women were notable in other arenas of production and distribution, such as New York theater owner and

producer Chelly Wilson; Radley Metzger's business partner at Audubon Pictures, Ava Leighton; and Russ Meyer's wife, Eve Meyer, who worked in running Eve Productions for Meyer. Some of their work will be detailed within this chapter; however, with that said, sexploitation film, though open to women's participation in a general sense, still operated as a mainly male operation on both the East and West Coasts.

8. Christian Hansen, Catherine Needham, and Bill Nichols, "Pornography, Ethnography and the Discourses of Power," in *Representing Reality: Issues and Concepts in Documentary*, ed. Bill Nichols, 201–28 (Bloomington: Indiana University Press, 1991).

9. Williams, *Hard Core*, 49–50.

10. Linda Hutcheon, *Irony's Edge: The Theory and Politics of Irony* (London: Routledge, 1995), 37.

11. James, *Allegories of Cinema*, 14.

12. Ibid., 283.

13. Schaefer, *Bold! Daring! Shocking! True!*, 80.

14. Chris Straayer, *Deviant Eyes, Deviant Bodies: Sexual Re-orientation in Film and Video* (New York: Columbia University Press, 1996), 186.

15. See Beth Bailey, *From Front Porch to Backseat: Courtship in Twentieth Century America* (Baltimore: Johns Hopkins University Press, 1989), and Bailey, *Sex in the Heartland* (Cambridge, Mass.: Harvard University Press, 2002); Jeffrey Escoffier, ed., *Sexual Revolution* (New York: Thunder's Mouth Press, 2003); Allyn, *Make Love Not War*; Miriam G. Reumann, *American Sexual Character: Sex, Gender, and National Identity in the Kinsey Reports* (Berkeley: University of California Press, 2005).

16. Bailey, "Sexual Revolution(s)," 237.

17. Seidman, *Romantic Longings*, 124.

18. On the relationship between the articulation of capitalism in the growth of urban centers and the development of gay and lesbian communities, see D'Emilio, "Capitalism and Gay Identity," in *Making Trouble: Essays on Gay History, Politics, and the University*, 3–16 (New York: Routledge, 1992).

19. D'Emilio and Freedman, *Intimate Matters*, 327.

20. Thomas Waugh, "Cockteaser," in *Pop Out: Queer Warhol*, ed. Jennifer Doyle, Jonathan Flatley, and Jose Munoz (Durham, N.C.: Duke University Press, 1996), 61.

21. Linda Williams discusses this dynamic of "exposure and concealment" in the striptease as articulated in an unpublished essay by David James in *Hard Core*, 77.

22. On the history of mail-order and underground distribution of adult films, see Eric Schaefer, "Plain Brown Wrapper: Adult Films for the Home Market, 1930–1969," in *Looking Past the Screen: Case Studies in American Film History and Method*, ed. Jon Lewis and Eric Smoodin, 201–26 (Durham, N.C.: Duke University Press, 2007).

23. Leon Hunt, *British Low Culture: From Safari Suits to Sexploitation* (New York: Routledge, 1998), 92–93.

24. For more on the development of the male consumer in relation to American magazine culture, see Tom Pendergast, *Creating the Modern Man: American Magazines and Consumer Culture, 1900–1950* (Columbia: University of Missouri Press, 2000); Keanon Brezeale, "In Spite of Women: *Esquire* and the Construction of the Male Consumer," *Signs: Journal of Women in Culture and Society* 20, no. 1 (1994): 1–22. On *Playboy* and the bachelor ethos of the 1950s, see Barbara Ehrenreich, "*Playboy* Joins the Battle of the Sexes," in *The Hearts of Men: American Dreams and the Flight from Commitment*, 42–51 (New York: Anchor, 1987).

25. Schaefer, *Bold! Daring! Shocking! True!*, 339.

26. Mark Gabor, *The Pin Up: A Modest History* (1972; repr., Cologne, Germany: Evergreen/Taschen, 1996); Despina Kakoudaki, "Pinup: The American Secret Weapon in World War II," in Williams, *Porn Studies*, 335–69; Maria Elena Buszek, *Pinup Grrrls: Feminism Sexuality, Popular Culture* (Durham, N.C.: Duke University Press, 2006).

27. Eric Schaefer, "'They Wear No Clothes!' Nudist and Burlesque Films," in *Bold! Daring! Shocking! True!*, 290–325. See also Robert Payne, "Beyond the Pale: Nudism, Race and Resistance in *The Unashamed*," *Film Quarterly* 54, no. 2 (2000–2001): 27–40.

28. On the fallen woman film in the context of the politics of the 1930s Production Code, see Lea Jacobs, *The Wages of Sin: Censorship and the Fallen Woman Film 1928–1942* (Berkeley: University of California Press, 1997).

29. Susan McLeland provides a detailed analysis of Liz Taylor's star image in the 1960s in "Elizabeth Taylor: Hollywood's Last Glamour Girl," in Radner and Luckett, *Swinging Single*, 227–51.

30. Alexander Doty, "Elizabeth Taylor: The Biggest Star in the World," in *New Constellations: Movie Stars of the 1960s*, ed. Pamela Robertson Wojcik, 34–54 (New Brunswick, N.J.: Rutgers University Press, 2012).

31. Parker Tyler, "The Awful Fate of the Sex Goddess," in *Sex Psyche Etcetera in the Film* (Baltimore: Penguin Books, 1969), 21.

32. David F. Friedman, interviewed by David Chute, "Wages of Sin," *Film Comment* 22, no. 5 (1986): 57.

33. Gordon Hitchens, "The Truth, the Whole Truth and Nothing but the Truth about Exploitation Films: With Barry Mahon," *Film Comment* 2, no. 2 (1964): 8–9.

34. Lynda Nead, *The Female Nude: Art, Obscenity, and Sexuality* (London: Routledge, 1992), 7.

35. Leslie Fiedler, "A Night with Mr. Teas," *Show* 1, no. 1 (1961): 118.

36. In his reading of the film, David Andrews suggests that "Teas' peeping does not culminate in masturbation or in signs of arousal. Besides Meyer's desire to avoid sex, anti-masturbatory norms that construct autoerotic gestures as effeminate (and

comic) inform this restraint." Andrews, *Soft in the Middle: The Contemporary Soft Core Feature* (Columbus: Ohio State University Press, 2006), 53.

37. Kristen Hatch discusses the implications of Meyer's aggressive female characters in his "middle period" films within the contexts of contemporary feminist revaluations of his films in "The Sweeter the Kitten the Sharper the Claws: Russ Meyer's Bad Girls," in *Bad: Infamy, Evil, and Slime on Screen*, ed. Murray Pomerance, 143–56 (Albany: SUNY Press, 2004).

38. Hitchens, "The Truth, the Whole Truth and Nothing but the Truth," 3–4.

39. Eric Schaefer observes this characteristic as well in numerous sexploitation films across the decade in "*Showgirls* and the Limits of Sexploitation," *Film Quarterly* 56, no. 3 (2003): 42–43.

40. Hitchens, "The Truth, the Whole Truth and Nothing but the Truth," 4.

41. Mahon also mentions an exception in his film *She Should Have Stayed in Bed* (1963), which the New York State Board of Regents denied a license. The film attempted to use the premise of a "roving photographer making a movie in a building inhabited mostly by women. Periodically, he lets his camera stray into their apartments rather than sticking to the job at hand. . . . The censors felt that it was a peeping tom operation." Ibid., 4. This film contains a voice-over commentary, presumably of the cameraman, who punctuates the images and makes self-referential comments such as, "This picture's the worst I ever worked on!"

42. For varying accounts of Yves Klein and his art career in the contexts of the European postwar avant-garde, see Benjamin Buchloh, *From Neo Avant-garde to Culture Industry: Essays on European and American Art from 1955 to 1975* (Cambridge, Mass.: MIT Press, 2001), 257–84, and Buchloh, "Klein and Poses," *ArtForum International* (June 1995); Hannah Weitemeier, *Yves Klein: 1928–1962: International Klein Blue* (New York: Taschen Books, 2001); Sidra Stitch, ed., *Yves Klein* (Vienna: Cantz, 1994); Amelia Jones, *Body Art/Performing the Subject* (Minneapolis: University of Minnesota Press, 1998), 53–103.

43. Body painting would figure in mid- to late-1960s sexploitation as a cultural symbol of youth practices and sexual openness resignified as aesthetic experimentation, especially in the pseudo-documentary counterculture exposés, such as *Free Love Confidential* (Gordon Heller, 1967), *Like It Is* (William Rotsler, 1968), *The Hippie Revolt* (Edgar Beatty, 1967), *The Filth Shop* (Looney Bear, 1969), and others.

44. Yeager was her own cottage industry, authoring more than thirty books on pinup photography, with titles including *How I Photograph Nudes, Bunny's Bikini Beauties, Bettie in Jungle Land,* and *100 Girls.* According to Legs McNeil and Jennifer Osborne's interviews with Yeager, she was also involved in the production of a small number of her own sexploitation films in the late 1960s, as well as having some interaction with Linda Lovelace's infamous husband, Chuck Traynor. McNeil and Osborne, *The Other Hollywood: The Uncensored Oral History of the Porn Film Industry* (New York: HarperCollins, 2005). The titles of the films include *Sextet, Room 11* (credits have Bud Irwin as director), and *Orgy of Revenge*

(dates for all three films are unverified, but all were likely made in the late 1960s). Until her death in 2014, Yeager maintained her own website and continued creating calendar-style pinup photographs, selling both her historical and contemporary photos. For a recent account of Yeager's self-portraiture and celebrity, which briefly discusses Mahon's *Nude Camera,* see Ellen Wright, "Having Her Cheesecake and Eating It: Performance, Professionalism, and the Politics of the Gaze in Bunny Yeager's Self-Portraiture," *Feminist Media Histories* 2, no. 4 (2016): 116–42.

45. Michael Fessier Jr., "Anatomy of Nude Film Biz: Chary Theatres as Main Hurdle," *Variety,* June 19, 1963, 5.

46. Murray Schumach, "Union Opposing Nudity in Films," *New York Times,* October 1, 1962, 54.

47. Monroe's last, uncompleted film, *Something's Got to Give* (George Cukor, 1962), was widely known to have included a nude swimming pool scene. Jayne Mansfield gained the mantle of the first known star to appear nude in *Promises! Promises!* (King Donovan, 1963). Carroll Baker, who had appeared in the controversial Elia Kazan film *Baby Doll* (1956), became a vocal advocate on behalf of her own choice to do nude scenes in Hollywood films. Murray Schumach, "Hollywood Candor: Carroll Baker Defends Her Nudity in Films," *New York Times,* June 14, 1964, X9.

48. Vernon Scott, "Nudie Films Irk 'Cleavage Girl,'" *The Independent* (Long Beach, Calif.), December 31, 1965, 7.

49. Murray Schumach, "Producer Defies MGM on Nudes," *New York Times,* November 17, 1963, 43, and Schumach, "Producer Decries Movie Nudity Ban," *New York Times,* March 19, 1964, 37.

50. Schumach, "Hollywood Candor."

51. "The Trade: Nude Wave," *Time,* October 20, 1967, 101.

52. Friedman and Lewis's excursion into and reconfiguration of the horror film formula in *Blood Feast* (1963) is also deployed to mark this break, as a signpost or milestone that gestures toward the transition to the more violent roughies—even though it represents an offshoot to a different, non-sexploitation-oriented cycle, the "ghoulie" film, which led the way toward the gore and splatter films of the 1970s and 1980s. *Blood Feast* used its blaring color and new advances in fake blood to offer audiences a more graphic—also self-consciously stagy and artificial—dismemberment and blood-letting of young women than had been previously available on motion picture screens. I am choosing not to discuss the ghoulies because of their departure from overt concerns of sexuality, despite both this linkage on the level of production personnel and the film and its sequels' relationships to the historiography of the roughies and kinkies. Lewis would go on to direct numerous other gore films and return to sexploitation in the late 1960s with films such as *Suburban Roulette* (1968) and *She Devils on Wheels* (1968).

53. Turan and Zito, *Sinema,* 17–18.

54. Schaefer, *Bold! Daring! Shocking! True!,* 330–37.

55. Mark Betz, "Art, Exploitation, Underground," in *Defining Cult Movies:*

The Cultural Politics of Oppositional Taste, ed. Mark Jancovich, Antonio Lazaro-Reboll, Julian Stringer, and Andy Willis, 202–22 (Manchester, UK: Manchester University Press, 2003).

56. See ibid.; Schoonover, *Brutal Vision,* 69–108.

57. Schaefer, "Adults Only," 30.

58. Ibid., 47–51.

59. Andrews gives these two directors a pivotal place in the ways that sexploitation became "feminized" and oriented more around female protagonists and narratives of "sexual awakening." Andrews, *Soft in the Middle,* 45–76.

60. While the AFI film catalog lists Sarno as the credited director, the press book materials list no discernible director. *Nude in Charcoal* press book, William K. Everson Collection, New York University. According to Sarno biographer Michael Bowen, Sarno was asked at first to write the script of the film for Philip Melillo and subsequently took the helm of directing. Thanks to Michael Bowen for clarifying this information. While the film could have been released closer to its production date in 1961, advertisements for the film evidence its exhibition in early 1963 in Hartford, Connecticut, and Los Angeles, with subsequent screenings later in the year in Chicago. Display ads, *Hartford Courant,* February 16, 1963, 16E; February 18, 1963, 6; film listings, *Los Angeles Times,* March 7, 1963, 28; film listings, *Chicago Tribune,* October 20, 1963, F15.

61. Film synopsis, *Nude in Charcoal* press book, William K. Everson Collection, New York University.

62. Ibid.

63. Ibid.

64. Moya Luckett also cites Lisa Petrucci, who suggests that the earliest roughie spans back to 1962 with the release of Roberta and Michael Findlay's *The Festival Girls.* Luckett, "Sexploitation as Feminine Territory: The Films of Doris Wishman," in Jancovich et al., *Defining Cult Movies,* 144.

65. Display ad, *Chicago Tribune,* February 26, 1964, A5.

66. Foucault, *History of Sexuality, Vol. 1.* Foucault of course was interested in challenging the normative function of the repressive hypothesis in its structuring of knowledge about sexuality from the Victorian era into the 1960s, and his critique was a response to some of the sexual liberationist rhetoric of thinkers embraced by the counterculture, such as Herbert Marcuse and Wilhelm Reich. Yet in the vernacular understanding within which sexploitation producers worked, the "repressive hypothesis" was the dominant understanding of sexual change and provided a commonplace structure around which sexual ideologies could be organized. However, there is a way that in refusing a notion of the possibility of sexual freedom, sexploitation films are more Foucauldian than they at first seem. The double-edged logic of necessitating repression and censorship in order to toe the line or break it, on the industrial and legal levels, attests to the complexity of Foucault's argument.

67. This film was recently recovered and is discussed in the AFI 1961–70 cata-

log and in Turan and Zito, *Sinema,* 52–53; Richard Krafsur, ed., *The American Film Institute Catalog, Feature Films 1961–70* (New York: R. R. Bowker, 1976).

68. Chute, "Wages of Sin," 47.

69. Eithne Johnson and Eric Schaefer, "Soft Core/Hard Gore: Snuff and the Crisis in Meaning," *Journal of Film and Video* 45, no. 2/3 (1993): 40–59.

70. Williams, *Hard Core,* 164.

71. It is hardly ironic that *The Beatniks* seemed far more in the mold of the juvenile delinquent or teenpic than any verisimilar depiction of "authentic" beat culture or ideals. *The Defilers* itself bears more than a passing resemblance to the JD pictures of the 1950s in its indulgence in formulaic violence and the recipe of disaffected youth.

72. Mabe had previously appeared in Mahon's *1,000 Shapes of a Female* and *The Beast That Killed Women* (1965) and had come to Los Angeles from New York with a recommendation from Mahon. Mabe would go on to direct his own films under the tutelage of Friedman, starting with *A Smell of Honey, a Swallow of Brine* in 1966 as well as *She Freak* (1967), *The Acid Eaters* (1968), *The Lustful Turk* (1968), and others.

73. Helen Gurley Brown's *Sex and the Single Girl* as well as Betty Friedan's *The Feminine Mystique* can be seen as two operative poles of this emerging discourse that would lead to the flowering of the women's liberation movement, the former accounting for women's lives in the public sphere of work and urban life, the latter contending with the private, domestic, and suburban. Gurley Brown, *Sex and the Single Girl* (New York: Random House, 1962); Friedan, *The Feminine Mystique* (New York: Dell, 1963).

74. Barbara Ehrenreich has an extended and illuminating chapter on the function of the beats within the landscape of transforming masculine identity in the postwar period in *The Hearts of Men: American Dreams and the Flight from Commitment* (New York: Doubleday, 1983), 52–67. In her analysis, she suggests that the beat ethos was one that emerged out of a decidedly lower-class affiliation, or at least a desired downward mobility. In this sense, *The Defilers* parts company with a beat aesthetic here, in that sexual dysfunction is seen to emerge from a certain class privilege, a side effect that comes from easy wealth.

75. Estelle Freedman, "'Uncontrolled Desires': The Response to the Sexual Psychopath, 1920–1960," in *Passion and Power: Sexuality in History,* ed. Kathy Peiss and Christina Simmons (Philadelphia: Temple University Press, 1989), 213.

76. Ehrenreich writes, regarding the association of homosexuality with any symptom of failed masculinity in the postwar period, "In psychiatric theory and popular culture, the image of the irresponsible male blurred into the shadowy figure of the homosexual. Men who failed as breadwinners and husbands were 'immature,' while homosexuals were in psychiatric judgment 'aspirants to perpetual adolescence.'" Ehrenreich, *Hearts of Men,* 24.

77. *The Defilers* press book, Pressbook Files, William K. Everson Collection, New York University.

78. For a definitive overview of Wishman's career, see Michael Bowen, "Embodiment and Realization: The Many Film-Bodies of Doris Wishman," *Wide Angle* 19, no. 3 (1997): 64–90. See also a reconsideration of Wishman's work from feminist film critic Tania Modleski in "Women's Cinema as Counterphobic Cinema: Doris Wishman as the Last Auteur," in *Sleaze Artists: Cinema at the Margins of Taste, Style, and Politics,* 47–70 (Durham, N.C.: Duke University Press, 2007).

79. The notion of the "rape discourse" is prominent in David Andrews's analysis of 1960s sexploitation films in *Soft in the Middle,* 46–62.

80. Moya Luckett elaborates on some of the broader stylistic features and motifs of Wishman's work, particularly Wishman's cultivation of a female spectatorial position and her circumvention of the codes of sexploitation spectacle in "Sexploitation as Feminine Territory."

81. For a reading of sexploitation cinema as an entry point into the development of soft-core, see Andrews, *Soft in the Middle,* 3–6.

3. Girls with Hungry Eyes

1. Gurley Brown, *Sex and the Single Girl.*
2. Jennifer Scanlon, *Bad Girls Go Everywhere: The Life of Helen Gurley Brown* (Oxford: Oxford University Press, 2009). See also Julie Berebitsky, "The Joy of Work: Helen Gurley Brown, Gender, and Sexuality in the White Collar Office," *Journal of the History of Sexuality* 15, no. 1 (2006): 89–127.
3. Radner, "Queering the Girl," 14.
4. Ibid., 15–16.
5. Friedan, *Feminine Mystique,* 366.
6. Ibid., 369.
7. Ibid., 366.
8. For analyses of white slavery scares in the teens in relation to *Traffic in Souls,* see Christopher Diffee, "Sex and the City: The White Slavery Scare and Social Governance in the Progressive Era," *American Quarterly* 57, no. 2 (2005): 411–37; Shelley Stamp Lindsey, "Wages and Sin: *Traffic in Souls* and the White Slavery Scare," *Persistence of Vision,* no. 9 (1991): 92; Tom Gunning, "From the Kaleidoscope to the X-Ray: Urban Spectatorship, Poe, Benjamin, and *Traffic in Souls,*" *Wide Angle* 19, no. 4 (1997): 25–61; Janet Staiger, *Bad Women: Regulating Sexuality in Early American Cinema* (Minneapolis: University of Minnesota Press, 1995), 116–47.
9. Andrews, *Soft in the Middle,* 57.
10. Raymond Durgnat, *Sexual Alienation in the Cinema* (London: November Books, 1972), 245–46.
11. Ibid., 248.
12. When contrasted to the underground queer cinema being produced contemporaneously to it in 1960s New York, such as Jack Smith's *Flaming Creatures* (1963) or the work of George and Mike Kuchar or Barbara Rubin, *Chained Girls* is without a doubt operating with aesthetic aims far removed from artisanal experimental practices and politics of avant-garde cinema. However, it articulates

some of the social and cultural associations of gay, lesbian, and nonheteronormative sexuality with urban places and spaces and with an imaginary embedded in an idea of eroticism dynamized by city dwelling.

13. Smith worked as cinematographer on a number of Doris Wishman roughies and soft-core films, including *Bad Girls Go to Hell, Another Day, Another Man* (1966), *A Taste of Flesh* (1967), *Indecent Desires* (1967), *Too Much Too Often* (1968), and *Double Agent 73* (1974), among many others. Smith also directed a number of his own films, including *To Turn a Trick* (1967) and *The Girl from S.I.N.* (1966).

14. Chuck Kleinhans, "Pornography and Documentary: Narrating the Alibi," in Sconce, *Sleaze Artists*, 107–8.

15. David Reuben, *Everything You Wanted to Know about Sex but Were Afraid to Ask* (New York: David MacKay, 1969); Albert Ellis, *The Art and Science of Love* (New York: Bantam, 1966).

16. Janice Irvine, *Disorders of Desire: Sex and Gender in Modern American Sexology* (Philadelphia: Temple University Press, 1990), 14.

17. Some social scientific texts that detail "deviant" subcultures include Kai T. Erickson, "Notes on the Sociology of Deviance," *Social Problems* 9, no. 4 (1962): 307–14; R. E. L. Masters, *The Homosexual Revolution: A Challenging Expose of the Social and Political Directions of a Minority Group* (New York: Julian, 1962); Howard Becker, *Outsiders: Studies in the Sociology of Deviance* (New York: Free Press, 1963); Albert Cohen, "The Sociology of the Deviant Act: Anomie Theory and Beyond," *American Sociological Review* 30, no. 1 (1965): 5–14; Ned Polsky, *Hustlers, Beats, and Others* (Chicago: Aldine, 1967); John Gagnon and William Simon, "Sexual Deviance in Contemporary America," *Annals of the American Academy of Political and Social Science* 376 (1968): 106–22; Laud Humphreys, *Tearoom Trade: Impersonal Sex in Public Places* (London: Duckworth, 1970); Erich Goode and Richard R. Troiden, eds., *Sexual Deviance and Sexual Deviants* (New York: William Morrow, 1975).

18. This tagging or identification of "underground" with the sex film was common in advertisements for films but also appears in journalism. For a discussion of some misrecognitions, overlaps, and associations between sexploitation and experimental cinemas, see James Lithgow and Colin Heard, "Underground USA and the Sexploitation Market," *Films and Filming*, August 1969, 18–29.

19. Jimmy McDonough, *The Ghastly One: The Sex-Gore Netherworld of Filmmaker Andy Milligan* (Chicago: A Cappella Books, 2001), 75–95.

20. On the notion of incoherence or incongruity in the cult film text more broadly, see Sconce, "Trashing the Academy"; William Routt, "Bad for Good," *Intensities: The Journal of Cult Media*, Autumn/Winter 2011, https://intensitiescultmedia.files.wordpress.com/2012/12/routt-bad-for-good.pdf; and J. Hoberman, "Bad Movies," in *Vulgar Modernism*, 13–22 (Philadelphia: Temple University Press, 1991).

21. Craig Fischer, "*Beyond the Valley of the Dolls* and the Exploitation Genre," *Velvet Light Trap* 30 (Fall 1992): 18–33.

22. Schaefer, *Bold! Daring! Shocking! True!*, 93–94.

23. Susan Stryker, *Queer Pulp: Perverted Passions from the Golden Age of the Paperback* (San Francisco: Chronicle Books, 2001), 8.

24. Yvonne Keller, "Ab/normal Looking: Voyeurism and Surveillance in Lesbian Pulp Novels and US Cold War Culture," *Feminist Media Studies* 5, no. 2 (2005): 177–95.

25. Ibid., 191.

26. Andrews, *Soft in the Middle*, 53–54.

27. Schaefer, "Gauging a Revolution," 6.

28. Vincent Canby, "*I, a Woman* a Hit Despite Its Origin," *New York Times*, August 10, 1967, 44.

29. Ed Murnane, "I, a Reporter, See 'Hot' Film," and Hester Kline, "*I, a Woman* Film Pulled: Police Act after Calls," *Rolling Meadows Daily Herald* (Arlington Heights, Ill.), October 11, 1967, 1.

30. Film advertisement, Queen Theater, *Daily Eagle* (Bryan, Tex.), April 3, 1967, 6.

31. For discussion of the implications of Masters and Johnson's "discovery" of clitoral orgasm, see Barbara Ehrenreich, Elizabeth Hess, and Gloria Jacobs, *Remaking Love: The Feminization of Sex* (New York: Anchor Books, 1987), 39–73; Irvine, *Disorders of Desire*, 86–103.

32. Williams, *Screening Sex*, 168.

33. Radner, "Queering the Girl," 11.

34. Turan and Zito, *Sinema*, 56.

35. For a historical contextualization of the invisibility of lesbians in Hollywood films during the reign of the Production Code, see Patricia White, *Uninvited: Classical Hollywood Cinema and Lesbian Representability* (Bloomington: Indiana University Press, 1999).

36. Jeffrey Sconce, "Altered Sex: Satan, Acid, and the Erotic Threshold," in Schaefer, *Sex Scene*, 235–64.

37. Beth Bailey, "Sex as a Weapon: Underground Comix and the Paradox of Liberation," in *Imagine Nation: The American Counterculture of the 1960s and 1970s*, ed. Peter Braunstein and Michael William Doyle (London: Routledge, 2002), 307.

38. Eberwein, *Sex Ed*, 1–9.

39. Lewis, *Hollywood v. Hardcore*, 147.

40. Kevin Heffernan, "Prurient (Dis) Interest: The American Release and Reception of *I Am Curious (Yellow)*," in Schaefer, *Sex Scene*, 115.

41. Richard Corliss, "Confessions of an Ex-Pornologist," *The Village Voice*, June 3, 1971, 64.

42. Ibid.

43. By 1971, Friedman, president of the AFAA, distinguished sexploitation productions from the emergent creep of hard-core 16mm films by making an economic argument—that his films produced on budgets of one hundred thousand dollars had class and respectability and were distributed by known entities, and that the same was not borne out by the twenty-five hundred dollar budgets of the

hard-core features, which were shot in two days' time. Vernon Scott, "Exploitation Films 'Don't Exploit Sex,'" *Chicago Tribune*, March 14, 1971, E6.

44. Andrews, *Soft in the Middle*, 60–63.

45. Ibid.

4. Watching an "Audience of Voyeurs"

1. Eric Schaefer, "Pandering to the Goon Trade: Framing the Audience through Sexploitation Advertising," in Sconce, *Sleaze Artists*, 19–46.

2. Of course, film history and reception studies have taught us that no historical spectator can be relegated to the position of naïveté so glibly. Tom Gunning's challenging of the generative myth of early cinema audiences' first viewing of the Lumières' *The Arrival of a Train in the Station* (1895) has particular bearing on this seemingly unrelated characterization of adult film audiences in that both myths presume the naïveté of the viewer, one in terms of the realism employed by the medium and the other by the uses of realism toward a promise of erotic spectacle. Gunning, "An Aesthetic of Astonishment: Early Film and the (In)credulous Spectator," *Art and Text*, no. 34 (Spring 1989): 31–45.

3. *Report of the Commission on Obscenity and Pornography* (New York: Bantam Books, 1970), 162.

4. Jeffrey Escoffier, "Beefcake to Hardcore: Gay Pornography and the Sexual Revolution," in Schaefer, *Sex Scene*, 319–50; Jose Capino, "Homologies of Space: Text and Space in the All Male Adult Theater," *Cinema Journal* 45, no. 1 (2005): 50–65. On the emergence of gay adult cinema, see Tom Waugh, *Hard to Imagine: Gay Male Eroticism in Photography and Film from Their Beginnings to Stonewall* (New York: Columbia University Press, 1996), 253–73, 351–66; Jack Stevenson, "From the Bedroom to the Bijou: A Secret History of American Gay Sex Cinema," *Film Quarterly* 51, no. 1 (1997): 24–31; Whitney Strub, "Mondo Rocco: Mapping Gay Los Angeles Sexual Geography in the Late 1960s Films of Pat Rocco," *Radical History Review*, Spring 2012, 13–34.

5. Monaco, *The Sixties*, 40–55.

6. Leigh Anne Wheeler, "Publicizing Sex through Consumer and Privacy Rights: How the American Civil Liberties Union Liberated Media in the 1960s," in Schaefer, *Sex Scene*, 351–82.

7. For a useful summary of reception and audience studies in the discipline of film studies, see Henry Jenkins, "Reception Theory and Audience Research: The Case of the Vampire's Kiss," in *Reinventing Film Studies*, ed. Christine Gledhill and Linda Williams, 165–82 (London: Arnold, 2000).

8. This notion of "use-value" is drawn from Janet Staiger's discussion of historical reception studies in her book *Interpreting Films: Studies in the Historical Reception of American Films* (Princeton, N.J.: Princeton University Press, 1992).

9. The "orgone box" of course referred to the ideas of Austrian émigré and doctor Wilhelm Reich and his thinking on sexual revolutions and the need to rid

society of its ills through the harnessing of repressed and misdirected sexual energy. He developed his ideas on sexual repression and its links to political authoritarianism in the United States in the 1930s and 1940s after fleeing Germany in 1933. *Orgone* became the term for the orgasmic energy that needed to be managed, and he developed a therapy that involved patients' use of an "orgone accumulator" that he had begun to build and distribute. Reich was arrested and imprisoned for his research and died while in jail. His ideas gained extraordinary currency during the 1960s, giving voice to the antiauthoritarian and hedonistic experience–seeking elements of the counterculture. "The Second Sexual Revolution: A Survey," *Time*, January 24, 1964, reprinted in Henry Anatole Grunwald, ed., *Sex in America* (New York: Bantam Books, 1964), 1, 3.

10. Vincent Canby, "Wider Public for Sexy Films: Folks 'Tsk-Tsk' but Buy Tickets," *Variety*, February 10, 1965, 1.

11. Paul Monaco, "Runaway Audience," in *The Sixties*, 54.

12. Schaefer, *Bold! Daring! Shocking! True!*, 336.

13. *Art Films International* 1, no. 3 (1963): 25–30, 38–45.

14. David Friedman, with Don De Nevi, *A Youth in Babylon: Confessions of a Trash Film King* (Buffalo, N.Y.: Prometheus Books, 1990), 100.

15. Tom Brinkmann has exhaustively documented the sexploitation film magazine as one form of postwar pulp magazine production on his website (http://www.badmags.com/bmsexploitation.html) and in his book *Bad Mags: The Strangest, Most Unusual and Sleaziest Periodicals Ever Published* (London: Headpress/Critical Vision, 2007). See also David Church on the role of the sex film magazines in the career of impresario William Rotsler in "Between Fantasy and Reality: Sexploitation, Fan Magazines, and William Rotsler's 'Adults-Only' Career," *Film History: An International Journal* 26, no. 3 (2014): 106–43.

16. David Moller, "Nuderama," *Art Films International* 1, no. 5 (1964): 20–22.

17. Patrice Petro, "Aftershock, between Boredom and History," in *Aftershocks of the New: Feminism and Film History* (Camden, N.J.: Rutgers University Press, 2002), 61, 63.

18. Ibid, 22.

19. Ibid.

20. This notion of a "special interest group" has been discussed in relationship to art houses in the 1950s and early 1960s in Staiger, *Interpreting Films*, 184–85; John Twomey, "Some Considerations on the Rise of the Art-Film Theater," *Quarterly of Film, Radio, and Television* 10 (Spring 1956): 239–47.

21. "Life along Cinema Raw," *Los Angeles Times*, February 4, 1968, B21.

22. *The Realist* was an early staple in the development and outgrowth of the underground press in the 1960s, fueled by the kinds of questioning of traditions and social institutions that enlivened performative and protest movements. Started in 1958 by writer Paul Krassner, the New York–based newspaper was a contrarian's delight, intent on exposing hypocrisy and juxtaposing searing pieces of satire with investigative journalism. At its height, the newspaper had a subscription of

one hundred thousand. For more on *The Realist* in the context of other independent, countercultural presses, see Abe Peck, *Uncovering the Sixties: The Love and Times of the Underground Press* (New York: Citadel, 1985), 10–13.

23. Michael Valenti, "The Lonely Private World of Dirty Movies," *The Realist*, October 1965, 5.

24. Radley Metzger, one of the foremost dubbers and importers of foreign films for U.S. release in the early 1960s (that is, before he would switch to subtitling with *I, a Woman*), would pen an article in *Art Films International* defending dubbed films against the snobbery of cineastes and explaining the multiple circumstances through which a film might get dubbed in both its original production context and abroad. Metzger, "Dubbing: They Took the Words Right Out of My Mouth," *Art Films International* 1, no. 3 (1963): 14–17.

25. Valenti, "Lonely Private World," 5.

26. Ibid., 6.

27. Ibid.

28. Ibid.

29. Ibid.

30. "Sexploiters Pushing into New and More Erotic Areas; Their Legal Cases Open New Vistas for Films," *Variety*, August 23, 1967, 7.

31. Kevin Thomas, "Meaning of Exploitation," *Los Angeles Times*, April 30, 1967, C1.

32. Ado Kyrou, "The Marvelous Is Popular," in *The Shadow and Its Shadow: Surrealist Writings on Cinema*, ed. Paul Hammond, 68–70 (London: British Film Institute, 1978); Bela Balazs, *Theory of the Film: Character and Growth of a New Art* (London: Dennis Dobson, 1952).

33. Fred Chappell, "Twenty Six Propositions about Skin Flicks," in *Man and the Movies*, ed. William R. Robinson and W. George Garrett (Baton Rouge: Louisiana State University Press, 1967), 53–54.

34. Susan Sontag, "One Culture and the New Sensibility," in *Against Interpretation and Other Essays*, 293–304 (New York: Farrar, Straus, and Giroux, 1966).

35. Chappell, "Twenty Six Propositions about Skin Flicks," 55.

36. Ibid., 56.

37. Ibid., 57.

38. Ibid., 58.

39. Roland Barthes, "The Death of the Author," in *Image, Music, Text*, ed. and trans. Stephen Heath, 142–48 (New York: Hill and Wang, 1977).

40. Andrew Sarris, "Notes on the Auteur Theory in 1962," *Film Culture*, no. 27 (Winter 1962–63): 1–8.

41. Roger Ebert, "Exploitation Films: Spice and Things Not So Nice," *Los Angeles Times*, May 21, 1967, 11.

42. Ibid.

43. Kevin Thomas, "*Mudhoney* Unspoiled Sex Farce," *Los Angeles Times*, April 19, 1966, 30. Just two years prior, in a review of Meyer's *Lorna* in the *LA*

Times, notably by a female reviewer, Meyer's film was indicted as being "afflicted with terrible taste" and the filmmaker himself "without a shred of talent." Margaret Harford, "*Lorna* Caricatures Adult Art Features," *Los Angeles Times*, September 18, 1964, C10.

44. Thomas, "*Mudhoney*," 30.

45. Quoted in Steven Lovelady, "King Leer: Top Nudie Film Maker Russ Meyer, Scrambles to Outshock Big Studios," *Wall Street Journal*, April 24, 1968, 1.

46. Vincent Canby, "Films Exploiting Interest in Sex and Violence Find Growing Audience Here," January 24, 1968.

47. Kevin Thomas, "*Ingrid* Film Playing on Canon Screen," *Los Angeles Times*, March 19, 1969, G14.

48. Vincent Canby, "Essy the Spirit, Essy the Body," *New York Times*, May 26, 1968, 22.

49. R. Albarino, "Stranglehold on Sex Gasps: Majors Giving Indies a Lesson," *Variety*, October 12, 1966, 7.

50. J. Doerfler, "Radley Metzger: Let 'Em See Skin . . . ," *Boston after Dark*, February 9, 1971, 16.

51. Kevin Thomas, "*Carmen Baby* Screens at the Cinema Theater," *Los Angeles Times*, December 23, 1967, B7.

52. Renata Adler, "Lost Innocence: *Therese & Isabelle* Opens at Two Theaters," *New York Times*, May 15, 1968, 41.

53. Canby, "Essy the Spirit, Essy the Body," 22.

54. Douglas Brode, "Radley Metzger: Master of the Erotic on Film," *Show* 2, no. 7 (1971): 42–45; Richard Brown, "Radley Metzger: Auteur of the Erotic," *Film Comment*, June [1971], 26–29, 65–66; Richard Corliss, review of *Camille 2000* in the *Village Voice* (1969), quoted in *Camille 2000*, new acquisitions screening, program notes, April 1–30, 1976, Museum of Modern Art Film Study Center, Radley Metzger Clippings File.

55. Kevin Thomas, "*Laughing Woman* New Radley Metzger Film," *Los Angeles Times*, August 7, 1970, G9.

56. Nat Freedland, "Russ Meyer: Beyond Nudies," *Entertainment World*, January 30, 1970, 12–14.

57. Richard Schickel, "Porn and Man at Yale," *Harper's*, July 1970, 34, 36–38; Arthur Knight and Kevin Flanagan, "Porn Goes to College: American Universities, Their Students, and Pornography, 1968–1973," in Schaefer, *Sex Scene*, 407–34.

58. "Cineprobe: An Evening with Radley Metzger," January 26, 1971, sound recording 71.5, Sound Recordings of Museum Related Events, Museum of Modern Art Archives; "An Evening with Russ Meyer," July 22, 1971, Museum of Modern Art Program Notes; "Cineprobe: A Question of Censorship" program notes, October 12, 1971. Russ Meyer Clippings File, Museum of Modern Art Film Study Center.

59. Mark Finston, "Picasso Upstairs but *Dolls* in the Basement: X Marks the Spot at the Museum of Modern Art," *Star Ledger* (Newark, N.J.), July 26, 1971, 8.

60. Ibid.

61. Margot Hentoff, "Notes from above Ground," *New York Review of Books* 12, no. 10 (1969): 3.

62. "Sex as a Spectator Sport," *Time*, July 1, 1969, 61–66.

63. Robert Sklar, "Nadir and Revival," in *Movie-Made America*, 321–38 (New York: Vintage, 1975). See also Lewis, *Hollywood v. Hardcore*, 135–91; Monaco, *The Sixties*, 24–66.

64. MPAA audience survey findings, 78–81, Commission Correspondence file, box 43, Commission on Obscenity and Pornography Collection, LBJ Presidential Library, Austin, Tex.

65. David Isaacson, "The Need for an Adult Film Association," *Independent Film Journal*, October 14, 1969, 20; "Green: 'Curious' Reception Harms Rest of Market," *Independent Film Journal*, October 14, 1969, 24.

66. "The Trade: Nude Wave," *Time*, October 20, 1967, 101.

67. *Technical Report of the Commission on Obscenity and Pornography*, vol. 3, *The Marketplace: The Industry* (Washington, D.C.: U.S. Government Printing Office, 1971), 50–52; "The Sex Exploitation Explosion," *Independent Film Journal*, October 14, 1969, 17.

68. "Sex Exploitation Explosion," 17; "'Profits Lie in Booming Exploitation Market,' Maintains AIM Manager," *Independent Film Journal*, October 14, 1969, 22.

69. See Lewis, *Hollywood v. Hardcore*, 166; "X Rating a Sales Gimmick?," *Variety*, December 17, 1969, 6; "Film Prods. Many Now Self-Apply X Rating," *Variety*, January 22, 1969, 1, 62.

70. "What Is ARTISEX? A Statement Concerning Its Policy and Raison d'Etre," *Artisex* 1, no. 2 (1968): 2, Pornography Clippings File, Museum of Modern Art Film Study Center.

71. *Artisex* 2, no. 9 (1969): 3, Joseph A. Labadie Collection, University of Michigan Library, Ann Arbor.

72. *Deep Inside* review, ibid., 2.

73. Schaefer, "Gauging a Revolution."

74. "Hello Sucker!," *Artisex* 3, no. 7 (1970): 1, Kinsey Institute of Research on Sex, Gender, and Reproduction Special Collections.

75. "Ticket Sales Need More Than Sex and Nudity: Hessel" and "Social Consciousness Is Pebble's Direction for Low-Budgeters," *Independent Film Journal*, October 14, 1969, 24; "Pioneer's Borden: Many Films Pass No Return Point," *Independent Film Journal*, October 14, 1969, 22.

76. E.g., see Richard Gilman, "There's a Wave of Pornography/Obscenity/Sexual Expression," *New York Times Magazine*, September 8, 1968, 69.

77. William Kling, "House OK's Panel to Study Obscenity," *Chicago Tribune*, August 8, 1967, 1.

78. Among the studies done by the commission grouping adult bookstores, film theaters, and other sex businesses into a research category, see Morris Massey,

"A Marketing Analysis of Sex-Oriented Materials in Denver, August 1969"; Marvin Finkelstein, "The Traffic in Sex Oriented Materials in Boston"; Harold Nawy, "The San Francisco Erotic Marketplace"; and Charles Winick, "Some Characteristics of Patrons of Adult Theaters and Bookstores," in *Technical Report of the Commission of Obscenity and Pornography*, vol. 4, *The Marketplace: Empirical Studies* (Washington, D.C.: U.S. Government Printing Office, 1971), 3–98, 99–155, 155–224, 225–44.

79. *Report of the Commission on Obscenity and Pornography*, 162; see also Edward Cody, "Businessmen Most Frequent Patrons of Theaters Showing Skin Flicks," *High Point Enterprise* (High Point, N.C.), November 16, 1969, 14A.

80. Charles Winick, "A Study of Consumers of Sexually Explicit Materials: Some Functions Served by Adult Movies," in *Technical Report of the Commission on Obscenity and Pornography*, 4:245–62.

81. Ibid., 248.

82. Ibid., 249.

83. Ibid.

84. Ibid., 256–57.

85. Ibid., 251.

86. *Report of the Commission on Obscenity and Pornography*, 162.

87. MPAA audience survey findings, 78–81, Commission Correspondence file, box 43, Commission on Obscenity and Pornography Collection, LBJ Presidential Library.

88. Hentoff, "Notes from above Ground," 3.

89. For a history of the Combat Zone in the 1970s and 1980s, see Eric Schaefer and Eithne Johnson, "Quarantined! A Case Study of Boston's Combat Zone," in *Hop on Pop*, ed. Henry Jenkins, 430–54 (Durham, N.C.: Duke University Press, 2003).

90. Alan Murray, "Skin Flicks: A Layman's Guide to Washington Street," *Fusion*, March [1969 or 1970], 17–19, 21.

91. Winick, "A Study of Consumers of Sexually Explicit Materials," 251, 255.

92. Ibid., 252.

93. Memo by Freeman Lewis, Presidential Commission on Obscenity and Pornography Records, Memorandum file, January 13, 1970, box 50, LBJ Library.

94. Justin Wyatt, "Selling Atrocious Sexual Behavior: Revising Sexualities in the Marketplace for Adult Film in the 1960s," in *Swinging Single: Representing Sexuality in the 1960s*, ed. Moya Luckett and Hilary Radner (Minneapolis: University of Minnesota Press, 1999), 114, 117.

95. Ibid., 118.

96. *Technical Report of the Commission on Obscenity and Pornography*, 3:53. The commission researchers defined "hybrid and new genre" films as those that broke out of the sexploitation/grind house ghetto in terms of exhibition due to their art house aesthetic, stronger production values, and deployment of sexual situations.

97. Schaefer, "Gauging a Revolution," 3–26.

98. Steven V. Roberts, "Pornography in U.S.: A Big Business," *New York Times*, February 22, 1970, 1; Alan S. Oser, "Times Square Finds Erotica Has Impact," *New York Times*, August 23, 1970, R1.

99. See Peck, *Uncovering the Sixties*; and Sandra Levinson, "Sexploitation in the Underground Press," *Ramparts*, 1969.

100. David Allen Karp, "Public Sexuality and Hiding Behavior: A Study of the Times Square Sexual Community," PhD diss., New York University, October 1971.

101. Corliss, "Confessions of an Ex-Pornologist," 62.

102. Karp, "Public Sexuality and Hiding Behavior," 152–68. In comparison to the Capri, which at the time was showing explicit 16mm films, based on the four to five dollar ticket price reported, Karp ventured to the ninety-nine cent theaters along 42nd Street, in which the content was less explicit (sexploitation and other low-budget adult films, based on his description) and the crowd was more vociferous, with audience members displaying a more casual bodily comportment, raising legs aloft on seats and laughing and talking back to the screen.

103. Philip Brian Harper, *Private Affairs: Critical Ventures in the Culture of Social Relations* (New York: New York University Press, 1999), 60–88; Gertrud Koch, "The Body's Shadow Realm," in *Dirty Looks: Women Pornography Power*, ed. Pamela Church Gibson (London: British Film Institute, 1993), 25–26.

104. "A Report on the Undergrounds," *Artisex* 3, no. 1 (1970): 2, Labadie Collection, University of Michigan Library Special Collections.

105. Wyatt, "Selling Atrocious Sexual Behavior," 121.

106. "Rating Criteria," *Artisex* 3, no. 1 (1970): 7.

107. *Artisex*, Last Issue, September 13, 1971, 1, Kinsey Institute for Sex Research.

108. Richard Corliss, "Film and Other Four Letter Words," *National Review*, July 29, 1969, 760.

109. Ed Wallace, "Sexploitation: The Skin Flicks," *New York Sunday News*, January 18, 1970, 16.

110. Jerry Tallmer, "Adults Only: And They Sit Like Granite," *New York Post*, January 9, 1971, 27 (magazine p. 5).

111. Charles Champlin, "Skin Flicks Are Chafing," *Los Angeles Times*, November 27, 1970, 11.

112. Ibid.

113. Bob Lardine, "The Smut Glut Is Cutting into Blue Movie Profits," *Sunday News*, April 25, 1971, section 2, p. 1.

114. Sarris, "Ethos of the 'Doity Movie,'" 59, 76.

115. Ibid., 59.

116. Ibid., 76.

117. Ralph Blumenthal, "Porno Chic: Hard-Core Grows Fashionable and Very Profitable," *New York Times*, January 21, 1973, 28, 30–33.

118. Ibid.

119. Vincent Canby, "What Are We to Think of *Deep Throat?*," *New York Times*, January 21, 1973, A1, 33.
120. Paul Montgomery, "*Throat* Obscene, Judge Rules Here," *New York Times*, March 2, 1973, 1, 18.
121. Charles Champlin, "*Tango, Throat*: High and Low of Sex on Screen," *Los Angeles Times*, February 3, 1973, 18.
122. Wyatt, "Selling Atrocious Sexual Behavior," 123–24.
123. Ibid., 126–27.
124. On the instrumentality of video to the changing porn market, see Peter Alilunas, *Smutty Little Movies: The Creation and Regulation of Adult Video, 1976–1986* (Berkeley: University of California Press, 2016).
125. Schaefer, "Gauging a Revolution," 4.

Conclusion

1. The film originally released with an X rating in 1969 and then rereleased with an R rating in early 1970. Rapp was an independent producer-director who had previously worked with Roger Corman's AIP on *The Wild Angels* (1968) and had assistant produced the homophobic farce about draft dodging *The Gay Deceivers* (1969).
2. William Wolf, "Wolf on Movies: Needed: An Honest Approach to Movie Pornography," *Cue*, December 28, 1968, 7.
3. Ibid.
4. Eric Schaefer, "Introduction: Sex Seen: 1968 and the Rise of 'Public Sex,'" in *Sex Scene*, 13–18.
5. Jeffrey Sconce, "'Trashing' the Academy: Taste, Excess and an Emerging Politics of Cinematic Style," *Screen* 36, no. 4 (1995): 371–93.
6. For an extended analysis of this film and an account of its "dated" aesthetic, see Elena Gorfinkel, "Dated Sexuality: Anna Biller's *Viva* and the Retrospective Life of Sexploitation Cinema," *Camera Obscura* 78 26, no. 3 (2011): 94–135.
7. Recent accounts about the longing for the grind house in the sphere of reception have considered its relationship to the historicity of film and video as medium and addressed the ways that exploitation cinema has circulated through underground and mainstream venues. See Caetlin Benson Allott, *Killer Tapes and Shattered Screens: Video Spectatorship from VHS to File Sharing* (Berkeley: University of California Press, 2013), 132–66; David Church, *Grindhouse Nostalgia: Memory, Home Video and Exploitation Movie Fandom* (Edinburgh: Edinburgh University Press, 2014); Kevin Esch, "'The Lesser of the Attractions': Grindhouse and Theatrical Nostalgia," *Jump Cut* 54 (Fall 2012), http://www.ejumpcut.org/archive/jc54.2012/EschGrindhouse/text.html.
8. Mekado Murphy, "Nicolas Winding Refn on *The Act of Seeing*," *New York Times*, September 25, 2105, http://www.nytimes.com/interactive/2015/09/25

/movies/25nicolas-winding-refn.html; Elizabeth Wagmeister, "HBO Orders David Simon Pilots Including Porn Industry Drama Starring James Franco," *Variety,* August 6, 2015, http://variety.com/2015/tv/news/hobo-the-deuce-david-simon-james-franco-porn-1201557801/; Lacey Rose, "David Simon Reveals Plans for 1970s Times Square Porn Project at HBO," *Hollywood Reporter,* June 17, 2015, http://www.hollywoodreporter.com/live-feed/david-simon-reveals-plans-1970s-803073.

FILMOGRAPHY

DVD Distributors

Something Weird Video

http://www.somethingweird.com
The largest distributor of sexploitation, exploitation, B films, and sex cinema, with an extensive collection of hundreds of titles.

Vinegar Syndrome

https://vinegarsyndrome.com/
A young preservation-minded distributor that specializes in the digital restoration of sexploitation, grind house, horror, soft- and hard-core, and 1970s and 1980s genre oddities.

Alternative Cinema

https://www.alternativecinema.com/studio/retro-seduction-cinema
This distributor's Retroseduction line has released a number of undistributed Joe Sarno titles as well as other notable 1960s and 1970s sexploitation films.

Cult Epics

http://www.cultepics.com/
This distributor has released some Radley Metzger and other sexploitation and soft-core titles.

Films

1,000 Shapes of a Female. Dir. Barry Mahon. Artlife Pictures. 1963.
50,000 B.C. (Before Clothing). Dir. Warner Rose. Biolane Corp. 1963.
The Abnormal Female. Dir. George Rodgers. Dove Prod. 1969.

A Bride for Brenda. Dir. Tommy Goetz. Kirt Films International. 1969.
The Acid Eaters. Dir. Byron Mabe (as B. Ron Elliot). III Lions. 1968.
The Adventures of Lucky Pierre. Dir. Herschell Gordon Lewis (as Lewis H. Gordon). Lucky Pierre Enterprises. 1961.
A Free Ride (Alt. *A Grass Sandwich*). Dir. A Wise Guy (pseud.). Gay Paree Picture. 1915.
Africa Addio. Dir. Gualtiero Jacopettie and Franco Prosperi. Cineriz. 1966.
Agony of Love. Dir. William Rotsler. Boxoffice International Pictures. 1966.
A History of the Blue Movie. Dir. Alex de Renzy. Graffiti Prod. 1970.
All about Eve. Dir. Joseph Mankiewicz. Twentieth Century Fox. 1950.
The Alley Cats. Dir. Radley Metzger (as Radley H. Metzger). Spear Prod.–J. C. Production Co. 1966.
All Women Are Bad. Dir. Larry Crane. American Film Distributing Corp. 1969.
The Americanization of Emily. Dir. Arthur Hiller. MGM. 1964.
And God Created Woman. Dir. Roger Vadim. Cocinor. 1956.
Another Day, Another Man. Dir. Doris Wishman. Juri Prod. 1966.
Anything for Money. Dir. Joe Sarno. Howard Farber Films. 1967.
Aroused. Dir. Anton Holden. Plaudit Prod. 1966.
Artists Studio Secrets. Dir. J. M. Kimbrough. Avanti Pictures. 1964.
A Smell of Honey, a Swallow of Brine. Dir. Byron Mabe (as B. Ron Elliott). Essaneff. 1966.
A Stranger Knocks (En fremmed banker på). Dir. Johan Jacobsen. Flamingo. 1959.
A Taste of Flesh. Dir. Doris Wishman (as Louis Silverman). Mostest Prod. 1967.
A Thousand Pleasures. Dir. Michael Findlay. Rivamarsh Prod. 1968.
Austin Powers. Dir. Jay Roach. Capella International. 1997.
Baby Doll. Dir. Elia Kazan. Newtown Prod. 1956.
Bad Girls Go to Hell. Dir. Doris Wishman. Juri Prod. 1965.
Barbarella. Dir. Roger Vadim. Dino de Laurentiis Cinematografica. 1968.
The Beast That Killed Women. Dir. Barry Mahon. Barry Mahon Prod. 1965.
The Beatniks. Dir. Paul Frees. Glenville. 1960.
Behind the Green Door. Dir. Artie Mitchell and Jim Mitchell. Cinema 7 Film Group. 1972.
Bell, Bare and Beautiful. Dir. Lewis H. Gordon. Griffith Prod. 1963.
Belle du Jour. Dir. Luis Buñuel. Paris-Films Prod. 1967.
The Best of Everything. Dir. Jean Negulesco. Twentieth Century Fox. 1959.
Beyond the Valley of the Dolls. Dir. Russ Meyer. Twentieth Century Fox. 1969.
Bike Boy. Dir. Andy Warhol. Factory Films. 1967.
Bitter Rice. Dir. Giuseppe De Santis. Lux Film. 1949.
Blonde on a Bum Trip. Dir. Ralph Mauro. Niles Street Films. 1968.
Blood Feast. Dir. Herschell G. Lewis. Box Office Spectaculars. 1963.
Blow-Up. Dir. Michelangelo Antonioni. Bridge Films. 1966.
Blue Movie (Alt. *Fuck*). Dir. Andy Warhol. Factory Films. 1969.
Bob & Carol & Ted & Alice. Dir. Paul Mazursky. Frankovich Prod. 1969.

Body of a Female. Dir. John Amero and Michael Findlay (as J. Ellsworth and Julian Marsh). Amlay Pictures. 1965.
Bunny Yeager's Nude Camera. Dir. Barry Mahon. Cinema Syndicate. 1963.
Bunny Yeager's Nude Las Vegas. Dir. Barry Mahon. Barry Mahon Prod. 1964.
Butterfield 8. Dir. Daniel Mann. Afton-Linebrook. 1960.
Camille 2000. Dir. Radley Metzger. Spear Prod. 1969.
Carmen, Baby. Dir. Radley Metzger. Amsterdam Film Corp. 1967.
Carnal Knowledge. Dir. Mike Nichols. Embassy Pictures. 1971.
The Carpetbaggers. Dir. Edward Dmytryk. Embassy Pictures. 1964.
Cat on a Hot Tin Roof. Dir. Richard Brooks. MGM. 1957.
Censored. Dir Barry Mahon. Barry Mahon Prod. 1965.
Chained Girls. Dir. Joseph P. Mawra. American Film Distributing Corp. 1965.
Chelsea Girls. Dir. Andy Warhol. Andy Warhol Films. 1966.
The Collector. Dir. William Wyler. Collector Co. 1965.
Coming Apart. Dir. Milton Moses Ginsberg. Kaleidoscope Films. 1969.
Confessions of a Bad Girl. Dir. Barry Mahon. Barry Mahon Prod. 1965.
The Curious Female. Dir. Paul Rapp. Fanfare Film Prod. 1969.
The Curse of Her Flesh. Dir. Michael Findlay (as Julian Marsh). Rivamarsh Prod. 1968.
David Holzman's Diary. Dir. Jim McBride. Jim McBride. 1968.
Deep Inside. Dir. Joe Sarno. Cannon Prod. 1968.
Deep Throat. Dir. Gerard Damiano. GDFP. 1972.
The Defilers. Dir. Lee Frost. Essaneff Pictures. 1965.
The Devil in Miss Jones. Dir. Gerard Damiano. Pierre Prod. 1973.
The Dirty Girls. Dir. Radley Metzger. Charles Film Prod. 1965.
Double Agent 73. Dir. Doris Wishman. Juri Prod. 1974.
Dr. Sex. Dir. Ted Mikels. RS Prod. 1964.
Electronic Lover. Dir. Jesse Berger. Generation Films. 1966.
Emmanuelle. Dir. Just Jaeckin. Trinacra Films. 1974.
Eve and the Handyman. Dir. Russ Meyer. Eve Prod. 1961.
Eveready Harton in Buried Treasure (Alt. *Buried Treasure*). Dir. E. Hardon (pseud.). Climax Fables. 1928.
Faster Pussycat! Kill! Kill! Dir. Russ Meyer. Eve Prod. 1965.
File X for Sex. Dir. C. Davis Smith. Sam Lake Entertainment. 1967.
The Filth Shop. Dir. Looney Bear. 1969.
Fireworks. Dir. Kenneth Anger. 1947.
Flaming Creatures. Dir. Jack Smith. Film-Makers' Cooperative. 1963.
The Fourth Sex (Alt. *Le Quatrieme Sexe*). Dir. Michel Wichard. Condor Films. 1963. U.S. release, Audubon Films.
The Fox. Dir. Mark Rydell. Motion Pictures International. 1967.
Free Love Confidential. Dir. Gordon Heller. Boxoffice International Pictures. 1967.
The Garden of Eden. Dir. Max Nosseck. Excelsior Pictures Corp. 1954.
The Gay Deceivers. Dir. Bruce Kessler. Fanfare Films. 1969.

The Girl from S.I.N. Dir. C. Davis Smith. Bobmaral. 1966.
Girl in Trouble. Dir. Brandon Chase (as Lee Beale). Vanguard Prod. 1963.
The Girl with the Hungry Eyes (Alt. *The Face of Sin*). Dir. William Rotsler. 1967.
Good Time with a Bad Girl. Dir. Barry Mahon. Cinema Syndicate. 1967.
The Graduate. Dir. Mike Nichols. Lawrence Turman Inc. 1967.
Have Figure, Will Travel. Dir. Leo Orenstein (as Alan Overton). Green Bush Films. 1963.
Hells Angels on Wheels. Dir. Richard Rush. Fanfare Films. 1967.
Her Odd Tastes. Dir. Don Davis. Hollywood Cinema Associates. 1969.
Hideout in the Sun. Dir. Doris Wishman (uncredited, dir. credit as "Lazarus Wolk"). Wica Pictures. 1960.
The Hippie Revolt (Alt. *Something's Happening*). Dir. Edgar Beatty. Belish-Fremont Associates. 1967.
Hollywood Nudes Report. Dir. Barry Mahon. Cinema Syndicate. 1964.
Hollywood's World of Flesh. Dir. Lee Frost (as R. L. Frost). Olympic International Films. 1963.
The Hookers. Dir. Jalo Miklos Horthy. 1967.
Hot Skin, Cold Cash. Dir. Barry Mahon. Barry Mahon Prod. 1965.
Hot Spur. Dir. Lee Frost (as R. L. Frost). International Theatrical Amusements. 1968.
How Many Times. Dir. Don Walters (as Arlo Shiffen). Cine-Systems. 1969.
Hurry Sundown. Dir. Otto Preminger. Otto Preminger Films. 1967.
I, a Man. Dir. Andy Warhol. Andy Warhol Films. 1967.
I Am Curious (Yellow). Dir. Vilgot Sjoman. Sandrews See. 1967.
I, a Woman. Dir. Mac Ahlberg. Nordisk Film/Europa Film/Novaris Film. 1965. U.S. release, Audubon Films, 1966.
I Crave Your Body. Dir. Abe Lutz. Dove Prod. 1967.
The Immoral Mr. Teas. Dir. Russ Meyer. Pad-Ram Enterprises. 1959.
Indecent Desires. Dir. Doris Wishman. Mostest Prod. 1968.
I Was a Man. Dir. Barry Mahon. Sack Amusement Enterprises. 1967.
Jules and Jim. Dir. François Truffaut. Films du Carrosse. 1962.
The Killing of Sister George. Dir. Robert Aldrich. Associates and Aldrich Co. 1968.
Kiss Me Quick. Dir. Peter Perry. Fantasy Films. 1964.
The Kiss of Her Flesh. Dir. Michael Findlay (as Julian Marsh). American Film Distributing Corp. 1968.
La Dolce Vita. Dir. Federico Fellini. Riama Film. 1960.
Lady Chatterley's Lover. Dir. Marc Allegret. Orsay Films. 1955.
The Language of Love. Dir. Torgny Wickman. Swedish Film Prod. 1969.
Last Tango in Paris. Dir. Bernardo Bertolucci. United Artists. 1972.
The Laughing Woman. Dir. Piero Schivazappa. Cemo Film. 1970.
The Layout. Dir. Joe Sarno. DeLuxe Pictures. 1969.
The Libertine. Dir. Pasquale Festa. Clesi Cinematografica. 1969.
The Lickerish Quartet. Dir. Radley Metzger. Cinemar Prod. 1970.

Like It Is. Dir. William Rotsler. Lima Prod. 1968.
Logan's Run. Dir. Michael Anderson. MGM. 1976.
Lolita. Dir. Stanley Kubrick. MGM. 1962.
Lonesome Cowboys. Dir. Andy Warhol. Factory Films. 1968.
Lorna. Dir. Russ Meyer. Eve Prod. 1964.
Love Camp 7. Dir. Lee Frost (as R. L. Frost). Olympic International Films. 1969.
Love Is a Four Letter Word. Dir. Lee Frost (as R. L. Frost). Temarro Films. 1966.
Love Island. Dir. Bud Pollard. Elliot-Shelton Films Inc. 1952.
Love Me . . . Please! Dir. Victor Petrashevic (as Victor Peters). CineCentrum Inc. 1969.
The Lovers. Dir. Louis Malle. NEF. 1958.
The Lustful Turk. Dir. Byron Mabe (as B. Ron Elliott). B&B Prod. 1968.
The Lusting Hours. Dir. John Amero and Lem Amero. American Film Distributing Corp. 1967.
Madame Olga's Massage Parlor. Dir. Joseph P. Mawra. American Film Distributing Corp. 1965.
Man and Wife. Dir. Marv Miller. New World Studios. 1969.
Mantis in Lace. Dir. William Rotsler. Boxoffice International Pictures. 1968.
The Man with the Golden Arm. Dir. Otto Preminger. Carlyle Prod. 1955.
Mickey One. Dir. Arthur Penn. Florin-Tatira Prod. 1965.
Midnight Cowboy. Dir. John Schlesinger. Jerome Hellman Prod. 1969.
The Miracle (Il Miracolo). Dir. Roberto Rossellini. Finecine. 1948.
The Molesters. Dir. Franz Schnyder. Praesens Film. 1964.
Mona (Alt. *Mona the Virgin Nymph*). Dir. Bill Osco. Graffitti Prod. 1970.
Mondo Bizarro. Dir. Lee Frost (uncredited). Olympic International Films. 1966.
Mondo Cane. Dir. Paolo Cavara, Gualtiero Jacopetti, Franco Prosperi. Cineriz. 1962.
Mondo Freudo. Dir. Lee Frost (as R. L. Frost). Olympic International Films. 1966.
Mondo Keyhole. Dir. Jack Hill, John Lamb. Horizon Prod. 1966.
Mondo Mod. Dir. Peter Perry. Timely Motion Pictures. 1967.
Mondo Oscenita. Dir. Joseph P. Mawra (as Carolo Scappine). American Film Distributing Corp. 1966.
Monique, My Love. Dir. Peter Woodcock. Dekko Films. 1969.
The Moon Is Blue. Dir. Otto Preminger. Otto Preminger Films. 1953.
Moonlighting Wives. Dir. Joe Sarno. Morgan Pictures. 1966.
Motel Wives. Dir. Adam Clay. Mitam Prod. 1968.
Mr. Peter's Pets. Dir. Dick Crane. Sonney Amusement Enterprises. 1963.
Mudhoney. Dir. Russ Meyer. Eve Prod. 1965.
My Body Hungers. Dir. Joe Sarno. Amalfi Films. 1967.
My Brother's Wife. Dir. Doris Wishman. Juri Prod. 1966.
Nature Camp Diary (Alt. *Nature Camp Confidential*). Dir. Doris Wishman. Dawn Prod. 1961.
The Naughty Shutter. Dir. Sammy Helm. Sack Amusement Enterprises. 1963.
Not Tonight Henry. Dir. W. Merle Connell. Foremost Films. 1960.

Nude in Charcoal. Dir. Joe Sarno. Tempest Prod. 1961.
Nude on the Moon. Dir. Doris Wishman. Moon Prod. 1961.
Nude Restaurant. Dir. Andy Warhol. Factory Films. 1967.
Nudes Inc. Dir. Barry Mahon. Barry Mahon Prod. 1964.
Nympho. Dir. Nick Millard (as Alfredo Nicola). IRMI Films. 1965.
Nymphs Anonymous. Dir. Manuel S. Conde. Great Empire Films. 1968.
Odd Obsession. Dir. Kon Ichikawa. Daiei Motion Picture. 1959.
Office Love-In, White Collar Style. Dir. Stephen Apostolof (as A. C. Stephen). AFPI Prod. 1968.
Olga's Dance Hall Girls. George Weiss Prod. 1969.
Olga's Girls. Dir. Joseph P. Mawra. American Film Distributing Corp. 1964.
Olga's House of Shame. Dir. Joseph P. Mawra. American Film Distributing Corp. 1964.
One Naked Night. Dir. Albert T. Viola. Four Seasons Prod. 1963.
The Opening of Misty Beethoven. Dir. Radley Metzger (as Henry Paris). Crescent Films. 1976.
Orgy at Lil's Place. Dir. Jerald Intrator (as J. Nehemiah). Extraordinary Films. 1963.
Pardon My Brush. Dir. John K. McCarthy. Active-Stardust. 1964.
The Pawnbroker. Dir. Sidney Lumet. Landau Co. 1964.
The Peek Snatchers. Dir. Joseph Mawra. 1965.
Peeping Tom. Dir. Michael Powell. Michael Powell Prod. 1960.
Persona. Dir. Ingmar Bergman. Svensk Filmindustri. 1966.
Peyton Place. Dir. Mark Robson. Twentieth Century Fox. 1957.
Playgirls International. Dir. Doris Wishman. Westfield Prod. 1963.
The Pleasure Lovers. Dir. Charles Saunders. Butchers Film. 1959. U.S. release, Joseph Brenner Associates, 1964.
Point Blank. Dir. John Boorman. MGM. 1967.
Portrait of Jason. Dir. Shirley Clark. Shirley Clark Prod. 1967.
P.P.S. (Prostitutes Protective Society). Dir. Barry Mahon. Barry Mahon Prod. 1966.
Promises! Promises! Dir. King Donovan. Noonan-Taylor Prod. 1963.
Psycho. Dir. Alfred Hitchcock. Shamley Prod. 1960.
Rent-a-Girl. Dir. William Rose. Corsair Films. 1965.
Revenge at Daybreak. Dir. Yves Allégret. Hoche Prod. 1952.
Riot on the Sunset Strip. Dir. Arthur Dreifuss. Four Leaf Prod. 1967.
Room at the Top. Dir. Jack Clayton. Romulus Films. 1959.
Rope. Dir. Alfred Hitchcock. Warner Bros. 1948.
The Sarnos: A Life in Dirty Movies. Dir. Wiktor Ericsson. Anagram. 2013.
Saturday Night and Sunday Morning. Dir. Karel Reisz. Woodfall Film Prod. 1960.
The Scavengers. Dir. Lee Frost (as R. L. Frost). Cresse-Frost Prod. 1969.
Schlock! The Secret History of American Movies. Dir. Ray Greene. Pathfinder Pictures. 2001.
Scorpio Rising. Dir. Kenneth Anger. Puck Film Prod. 1964.

Scum of the Earth. Dir. Herschell Gordon Lewis (as Lewis H. Gordon). Box Office Spectaculars. 1963.
Seconds. Dir. John Frankenheimer. Douglas and Lewis Prod. 1966.
The Sex Killer. Dir. Barry Mahon (uncredited). Barry Mahon Prod. 1967.
The Sex Perils of Paulette. Dir. Doris Wishman. Juri Prod. 1965.
The Sexperts—Touched by Temptation. Dir. Jerald Intrator (as J. Nehemiah). William Mishkin. 1966.
The Sexploiters. Dir. Al C. Ruban. Esquire Pictures. 1965.
Sexual Freedom in Denmark. Dir. John Lamb (as M. C. Von Hellen). Horizon Prod. 1970.
Sexy Proibitissimo. Dir. Marcello Martinelli. Gino Mordini Produzione Cinematografiche. 1964.
She-Devils on Wheels. Dir. Herschell Gordon Lewis. Mayflower Pictures. 1968.
She Freak. Dir. Byron Mabe, Donn Davison (uncredited). Sonney-Friedman Pictures. 1967.
She Mob. Dir. Harry Wuest. Lorenzo Prod. 1968.
She Should Have Stayed in Bed. Dir. Barry Mahon. Barry Mahon Prod. 1963.
The Silence. Dir. Ingmar Bergman. Svensk Filmindustri. 1963.
Sin in the Suburbs. Dir. Joe Sarno. Lojeare Prod. 1964.
The Sin Syndicate. Dir. Michael Findlay. Joseph Brenner Associates. 1965.
The Skin Game. Dir. Arnold Louis Miller. Searchlight Prod. 1965.
Smoke and Flesh. Dir. Joe Mangine. Imperial Pictures. 1968.
Something's Got to Give. Dir. George Cukor. Twentieth Century Fox. 1962.
Splendor in the Grass. Dir. Elia Kazan. Warner Bros. 1961.
The Spy Who Came. Dir. Ron Werthheim. Cinex Film Industries. 1969.
Starlet! Dir. Richard Kanter. ADO Prod. 1969.
Strange Compulsion. Dir. Irvin Berwick. Ivmar. 1964.
The Strange One. Dir. Jack Garfein. Columbia Pictures Corp. 1957.
Strange Rampage. Dir. Harry Kerwin (as Ignatius Volpe). Monique Prod. 1967.
The Subterraneans. Dir. Ranald MacDougall. MGM. 1960.
Suburban Roulette. Dir. Herschell Gordon Lewis. Unusual Films International. 1968.
Suburbia Confidential. Dir. Stephen C. Apostolof (as A. C. Stephens). AFPI Prod. 1966.
Summer with Monika. Dir. Ingmar Bergman. Svensk Filmindustri. 1953.
The Swap and How They Make It. Dir. Joe Sarno. General Studios. 1966.
Tales of a Salesman. Dir. Don Russell. Lawtone Prod. 1965.
Target Smut. Citizens for Decent Literature Inc. 1968.
Tea and Sympathy. Dir. Vincente Minnelli. MGM. 1956.
Thar She Blows. Dir. Richard Kanter. Ado Prod. 1968.
That's Sexploitation! Dir. Frank Henenlotter. Something Weird Video. 2013.
Therese and Isabelle. Dir. Radley Metzger. Amsterdam Film Corp. 1968.

The Third Sex (Alt. *Bewildered Youth,* Orig. *Anders als du und ich*). Dir. Veit Harlan. Arca Filmproduktion GMBH. 1957.

Too Much Too Often! Dir. Doris Wishman (as Louis Silverman). Mostest Prod. 1968.

To Turn a Trick. Dir. C. Davis Smith (as Charles Andrew). Sam Lake Enterprises. 1967.

The Touch of Her Flesh. Dir. Michael Findlay (as Julian Marsh). Rivamarsh Prod. 1967.

Traffic in Souls. Dir. George Loane Tucker. Universal Film Manufacturing Co. 1913.

The Twilight Girls. Dir. Andre Hunebelle, as *Les Collegienes.* Safia-Sirius-Contact Organization. 1957. Rereleased in the United States by Audubon Pictures, 1961.

Vapors. Dir. Andy Milligan. 1965.

Venus in Furs. Dir. Joseph Marzano. Cam-Scope Pictures. 1967.

Vibrations. Dir. Joe Sarno. Morris Kaplan Prod. 1969.

The Virgin Spring. Dir. Ingmar Bergman. Svensk Filmindustri. 1960.

Viridiana. Dir. Luis Buñuel. Films 59. 1961.

Viva. Dir. Anna Biller. Anna Biller Prod. 2007.

Vixen. Dir. Russ Meyer. Eve Prod. 1968.

The Voyeur. 1970.

Walk on the Wild Side. Dir. Edward Dmytryk. Famous Artists Prod. 1962.

The Weird Lovemakers (The Warped Ones/Kyonetsu no Kisetsu). Dir. Koreyoshi Kuruhara. Nikkatsu. 1960. U.S. release, Audubon Pictures, 1963.

Whip's Women. Dir. Jerry Denby. Jode Prod. 1968.

White Slaves of Chinatown. Dir. Joseph P. Mawra. 1964.

Who's Afraid of Virginia Woolf? Dir. Mike Nichols. Warner Bros. 1966.

The Wild Angels. Dir. Roger Corman. American International Pictures. 1966.

Wild Gals of the Naked West. Dir. Russ Meyer. Pacifica Films. 1962.

Without a Stitch. Dir. Annelise Meineche. Palladium. 1968.

Women of the World. Dir. Gualtiero Jacopetti. Cineriz. 1963.

INDEX

Abnormal Female, The, 170
Acid Eaters, The, 185
Adler, Judy, 133
adult film, 196, 200, 222, 261–62, 264, 276
Adult Film Association of America (AFAA), 90, 92, 95, 238, 284
"adults only," 13, 31, 65–66, 87, 131, 200, 202, 206, 228, 232, 238, 264n26
advertising, 50, 62–63, 74, 79–80, 109, 202, 222, 226, 235, 264; sexploitation films, 55, 63, 106, 130, 197, 202–3, 205, 239, 270, 283
Africa Addio, 210
Agony of Love, 7, 188, 235
Agnew, Spiro, 84
All Women Are Bad, 17, 106
Alternative Cinema, 22
amateur performers, 112–13, 116, 166
American Civil Liberties Union (ACLU), 77, 200
American Genre Film Archive, 18
American International Pictures (AIP), 6, 185, 214, 292, 185
Americanization of Emily, The, 129
American Motion Picture Producer's Association, 46
anachronism, 18, 22, 26, 76, 92–93, 100, 121, 137, 166, 173, 246, 250

And God Created Woman, 131, 283
Andrews, David, 194–95
Anthropometrie de l'epoque bleue, 122–23
anti-obscenity actions, 46–47, 73, 74–75, 86, 221, 273
anti-pornography, 77
Antonioni, Michelangelo, 10
Apostolof, Steven, 91
A Quantity of Copies of Books v. Kansas (1964), 72–73
archives, 17–19, 226; amateur histories, 17–19, 253
Aroused, 135
art cinema, 94, 130–31, 200–203; definition of, 60, 69, 122, 192–93, 202, 214; exhibition, 38, 191–92, 201–2, 206–8, 261, 264; market, 5
Art Films International (Adult Art Films), 202, 204, 287
Artisex, 222–26, 229, 234–37
Artists Studio Secrets, 110
Astro–Jemco, 95
audience, 1–26, 31–35, 59–61, 66–68, 71, 81, 101, 103, 127–30, 165, 169, 207–10, 219–28, 234–35, 238, 253; adult, 12, 28, 31, 37, 40–41, 52, 87–88, 197–202, 227–32, 241–43; cultivation of, 1–8, 12–13, 25, 38, 40, 65–66, 96, 109, 175, 214–17;

dupe, 25, 112, 197–98, 205–7, 225–26; "erotica consumer," 200, 225, 228, 243–44; female, 13, 100, 113, 174, 177, 210, 253; home, 18, 21, 22; male, 100, 106, 111, 113, 138–39, 198, 205, 228, 232, 277; youth, 8, 20, 65–66, 73, 76, 78, 86, 89, 184–85, 200, 207, 229–32, 267. *See also* homosociality
Audubon Films, 52–53, 59, 68, 72, 83, 175–76, 201, 218, 276
autoeroticism, 117, 134, 174–75, 178–79, 209, 232, 233–34, 277

Baby Doll, 129, 279
Baker, Carroll, 129
Barbarella, 175, 178
Barrington, Pat, 22
Bataille, Georges, 37
Beatniks, The, 145, 281
Behind the Green Door, 242
Bell, Bare and Beautiful, 64
Belle du Jour, 175
Bennett, Darlene, 113, 168
Bennett, Dawn, 113
Benveniste, Michael, 196
Berry, Sid, 30, 32, 34
Best of Everything, The, 40
Betz, Mark, 13, 131
Bibo, Walter, 45
Bike Boy, 230
Blonde on a Bum Trip, 185
Blow-up, 186, 192
Blue Movie. See *Fuck*
Bob & Carol & Ted & Alice, 191
Body of a Female, 17, 71
Boxoffice International, 193
Boyce, Linda, 113
Brennan, William, 38–39
Brenner, Joseph, 131
Bride for Brenda, A, 114, 180, 182–83
Broadway Association, 76
Buried Treasure, 195
burlesque, 43, 56, 64, 111, 113–14, 116–18
Butterfield 8, 46, 111–12

Cambist Films, 94
Campbell, Audrey, 22, 155, 161
CARA Ratings (MPAA), 40, 79, 221–22
Carnal Knowledge, 242
Catholic Legion of Decency, 39, 74
Cat on a Hot Tin Roof, 40
censorship, 10, 14, 24, 27–28, 32–42, 47–52, 55–56, 62–67, 71, 88–93, 128, 153, 223, 266, 268; and art, 37, 54; informal, 74, 77, 91; as marketing, 30, 55, 79, 90, 221
Chained Girls, 167, 171, 177, 282
Chappell, Fred, 211–13
Chelsea Girls, 171, 210
Chinese Consolidated Benevolent Association, 75
Cinema Syndicate, 63
Citizens for Decent Literature (CDL), 74, 76–78, 83–84, 86, 227, 273
Clancy, James, 83
Coming Apart, 191, 230
connoisseurship, 17, 68, 130, 204, 216–17, 222–23, 225–26, 229, 234–37, 243–44
Coppola, Francis Ford, 11
Corliss, Richard, 192–93, 217, 233–34, 237, 243
Corman, Roger, 6, 243, 263, 292. *See also* American International Pictures
counterculture, 8, 94, 97, 147, 184–86, 231, 250, 278
Cresse, Bob, 92–94, 112
Cult Epics, 22
Curious Female, The, 193, 245–51, 253

Dales, John L., 46
Damiano, Gerard, 95–96
Darlene, Gigi, 113, 149
David Holzman's Diary, 191
Davis, Don, 91
Davis, George, 91
DeCenzie, Peter, 43
Deep Throat, 96, 196, 240–42
de Grazia, Edward, 38
D'Emilio, John, 98, 105
De Palma, Brian, 11

INDEX

de Renzy, Alex, 95
Detention Girls, 227
Deuce, The, 255
Devil in Miss Jones, The, 242
Di Carlo, Joseph, 75
Distribpix, 22, 191
Dolce Vita, La, 48, 59
Don Giovanni, 66
Don Juan Decision (*Times Film Corp. v. City of Chicago*; 1961), 67
Doty, Alex, 112
Dr. Sex, 110, 128
drugs, 72, 160–61, 186, 271–72; drug culture, 161, 173, 185–87; film content, 6, 21, 75, 160, 164–65

Eberwein, Robert, 189–90
Emmanuelle, 243
Entertainment Ventures Incorporated (EVI), 193
Esquire, 110
Eve Productions, 79, 276
experimental films, 171
exploitation film, 6–7

Fadiman, William, 41
Falbo, Billy, 118
Fanfare Films, 185
female body, 2, 123–25, 154, 162, 174, 212
female desire, 25, 141–42, 145, 154, 158, 175, 181, 190, 198
female orgasm, 178–79, 284
female subjectivity, 135, 142, 149, 154–55, 157, 172, 174, 178, 186–87, 254
Feminine Mystique, The, 158, 281
feminism, 20, 145–46, 158, 178, 190–91, 278, 282; women's movement, 8
Festival Girls, The, 280
fetishism, 159–61
Fiedler, Leslie, 116–17
50,000 B.C. (Before Clothing), 110
File X For Sex, 167–70
Film Comment, 204

film culture, 10, 38; criticism, 94, 204, 210–11, 222–25, 241–42; critics, 45, 204, 223; magazines, 18, 20, 40, 45
Findlay, Michael and Roberta, 13, 22, 135, 275; *The Curse of Her Flesh,* 13; *The Kiss of Her Flesh,* 13; *The Sin Syndicate,* 106; *A Thousand Pleasures,* 181; *The Touch of Her Flesh,* 8, 13, 135
Fireworks, 171
First Amendment, 72, 74, 84
Fleishman, Stanley, 56, 58–59, 73, 91
Fonda, Jane, 178
Foucault, Michel, 28
Fourth Sex, The, 131
Fox, The, 191
Freedman, Estelle, 98, 105
Freedman v. Maryland (1965), 66–69, 71
Free Love Confidential, 25, 185–87, 278
Freeman, Y. Frank, 46
Friedman, David, 21, 22, 45, 88–90, 103, 112, 136, 191, 193, 202, 230, 238, 284; *The Adventures of Lucky Pierre,* 25, 117–21, 124–25; *Blood Feast,* 63, 279; *The Defilers,* 25, 130, 144–50, 160, 198, 281; *Scum of the Earth,* 130, 136–39, 149; *Starlet!,* 25, 193–95
Friedman, Jane, 83–84
Fuck, 237

Gabor, Eva, 205
Garden of Eden, The, 41–43, 45, 58, 111, 121, 268
Gavara, Paola, 123
Gavin, Erica, 78
gay: adult films, 198, 285; cruising, 233–34; desire, 146, 171; films, 77, 171; identity, 170, 276, 281, 283; representation, 53, 170–71, 173, 246
gender, 139, 170, 275–76; femininity, 125, 141, 151, 159, 278, 280; identity, 162; masculinity, 99, 140–42, 144–47, 198, 234, 281

Gent, 110
Ginzburg v. United States (1966), 84
Girl in Trouble, 114
Goodman, Paul, 37
Graduate, The, 175
Grass Sandwich, A, 195
guilty expenditure, 14, 97

hard-core, 15, 28, 62, 79, 92, 94–95, 100–101, 112, 145, 192–96, 232, 237, 239–40, 243, 264; generic dominance, 13, 17, 22, 103, 225, 228, 235, 242, 247, 274
hard-core sex, 192, 193
Have Figure, Will Travel, 43
Hells Angels on Wheels, 185
Henry, Hank, 55, 59
Hentoff, Margot, 220, 230, 248
Her Odd Tastes, 179
Hessel, Lee, 94
Hippie Revolt, The, 185, 278
History of the Blue Movie, A, 195, 247
Hollywood's World of Flesh, 93
homosociality, 141, 144–48, 198, 209, 232–34
Hookers, The, 8, 188, 263
Hoover, J. Edgar, 74
Horowitz, Bernard, 90, 95
Hot Spur, 93, 193
How Many Times, 8, 158
Hurry Sundown, 210
Hutcheon, Linda, 101

I, A Man, 230
I, A Woman, 72, 83, 86, 175–76, 217, 221, 287
I Am Curious (Yellow), 68, 78, 90, 192, 221, 251
I Crave Your Body, 158
Incredibly Strange Films, 18

Jacobellis v. Ohio (1964), 36, 62, 153
Jacopetti, Gualtiero, 123
James, David, 101
Jansson, Mai, 145
Janus Films, 53, 55–56, 58, 61

Jordan, Marsha, 22
Jules and Jim, 59

Kansas, Ansa, 170
Karp, David Allen, 232–34, 291
Kaufman, Pete, 88, 95
Keating, Charles H., Jr., 77, 79, 81–82, 84–85, 273
Keating, Kenneth, 77
Kellery, Yvonne, 173
Kent, Sharon, 113
Killing of Sister George, The, 191
Kim's Video, 19, 21
Kingsley International Pictures v. Board of Regents (1959), 39
Kinsey, Alfred, 104–5, 169
Kiss, 232
Klaw, Irving, 161
Klein, Yves, 122–23
Kleinhans, Chuck, 168
Klinger, Barbara, 23
Kovács, László, 11
Krafft-Ebing, Richard von, 135

labor, 95, 138
Lady Chatterley's Lover, 39, 68
Lake, Sam, 88, 132
Language of Love, The, 196
Last Tango in Paris, 242
Laughing Woman, The, 217
Laurent, Agnès, 53
Lease, Maria, 182
Leighton, Ava, 52–53, 201, 276
lesbian: identity, 8, 167–68, 173–74, 246, 276; pulp, 173–74; representation, 53–54, 69, 150–51, 154, 283–84; sexuality, 25, 78, 81–82, 166, 170–71, 179–82
Lewis, Freeman, 89
Lewis, Herschell Hordon, 18, 22
Lewis, Jon, 74
Libertine, The, 218
Like It Is, 185, 278
Linville, Alice, 155
Lolita, 40
Lonesome Cowboys, 76

Love Camp 7, 93
Love Is a Four Letter Word, 93
Love Island, 205
Love Me . . . Please!, 7, 13
Lovers, The, 36, 59, 68, 131, 153
Lusting Hours, The, 171

Madame Olga's Massage Parlor, 160
Mahon, Barry, 21, 28, 30, 32, 33, 45, 62, 113, 121–22, 125, 128, 133; *The Beast That Killed Women*, 281; *Bunny Yeager's Nude Camera*, 25, 122, 125–27; *Bunny Yeager's Nude Las Vegas*, 122, 125–26; *Censored*, 28, 30–37, 50–51, 60, 165; *Confessions of a Bad Girl*, 133, 155; *Good Time with a Bad Girl*, 158; *Hollywood Nudes Report*, 63; *Hot Skin, Cold Cash*, 188; *I Was a Man*, 170; *Nudes Inc.*, 62, 128; *1,000 Shapes of a Female*, 110, 122–25, 281; *P.P.S. (Prostitutes Protective Society)*, 106; *The Sex Killer*, 135; *She Should Have Stayed in Bed*, 278
Malibu Inc., 79
Man and Wife, 196, 225
Man with the Golden Arm, The, 39
Mansfield, Jayne, 129, 279
Man's World, 110
Mantis in Lace, 185
Marcus, Steven, 14
Marriage Manual films, 195
Maryland State Censor Board, 43, 47–48, 51, 68–69
masturbation, 180, 233–34, 277. *See also* autoeroticism
Melillo, Philip, 132
Memoirs v. Massachusetts (1966), 36
Metzger, Radley, 13, 19, 20, 22, 24, 52–55, 60, 69–70, 115, 131, 154–55, 177, 191, 193, 214–19, 221–22, 238, 269, 287; *The Alley Cats*, 210; *Camille 2000*, 218; *Carmen, Baby*, 73, 81, 217, 221; *The Dirty Girls*, 68–70, 131, 154, 177–80, 207; *The Lickerish Quartet*, 219; *The Opening of Misty Beethoven*, 242; *Therese and Isabelle*, 86, 171, 217–18, 221, 225, 251
Meyer, Eve, 276
Meyer, Russ, 13, 18, 19, 20, 22, 43, 51, 69, 77–79, 112, 117, 140, 177, 191–93, 214–19, 221–22, 263, 277; *Beyond the Valley of the Dolls*, 79, 192, 218–19; *Eve and the Handyman*, 140; *Faster Pussycat! Kill! Kill!*, 8, 117, 190, 216, 263; *The Immoral Mr. Teas*, 13, 25, 43, 44, 46, 48, 51, 110, 115–17, 121, 125, 205, 269, 277–78; *Lorna*, 25, 69, 130, 139–44, 149–50, 154, 160, 165, 198, 208, 287–88; *Mudhoney*, 190, 215; *Vixen*, 77–86, 117, 175, 190, 221; *Wild Gals of the Naked West*, 140
Midnight Cowboy, 191
Miller v. California (1973), 84, 96, 242
Milligan, Andy, 17, 22, 170
Miracle, 5, 38. *See also* Miracle Decision
Miracle Decision (*Joseph Burstyn, Inc. v. Wilson*; 1952), 5, 38, 45
Miranda, Julian, 56, 58
Mishkin, William, 17, 51, 131, 191, 269
mode of address, 4, 12, 24–25, 30–32, 36, 144, 171–72, 185, 208, 249–50; advertising, 11, 109, 147; alibi, 7, 32, 58, 116, 167–68, 172, 197, 201, 204–5, 209, 217, 225, 231; direct address, 34–35, 116–18, 138–41, 165; dialogue and narrative, 137, 193; narration, 7, 102, 121, 123, 134, 144, 159, 161, 164–68, 180–81; tease, 11, 105–6, 119, 121, 198, 208, 249–50
Modern Man, 110
Molesters, The, 131
Moller, David, 204–5
Mona, 196, 233, 240–41
Monaco, Paul, 5
Mondo Bizarro, 93, 123
Mondo Cane, 123
Mondo Freudo, 93, 123

Mondo Mod, 185
Mondo Oscenita, 123
Monika, 131
Monique, My Love, 25, 181, 183
Monroe, Marilyn, 129
Moon Is Blue, The, 39
Morris, Barbara, 1
Motel Wives, 158
Motion Picture Association of America (MPAA), 39, 73, 92, 229; Production Code Administration (PCA), 40
Mr. Peter's Pets, 110
Murder a la Mod, 263
Mutual Film Decision (*Mutual Film Corp. v. Industrial Commission of Ohio*; 1915), 38, 45, 60–61, 67

National Association of Theater Owners, 73
National Catholic Office for Motion Pictures, 74
Naughty Shutter, The, 110, 128
Nead, Lynda, 114–15
Newman, Roger, 38–39, 82
New Hollywood, 22, 263
New York State Board of Appeals Decision (1957), 7
New York State Board of Regents, 39, 49–50, 53, 55, 65, 268, 278
New York State Censor Board, 28, 48–56, 58, 60, 64, 66, 71, 268
Nocolo, Loloni, 166
nostalgia, 18–21, 237, 239, 247, 254–55
Not Tonight Henry, 55–61, 110, 269; Modesto legal case, 59
Novak, Harry, 21, 22
Nude Restaurant, 230
nudist camp films, 41–43, 45, 52, 110–11, 113, 116, 149
nudity, 41–43, 45–46, 50–53, 56, 58, 61, 63, 75, 98, 106, 109–16, 119, 121–23, 128–29, 135, 137, 144, 170, 174, 179, 184, 201–2, 205, 212–13, 279
Nympho, 158
Nymphs Anonymous, 190–91

obscenity law, 5, 10, 28, 31, 33, 36–37, 42, 52, 56, 59, 62–68, 72–73, 76, 79, 83, 96, 121, 198, 221; definition of obscenity, 37–43, 45, 58, 65, 68, 71–72, 77, 87–89, 94, 153, 158, 160, 191, 196, 242, 261, 271–72; Roth Test (Roth Doctrine), 1, 32, 41
obsolescence, 16–17, 22, 96, 238–40, 244, 247, 249, 251–52; legal standards, 49, 66, 93
Odd Obsession, 59
Office Love-In, White Collar Style, 25, 188–90
Olga's Dance House Girls, 160
Olga's Girls, 8, 160, 162–63, 166
Olga's House of Shame, 7, 160
One Naked Night, 1–4, 8, 10, 155
Orgy at Lil's Place, The, 7, 17, 210
Ostrov, Herbet, 85

Pad-Ram, 43, 45
Page, Bettie, 161
Paramore, Ted, 34, 59–61
Pardon My Brush, 110
Paris, Henry. *See* Metzger, Radley
Pawnbroker, The, 129
Peeping Tom, 99
Persona, 151
Persson, Essy, 175–76
Pesce, Louis, 49, 51, 52, 58, 62–63, 71
Peyton Place, 40
Pickett, Lowell, 95
Playboy, 43, 104, 106, 110, 114, 125
Pleasure, 232
Pleasure Lovers, The (Naked Fury), 158, 208
pornography, 61, 87–88, 99, 105, 192, 275; hard-core, 4, 13, 61, 69, 82, 89, 96, 99–101, 153, 163, 198, 220, 234, 238, 251–52, 262; soft-core, 220, 231–32, 239, 282
Portrait of Jason, 171
Premier Pictures Company, 132, 192
Preminger, Otto, 39
Presidential Commission on Obscenity

and Pornography, 13, 28, 77, 83, 85, 87, 89–90, 228, 231
Prevost, Marianne, 182
privacy, 74, 81–82, 85, 88, 135, 170, 233
Production Code (MPAA), 6, 39, 40, 53, 92, 129, 277, 284
Prosperi, Franco, 123
prostitution, 7, 75, 87, 160, 171, 228
Psycho, 99
Psychopathia Sexualis, 135
pulp paperbacks, 4, 112, 161, 172–74, 286
Pussycat Theaters, 191

Rabe v. Washington (1964), 73
race, 78, 188, 262–63; whiteness, 8–9, 100, 166
Radner, Hilary, 9, 178–79
Randall, Richard, 55, 74
Ransohoff, Martin, 129
Realist, The, 207, 286–87
reception, 40, 45, 46, 71, 58, 84, 101–2, 104, 199, 204–7, 213, 225, 230, 242, 243, 285, 292
reflexivity, 33, 35, 98, 101–2, 116, 128, 138, 165, 189–90, 193–95, 247, 251
Reich, Wilhelm, 280, 285–86
Rent-a-Girl, 8, 71, 159
representation: bodies, 111, 114, 118, 121, 154; conventions, 65, 90, 110–12, 194, 239, 250; nudity, 42, 45–46, 123, 174; sex, 4, 43, 52, 79, 81–82, 98–99, 104, 153, 159, 166, 195–96, 232, 235; strategies, 93–94, 131, 134, 158, 179, 183, 212
Revenge at Daybreak, 66
Roberts, June, 113–14
Room at the Top, 59
Roth v. United States (1957), 38, 47, 68, 83, 160, 266
Russell, Jane, 129

Sampson, John, 88
Sarno, Joe, 13, 18, 20, 21, 22, 107–9, 132, 154–55, 182–83, 188, 238, 239, 280; *Anything For Money*, 155; *Deep Inside*, 223; *The Layout*, 179; *Moonlighting Wives*, 17, 155; *My Body Hungers*, 158; *Nude in Charcoal*, 110, 132–34; *Sin in the Suburbs*, 25, 106, 131, 154–56, 184, 238; *The Swap and How They Make It*, 107–9; *Vibrations*, 13, 179, 182–83
Sarnos, The, 20, 255
Sarris, Andrew, 11
Saturday Night and Sunday Morning, 59
Scavengers, The, 93
Schaefer, Eric, 6, 9, 14–15, 19, 102, 111, 130, 134, 172, 193, 197, 202, 231, 252–53
Schlock!, 20
Schoonover, Karl, 12, 13
Sconce, Jeffrey, 15, 18
Scorpio Rising, 147
Screen Actors Guild, 128
Screw, 226, 232
Seconds, 151
Seidman, Steven, 105
Sex and the Single Girl, 104, 157, 281
sexploitation films, 4, 7, 11, 27, 168, 172, 192, 198, 249, 262; and art films, 45, 55, 60, 68, 95, 118, 121, 210–11, 214–15, 217, 219–20, 223, 275; "artist's model," 121–22, 127, 133; distribution, 49, 54, 62–64, 71, 175, 191, 222; economics, 46, 63, 105, 284; exhibition, 48, 52, 62–67, 71, 73–74, 76–77, 83, 91, 94, 130, 132, 175, 198, 201, 219, 221, 231, 268, 291; genre, 5, 7–8, 33, 43, 63, 89, 97, 100, 102, 114, 117, 122, 129–34, 150–51, 153, 155, 158–59, 170, 173, 219, 263, 274, 275, 279, 284, 290; "kinky," 130, 160, 172; "nudie cutie," 43–44, 55, 98, 109–11, 113–15, 117, 121, 128–30, 132–34, 137, 174; "roughie," 98–99, 129–30, 132–36, 139, 144, 147, 157, 160, 172, 280; "sex exposé," 167; "social problem," 173

Sexploiters, The, 17, 76
Sexual Freedom in Denmark, 195, 240
sexuality, 225, 231, 234, 250–51, 253, 274–75, 280–83, 285–86; acts, 154–55, 164, 167, 174, 179, 225; agency, 175; female, 81, 135, 140–41, 144, 157–58, 178, 184, 231, 240; homosexuality, 170–73, 234; identity, 100, 104–5, 154; labor, 101, 137, 155, 157, 159, 184, 187–89; perversion, 145–46, 159–60, 166, 170, 175, 182; pleasure, 3, 15, 99, 178–79, 186; practices, 112, 185–86, 230; sexual pathology, 130, 135, 146–47, 167; "sexual psychopath," 8, 34, 135, 146–47
sexual revolution, 9–10, 104–6, 184, 201, 247, 249, 252–53, 263, 285–86; sexual liberation, 122, 186–87, 190, 281
sexual science, 128, 168–70, 178; *Human Sexual Response,* 178; Kinsey Institute, 17, 135
Sexy Probitissimo, 76
She Mob, 8, 182
Sher, Louis, 88, 171
Sherpix, 171, 191
Show, 116
Shurlock, Geoffrey, 40
simulation, 27, 82, 84, 98, 101, 132, 151, 172, 174, 179, 183–84, 198, 252
Sinister Cinema, 18
Skin Game, The, 9, 131
soft-core, 89–90, 92, 95–96, 101, 118, 132, 183, 193–94, 225, 238, 243, 251
Something's Got to Give, 279
Something Weird Video, 18, 21–22, 265
Sontag, Susan, 37
spectacle, 102–3, 114, 117, 136, 150, 168, 171, 183–84, 229, 250, 275
spectatorship, 2, 10, 12, 23, 175, 226, 285; arousal, 198; body of, 97, 103, 115, 214, 252; boredom, 205–6, 237–38; cinephilia, 19–20, 225, 243, 249–50; desires, 71, 141, 144, 208; erotic consumption, 11, 35, 102, 139, 200, 234–35; female spectator, 163, 177, 249, 253, 282; gawker, 99, 115, 119; gullible, 197; male spectator, 116–17, 142, 200; participation, 137; privacy of, 76–77, 84–85; "seeing and doing," 190; unintended spectator, 67, 74
Spelvin, Georgina, 53
Splendor in the Grass, 46
Stag, 111
stag film, 2, 106, 136, 190, 194–95, 237
Starr, Blaze, 114
St. Cyr, Lili, 111, 114
Stephens, A. C. *See* Apostolof, Steven
Stewart, Potter, 62
Storm, Tempest, 111
Straayer, Chris, 103–4
Strange Compulsion, 8, 135
Strange One, The, 40
Strange Rampage, 170
Stranger Knocks, A, 71, 266
striptease, 1, 106, 172, 232, 276
Stryker, Susan, 173
Sturges, Solomon, 135
Subterraneans, The, 145
Suburbia Confidential, 189
Swank, 111
swinging, 8, 25, 155, 172, 184–85, 189, 236, 250, 253

Tales of a Salesman, 110
Target Smut, 83
Taylor, Elizabeth, 111–14
Tea and Sympathy, 40
Teas, Bill, 43
Teitel, Charles, 72
Thar She Blows, 225
That's Sexploitation!, 20
theater owners, 65, 66, 75–77, 86
theaters, adult, 16, 45, 66, 191–92, 197, 209–10, 226, 230, 232–33
theaters, art, 210, 222
Third Sex, The, 59

Thorne, Dyanne, 155
Times Square, 19, 30, 75–76, 188, 199, 204, 207, 209, 230, 232, 255
Tonight for Sure, 263
Torrell, Frank, 64
Traffic in Souls, 160, 282
Tri-State Theater Service, 79
Turan, Kenneth, 78, 130
Twilight Girls, The, 52–55, 60, 131
Tyler, Parker, 112

underground films, 6, 18–20, 138, 170–71, 199–200, 231, 234, 245, 248, 262, 276, 282–83, 292
U.S. Supreme Court, 5, 38, 39, 41, 51–52, 59, 66–67, 73, 83–84, 95
U.S. v. Paramount Pictures, Inc. (1948), 5, 12, 37

Valenti, Jack, 92
Valenti, Michael, 207–9
Vapors, 170–71
Variety, 90, 201, 210, 270
video, 17–19, 21, 134, 243, 253, 292
Video Vault, 18
Vinegar Syndrome, 22
Virgin Spring, The, 142
Viola, Albert, 4
violence, 63, 134–35, 139, 146–47, 159–60, 188
Viridiana, 59
Viva, 253–55, 292
Voyeur, The, 225
voyeurism, 115, 135, 141, 166, 173–74, 180–81, 207–8, 221, 234

Walk on the Wild Side, 46
Warhol, Andy, 76–77, 171, 210, 230, 237
Watson, Paul, 11

Waugh, Thomas, 11, 105
Weird Lovemakers, The, 131
Weiss, George, 22, 62
White Coater film. *See* Marriage Manual films
white slavery, 33, 160, 164, 282. See also *White Slaves of Chinatown*
White Slaves of Chinatown, 25, 62, 75, 130, 160–67, 173
Who's Afraid of Virginia Woolf?, 191
Wild Angels, The, 185
Williams, Linda, 4, 14–15, 100–101, 178
Willie, John, 161
Wilson, Chelly, 276
Winick, Charles, 228–29
Winters, Cherie, 113
Wise, Henry, 63
Wishman, Doris, 18, 20–22, 45, 100, 149, 282–83; *Another Day, Another Man,* 151; *Bad Girls Go to Hell,* 25, 114, 149–51, 283; *Double Agent 73,* 20, 283; *Hideout in the Sun,* 205; *Indecent Desires,* 151, 283; *My Brother's Wife,* 151; *Nature Camp Diary (Nature Camp Confidential),* 71; *Nude on the Moon,* 110; *Playgirls International,* 134; *The Sex Perils of Paulette,* 50, 51, 76, 151; *A Taste of Flesh,* 283; *Too Much Too Often!,* 283
Without a Stitch, 225, 230–31
Wolf, William, 251–53
Wood, Barbara, 159

X rating, 79, 222, 232, 292

Yeager, Bunny, 125, 128, 278–79

Ziehm, Howard, 196
Zito, Stephen, 130

ELENA GORFINKEL is senior lecturer in film studies at King's College London and coeditor of *Taking Place: Location and the Moving Image* (Minnesota, 2011).